P & R PUBLICATIONS
Second Edition

COLLECTORS' GUIDE TO
SPORTS ILLUSTRATED®
&
SPORTS PUBLICATIONS

Philip W. Regli

P & R Publications
Las Vegas, Nevada

Published by P & R Publications
P.O. Box 26596
Las Vegas, NV 89126-0596

Catalog Number: PR-CGSP-002

Second Edition

Publisher's Cataloging in Publication
(Prepared by Quality Books Inc.)

Regli, Philip W.
    Collectors' guide to Sports Illustrated and sports publications
/ Philip W. Regli. -- 2nd ed.
    p. cm.
    ISBN 0-9655697-1-3

    1. Sports--Periodicals--Prices. 2. Sports journalism--
Collectors and collecting. 3. Sports--Periodicals--Collectors and
collecting.   I. Title.

PN4784.S6R44 1996   796
                                    QBI96-40718

TABLE OF CONTENTS

A NOTE ON THE AUTHOR

Phil Regli has been a national sports memorabilia dealer since 1976 and is recognized as a leading authority on Sports Publications. He owns and operates Sports Publication Clearinghouse, one of the largest Sports Publications trading houses in the country. He has written various articles for trade magazines and publishes the *Sports Publications Newsletter* on collecting sports publications. He has masters degrees in economics and business and has published in the areas of finance and statistics. His address is: P.O. Box 26596, Las Vegas, NV 89126-0596. (702) 228-9902 evenings.

ACKNOWLEDGMENTS

This book is a "team effort" in more ways than one. Many dealers and collectors have assisted me in bringing it to publication, and I would like to thank them for all their help. Among the folks on my "team" are folks at Sports Illustrated who provided current publication information. Collectors and dealers in sports publications have made contributions in prices and information. These people are: Steve Prothero, Scott Smith, Rich Behrens, Steven Shaff, Stan Keen, Ed Taylor, Joe Esposito, Joe Campius, Lou Madden, and the thousands of *SI* collectors we have met over the years. Special acknowledgment to Steve Prothero for his work on the first edition of the collector guide.

In addition to these experts, I would like to thank my wife, Carol, for editing the book and my children for realizing daddy dreams. I also would like to acknowledge Diane Durham, Valerie Durham and Jessie Goss for contributing to the project.

INTRODUCTION

Why a book on collecting *Sports Illustrated, Sport, Time, Life, Becketts, Sports Illustrated for Kids,* and autograph sports publications? First, *Sports Illustrated* (a.k.a. *SI*), is an American institution with over 3 million subscribers. *Sport* magazine is celebrating it's 50th anniversary this year. *Time* is the most read weekly magazine and has some of the most sought after sports covers. *Life* is one of the most popular magazines for autograph purposes. *Sports Illustrated for Kids* is a child of *Sports Illustrated* and needs to be recognized as part of *Sports Illustrated*. *Becketts* is actually collected by many card enthusiasts who like to get their issues autographed. The list can go on, but these are the main publications collected and used for autographing and prior to this, there was no leading authoritative guide to help the collector on collecting them.

Sports Illustrated is by far the most sought after and most collected. The cover photos of *Sports Illustrated* are rightfully famous. Taken by some of the world's finest sports photographers, *SI* covers record many of the greatest moments in American sports history: the victory of Joe Namath's Jets in Super Bowl III, Hank Aaron's 715th home run, and the U.S. hockey team's Olympic "miracle" in the 1980 games (to name just a few). Thought by many to be powerful enough to "jinx" the athletes whom it features, the *SI* cover is as much an American institution as the magazine itself.

Sport magazine is known as 'the golden era sports magazine'. The magazine captures the best photos and stories of the 1940's-1950's. The magazine is heavily collected by those who love the sports game and want to read about their favorite stars. *Sport* magazine color photos were heavily used as pinups in kids' bedrooms and many were used as autograph instruments during that era. It is not uncommon to find a beautiful *Sport* magazine with its photos cut out.

Since the 1920's and 30's *Time* and *Life* magazines have captured American and world history. Part of that great heritage is capturing sports hero's on the cover and in the written. If you are a serious collector of old time sports heroes *Time* and *Life* magazines are a must. I find that both make great autographed items and are wonderful gifts for serious sports collectors.

A second reason for this book is the fact that *Sports Illustrated* and sports publications collecting is one of the fastest-growing niches in the sports memorabilia market. No more than five years ago only a handful of dealers stocked sports publications. Now ads offering magazines abound in hobby publications and collectors compete fiercely for choice issues. *Sports Illustrated's* are popular because they are inexpensive, informative, and attractive. While a Mickey Mantle rookie card in nice condition will set you back thousands of dollars, an equally nice copy of Mantle's first *SI* cover (the magazine collector's equivalent of a rookie card) can be had for about $150. And while Topps makes an effort to provide information about a player on his card, a *SI* feature written by a top-flight sports journalist obviously offers greater insights. *SI* covers are also a much more attractive medium for signatures than are sports cards. Get your magazine cover signed and framed, and you have a spectacular and valuable display piece for your home or office.

A third and final reason for this update is the tremendous growth in autograph collecting on *Sports Illustrated* over the last two years. Many fellow collectors want a reference that shows them the value of getting their magazine autographed. Until now, only a handful of nationally known dealers have any idea of the scarcity of autographed Sports Illustrateds.

So what should you expect from this book? The first chapter, "Collecting *Sports Illustrated*," explains why *SI* is the most popular magazine among sports collectors. This chapter details the magazine's history from its beginnings in August of 1954 until this, its 42nd season, and discusses some of the most popular cover stars. It also suggests a number of ways to build a *SI* collection.

"Autographed Sports Publications," the second chapter, also responds to inquiring collectors. "What is the best way to get *SI*'s (or any publication) autographed?" "Should I send them through the mail?" "If so, how can I maximize the chances that I'll get them back signed and in good shape?"

In addition to answering these questions, the book includes in its third chapter, "Address List," hundreds of addresses you can use to contact individuals who have appeared on a publication cover. In an effort to respect the privacy of cover stars, I have listed institutional rather than individual addresses -- teams, colleges, halls of fame, etc. Many of these teams and organizations will gladly forward mail to athletes.

A fourth chapter responds to the questions, "How should I grade my magazines?" and "How should I store and preserve them over time?" Grading, of course, is an inexact science, but here I have done my best to make the art more exacting. And I have offered tips on how to keep your *SI*'s in tip-top shape.

Although I have done my best to respond to a wide variety of questions about *Sports Illustrated*, the price guide lies at the heart of the book. Mindful of the fact that the values of magazines vary, like sports cards, according to condition, I have listed not one but three prices for each. But the price guide, which constitutes Chapter Five, contains much more information than current values for mint (MT), excellent-to-mint (EM), and very good (VG) copies. For example, it lists not only the cover athlete but also his or her team or sport.

Just as critical as condition to a magazine is whether or not it is autographed. The autograph price applies to clean and clear signatures on a Mint (Mt) or Excellent Mint (Em) sports publication. Autograph prices are more subjective than magazine prices. The value for some of the deceased players covers are not known because an autographed magazine may not even exist! However, in most situations, the autographed magazine cover carries the same or more value than an 8x10. For example, deceased baseball player autograph values would range between an 8x10 and a clean single signed baseball. It also lists key feature articles and ads. Over the years, I have been asked for magazines that contain articles on "Pistol Pete" Maravich, Roberto Clemente, and other athletes that command a strong collectors' following. Corvette enthusiasts, for example, have asked me for magazines with ads of that classic American car, and Sam Snead fans have requested ads featuring "Slammin' Sam." In response to this interest, I have listed articles and ads that in my experience have been widely collected. I have also informed my readers which famous athletes have appeared as youngsters on the popular "Faces in the Crowd" (FIC) page.

In a number of cases, I have also noted when a particular athlete is appearing on the cover for the first time (FC = first cover). I have done this because, like rookie cards, first cover appearances typically bring a premium price. Some collectors, in fact, insist on nothing less than a star's first cover. Because some athletes shared cover honors with others the first time they appeared on it, I have also noted in some cases when an athlete earned his or her first solo cover (FSC).

The sixth chapter is devoted to *Sports Illustrated for Kids*. This is the child of SI and is geared toward the youth market (6-13). Each magazine has a great cover with great ads and a set of nine sports cards that cover every sport imaginable! Many of these cards are sought after by the player collector (Michael Jordan fans stand up) and usually drive the price of the individual issues. I listed every magazine cover and the cards since both drive the market for these collectibles.

The seventh chapter is devoted to *Time* and *Life* magazines with sports covers. This is one of my favorite subjects and is usually the section that everyone asks me about. The covers and pricing is similar to the *Sports Illustrated* chapter except there are more cover variations.

The eighth chapter is devoted to *Sport* Magazine. This chapter celebrates *Sport* magazine's 50th anniversary by going into every issue and examining its cover, its photo's, its feature articles and its ads. Though the number of autograph Sport magazine collectors is small, *Sport* magazines has some players that do not appear on *Sports Illustrated* (Bob Feller, Bob Lemon, etc.) and so many autograph sports magazine collectors seek out *Sport* magazine as a good substitute.

The ninth chapter is devoted to *Becketts* monthly price guides. This book recognizes *Becketts* as an alternative collectible for many collectors who want to collect more current and popular players. Many players appear on *Becketts* that do not grace the cover of *Sports Illustrated* and therefore it has become an alternative for collectors.

The final chapter is an Alphabetical Index of Sports covers by player. It lists every player and then the magazines on which he/she appeared. This feature was added because of frequent requests by people who like to collect by player or who like to know if a particular star ever appeared on a sports publication.

The book has three appendices. The first lists various types of *Sports Illustrated* games, posters, prints, etc. that have been released over the last 40 years. The second deals with the list of stars who appeared on *Sports Illustrated*. The final appendice concludes the book with sources for magazine supplies, materials, dealers and suppliers. The dealers and providers mentioned have contributed to the sports publication hobby and are worth noting in this second edition of the Collectors guide.

CHAPTER ONE:

COLLECTING *SPORTS ILLUSTRATED*

Sports Illustrated is an adolescent in the family of American sports magazines. Begun in 1954, it is far younger than, for example, the *Sporting News* (est. 1886) yet much older than its closest kin, *Sports Illustrated for Kids*, which began in 1989. Because of its intermediate age, *Sports Illustrated* is not scarce but chasing down early issues in nice condition is a challenge. This factor, combined with the magazine's runaway popularity among sports fans and the fact that its colorful covers are a near-perfect medium for autograph hunters, contribute to its unparalleled collectibility.

The inspiration behind *Sports Illustrated*, which is now America's most widely-read sports weekly, was publishing giant Henry R. Luce. Determined to capitalize on the postwar interest among well-to-do American men in the sporting life, Luce (who as the publisher of *Time*, *Life*, and *Fortune* obviously had a penchant for catchy, one-word magazine titles) attempted to buy the name of *Sport* from McFadden Publications, which in September of 1946 had started the monthly that would become *SI*'s chief rival. Although Luce offered $200,000 for the name, McFadden Publications insisted on a quarter of a million, so Luce shopped around for another title. Jokingly, Luce's associates dubbed his new venture "Jockstrap." But Luce finally settled on "Sports Illustrated."

Unfortunately that moniker too was already taken -- by a gentleman named Stuart Scheftel who had inaugurated his monthly *Sports Illustrated* in an oversized format in the late 1930s. More reasonable than the owners of *Sport*, Scheftel (who had lent the "Sports Illustrated" name to Dell Publications for a brief run in the 1940s) settled for "something in the low five figures" -- plus a lifetime subscription to the new publication -- and today's *Sports Illustrated* was born.

Like Scheftel's *Sports Illustrated*, which eventually merged with *Golf Illustrated*, Luce's new magazine began (at a relatively pricey $7.50 a year!) as a highbrow publication aimed at elite sportsmen who had both the money and the leisure to enjoy a week of marlin fishing in the Pacific or an extended safari in East Africa. This fact is reflected in many of the sporting images (now not widely collected) that filled the *SI* cover in its inaugural year: yacht racers on Long Island Sound, a steeplechase race, a dog with its pheasant prey, etc. Although this well-heeled club had money, it did not have enough members, and *Sports Illustrated* lost money throughout the 1950s.

In the early 1960s, however, the magazine found its current niche, as a profitable publication devoted primarily, if not exclusively, to major spectator sports such as football, baseball, basketball, hockey, boxing, golf, and tennis. Accompanying this shift in editorial focus (and profitability) was a parallel shift in cover images. Although *Sports Illustrated*'s cover featured some superstars in the mid-1950s -- Y.A. Tittle, Ben Hogan, Ted Williams, Rocky Marciano, and Bob Cousy among them -- its editors did not discover until later in the decade that covers of dogs and fish and birds would not pay the bills. The decision to jettison the emphasis on the pastimes of elites in favor of an emphasis on popular spectator sports opened the door not only for *Sports Illustrated*'s profitability but also for its current collectibility.

BASEBALL CARD ISSUES

Another factor that contributed to *SI*'s collectibility was its editors' decision to include baseball card inserts in four early issues. The first issue of *Sports Illustrated*, which hit the newsstands on August 16, 1954, featured on its cover Milwaukee Braves' slugger Eddie Mathews swinging for the fences of Milwaukee's County Stadium. (New York Giants catcher Wes Westrum and umpire Augie Donatelli are also in the shot.) Inside were three fold-out pages of baseball cards made after the manner of regular 1954 Topps cards but printed on paper stock. Among the superstars who appeared on these cards were Willie Mays, Ted Williams, Duke Snider, Richie Ashburn, Jackie Robinson, Ted Kluszewski, and Mathews himself.

SI's second issue, which appeared on August 23, 1954, also included card inserts. Its cover was less interesting (golf bags at the Masters) but its cards are more valuable. Also produced by Topps, this second three-page foldout featured the entire New York Yankee team which included, among them Yogi Berra, Whitey Ford, and Mickey Mantle. Because contractual disagreements prevented Topps from releasing a regular issue card of Mantle, this is the only 1954 Topps Mantle "card" available to collectors.

Conventional wisdom would seem to dictate that the premier issue of a magazine would command the premium price, but conventional wisdom is sometimes wrong. Although *SI* #1 typically sells for $200 to $300 (a healthy increase over its original price of 25¢), *SI* #2 retails for around $300 to $400. Why? First and most obviously, the second issue contains not only Yankees cards but a Mantle, and sports collectors are crazy about both New York's most famous team and arguably its most famous modern superstar. Secondly, there were far fewer issues of #2 produced. Luce sent out numerous promotional copies of its inaugural issue, but only subscribers received its next offering. Even today a warehouse find a few years ago has caused the market to be flooded with mint SI #1 issues. *Sports Illustrated* also has made two recent offerings of its premiere issue through advertisements on its pages and through its collectible marketing arm called the Sports Illustrated Store.

In the spring of 1955, *SI* produced two more magazines with baseball card inserts. The April 11, 1955 issue showed Giants' legend Willie Mays with Leo Durocher and his wife Laraine Day on the cover. Inside it contained a one-page insert, again produced by Topps but made this time in the image of 1955 cards. Among the stars who appeared on these eight cards were Ernie Banks, Warren Spahn, and Dick Groat. One week later, on April 18, 1955, *Sports Illustrated* included another page of baseball cards in an issue whose cover featured Cleveland Indians slugger Al Rosen. This less interesting insert contained, along with Rosen, only second-tier stars such as Ferris Fain, Bob Turley, and Roy Sievers.

BUILDING A COLLECTION

There are many ways to build a collection of *Sports Illustrated*. Usually the easiest way is to subscribe and to save each issue as it is delivered. Many collectors have a run of 10 years or so and are eager to fill in the missing years. The two ways to store entire runs is either with magazine boxes that can be stacked or a library file system in the home that requires magazine (verticle) boxes that are used in libraries.

If, like most collectors, your goal is something less than a complete collection, your first acquisition should be the 35th anniversary issue published as a special supplement by *SI* on March 26, 1990. Entitled "35 Years of Covers," this magazine pictures every *Sports Illustrated* cover from 1954 through 1989. Flip through this issue and see what catches your eye. Then fix upon a collecting strategy and stick to it.

One time-honored strategy for *SI* collecting is to concentrate on a certain sport. This cuts down on both cost and space, but can still be a daunting task. Of all the sports featured on *SI* covers, football is #1 at 523 covers as of the end of 1995 (not including SI Presents). Baseball and basketball follow with 428 and 324 covers, respectively. Golf (136), boxing, (121), and track (93) come next in popularity, trailed by hockey (83), tennis (73), horseracing (54), and skiing (44).

A third approach is to focus on only your favorite player (or players). Muhammad Ali (a.k.a. Cassius Clay) held the all-time record for cover appearances with 33 until 1996 when Michael Jordan passed it. Third with 28 covers is UCLA Basketball phenom Kareem Abdul-Jabbar [Lew Alcindor], who first appeared on the *SI* cover on December 5, 1966. Rounding out the current top five are Jack Nicklaus and "Magic" Johnson [see Appendix 1 for cover leaders].

Oddly enough, some *SI* collectors eschew sports stars entirely, focusing on non-sport celebrities that have appeared on the cover. In this crew are Gary Cooper, Bob Hope, Shirley MacLaine, Steve McQueen, Ernest Hemingway, Burt Reynolds and Arnold Schwarzenegger. Among U.S. Presidents, Ronald Reagan, Gerald Ford, Jack Kennedy and, most recently, Bill Clinton have served as *SI* cover models.

Clearly the most popular "non-sport" covers, however, are *Sports Illustrated*'s annual swimsuit issues. Swimsuit models appeared on the cover as early as *SI*'s third offering in 1954, but the swimsuit issue did not begin officially until Babette March graced the cover on January 20, 1964. Now a *SI* institution, this controversial issue prompts cancellations from subscribers every year, but it is also far and away the best seller on the newsstands. A complete run of 33 swimsuit issues from 1964 to 1996 will set a collector back a few hundred dollars.

Given the popularity of the "Sportsman of the Year" (SOY) issue, which *Sports Illustrated* began on January 3, 1955 with its selection of miler Roger Bannister as 1954's "Sportsman," it should not be surprising that there are collectors who have put together runs of Sportsman (or Sportswoman) of the Year covers. This list includes legends such as Arnold Palmer, Stan Musial, Michael Jordan, Bill Russell, and Billie Jean King (the first Sportswoman of the Year) as well as relative unknowns such as sprinter Bobby Morrow, college quarterback Terry Baker, and miler Jim Ryun.

Collectors specializing in the memorabilia of a particular player may want to track down issues that contain articles featuring their chosen star. There are, moreover, some very interesting and attractive advertisements in the magazine (Corvette ads, etc), especially in the 1950s and 1960s, and some collectors will search for those. (In order to assist those collectors, I have included in the price guide not only the issue date and cover subject but also significant articles and ads.) Nevertheless, collectors primarily interested in the content of the magazine are the exception rather than the rule. Covers, in short, generally drive *SI* collectibility.

Finally, a growing number of collectors gather only issues that they have a reasonable prospect of getting signed. These folks have merged *SI* collecting with autograph hunting. (For more on them and their passion, see Chapter 2.)

WHERE TO FIND SI's

There are a number of places to obtain *Sports Illustrated*s. For people with time on their hands and the desire for a great bargain in their hearts, yard sales, flea markets, and local auctions are good places to start. While the hope of finding baseball cards at bargain basement prices was extinguished years ago, it is still possible to find *SI*'s at these locations for as little as 10 cents a piece. This is especially true at yard sales, where homeowners are frequently ready to throw away anything that doesn't find a buyer over the weekend.

Used book stores, comic book shops, and magazine shops are another good possibility. Most major cities have at least one store devoted exclusively to magazines.. Cities that don't have shops specializing in magazines will, no doubt, have stores devoted to used books and comics. These also provide a good opportunity. If when you visit these locations you don't see any *SI*'s, don't give up. Tell the shop owner that you are looking for *Sports Illustrated*. The next time he's offered a lot, he may give you a call!

If you don't have any luck with these local options, you might want to try national mail-order dealers that specialize in sports-related publications (see Appendix III). You will, of course, pay a little more this way. But your search will be less time consuming, and you are more likely to find the issues you need in collectible condition.

"PERIPHERAL" COLLECTIBLES

Some die-hard *SI* collectors also chase "peripheral" *SI* collectibles such as the two "dummy" issues that preceded the magazine's official debut on August 16, 1954. Because Luce hadn't yet settled on a moniker for his new venture, the first "dummy" (December 1953), which featured a crowd of spectators at a football stadium on its cover, was called *The New Sport Magazine*. The second cover (April 1954) showed a golfer at Pebble Beach and was dubbed, simply, *Dummy*. These issues, which are frequently accompanied by a letter from Luce asking the reader for helpful comments and criticisms, typically sell for about $400 each in near mint shape.

Also collected by *SI* buffs are pre-1954 SI's produced either by Scheftel or by Dell. Tops on this list is a May of 1949 *Life*-sized issue that features Yankee slugger Joe Dimaggio on its cover. Because Dimaggio did not appear on the cover of the "real" *SI* until 1993, this issue is widely sought-after by *SI* enthusiasts. It typically commands about $500-700 in nice shape.

Perhaps most difficult to track down are the many "spoofs" of *Sports Illustrated* published over the years, often by college humor magazines. The most famous and accessible of these is a 1974 parody published by the Harvard Lampoon. Others include *Sports Illuminated* (1956, Valparaiso), *Sports Ill-rated* (1956, Maryland), *Sports Frustrated* (1958, Stanford), and *Sports Illiterate* (1959, Yale). *Mad!* magazine has also issued a number of *SI* parodies.

In addition to these publication "peripherals," some *SI* collectors also accumulate items sponsored by the magazine and sold through ads on its pages. In this category are *Sports Illustrated* posters, puzzles, calendars, games, movies, and videos (see Appendix 1). Probably the nicest of these "add-ons" are a set of autographed, limited-edition (1000 or 1500 copies) "Living Legends" lithographs offered to *SI* readers at $75 and $100 each in the mid-1970s. Some of these signed lithos feature two athletes: Joe Louis and Max Schmeling, Jack Dempsey and Gene Tunney, Wilt Chamberlain and John Havlicek. Others -- Stan Musial, Johnny Unitas, Eddie Arcaro, Jack Nicklaus, Rod Laver, Billie Jean King, Red Grange, Arnold Palmer, and Joe DiMaggio, among them -- focus on just one superstar. These signed litho's (in pencil) have commanded prices ranging from $75 - $1,500 depending upon scarcity and demand.

Tomorrow's *SI* collectibles are also available today through a new venture of Time, Inc.: _The Sports Illustrated Store_. The SI Store sells a variety of clothing and collectibles, including videos such as "Larry Bird: A Basketball Legend" and "Michael Jordan: Come Fly With Me". The store also sells oversized, framed lithographs of _SI_ covers signed by superstars such as Larry Bird, Joe Montana, Magic Johnson, Dan Marino, and Reggie Jackson. You can get their current catalog by calling (1-800-274-5200).

CHAPTER TWO:

SPORTS PUBLICATION AUTOGRAPHS

Hunting down signatures of *Sports Illustrated* cover superstars has in the past few years become an obsession for a growing number of collectors. While many sports fans still prefer autographs on cards, photos, bats, or balls, more and more are turning to magazines such as *Life*, *Time*, *Sport*, *Beckett*, *Sports Illustrated for Kids* and *Sports Illustrated* because of their attractive covers, their modest price-tags, and the fact that they are dated pieces with interesting historical content. Of all these magazines, *Sports Illustrated* is far and away the most popular among collectors of sports autographs. In fact, many categorically refuse to meddle with any other medium. This chapter will fill you in on the autographed publication craze and offer you some tips on how to get autographs for yourself.

GETTING STARTED

There are almost as many ways to build a collection of autographed *Sports Publications* as there are collectors. The key is to focus. Some autographed publication collectors chase only Heisman Trophy winners that have appeared on the cover. Others collect only baseball Hall of Famers, or *SI*'s Sportsmen and Sportswomen of the year, or footballers featured on the annual Super Bowl cover. Another simple method is to concentrate on a particular team or city. Start with the Los Angeles Lakers, for example, or, if you're from Philadelphia, fix your sights on the Phillies, Flyers, Sixers, and Eagles.

If you want a slightly broader collection, you might focus on a particular sport. If you're a baseball fan, don't worry about gymnast Mary Lou Retton. And if you're a gymnastics fan, forget about Red Sox slugger Carl Yastrzemski.

The most ambitious approach, of course, is to try to get as many different issues as possible signed. There are over 2100 different covers (and counting) of Sports Illustrated, but some can never be signed either because they appeared following a star's death (e.g. the Len Bias and

Reggie Lewis covers) or because they featured dogs, horses, or other non-signers. Collectors pursuing this difficult route should emulate Stan Keen of Oregon and Scott Smith of New Jersey, each of whom has amassed a collection of over a thousand signatures.

One modification of this approach adopted by slightly less ambitious collectors is to be satisfied with a single signed issue of any particular player. These folks forget about Muhammad Ali's 33 different covers or even Willie Mays' 8 and are satisfied with one cover signed per athlete (frequently, his or her first!). Even this approach, however, will send you off in hot pursuit of hundreds of different athletes.

If you are new to the signed *Sports Illustrated* game, you might want to emulate collectors who eschew marquee sports such as baseball, football, and basketball, and concentrate instead on less popular, but equally exciting sports where athletes are often genuinely glad to receive fan mail. These collectors frequently write to stars via their respective halls of fame, which are almost always willing to forward mail to their inductees. (For a list of hall of fame addresses, see Chapter 3.)

No matter which approach you take you will find adventure in each one. Most of the athletes that I meet who sign my cover are delighted to sign the magazine and usually have a story to add to it. For example, Jim 'Toy Cannon' Wynn told me he felt jinxed after he appeared on the cover in 1974. He was not to happy about the jinx but he is happy to sign his magazine cover today.

VALUES OF SIGNED *SI*'S

Because autographed *SI*'s are not as frequently bought and sold as, for example, signed 8 x 10 photos or "cut" signatures, establishing their value is a bit tricky. One thing is clear, however: unlike baseball cards, which frequently <u>decrease</u> in value when signed, *SI*'s always <u>increase</u> in price when autographed. One "rule of thumb" is that autographed *Sports Illustrated*s are worth about what the unsigned magazine is worth, plus the value of an autographed 8 x 10. So, for example, if an autographed Carl Yastrzemski 8 x 10 is worth about $25 and his 1967 "Sportsman of the Year" issue also runs $30 in EM shape, the signed (SOY) magazine should sell for approximately $55. This quick rule works best for relatively common autographs. Signed *SI* collectors are frequently willing to bid up the value of magazines autographed by "tough" signers or deceased superstars well beyond the combined value of the magazine and the 8 x 10. Signed Ben Hogan and Mickey Mantle SI's, for example, have sold for as much as $350 -- well over double what our "rule of thumb" would indicate. In this case (in fact in all cases!), signed *SI*'s are worth no more and no less than what the market will bear.

The price guide section has an autograph additional value to each issue. The autograph price is under the Mt and Em prices on the right hand section of the value list. These are market estimate 'guides' for nice clean autographs on a SI or other magazine. It is critical to note that the prices for tough autographed issues and those of deceased autographed players will be more likely to go for values higher than those prices listed. It should be noted that near mint magazines that are signed sell much faster than EM magazines with a label.

IN PERSON AUTOGRAPHS

The preferred way to obtain autographs is, of course, in person. Most big-time athletes do not sign through the mail, and almost all current athletes who are on the circuit get too much mail to answer. A few players have resorted to the dreaded autopen while others have been known to use an autograph stamp. So, personally witnessing a sports star signing your magazine is the only sure-fire way to know it's authentic. When you track down Wayne Gretzky after a practice and he agrees to sign your "Sportsman of the Year" *SI* cover, you <u>know</u> the autograph is legitimate, and you have a memory of your "brush with fame" to boot!

If you live in a major city, go to sporting events early and try to find participants there (before batting practice at the ballpark or before "shoot-around" at a basketball venue). Better yet, go the day before to where the team works out. Generally, you'll have better luck at the Atlanta Falcons' practice at Suwanee, Georgia than at their game at the Georgia Dome and more success at Pebble Beach practice rounds than at the U.S. Open itself.

These suggestions work for at least some of today's athletes, but what about retired superstars? One approach is to begin with your local paper and scan it carefully, especially the columns of your local purveyor of celebrity "gossip." There are hundreds and hundreds of *SI* cover subjects so chances are good that at least one of them will be passing through your city in a given month. If they're appearing at a press conference, playing in an exhibition, filming a commercial, or participating in a celebrity golf tournament, show up. And if you can find out where they are staying, park yourself in the hotel lobby. Some hotels now bar this practice, but many still permit it, especially if you are well-dressed and clean-shaven.

If you're persistent, prepared, and polite, you may get lucky. Bring along your Sharpie pen (the writing implement of choice for *SI* collectors), and get the attention of the athlete by holding up your magazine. You'll be amazed how frequently you'll hear a star say that he or she is surprised and delighted to see it. If you have duplicates, bring them along too. The athlete might want one or two for himself, and may be willing to sign multiples for you in return. Sound implausible? It's not. Remember that when superstars are in their prime they concentrate on winning championships, not on saving memorabilia. Recently a golf collector encountered Sam Snead after a charity golf tournament with a handful of *SI* covers. Snead was thrilled to see the November 12, 1962 cover featuring him with a young Arnold Palmer. The collector offered it to him, and he gratefully signed a number of his *SI* covers in return.

If preparedness is important, remember that the other two "P's" (politeness and persistence) also go a long way. Superstars may be great at shooting a basketball or reading a green, but they are people like you and I. They don't like folks shouting at them or interrupting their meals at restaurants. And believe it or not your chances of getting an autograph actually go up if you avoid pushing, shoving, and screaming. Nonetheless, persistence can pay off. After Jimmy Connors finished playing in a recent team tennis match, he was surrounded by autograph seekers and refused them all. Once he emerged from a press conference, a smaller group of fans besieged him, and again he refused. Undaunted, one *SI* collector followed him away from the stadium, walking on what he knew was his writing side (his left, of course!). He complimented him on his match, and politely asked Connors for his autograph. Connors, just before jumping into a waiting limousine, signed the magazine in a clear, bold hand.

AUTOGRAPH SHOWS

Sports memorabilia shows with autograph guests are another way to obtain "in person" signatures. Although this route is more expensive than obtaining autographs yourself before a workout or after a spring training game, it is certainly less time consuming. And depending on the athlete, you may also get a handshake and a short conversation for your autograph fee.

Charges for this service vary greatly from athlete to athlete and from show to show. The status of the star in his sport obviously has a lot to do with the cost of his or her autograph. That is why Phillies slugger Mike Schmidt (typically $50) costs more than, say, Pittsburgh shortstop Dick Groat (about $8). But scarcity also plays an important role. Bob Feller may be one of the greatest pitchers who ever lived, but he has been a regular on the baseball card show circuit for years, so his signature is inexpensive (also about $8). Prices really soar when a signer combines greatness with scarcity, as in the case of Celtic legend Bill Russell who until recently categorically refused virtually every autograph request. When he finally agreed to begin signing, collectors didn't blink at fees in triple figures.

If you have paid a lot of money for your autographed sports publication and there is a chance you might want to sell or trade it in the future, you might want to get it notarized. Frequently show promoters contract for the services of a notary public; you can typically obtain their certification on the spot for a nominal fee (about $3-$5). If the autographing fee was modest or you don't want to shell out the money for the notary, save your stamped autograph ticket or a flyer advertising the show. Even better, have your photograph taken with your hero. Some show promoters still allow this, despite the fact that it slows down the line, and you can pull the picture out in the future for "evidence" of your signature's authenticity.

For people who don't live in the vicinity of major card shows, it is possible to obtain autographs from show promoters through the mail. If this is the route you want to go, get references to be sure you are dealing with a legitimate and considerate promoter. In order to preserve the condition of your magazine, take pains to pack your magazine with a backing board and to mail it in a padded manila envelope. If the show promoter wants you to include return postage (and they usually do), be sure to include a SASE (self-addressed stamped envelope [Priority Mail from the Post Office]) for your *SI*'s safe return trip. However, here is my additional advice on making sure you get your magazine back the same way you sent it.

Type a very clear letter stating the following issues:

> a. EXACTLY how you want the magazine signed,
>   (Location & personalization & HOF date, etc.)
> b what you want it signed with (Pen, Sharpie, etc.),
> c. how you want the magazine handled
> d. how you want it repackaged
> e. How you want it reshipped.
> f. State how to identify your magazine (be it with the mailing
>   label name or with your signature penciled lightly on a page
>   inside the magazine.

Be very clear with your instructions. Believe me, it is worth the time. I thought I was getting a super deal from one promoter but found that my magazine was damaged and my complaints were ignored. Also promoters may mix your mint 1955 Sports Illustrated Ted Williams with someone else's, so tagging your magazine with a pencil mark inside on a specific page (how's page 10) is not a bad idea (your signature is usually good - make sure you can erase it without leaving a mark).

AUTOGRAPHS BY MAIL

Collectors who can't afford to shell out the cash commanded by stars at card shows or who desire signatures of athletes not currently on the autographing circuit will want to contact their heroes directly by mail. The most surprising thing about this strategy is how frequently it works!

The first hurdle to this approach is, of course, obtaining a current address. Here the lists published by autograph collecting newsletters are invaluable. More up-to-date than lists published in a book format, these monthly or bimonthly newsletters routinely publish reports from subscribers regarding addresses that have worked (or failed) and the signing policies of individuals. Clearly the best value of these is "The Autograph Banker," which is published occasionally by George Haggas of Audubon, New Jersey. An old-fashioned collector, Haggas does his newsletter just for the fun of it. He charges no subscription fees, and asks only that you send him SASE's for as many of his upcoming newsletters as you want. You can reach him at: P.O. Box 42, Audubon, New Jersey 08106. Another source is the Sports Publication Newsletter, PO Box 26596, Las Vegas , NV 89126-0596 ($24/yr) which focuses only on people who have appeared on a sports cover.

If you can't get an individual address for an athlete, try his or her college athletic department, pro team, agent, or sponsoring company. (Our address list will help you here.) In fact, sports stars frequently prefer that you write them in this indirect manner, freeing up their home mailboxes for family matters. You will generally have better luck during the off-season or pre-season, when athletes have both less mail and more free time to answer it.

Unfortunately, a few of America's most famous superstars will not sign anything through the mail. Don't be too harsh on them, however. Some get practically as much mail as the President and have as little free time. Anything you send to these marquee players will either be returned or, worse, thrown away. As a general rule, therefore, you should never send anything through the mail that you cannot absolutely, positively live without.

Those who will sign through the mail frequently have clear, if unannounced, policies regarding what they will and will not sign, so it may be worth sending a letter (with a SASE) inquiring about policies before you send your publication. Some athletes will return an autographed photo to admirers but will refuse to sign items sent to them. Others will sign only one item, while others will sign up to three. Still others will write back, requesting a fee or referring you to a fan club that offers signed items for sale. In an attempt to frustrate the efforts of dealers who sell autographed items obtained through the mail, some will insist on personalizing (e.g., "To Bill . . ."). Others will refuse to personalize anything on the grounds that it takes up too much time. Sometimes, the secretaries of athletes who are gracious enough to sign through the mail keep track of writers whom their employees have previously accommodated. These athletes will respond to your first request but return a second or third unsigned. The bottom line here is that there are no hard and fast rules about athletes' autographing policies.

IMPROVING YOUR CHANCES

You can do at least four things to improve your chances of getting your *SI* signed and returned from your favorite athletes. The first rule is to save the athlete both time and money by including a SASE with sufficient return postage. For stars residing outside the United States, use International Reply Coupons (IRC's), which can be exchanged in foreign countries for stamps.

The second rule is to send a thoughtful letter. This letter should be handwritten but legible. It should be concise and to the point. You should tell the athlete why <u>you</u> are writing to <u>him</u> (or <u>her</u>) -- you run track, you love three-point shooters, you went to UCLA like he did, you share the same birthday, etc. In short, you should do everything you can to distinguish yourself from all the other requests the athlete receives. DO NOT send a copied letter with the athlete's name filled in, and DO NOT tell the athlete she is the hundred-and-first person you have written to this year (even if she is). Such approaches are, for obvious reasons, doomed to fail.

The third rule is to pack your magazine carefully. My recommendation is the following:

#1　　Put the *SI* and backboards in a plastic magazine bag with a backboard on the outside to prevent the magazine from getting bent.

#2　　Put a RETURN SASE U.S. POST OFFICE PRIORITY MAILER WITH YOUR RETURN ADDRESS and Stamp (first class) inside the package, preferable next to the magazine.

#3　　Put your letter in front of the magazine in the plastic magazine bag, state in the letter how you want the magazine to be shipped back to you. Also attach any donation or check to the letter.

#4　　Put the bagged *SI* in a bubble-wrapped manila envelope that you get from an office supply center.

#5　　Place the bubble-wrapped manila envelope (with the magazine inside it) inside a U.S. Post Office Priority mailer.

These five steps sound like a lot of work, but in my experience it is better to be safe than sorry. The good news, is that, players usually treat your magazine better than promoters. This is because promoters sometimes hire people to handle the 'mail' who are just not in tune with the hobby at all.

Finally, you might want to include a small check ($2-$10) to speed up the process. Some players will donate the money to charity, while many more will return the check uncashed.

If you are just starting out collecting autographed sports publications through the mail, you might want to begin with individuals who receive only a few pieces of fan mail a month rather than a few hundred a day. Skip big sports names in baseball, and focus on other sports like basketball or football. If you want to make a retired athlete's day, try swimmers or track and field stars.

If you don't have these athletes' individual addresses, try the appropriate hall of fame. If they've been on an *SI* cover, chances are that they've been inducted into their respective hall. The vast majority of halls of fame are happy to forward mail to their inductees. (For a list of these addresses, see Chapter 3.)

Gathering sports publication autographs through the mail may be a bit risky but it is lots of fun. You will probably, at one time or another, receive a "ghost" signature and you may lose some magazines in the process, but you will go to your mailbox each day with a new sense of adventure!

AUTOGRAPH DEALERS AND OTHER STRATEGIES

If you are serious about collecting autographed sports publications, you may want to call on the services of a reputable autographed publications dealer. Basketball superstar Michael Jordan doesn't do card shows, doesn't sign through the mail, and is a very tough signature in person, so if you absolutely, positively must have an autographed Jordan cover, you will probably have to go through a dealer. The same is true, for obvious reasons, if you want an autographed *SI* cover of deceased athletes such as Arthur Ashe or if you want a "cut" autograph to frame with an unsigned *SI*.

When buying through a dealer, the most important advice is to be cautious. There are some cheats out there, so get references. Ask about how and when the dealer obtained the autograph and why he or she thinks it's legitimate. Then, after you are convinced of the story, get a money-back guarantee (It should be automatic and save your receipts!). Finally, don't put too much stock in so-called "certificates of authenticity." If a dealer is unscrupulous enough to be peddling fake autographs, he is probably not going to worry too much about distributing fake "certificates."

Once you have determined that a dealer is reputable, educate yourself about the value of autographs. Sections of this book are devoted to helping educate the collector on the autograph value of a sports publication. However, it is also good to know why certain autographs are more valuable than others. Celtics great Bill Russell is a tough signature and his signed *SI* (assuming you can find one) rightfully commands a premium price ($250-$300) because he has only done three signings in his entire career! But Eddie Mathews is a show circuit regular whose signature doesn't add more than $10 or $15 to the cost of his magazine covers. Some autographs are hard to obtain because they do not sign through the mail and do not do shows. Try, for example, finding autographed SI's of great Russian athletes...good luck.

Finally, be picky about condition. Don't pay a "mint" price for a "very good" magazine. Make sure the signature is legible and placed in a good spot on the cover. The bottom line here is that you should be certain the cover is something you would be proud to frame and display before you agree to buy it.

There are, of course, other ways to get your magazines signed. If you have a friend who's going to spring training, give him two of your Frank Robinson covers and tell him you expect one back, signed, in return. You might also want to engage in the ancient practice of horse trading. Even if you are only interested in one signed *SI* per player, get two whenever you have a chance. The second can be used in the future for "trade bait." The lesson here is to keep your ears and options open. Get to know other collectors. Let friends know that you collect autographed *SI*'s. Soon you will discover that a co-worker lives next door to swimming great Donna de Varona or that an acquaintance works for a network and can hit up ex-Steeler Terry Bradshaw. Before you know it, you'll be on your way!

CHAPTER THREE:

ADDRESS LIST

What follows is a list of addresses you can use to contact sports publication cover subjects. I have not listed individual addresses for two reasons. First, I want to respect the privacy of cover stars who understandably prefer not to be contacted, even by their most admiring fans, at their homes. Second, I have discovered over the years that many athletes prefer to be reached indirectly (via their team, for example) rather than directly (via their residence). As a result, you are in many cases likely to have greater signing success through the institutional addresses I have listed here than through home addresses.

Among the addresses I have included are those for MLB, NBA, NFL, and NHL teams and for colleges whose stars have appeared on the *SI* cover. I also fill you in on how you can contact key halls of fame and I have provided listings for other associations and key corporations through which you are likely to have signing success. If you need home, business or charity addresses you can request that by subscribing to the SPN, at PO Box 26596, Las Vegas NV 89126-0596 ($24/yr). Many collectors share addresses of people who sign through the mail. The chapter concludes with a list of deceased sports publication cover stars dated through June of 1996.

Major League Baseball Team Addresses

Atlanta Braves
P.O. Box 4064
Atlanta-Fulton County Stad.
Atlanta, GA 30312

Baltimore Orioles
333 West Camden St.
Baltimore, MD 21201

Boston Red Sox
Fenway Park
24 Yawkey Way
Boston, MA 02215

California Angels
P.O. Box 2000
Anaheim Stadium
Anaheim, CA 92803

Chicago Cubs
1060 W. Addison St.
Wrigley Field
Chicago, IL 60613

Chicago White Sox
333 W. 35th St.
Comiskey Park
Chicago, IL 60616

Cincinnati Reds
100 Riverfront Stadium
Cincinnati, OH 45202

Cleveland Indians
Jacobs field
2401 Ontario St.
Cleveland, OH 44114

Colorado Rockies
Mile High Stadium
1700 Broadway #2100
Denver, CO 80290

Detroit Tigers
Tiger Stadium
2121 Trumbull Ae
Detroit, MI 48216

Florida Marlins
2267 NW 199th St.
Opa Locka, FL 33056

Houston Astros
P.O. Box 288
The Astrodome
Houston, TX 77001-0288

Kansas City Royals
P.O. Box 419969
Royals Stadium
Kansas City, MO 64141

Los Angeles Dodgers
1000 Elysian Park Ave.
Dodger Stadium
Los Angeles, CA 90012

Milwaukee Brewers
Milwaukee County Stadium
Milwaukee, WI 53214

Minnesota Twins
501 Chicago Ave. S.
H.H. Humphrey Metrodome
Minneapolis, MN 55415

Montreal Expos
P.O. Box 500, Station M
Olympic Stadium
Montreal, Quebec
CANADA H1V 3P2

New York Mets
Shea Stadium
Flushing, NY 11368

New York Yankees
Yankee Stadium
Bronx, NY 10451

Oakland A's
Oakland-Alameda County
Stadium
Oakland, CA 94621

Philadelphia Phillies
P.O. Box 7575
Veterans Stadium
Philadelphia, PA 19101

Pittsburgh Pirates
P.O. Box 7000
Three Rivers Stadium
Pittsburgh, PA 15212

San Diego Padres
PO Box 2000
San Diego, CA 92120

San Francisco Giants
Candlestick Park
San Francisco, CA 94124

Seattle Mariners
P.O. Box 4100
The Kingdome
Seattle, WA 98104

St. Louis Cardinals
250 Stadium Plaza
Busch Stadium
St. Louis, MO 63102

Texas Rangers
P.O. Box 1111
Arlington, TX 76010

Toronto Blue Jays
Skydome
300 Brenner Blvd #3200
Toronto, Ontario
CANADA M5C 3b3

Major League Baseball Spring Training Addresses

Atlanta Braves
Municipal Stadium
715 Hank Aaron Dr.
P.O. Box 2619
West Palm Beach, FL
33402-2619

Baltimore Orioles
Twins Lake Park
6700 Clark Rd.
Sarasota, Fl 34241

Boston Red Sox
City of Palms Park
2201 Edison St.
Ft. Myers, FL 33901

California Angels
Diablo Stadium
2200 W. Alameda Dr.
Tempe, AZ 85282

Chicago White Sox
Ed Smith Stadium
1090 N. Euclid
Sarasota, FL 34237

Chicago Cubs
HoHoKam Park
1235 N. Center St.
Box 4066
Mesa, AZ 85201

Cincinnati Reds
Plant City Stadium
1900 S. Park Rd.
Box 2275
Plant City, FL 33564

Cleveland Indians
Cypress Gardens Blvd.
Winter Haven, Fl 33880

Colorado Rockies
Hi Corbett Field
Randolph Park
3400 E. Camino Compestre
Tucson, AZ 85716

Detroit Tigers
Joker Marchant Stadium
Lakeland Hills Blvd.
Box 90187
Lakeland, FL 33804

Florida Marlins
Cocoa Expo
500 Friday Rd.
Cocoa, FL 32926

Houston Astros
Osceola County Stadium
100 Osceola Blvd.
Box 422229
Kissimmee, FL 34744

Kansas City Royals
Baseball City Stadium
Interstate 4 and U.S. 27
Baseball City, FL 33844

Los Angeles Dodgers
Holman Stadium
4001 26th St.
Vero Beach, FL 32961-2887

Milwaukee Brewers
Compadre Stadium
1425 W. Ocotillo Rd.
P.O. Box 2650
Chandler, AZ 85244

Minnesota Twins
Lee County Sports Complex
14100 Six Mile
Cypress Pkwy.
Fort Myers, FL 33912

Montreal Expos
Municipal Stadium
715 Hank Aaron Dr.
Box 3566
West Palm Beach, FL
33402

New York Mets
Thomas J. White Stadium
525 NW Peacock Blvd.
Port St. Lucie, Fl 34986

New York Yankees
Ft. Lauderdale Stadium
5301 NW 12th Ave.
Ft. Lauderdale, FL 33309

Oakland Athletics
Phoenix Stadium
5999 E. Van Buren
Phoenix, AZ 85258

Philadelphia Phillies
Jack Russell Stadium
800 Phillies Dr.
Box 10336
Clearwater, FL 34617

Pittsburgh Pirates
McKechnie Field
17th Ave. W & 9th St.
Box 1359
Bradenton, Fl 34206

St. Louis Cardinals
Al Lang Stadium
180 Second Ave. SE
St. Petersburg, Fl 33701

San Diego Padres
Desert Sun Stadium
Ave. A at 35th St.
Box 4668
Yuma, AZ 85246

San Francisco Giants
Scottsdale Stadium
7402 E. Osborn Rd.
Scottsdale, AZ 85251

Seattle Mariners
Peoria Complex
15999 N. 81st Ave.
Peoria, AZ 85345

Texas Rangers
Box 3609
Port Charlotte, FL 33949-
3609

Toronto Blue Jays
Grant Field
311 Douglas Ave.
Box 957
Dunedin, Fl 34697

National Basketball League Team Addresses

Atlanta Hawks
1 CNN Center
South Tower, #405
Atlanta, GA 30303

Boston Celtics
151 Merrimac St.
5th Floor
Boston, MA 02114

Charlotte Hornets
100 Hive Drive
Charlotte, NC 28217

Chicago Bulls
1 Magnificent Mile
980 N. Michigan Ave.
Suite 1600
Chicago, IL 60611

Cleveland Cavaliers
2923 Streetsboro Rd.
Richfield, OH 44286

Dallas Mavericks
Reunion Arena
777 Sports St.
Dallas, TX 75207

Denver Nuggets
1635 Clay St.
Denver, CO 80204

Detroit Pistons
Palace of Auburn Hills
2 Championship Dr.
Auburn Hills, MI 48057

Golden State Warriors
Oakland Coliseum Arena
7000 Coliseum Way
Oakland, CA 94621

Houston Rockets
The Summit
10 Greenway Plaza
Houston, TX 77046

Indiana Pacers
300 East Market St.
Indianapolis, IN 46204

Los Angeles Clippers
L.A. Sports Arena
3939 S. Figueroa St.
Los Angeles, CA 90037

Los Angeles Lakers
Great Western Forum
3900 W. Manchester Blvd.
Inglewood, CA 90306

Miami Heat
Miami Arena
Miami, FL 33136-4102

Milwaukee Bucks
Bradley Center
1001 N. 4th St.
Milwaukee, WI 53203

Minnesota Timberwolves
Target Center
600 1st Ave. North
Minneapolis, MN 55403

New Jersey Nets
Meadowlands Arena
E. Rutherford, NJ 07073

New York Knickerbockers
Madison Square Garden
2 Penn Plaza, 3rd Floor
New York, NY 10001

Orlando Magic
Orlando Arena
1 Magic Place
Orlando, FL 32801

Philadelphia 76ers
Veterans Stadium
Broad St. & Pattison Ave.
Philadelphia, PA 19148

Phoenix Suns
Box 1369
Phoenix, AZ 85001

Portland Trail Blazers
Suite 600 Lloyd Building
700 NE Multnomah St.
Portland, OR 97232

Sacramento Kings
1 Sports Parkway
Sacramento, CA 95834

San Antonio Spurs
Alamodome
100 Montana St.
San Antonio, TX 78203

Seattle Supersonics
190 Queene Anne, North
Suite 200
Seattle, WA 98109

Toronto Raptors
20 Bay st 1702
Toronto, Ontario,
Canada m5j 2n8

Utah Jazz
Delta Center
301 W. South Temple
Salt Lake City, UT 84101

Vancouver Grizzlies
General Motor Place
802 Griffith Way
Vancouver, BC Canada
V6B 6g1

Washington Bullets
1 Harry S. Truman Dr.
Landover, MD 20785

National Football League Team Addresses

Atlanta Falcons
Suwanee Road & I-85
Suwanee, GA 30174

Baltimore Ravens
11001 Owings Mills Blvd.
Owings Mills, MD 21117
(410) 654-6200

Buffalo Bills
One Bills Dr.
Orchard Park, NY 14127

Carolina Panthers
227 W. Trade st #1600
Charlotte, NC 28202

Chicago Bears
Halas Hall
250 N. Washington Rd.
Lake Forest, IL 60045

Cincinnati Bengals
200 Riverfront Stadium
Cincinnati, OH 45202

Dallas Cowboys
Cowboys Center
One Cowboys Parkway
Irving, TX 75063-4727

Denver Broncos
5700 Logan St.
Denver, CO 80216

Detroit Lions
1200 Featherstone Rd.
Pontiac, MI 48057

Green Bay Packers
1265 Lombardi Ave.
Green Bay, WI 54303

Houston Oilers
6910 Fannin St.
Houston, TX 77030

Indianapolis Colts
P.O. Box 535000
Indianapolis, IN 46253

Jacksonville Jaguars
1 Stadium Pl.
Jacksonville, Fl 32202

Kansas City Chiefs
One Arrowhead Dr.
Kansas City, MO 64129

Los Angeles Raiders
332 Center St.
El Segundo, CA 90245

Los Angeles Rams
2327 W. Lincoln Ave.
Anaheim, CA 92801

Miami Dolphins
Joe Robbie Stadium
2269 NW 199th St.
Miami, FL 33056

Minnesota Vikings
9520 Viking Dr.
Eden Prairie, MN 55344

New England Patriots
Sullivan Stadium, Rt. 1
Foxboro, MA 02035

New Orleans Saints
6928 Saints Ave.
Metairie, LA 70003

New York Giants
Giants Stadium
East Rutherford, NJ 07073

New York Jets
598 Madison Ave.
New York, NY 10022

Philadelphia Eagles
Broad St. & Pattison Ave.
Philadelphia, PA 19148

Phoenix Cardinals
P.O. Box 888
Phoenix, AZ 85001

Pittsburgh Steelers
Three Rivers Stadium
300 Stadium Circle
Pittsburgh, PA 15212

San Diego Chargers
San Diego-Jack Murphy
Stadium
9449 Friars Rd.
San Diego, CA 92120

San Francisco 49ers
4949 Centennial Blvd.
Santa Clara, CA 95054-
1229

Seattle Seahawks
11220 NE 53rd St.
Kirkland, WA 98033

Tampa Bay Buccaneers
One Buccaneer Place
Tampa, Fl 33607

Washington Redskins
P.O. Box 17247
Dulles Int'l Airport
Washington, DC 20041

National Hockey League Team Addresses

Boston Bruins
Boston Gardens
150 Causeway St.
Boston, MA 02114

Buffalo Sabres
Memorial Auditorium
Buffalo, NY 14202

Calgary Flames
Saddledome
Box 1540, Station M
Calgary, Alb. , T2P 3B9
CANADA

Chicago Blackhawks
Chicago Stadium
1800 W. Madison St.
Chicago, IL 60612

Colorado Avalanche
1635 Clay st
Denver, Co 80204

Dallas Stars
901 Main St., #2301
Dallas, TX 75202

Detroit Red Wings
Joe Louis Sports Arena
600 Civic Center Dr.
Detroit, MI 48226

Edmonton Oilers
Northlands Coliseum
Edmonton, Alberta
T5B 4M9, CANADA

Florida Panthers
100 N. 3d Ave., 10th Floor
Ft. Lauderdale, FL 33301

Hartford Whalers
274 Trumbell Dr.
Hartford, CT 06013

Los Angeles Kings
Box 17013
Inglewood, CA 90308

Mighty Ducks of Anaheim
c/o Disney Sports
Entertainment
1313 S. Harbor Blvd.
Anaheim, CA 92803

Montreal Canadiens
Montreal Forum
2313 St. Catherine St. West
Montreal, Quebec
H3H 1N2, CANADA

New Jersey Devils
Byrne Meadowlands Arena
Box 504
East Rutherford, NJ 07073

New York Islanders
Nassau Veterans Memorial
Coliseum
Uniondale, NY 11533

New York Rangers
Madison Square Gardens
4 Pennsylvania Plaza
New York, NY 10001

Ottawa Senators
301 Moodie Dr., #411
Neapean, Ontario
K2H 9C4, CANADA

Philadelphia Flyers
The Spectrum
Pattison Pl.
Philadelphia, PA 19148

Pittsburgh Penguins
Civic Arena
Pittsburgh, PA 15219

Quebec Nordiques
Colisee de Quebec
2205 Ave. du Colisee
Quebec City, Quebec
G1L 4W7, CANADA

St. Louis Blues
St. Louis Arena
5700 Oakland Ave.
St. Louis, MO 63110

San Jose Sharks
525 West Santa Clara St.
San Jose, CA 95113

Tampa Bay Lightning
Mack Center
501 East Kennedy Blvd.
Tampa, FL 33602

Toronto Maple Leafs
Maple Leaf Gardens
60 Carlton St.
Toronto, Ontario
M5B 1L1, CANADA

Vancouver Canucks
Pacific Coliseum
100 North Renfew St.
Vancouver, BC
V5K 3N7, CANADA

Washington Capitals
Capital Center
Landover, MD 20785

Winnipeg Jets
Winnipeg Arena
15-1430 Maroons Rd.
Winnipeg, Manitoba
R3G OL5, CANADA

Major College Addresses

University of Alabama
Tuscaloosa, AL 35487

University of Arkansas
Fayetteville, AR 72701

Army
West Point, NY 10996

Auburn University
Auburn, AL 36831

Boston College
Chestnut Hill, MA 02167

Brigham Young University
Provo, UT 84602

University of California
Berkeley, CA 94720

UCLA
Los Angeles, CA 90024

Clemson University
Clemson, SC 29633

University of Cincinnati
Cincinnati, OH 45221

University of Colorado
Boulder, CO 80309

Cornell University
Box 729
Ithaca, NY 14853

Davidson College
Davidson, NC 28036

Duke University
Durham, NC 27708

University of Florida
Gainesville, FL 32604

Florida State University
Tallahassee, FL 32316

Georgetown University
Washington, DC 20057

University of Georgia
Athens, GA 30613

Georgia Tech
Atlanta, GA 30332

Harvard University
60 John F. Kennedy St.
Cambridge, MA 02138

University of Houston
Houston, TX 77204

Indiana University
Bloomington, IN 47405

University of Iowa
Iowa City, IA 52242

University of Kansas
Lawrence, KS 66045

Kansas State University
Manhattan, KS 66506

University of Kentucky
Lexington, KY 40506

Louisiana State University
Baton Rouge, LA 70894

University of Louisville
Louisville, KY 40292

Marquette University
Milwaukee, WI 53233

Loyola Marymount
Los Angeles, CA 90045

University of Maryland
College Park, MD 20740

University of Miami
Coral Gables, FL 33124

University of Michigan
Ann Arbor, MI 48109

Michigan State University
East Lansing, MI 48824

University of Minnesota
Minneapolis, MN 55455

University of Mississippi
Oxford, MS 38677

Navy
Annapolis, MD 21402

University of Nebraska
Lincoln, NE 68588

UNLV
Las Vegas, NV 89154

University of North
Carolina
Chapel Hill, NC 27514

North Carolina State
Releigh, NC 27695

Northwestern University
Evanston, IL 60208

University of Notre Dame
Notre Dame, IN 46556

Ohio State University
Columbus, OH 43210

University of Oklahoma
Norman, OK 73109

University of Oregon
Eugene, OR 97403

Oregon State University
Corvallis, OR 97331

Penn State University
Univ. Park, PA 16802

University of Pittsburgh
Pittsburgh, PA 15213

Princeton University
Box 71/Jadwin Gym
Princeton, NJ 08544

Purdue University
West Lafayette, IN 47907

St. John's University
Jamaica, NY 11439

University of San Francisco
San Francisco, CA 94117

Santa Clara University
Santa Clara, CA 95053

Seton Hall University
South Orange, NJ 07079

University of South
Carolina
Columbia, SC 29208

Southern Methodist
University (SMU)
Dallas, TX 75275

USC
Los Angeles, CA 90089

Stanford University
Stanford, CA 94305

Syracuse University
Syracuse, NY 13244

Temple University
Philadelphia, PA 19122

University of Tennessee
Knoxville, TN 37901

University of Texas
Austin, TX 78713

Texas A&M
College Station, TX 77843

Texas Christian University
Fort Worth, TX 76129

University of Utah
Salt Lake City, UT 84112

Villanova University
Villanova, PA 19085

University of Virginia
Charlottesville, VA 22903

University of Washington
Seattle, WA 98195

Yale University
Box 208216A Yale Station
New Haven, CT 06520

Halls of Fame

College Football Hall of
Fame
5440 Kings Island Dr.
Kings Island, OH 45034

Collegiate Tennis Hall of
Fame
University of Georgia
Athens, GA 30613

Hall of Fame of the Trotter
240 Main St.
Goshen, NY 10924

Indianapolis Motor
Speedway Hall of Fame
Museum
4790 West 16th St.
Indianapolis, IN 46222

International Boxing Hall of
Fame
1 Hall of Fame Dr.
Canastota, NY 13032

International Gymnastics
Hall of Fame
227 Brooks St.
Oceanside, CA 92054

International Motorsports
Hall of Fame (NASCAR)
4000 Speedway Boulevard
Talladega, AL 35160

International Swimming
Hall of Fame
One Hall of Fame Dr.
Fort Lauderdale, FL 33316

Int. Tennis Hall of Fame
194 Bellevue Ave.
Newport, RI 02840

International Women's
Sports Hall of Fame
Eisenhower Park
East Meadow, NY 11554

Hockey Hall of Fame
Exhibition Place
Toronto, Ontario
Canada M6K 3C3

Museum of Yachting
Fort Adams State Park
Newport, RI 02840

Naismith Memorial
Basketball Hall of Fame
1150 W. Columbus Ave.
Springfield, MA 01101

National Baseball Hall of
Fame
Main Street
Cooperstown, NY 13326

National Bowling Hall of
Fame & Museum
111 Stadium Plaza
St. Louis, MO 63102

National Jockey Hall of
Fame
Pimlico Racetrack
Belvedere & Park Heights
Ave.
Baltimore, MD 21210

National Museum of Racing
and Hall of Fame
(Horseracing)
Union Ave. & Ludlow St.
Saratoga Springs, NY
12866

National Rowing
Foundation
Philadelphia Maritime
Museum
321 Chestnut St.
Philadelphia, PA 19101

National Soccer Hall of
Fame
5-11 Ford Ave.
Oneonta, NY 13820

National Track and Field
Hall of Fame
200 South Capitol
(One Hoosier Dome)
Indianapolis, IN 46225

National Wrestling Hall of
Fame
405 W. Hall of Fame Ave
Stillwater, OK 74075

PGA Golf Hall of Fame
SR 2
Pinehurst, NC 28374

PGA Hall of Fame
Box 109601
100 Ave. of Champions
Palm Beach Gardens, FL
33418

Pro Football Hall of Fame
2121 George Halas Dr. NW
Canton, OH 44708

Santa Cruz Surfing
Lighthouse Point
Santa Cruz, CA 95060

Speedskating Hall of Fame
371 Washington St.
Newburgh, NY 12550

Stock Car Hall of Fame
SR 34 & US 52
Darlington, SC 29532

U.S. Bicycling Hall of Fame
34 East Main St.
Somerville, NJ 08876

U.S. Hockey Hall of Fame
Frontage & Hat Trick
Eveleth, MN 55734

U.S. National Ski Hall of
Fame
Route 41
Ishpeming, MI 49849

U.S. Olympic Committee
Hall of Fame
1750 East Boulder St.
Colorado Springs, CO
80909-5760

World Figure Skating Hall
of Fame
20 First St.
Colorado Springs, CO
80906

Other Sports Addresses

ABC Sports
47 W. 66th St., 13th Fl.
New York, NY 10023

Association of Tennis
Professionals
200 ATP Tour Blvd.
Ponte Vedra Beach, FL
32082

CBS Sports
51 W. 52nd St., 25th Fl.
New York, NY 10019

ESPN
ESPN Plaza
Bristol, CT 06010

Harlem Globetrotters
15301 Ventura Blvd., Suite
430
Sherman Oaks, CA 91403

IndyCar
390 Enterprise Court
Bloomfield Hills, MI
48302

Ladies' Pro Golf Ass.
2570 Volusia Ave., #B
Daytona Beach, FL 32114

NASCAR
Box 2875
Daytona Beach, FL 32120

NBC Sports
30 Rockefeller Plaza
New York, NY 10112

PGA Tour
112 TPC Blvd.
Ponte Vedra Beach, FL
32082

U.S. Figure Skating
Association
20 First St.
Colorado Springs, Co
80906

U.S. Olympic Committee
1 Olympic Plaza
Colorado Springs, CO
80909

U.S. International
Speedskating Association
Box 16157
Rocky River, OH 44116

U.S. Skiing
Box 100
1500 Kearns Blvd.
Park City, UT 84060

U.S. Swimming, Inc.
1 Olympic Plaza
Colorado Springs, CO
80909

U.S.A. Gymnastics
Pan American Plaza, #300
201 South Capitol Avenue
Indianapolis, IN 46225

U.S.A. Track & Field
1 Hoosier Dome, #140
Indianapolis, IN 46225

Women's Tennis
Association
133 1st St. NE
St. Petersburg, FL 33701

HEAVEN HALL OF FAME

Deceased Cover Stars of Sport, Sports Illustrated, Time and Life.

Allen, George
Alston, Walter (84)
Alzado, Lyle (93)
Armour, Tommy
Ashe, Arthur (94)
Barber, Jerry (95)
Bell, Gus (95)
Bell, Ricky
Bias, Len (86)
Boros, Julius (93)
Boyer, Ken (82)
Brown, Paul (93)
Bryan, Jim
Bryant, Paul (Bear) (83)
Burton, Ernest
Busch. A.
Busch, Gussie
Cagle, Christian
Campanella, Roy (93)
Carnera, Primo
Cerdan, Marcel (49)
Chabot, Lorne
Chandler, Happy(91)
Chambers, John
Clark, Jim (68)
Clemente, Roberto (73)
Cochrane, Mickey(62)
Conigliaro, Tony (95)
Connerly, Charles (96)
Cooper, Gary
Cosell, Howard (95)
Cox, Bill (96)
Cramm, Von Gottfried
Crawford, Jack
Cronin, Joe (84)
Davis, Ernie (62)
Dean, Dizzy (74)
Dempsey, Jack (83)
Dixon, Hewritt
Donatelli, Augie
Donohue, Mark
Drysdale,Don (93)
Durocher, Leo (91)
Dyer, Ed (64)
Finley, Charlie (96)
Fox, Nellie (66)
Foxx, Jimmy (67)
Galimore, Willie
Gathers, Hank (89)
Gehrig, Lou(41)
Goodman, Johnny
Gomez, Lefty(89)
Goren, Charles
Grange, Red (91)
Grove, Lefty (75)
Gutowski, Bob
Haney, Fred (77)
Harmon, Claude

Harmon, Tom (90)
Harris, Gypsy Joe
Hayes, Woodie (87)
Henie, Sonja(69)
Hill, Phil
Hill, Graham (75)
Hoad, Lew (95)
Hodges, Gil (72)
Holleder, Don
Holman, Nat (95)
Hornsby, Roger (63)
Howard, Elston(95)
Hubbell, Carl (88)
Jacobs, Louie
Jensen, Jackie (82)
Johnson, Floyd (46)
Johnson, Gus
Johnson, Jack (46)
Jones, Ben (61)
Jones, Bobby(71)
Jones, Calvin
Jones, Howard
Kennedy, John (63)
Kennedy, Jackie (94)
Kerr, Dave
Kim, Duk Koo
Kimberly, Jim
Kirby, Clay (95)
Kluszewski, Ted (88)
Krebs, Jim
Kuenn, Harvey (88)
Layne, Bobby (86)
Lavagetto, Cookie (90)
Leahy, Frank (73)
Lema, Tony
Lewis, Reggie (95)
Liston, Sonny (70)
Lombardi, Vince (70)
Long, Dale
Louis, Joe (81)
Luce, Clare Booth
Mack, Connie (56)
Maglie, Sal (94)
Mantle, Mickey (95)
Maravich, Pete (88)
Marciano, Rocky (69)
Maris, Roger (85)
Marston, Ann
Martin, Billy (89)
Matuszak, John
Mayer, Dick
McGraw, John (34)
McQuire, Frank (94)
McQueen, Steve
Monzon, Carlos (94)
Munson, Thurman (79)
Murchison, Clint
Murtaugh, Danny (76)
Nagy, Steve
Nance, Jim
Niarchos, Stavros (96)

Norgay, Tenzing
Nuthall, Betty
O'Connor, Pat
Olin, Mr./Mrs.
O' Malley, Walter (79)
Ott, Mel (58)
Owen, Lawrence
Peck, A. Wells
Perry, Fred (95)
Pietrosante, Nick
Pinson, Vida (96)
Plante, Jacques(86)
Post, Wally(82)
Prefontaine, Steve
Reynolds, Allie (95)
Repulski, Rep
Revson, Pete
Riggs, Bobby (95)
Rockne, Knute (31)
Robinson, Jackie (72)
Robinson, Sugar Ray (89)
Robinson, William (34)
Rodriguez, Ricardo
Roch, Max
Rupp, Adolph (77)
Ruppert, Jacob
Ruth, Babe (48)
Sanders, Mrs. Doug
Sawchuck, Terry
Schaddelee, Hugh
Shor, Toots
Sisler, George (73)
Snite, Betsy
Stagg, Nonagenarian (65)
Stengel, Casey (75)
Street, Gabby (53)
Sullivan, Ed
Sweikert, Bob
Tilden, Bill
Tunney, Gene (78)
Turner, Curtis
Valvano, Jim
Van Brocklin, Norm (83)
Vanderbilt, Alfred
Vanderbilt, Harold (70)
Veeck, Bill (86)
Vines Jr., Ellsworth
Werner, Buddy
Wilkinson, Bud
Willard, Jess
Williams, Edward B.
Wise, Mike
Wrigley, W.

CHAPTER FOUR:

GRADING AND PRESERVING MAGAZINES

The biggest change in collectors over the last two years is an increasing concern about the condition of their sports publications. This does not mean they are as fanatical as card collectors who demand PSA grades 8 or above, but it does mean that they will be more sensitive to condition than they are to price.

Grading, however, is only half the battle. Once you have obtained your *publications*, you will want to preserve them. Unlike baseball cards, which are printed on heavy stock, the thin pages of magazines are extremely sensitive to changes in temperature and humidity. As anyone knows who has seen *SI*'s that resided for years in a dank basement knows, poor storage circumstances can quickly transform prized magazines into worthless trash. Also using the proper bags and boards and storage material will make a difference in how well they are preserved.

GRADING

Basically there are four major grades with which everyone who buys or sells *Sports Publications* should be familiar with . In my price guide I refer to the first three of these grades as mint (MT), excellent/mint (EM), and very good (VG). The fourth grade is, basically, not collectible. While some would add to this list grades of Excellent (EX) and G (good), F (fair), and P (poor), I am convinced that such grading only confuses matters for *publication* collectors. While collectors of World Series programs might be willing to spring for a "good" copy of a 1913 program, knowledgeable collectors of *publications* simply won't be interested in a "good" example of even the most desirable magazines.

SI's that you might want to get signed and framed in order to display in your home or office typically fall into either the Mint (MT) or Excellent Mint (EM) categories.

Mint magazine are perfect with no mailing labels and no flaws.

Of course, only a magazine hot off the press is truly "mint." But what "mint" means here is that the magazine looks like new and, most importantly, has no mailing label. Because the vast majority of *Sports Illustrated* magazines (90-99%) are sold through the mail rather than off the newsstand, almost all have mailing labels. "Mint" issues without mailing labels are tremendously difficult to find and, as a result, command premiere prices (50% to 200% higher than EM items).

Excellent Mint (EM) magazines have a mailing label or minor cover flaws such as slight corner creases or some wear along the spine. But the flaws are only minor; covers will not have any significant creases (longer than one inch), water stains, finger smudging, loose bindings, etc. As a result, these magazines are desirable for showcasing. Magazines that have the label removed but still show marks are still graded Ex-Mt but may garner a little more if the marking are small and the buyer is willing.

VG or EX magazines, on the contrary, have enough cover flaws to make them unsuitable for autographing and framing. They might have, for example, a cover crease, smudging, significant binding wear or rolled bindings. But they will not have major cover flaws -- pen or pencil marks, tears or rips (including torn-away labels), water or coffee stains, etc. -- that drop them down to the not collectible category. These issues are generally collected for their contents (ads and features, especially) and not for their covers, so they must, like EM and MT issues, have all their pages intact.

PRESERVING MAGAZINES

Like other forms of collectible paper (old money, stamps, prints, etc.), magazines are extremely susceptible to variations in temperature and humidity. So ideally they should be stored in heated and air-conditioned rooms that are neither too humid in the summer nor too dry in the winter. Attics and basements make bad storage spots for *publications*! If you live in a house without central air conditioning, you might want to think about installing a window AC unit in the room where you keep your magazines. In addition to regulating the temperature, air conditioners also regulate humidity, so they will tend to keep your *publications* from mildewing.

Perhaps the simplest thing you can do to preserve your

publications is to bag, backboard, and box them. Some hobby dealers and comic book shops carry magazine bags with convenient fold-over flaps specifically designed for modern magazines but which may not meet your needs. For example, bags that I use are 9" x 12" with a 2" flap. I order them from a large distributor in the midwest (Appendix IV). As collectors of comics discovered long ago, bagging your magazines will tend to keep your collectibles free from the ill-effects of excess (or too little!) humidity and extreme temperatures. Bags will also prevent covers from picking up finger smudges, coffee stains, binding tears, etc. and protect your autographed magazine from getting smeared!!

Backing boards help to preserve your magazines by preventing them from bending. Slightly smaller than magazine bags, these boards are slipped into the bag behind the magazine before the bag is sealed with scotch tape. Because acid is a great destroyer of paper, a good bet here are acid-free boards.

I've found that boards 8 6/8" x 11 5/8" works well for early *Time, Sports Illustrated,* and *Sport* magazines. To get these bags and boards you might try one of the suppliers in the back (Appendix IV).

Magazine boxes also make it easy for you to thumb through your collection. Dealers who sell magazine bags and backing boards also typically offer magazine boxes, which like comic book boxes are designed to prevent binding damage by storing your collectibles standing up. Another way to store them, especially if you are only going to collect a few hundred is to buy specially made magazine shelf boxes. These will allow you to store them in your sports library along with your other sports memorabilia. It will give your office or sports den a very official look while preserving the magazines.

The cost of all of these preservation techniques adds up, but it is worth the expense. As our price guide indicates, there is a significant difference in value between a MT and EM and a VG *Sports Illustrated.* So 10¢ for a bag here and $5 for a box there is money well spent.

REMOVING LABELS

After you have taken pains not to ruin your magazines, you might be tempted to improve them. For most collectors, this means removing the mailing labels that appear on the covers of subscriber copies. Happily, this is a simple task for most issues in the 1980s and early 1990s. (Recently, *SI* jettisoned the mailing label entirely and began "inkjetting" addresses directly onto its covers; this ink, unfortunately, cannot be removed.) Mailing labels can also be removed rather simply from some random issues in the mid- to late-1970s, but it is impossible to be precise about which ones work and which ones don't.

Among the methods that will remove labels are steam, heat, lighter fluid, and turpentine. If you are using steam, a good source is your kitchen's tea kettle. Hold the label up to the steam and let a bit sink in. Be careful, however, that the water in the steam does not seep beyond the label into the cover, since that seepage could cause permanent water damage. If you don't mind the smell and the clean up afterwards, turpentine also works well. Take a Q-tip and lightly dab it on the label until it appears to be soaked. Then lift off. Probably the simplest method is the blow dryer. Turn it on, heat up the label for 30 seconds or so, and then peel away! With any of these methods, you should go slowly, being careful not to tear away any part of the cover as you lift off the label.

It is also possible to remove labels from 1950s and 1960s *Sports Illustrated*s, but because the printers used glues during those decades that discolored its covers, it will typically be obvious afterwards that the label has been removed. (Two or three unsightly white glue lines are the tell-tale signs.) In the future, *SI* collectors may join movie poster enthusiasts in employing paper conservators to remove labels and then to restore their magazines to something approximating their original condition, but for the time being, it is probably best, at least for pre-1980s issues, to leave your mailing labels alone.

The value of an EM issue after a label has been removed but which has a stain remaining changes little. It just makes it a nicer em issue. However, I have been lucky making some issues like new (mt). Before you take taking out your expensive issues and try removing your label, just remember that you can easily damage the issue as well!!!

CHAPTER FIVE:

SPORTS ILLUSTRATED PRICE GUIDE

The Sports Illustrated Price Guide section is the most comprehensive price guide on the subject. The guide works chronologically from the earliest known Sports Illustrated to June of 1996. If you need to find the issues of your favorite player, you need too first refer to Chapter 10: Alpha Index.

Each issue of Sports Illustrated is organized by date. Then the person or feature is listed. Under the Person name is either the team they played on (example 'Rams') or the sport (Swimming). Then this is followed by the key articles, features and ads. The advertisements are put into brackets. Under the Features/(Ads) section you will find Faces in the Crowd [FIC], Regional Cover mentions, cover variations, and other unique differences that are worth noting on the cover.

It should be noted that between 1954-1967 store variations may have a paper flap promoting a special feature in the issue. The paper flap will add at least a 10% premium to the mint issue and sometimes even more based on the content of the flap.
In some store variations there are actually differences in the headers and borders. These would add at least a 10% premium. During the 1950's for example, I have run across ½ off cover price as a promotion. The Canadian versions (1993-1995) will have Canada written on the top. These versions should have at least a 10% premium over the American editions.

Finally there are three prices for different graded Sports Illustrateds and one price for the added autographed value. The mint grade refers to magazines in nr-mt to mint condition. These magazines have no labels, no flaws and look new. A magazine that has no label but has a minor flaw (a bend in the corner, minor rubbing, minor corner bend or crease) will often be priced at a nr-mt to mt magazine and is usually worth it for pre 1980 magazines. However, when the mailing label is off and the magazine has a noticeable flaw, then the magazine will drop down to an EM price. Excellent-Mint price is for magazines that have a mailing label with no noticeable flaws. Most magazines will have a flaw but to be ex-mt it needs to be a clean cover with no cover creases, tears, or damage caused by water, oil, coke, etc. Magazines with a major flaw (crease, finger tears, cover wears, fingerprints) will be graded 'Excellent' and are very common to find at card shows and at the swap meet. These magazines tend to go for 50% of the EM grade. You will see a lot of these with the 50% off sign. The VG grade has serious cover problems (major crease or tear does it) and is only good for ads and articles.

The Autographed add value (+20) is shown below the Mt price. This means that the value of your *SI increases at least* by the added value. Sometimes the magazine goes for significantly more than the added value in auctions but it will at least be worth the noted added value for EM and MT prices. The added value does not necessarily apply to VG or EX grade or cover only magazines since collectors tend not to collect that grade. The only exception is autographed magazines of deceased athletes (Rocky Marciano) where the autograph is rarer than the magazine. This is especially true for rare autographed magazine covers. When there is more than one added value (+20/+15) it means the added value of the other person on the cover who is listed second. The (d) behind the (+20) means the person is deceased.

The most expensive *Sports Illustrated* tend to be the most popular stars in the sporting world. Therefore, the most expensive *SI's* tend to be 49' Joe Dimaggio, 55' Ted Williams and the 54' second edition with the baseball card fold out of Mickey Mantle and the rest of the 54 NY Yankee team cards.

The price guide is just a guide, built upon the opinions of nationally known dealers and collectors who sell or collect sports publications. When you use this guide to buy and sell, remember that the more expensive items tend to be the most popular and sell the quickest while the cheaper *SI's* are usually not heavily collected and should be treated like common baseball cards.

Pre 1954 Issues

DATE	COVER/Sport/Team	FEATURES /(ADS)	MT	EM	VG

Sports Illustrated (by Stuart Scheftel)

1930s The first incarnation of *Sports Illustrated*, this highbrow magazine eventually merged into *Golf Illustrated*. The magazine has great car ads and is sought after by advertising and golf enthusiasts. Here mass spectator sports such as football, baseball, and basketball take a back seat to skiing, fishing, golf, and other outdoor sporting activities. Magazine values range depending on ads.

	Typical Issues		200	100	50

Sports Illustrated (by Dell Publications)

The second *Sports Ilustrated*, this short-lived Dell Publications offering came in a large, *Life*-sized format (13 1/2" x 11"). The covers are color and the photos inside are black and white. The DiMaggio issue is the prize here.

DATE	COVER/Sport/Team	FEATURES /(ADS)	MT	EM	VG
2/49	Ralph Beard Kentucky BKB	Ben Hogan	200 +30	150	30
3/49	Marcell Cerdan Boxing	Casey Stengel	125 +1000(d)	75	20
4/49	Lou Boudreau Indians	Indians (Joan Crawford/Chesterfield)	150 +50	75	25
5/49	Joe DiMaggio Yankees		700 +200	400	100
6/49	Rex Barney Dodgers	Leo Durocher, Giants, Bob Hope/Chesterfield	150 +20	75	25

"Dummy" Sports Illustrated Issues (by Time-Life, Inc.)

These promotional issues were issued by Time-Life publisher Henry Luce to potential advertisers and other reviewers in an effort to "test the waters" for the publication that would follow. (The letters that Luce sent out with these issues are, by the way, also collectible.) Dummy #1 appeared as *The New Sport Magazine*. Its cover depicted a crowd rooting wildly at a football stadium. Dummy #2 was titled, simply, *Dummy*. Its cover depicted Pebble Beach and inside the magazine featured the Bing Crosby Pro-Am Tournament. The first *SI* golf issue, this second dummy is desired by golf collectors.

DATE	COVER/Sport/Team	FEATURES /(ADS)	MT	EM	VG
1953	Letter/Articles	Group of Articles	400	300	90
12/53	Stadium Fans	Dummy #1, Football	400	300	90
4/54	Pebble Beach	Dummy #2, Sam Snead, Ben Hogan	400	300	90

1954

DATE	COVER/Sport/Team	FEATURES //(ADS)	VALUE GUIDE		
			MT	EM	VG
8/16	Eddie Mathews* Braves	1st Issue, Baseball Cards (24 cards-Mays,Williams,etc) (*also Wes Westrum (Giants),Augie Donatelli (umpire))	270 +20	175	50
8/23	Masters Golf	Clubs US Amateur,Yankees Cards, (Mercury, Musial/Chesterfield) Wimbledon, (24 cards Mantle, Berra, etc)	400	300	150
8/30	Pamela Nelson Swimsuit	Yankee Stadium, Palmer, Indians, Eisenhower	40 +20	25	10
9/07	Sailing	Robin Roberts	40	25	10
9/14	Jim Kimberley Car Racing	College Football, Marciano, (Ford Skyline)	20 +50(d)	15	2
9/21	Cowboys	Football, Indians	15	10	2
9/28	Calvin Jones Iowa	Stadiums, Notre Dame, Rocky Marciano, (SI, Cadillac)World Series	20 +200(d)	12	2
10/04	Joyce Sellers Horserider	T-Birds, Baseball	15 +50(d)	10	2
10/11	Bandsman Oklahoma	Monroe/DiMaggio,Durocher, Giants, World Series, Mays Catch	15	10	2
10/18	Steeplechase	Porsche, Hockey Preview	15	10	2
10/25	English Setter Hunting	(T-Bird)	15	10	2
11/01	Football Fans Oklahoma Stadium		15	10	2
11/08	Surfcasting	Teddy Roosevelt, Pro Football, (Studebaker)	15	10	2
11/15	Snowbill Duck	Duck Foldout, (Model Toys)	20	10	5
11/22	Y.A. Tittle(FC) 49ers	Army/Navy Football, (55 Ford) Cover Variations - Newstand has strip at Top.	50 +20	30	10
11/29	Hef Parkins Old Cars	Beau Jack, Swimsuits, Hoover, (55 Lincoln)	15 +50(d)	10	2
12/06	African Lion	Redwings, (55 Mercury, Desoto)	15	10	2
12/13	Horse Show	Tom Gola, Churchill, Basketball Preview	15	10	2
12/20	Ken Sears Santa Clara BKB	Swimsuits Variation at Top: "First Weekly Golf Timp From a Top Pro"	25 +20	15	5
12/27	Klosters Skiing	Bowl Preview, Tom Gola, (Studebaker)	15	10	2

1955

DATE	COVER/Sport/Team	FEATURES /(ADS)	MT	EM	VG
1/03	**Roger Bannister** Track (SOY)	Mays, Cars	60 +25	30	5
1/10	**Horseracing** Santa Monica	Bowl Results, Dempsey, (Studebaker, Jaguar)	12	6	2
1/17	**Rafael Rodriquez** Bullfighting	(55 Ford)	12 +100(d)	6	2
1/24	**Dorris Hedberg** Maud Karten	Gordie Howe, Pistons, (55 Studebaker) Gymnasts	12 +20	6	2
1/31	**Jill Kilmont** Skier	James Naismith, College Basketball	12 +25	6	2
2/07	**Carol Heiss** Figure Skating	(Studebaker)	20 +25	10	2
2/14	**Great Dane**	Dog Foldout, Baseball Hall of Fame	12	6	1
2/21	**Betty DiBugnano** Swimsuit Model	Lakers/Knicks, Mays, (Studebaker) Bill Russell	20 +40	10	2
2/28	**Race Horses**	Mays, Lakers, (Corvette, Dodge)	12	6	2
3/07	**Jo Alston** Badminton	Branch Rickey, (T-Bird) Spring Training	12 +20	6	2
3/14	**Buddy Werner** Skier	Yankees, (Studebaker)	12 +100(d)	6	2
3/21	**Parry O'Brien** Shotputter	Giants, (DeSoto)	12 +20	6	2
3/28	**Steve Nagy** Bowler	Bill Russell, NCAA BKB Tourney	12 +20	6	2
4/04	**Ben Hogan (FC)** Golf	Masters	120 +150	60	20
4/11	**Willie Mays (FC) Leo Durocher Laraine Day** Giants	NL Baseball Review (Ted Williams Glove) Baseball Card Insert	250 +40/+100(d)/+40	125	50
4/18	**Al Rosen/B.Lope** Indians	AL Baseball Review Baseball Card Insert	100 +20/+10	50	25
4/25	**Tenzing Norgay** Mountain Climber	(Chrysler, Pepsi, Corvette, Ford) Nixon, A's	12 +100(d)	6	2
5/02	**Tom Courtney** Track	Brooklyn Dodgers	12 +20	6	2
5/09	**Shields/Fairbanks** Balloonists	Kentucky Derby, Swaps, Stadiums	12 +20each	6	2
5/16	**American Birds**	Swaps, Marciano, Bird Foldout Kentucky Derby	12	6	2
5/23	**Zale Perry** Skin Diver	Durocher, (Pepsi)	12 +20	6	2
5/30	**Herb Score** Indians	Durocher, Indy 500, (Snead, Corvette)	40 +20	20	5
6/06	**Rainbow Trout**	Durocher, Brigg Stadium (55 T-Bird)	12	6	2
6/13	**Magnus Johnson** Ocean Racing	LeMans Race, Swaps, (Kiner, Dodge) Indy 500	12 +20	6	2

1955

1956

DATE	COVER/Sport/Team	FEATURES //(ADS)	MT	EM	VG
1/02	Johnny Podres	Sports Year in Review	75	40	10
	Dodgers (SOY)	Classic American Cars	+20		
1/09	Bob Cousy (FC)	Bowls, Bill Russell, (56 T-Bird)	100	40	10
	Celtics		+45		
1/16	Mike Souchak	Hogan, Cousy, Crosby Pro-Am, (Corvette,	25	15	5
	Golf	Porsche)			
1/23	Jean Beliveau	Marciano	25	15	2
	Canadiens		+20		
1/30	Hayes Jenkins	Olympics, Floyd Patterson, (Studebaker,	12	6	2
	Tenley Albright	Plymouth)	+20 each		
	Figure Skating				
2/06	Ralph Miller	Olympics, (Porsche, Cadillac)	12	6	2
	Skier		+20		
2/13	Charles Maute	Olympic Results, Dick Irvin,	12	6	2
	Seton Hall	Track Classic American Cars	+15		
2/20	White Heron	Connie Mack's Death,	12	6	2
	Fish	(Porsche, Spring Training)			
2/27	Nashua	Baseball Owners	12	5	1
	Horseracing				
3/05	Stan Musial/Wally Moon/ Rip Repulski/		75	35	10
	Bill Virdon	(Jaguar, Studebaker, Porsche)	+20/+10 each		
	Cardinals	Spring Training			
3/12	Afghan Dog	Red Sox, Mercedes 300SL,	12	6	5
	Dog	(T-Bird)			
3/19	Alfred Glassell	Dodgers, Red Wings	12	6	2
	Marlin Fishing		+20		
3/26	Jim Kimberly	NCAA Basketball	15	7	5
	Auto Racing	(Trabert, Corvette, Jaguar)	+100(d)		
4/02	Al Wiggins	Spring Training, (Pepsi,	14	7	6
	Ohio State	T-Bird, Studebaker,Porsche)	+20		
4/09	56 Baseball	Cleveland Stadium,	50	25	10
	Issue	Flannels,(Robin Roberts) Campy,Berra			
4/18	Barbara Romack	Patterson,	12	6	5
	Golf	(Porsche, Corvette, Piersall)			
4/23	Billy Martin (FC)	Babe Didrikson, (Porsche, Jaguar)	30	20	10
	Yankees		+100(d)		
4/30	Trout Fisherman	Mantle, Bogart, Eisenhower	10	6	2
5/07	Needles	Marciano, (Kluszewski, Studebaker,	12	5	
	Kentucky Derby	Cadillac)			
5/14	Al Kaline (FC)	Didrikson, (T-Bird, Porsche,	50	25	10
	Harvey Kuenn	Snead, Mantle) Kentucky Derby,	+20/+100		
	Tigers				
5/21	John Landy	(Jaguar, Snead, Motorola)	10	6	4
	Miler	Athea Gibson [FIC]	+20		
5/28	Bob Sweikert	Sugar Ray Robinson (Chrysler, Porsche)	10	6	1
	Indy 500		+20		
6/04	Floyd Patterson	Dale Long, Pirate HR record	40	25	6
	Boxing (FC)		+20		
6/11	Sam Snead (FC)	U.S. Open, Indy 500, (Snead)	50	25	6
	Golf	(Sam Snead)	+25		
6/18	Mickey Mantle	Patterson, Gehrig,	250	125	65
	Yankees (FC)	(Pepsi, Jaguar, Continental)	+200		
6/25	Warren Spahn	US Open, Olympics, Swimsuits,	100	45	20
	Braves (FC)	(Corvette,Porsche, Chrsyler)	+20		

1956

VALUE GUIDE

1957

DATE	COVER/Sport/Team	FEATURES //(ADS)	MT	EM	VG
1/07	Bobby Morrow Texas Track (SOY)	NFL Championship, Olympics	20 +20	10	2
1/14	Wes/Betty Sime Skiers	Sugar Ray Robinson	12 +20 each	6	2
1/21	Johnny Lee Yale Basketball	(Chrysler)	12 +20	6	1
1/28	Bill Roberts, Jack Bionda, Cal Gardner, Allan Stanley John Peirson, Larry Regan Boston Bruins	Swimsuits, (Mercury)	40 +10 each	20	2
2/04	Huga Schaddlee Yachtsman	Yachting, (Triumph, Hogan)	12 +50(d)	6	3
2/11	Boxer Dog	Wilt Chamberlain,	12	6	2
2/14	Jim Krebs SMU Football	(Chrysler, Mercury)	12 +20	6	1
2/25	Johnny Saxton* Carmen Basilio Boxing	Birdie Tebbetts, (Corvette, Mercury)	25 +20 each	20	5
3/04	Mickey Mantle Yankees	Spring Training, (Chevrolet)	150 +200(d)	65	5
3/11	Ben Hogan Golf	Bob Cousy, Celtics Spring Training, (Corvette)	80 +150	40	10
3/18	Gordie Howe(FC) Ted Lindsay Red Wings	Ben Hogan, Basketball Braves, (Schoendienst)	110 +25/+15	45	5
3/25	Carroll Shelby Autoracing	Hogan, Roger Maris, B. Robinson (Chevrolet)NCAA Basketball	20 +20	10	2
4/01	Dan Hodge Oklahoma	Ben Hogan, Dodgers (Mercury, Robin Roberts)	30 +20	15	5
4/08	A.Wells Peck Fisherman	Ben Hogan, Indiana Basketball (Whitey Ford, Cousy, Pepsi)	14 +50(d)	7	3
4/15	1957 Baseball Issue	Williams, Ruth, Masters (Chrysler, Corvette)	60	30	10
4/22	Wally Moon Cardinals	(Plymouth,Triumph,Bing Crosby)	20 +20	15	3
4/29	Sugar Ray Robinson Gene Fullmer Boxing	Roger Maris, L. Burdette, (Chrysler, Mercury)	40 +150(d)/+20	20	2
5/05	Jockey	Kentucky Derby, Pirates, (Corvette)	12	6	5
5/13	Billy Pierce White Sox	(Ted Kluszenski,Jaguar) (Chrysler)	30 +20	15	3
5/20	Gussie Busch Horse Show	(Pontiac, Dodge)	12 +50(d)	6	1
5/27	Jim Bryan Indy 500	(Chrysler 300, Mercury)	12 +50(d)	6	1
6/03	Clem Labine Dodgers		20	15	2
6/10	Cary Middlecoff Golf	U.S. Open, (Mercury, Chrysler)	20	10	1
6/17	Eddie Arcaro Jockey	Hank Aaron, Yogi Berra (Triumph, Dodge)	25 +25	12	2
6/24	Bob Gutowski Pole Vaulter	US Open, Phillies, (Chrysler, Dodge)	12 +20	6	1

1957

DATE	COVER/Sport/Team	FEATURES /(ADS)	MT	EM	VG
7/01	Yachting Flags	Al Lopez	12	6	1
7/08	Ted Williams	All Star Preview	200	75	5
	Stan Musial		+150/+25		
	Red Sox/Cardinals				
7/15	Monkey	Wimbledon, Althea Gibson,	12	6	1
		(Mercury)			
7/22	Hank Bauer		40	20	1
	Yankees		+25		
7/29	Floyd Patterson	Orioles	30	15	2
	Boxing	(Plymouth, Porsche, Triumph)	+20		
8/05	Bonnie Prudden	Mays, PGA, Ted Williams	12	6	2
	Fitness		+20		
8/12	Russell Schleeh	Hank Aaron	12	6	5
	Hydroplanes	(Chrysler, Pepsi, Bud)	+50		
8/19	Johnny Simpson	Hickory Smoke	12	6	1
	Jockey	(Triumph, Mercury)	+20		
8/26	Consuelo Crespi	Braves	12	6	1
	Model		+50		
9/02	Althea Gibson	Nicklaus [FIC], Giants	20	10	6
	Tennis	(Bud, Kodak)	+35		
9/09	Roy McMillan	White Sox	30	12	2
	Reds		+20		
9/16	Carmen Basilio	Dodgers	25	12	2
	Boxing		+20		
9/23	1957 Football		25	12	2
	Preview				
9/30	Yankees Pitcher	World Series	40	20	5
10/07	Ollie Matson	Pro Football Issue	30	15	2
	Cardinals		+20		
10/14	Charles Goren	World Series, (Jaguar)	12	6	1
	Bridge		+50(d)		
10/21	Ducks	Hunting Preview	12	6	3
		(Frank Gifford)			
10/28	Autumn Trees	Hockey	12	6	1
11/04	Bobby Cox	Pro Basketball Preview	30	15	4
	Minnesota FB	Cousy, (58 Chevy)	+20		
11/11	Jay Utz	Car Issue, (Corvette, Jaguar)	12	6	5
	Horses		+20		
11/18	Oklahoma Band	Football	12	6	2
		(Imperial, MG, Lincoln)			
11/25	Willy Scherffler	(Triumph, Mercury)	12	6	2
		Skier	+20		
12/02	USSR Athlete	Army/Navy, Lions	12	6	2
		(Lincoln, Plymouth)	+50		
12/09	College BKB	Wilt Chamberlain	30	15	2
	Issue				
12/16	Amy Baird	49ers, (Mercury)	12	6	2
	Ski Fashion Model		+20		
12/23	Stan Musial	Bowl Preview, 49ers	75	35	3
	Cardinals (SOY)	Lions, (Lincoln), Sportsman	+25		

1958

DATE	COVER/Sport/Team	FEATURES /(ADS)	MT	EM	VG
1/06	Wasserman Family Vacation	Lions, (Plymouth)	25	15	1
1/13	Bill Mauldin	Bing Crosby, (Corvette)	20 +25	10	5
1/20	Neil Johston George Dempsey Warriors	NBA All Star Game,(Triumph) Boxing, Bobby Fischer[FIC],	30 +20 each	15	2
1/27	Willie Shoemaker Jockey	NY Rangers, (Lincoln, Imperial)	40 +100(can't sign)	20	5
2/03	Seals	Bill Russell,(Mercury, MG)	10	5	1
2/10	Henri Salem Diehl Matcer Squash	Wilt Chamberlain, (DeSoto) Elgin Baylor [FIC],	10 +20 each	5	3
2/17	Jacques Plante Canadiens Hockey	Bill Sharman, Celtics, (Triumph) Chevrolet, Bonneville)	30 +20	15	1
2/24	Phil Reavis Villanova Track	(Plymouth,Lincoln, Thunderbird)	10 +20	5	2
3/03	Andy Carey Yogi Berra, Enos Slaughter/Gil McDougald/Elston Howard Yankee Players	Spring Training, Musial, (Corvette, Porsche, Ford)	20 + Varies	15	6
3/10	Surf Australia	NCAA Basketball, Reds, (Lincoln, T-Bird)	14 +35	7	2
3/17	Sal Maglie Yankees	(Triumph, Bonneville, Mercury)	40 +50(d)	20	1
3/24	Carmen Basilio Boxing	LA Stadium, SF Stadium, NCAA Final Four, Walter O'Malley, Chevrolet)	20 +20	10	1
3/31	Roy Sievers Senators	Billy Martin, (T-Bird, Pepsi)	40 +20	20	4
4/07	Masters Golf	Basilio/Robinson, (Mathews, Ford)	30	15	3
4/14	1958 Baseball Issue	Masters, Snider, Mays, Braves, Cubs,Palmer (Pee Wee Reese, Ted Williams)	50	25	6
4/21	Del Crandall Braves	(Lincoln, Sam Snead)	50 +20	25	3
4/28	Silky Sullivan Horseracing	Kentucky Derby, Dodgers/Giants (Nellie Fox)	28	10	4
5/05	Gil McDougald Yankees	Dodgers, Giants, (Jaguar, Porsche)	40 +20	20	2
5/12	American Cup Yachting	White Sox, (Ed Mathews, Corvette, Ford)	20	10	6
5/19	Richie Ashburn Phillies	Musial, (Porsche)	60 +20	25	5
5/26	Pat O'Connor Indy 500	Indians, Orioles (Continental)	12 (Died week of)	5	1
6/02	Eddie Mathews Braves		75 +20	30	2
6/09	Dick Mayer Tennis	US Open Tennis, Yankees, (7-Up, Chevrolet)	20 +20	10	4
6/16	Lew Hoad Pancho Gonzales Tennis	Forest Hills, Mays, (Jaguar, Bud)	15 +20/+50(d)	5	2
6/23	Jackie Jensen Red Sox		40 +100(d)	15	2
6/30	Tennis Doubles	Dodgers, (Renault)	10	5	1

1958

DATE	COVER/Sport/Team	FEATURES /(ADS)	MT	EM	VG
7/07	Al-Star Preview* (T-Bird) [* Cover shows Mays, Musial, Banks Dell Crandall, Malzone, Jensen, Auto varies, Mantle, Triandos)]		70	35	5
7/14	Dog & Girl (Corvette, Kodak)		10	5	5
7/21	Chris Von Saltza		10	5	1
	Swimmer		+20		
7/28	Frank Thomas (Pepsi, Renault)		30	15	4
	Pirates		+20		
8/04	Vacationers		10	5	1
8/11	Clare Luce	Rafer Johnson, Giants	10	5	3
	Scuba Diving	(T-Bird, Chevrolet)	+100(d)		
8/18	Roy Harris	Cobb, Mantle	10	5	3
	Boxing		+20		
8/25	Pine Valley	Yankees,	30	12	4
	Golfer	(Pepsi, Lincoln, Triumph)			
9/01	Floyd Patterson/Roy Harris		30	15	2
	Boxing		+20/+100(d)		
9/08	Fisherman	(7-Up, Jaguar)	10	5	3
9/15	Sceptre Yacht	(Grange, Ted Williams, Bob Cousy)	10	6	6
	America's Cup				
9/22	1958 Football Issue	College Football Issue	20	10	3
9/29	World Series	Mantle, Hank Aaron	24	12	4
	Stadium Drawing	(7-Up, Ashburn)			
10/03	Goose Hunting	Stengel, YA Title	10	5	1
		(Jaguar, Buick)			
10/13	Ohio State Band	World Series Preview	10	5	3
10/20	James McCarthy	World Series Game 7,	10	5	4
	Cliff Hanging	(Feller, Ford, GM, Dodge)	+20		
10/27	Chick Zimmerman	Pro Basketball Preview,(7-Up)	18	9	3
	Syracuse Football		+20		
11/03	Hugh Wiley	Mercedes 300sl, (Chevy)	10	5	3
	Equestrian		+20		
11/10	Herb Elliott	Jim Brown, (Buick)	10	5	3
	Track		+20		
11/17	Mr./Mrs. Olin	(DeSoto)	10	5	1
	Hunters		+50 each(d)		
11/24	Pete Dawkins	Swimsuits,	40	20	5
	Walters, Anderson (7-Up, Arnett Rams, 59 Mercury)		+20 each		
	Army Football				
12/01	Montana Skiers	Montana Skiing	10	5	1
12/08	1958 BKB	College Basketball Issue,	30	15	5
	Preview	Oscar Robertson, (Mark 4)			
12/15	Barbara Wagner	(Mercury)	10	5	1
	Bob Paul		+20 each		
	Figure Skating				
12/22	Holiday Issue	Bowl Preview, (7-Up)	14	7	3

1959

DATE	COVER/Sport/Team	FEATURES /(ADS)	MT	EM	VG
1/05	**Rafer Johnson** Track (SOY)	Colts Championship, UCLA Track, Notre Dame Stengel	50 +35	25	4
1/12	**Andy Bathgate** Rangers	Davis Cup, Swimsuits, (Corvette, 7-Up)	30 +20	15	5
1/19	**Hal Roach** Phesant Hunter	Bob Pettit (Bing Crosby, T-Bird, Renault)	10 +50(d)	5	2
1/26	**Horseracers**	I. Johansson, Robertson (Studebaker, Dodge, Mercury)	10	5	2
2/02	**Ron Delany** Track	Black Hawks (DeSoto, Lincoln, Triumph)	10 +15	5	1
2/09	**Skiers**	Vince Lombardi, (Imperial)	10 +15	5	1
2/16	**John Longden** Jockey	(T-Bird, 7-Up, Corvette, Buick, Bob Hope, Desoto)	10 +15	8	8
2/23	**Bill Cox** Sailing	(Coke, MG, Rambler)	10 +50(d)	5	5
3/02	**Casey Stengel** **Fred Haney.Umpire** Yankees/Braves	Spring Training, Yogi Berra, (Volvo, Triumph, Continental)	25 +200/+100(d)	17	2
3/09	**Ed Sullivan** Golf	Hot Rod Henley (Corvette, Mercedes, Austin)	15 +200(d)	7	5
3/16	**Phil Hill** Autoracing	Pirates, Basketball Issue, (T-Bird, Coke, 7-Up, Jaguar)	10 +20	5	5
3/23	**Aly Khan** Polo	Giants, Ashburn, (Willie Mays, Lincoln, Dodge)	10 +50(d)	5	5
3/30	**Tommy Armour** Golf	NCAA Final Four (Stengel, Chevy, Gill McDonald)	10 +50(d)	6	1
4/06	**Bobby Jones** Golf	Masters, Elgin Baylor, Lakers, (Palmer, Mercedes)	75 +1500(d)	35	5
4/13	**Willie Mays(FC)** Giants	59 Baseball Issue, Masters, (Stengel, Dodge, 7-Up, Ted Williams, T-Bird)	40 +40	25	10
4/20	**Bill Talbert** Tennis	Ingemar Johansson Poster (Bob Hope, Coke, Jaguar, Chevrolet)	10 +10	5	5
4/27	**Silver Spoon** Horseracing	Kentucky Derby (Bob Cousy, Continental)	10	5	2
5/04	**Bob Turley** Yankees	(Triumph, MG)	20 +15	12	1
5/11	**Gambling**	Swimsuits, Indians, Patterson (T-Bird, 7-Up, Hogan/Snead)	10	5	1
5/19	**Bob/Bus Mosbacher** Yachting	Tigers, Ben Hogan, Oscar Robertson, (Mays, Hank Aaron, Chrysler)	10 +20 each	5	4
5/25	**Indy 500 Cars**	Yankees, Hank Aaron (Coke, Ted Williams, Corvette)	10	5	5
6/01	**Gary Cooper/Family** Scuba Diving	Yankees, Killebrew, (Ashburn, Corvette, Gifford)	10 +100(d)	5	5
6/08	**Tom Bolt** **Art Wall** **Don Finsterwald** **Peter Thomson** Golf	US Open, Indy 500, Braves, (Coke)	25 +20 each	12	4
6/15	**Dodger Stadium**	Mickey Mantle, Willie Mays, Dodgers, (Mercedes, T-Bird, Venturi)	15	10	4
6/22	**Ingemar Johansson** Boxer	US Open, Arcaro, Casper, (Snead, Chrysler, Continental)	20 +35	10	3
6/29	**Golden Eagle**	Mantle, Wilhelm, Colavito Poster (Plymouth)	10	5	5

1959

DATE	COVER/Sport/Team	FEATURES /(ADS)	MT	EM	VG
7/06	Ingemar Johansson	All Star Game, Tigers,	30	15	4
	Floyd Patterson	(Mantle, Imperial, 7-Up)	+35/+20		
	Boxing				
7/13	Becky Collins	Patterson/Johansson,	10	5	7
	Swimmer	(Corvette, Coke, Lincoln)	+20		
7/20	Vasily Kuznetsov	Dodgers	10	5	2
	USSR Track	(Mercedes, Rambler)	+50		
7/27	Toots Shor/	Track, Indians	10	5	2
	John Wayne	(Drysdale, Chrysler)	+50(d)/+200(d)		
8/03	Horsetrotter	Giants, (7-Up, VW)	10	5	3
8/10	Nellie Fox/	McCovey,	95	35	4
	Luis Aparicio	(Wheaties, Coke, VW, Chevy, MG)	+20/+150(d)		
	White Sox				
8/17	Anne Quast	Ernest Hemingway, Willie McCovey	10	5	1
	Golf		+20		
8/24	Stavros Niarchos	Archie Moore, Dodgers,	10	5	5
	Yachting	Yaz [FIC], (VW)	+100(d)		
8/31	Parry O'Brien	Braves, Dodgers	10	5	5
	Shot Putter	Drysdale Poster,	(7-Up)		
9/07	Alex Olmedo	Giants, White Sox, Davis Cup	10	5	5
	Tennis	(Crandall, Coke)			
9/14	Charlie Coe	Yankees	10	5	3
	Golf	(Warren Spahn, Pat Boone, Roy Rogers)			
9/21	1959 Football	Dodgers, Reds, Giants,	30	15	2
	Issue	(Spahn, Triumph)			
9/28	White Sox Team	Nicklaus, World Series,	60	30	5
	Aparicio,Fox, ETC	(Colavito, Spahn)	+ varies		
10/05	Johnny Unitas (FC)	Pro Football Preview	75	35	10
	Colts	Dodgers, (Mickey Mantle, Bob Hope)	+25		
10/12	Duck Hunting	World Series, Sam Snead	10	5	1
		(Falcon, VW, Dodge)			
10/19	Auto Racing	Dodgers, World Series	10	5	1
		(Plymouth, Porsche)			
10/26	George Izo	Pro Basketball Issue,	40	20	5
	Notre Dame	Gifford Poster, Football Issue	+20		
		(Gifford, Mercedes, 7-Up)			
11/02	Golfers	(Coke, Desoto, Corvair)	10	5	3
11/09	Bob/Mrs. Lackey	(Tennis, Triumph, Mercury)	10	5	1
	Texas Football		+20		
11/16	Daytona 500	Russell/Wilt Chamberlain	10	5	2
	NASCAR	(Imperial, VW, Snead)			
11/23	Ski Season	(Mercedes, Andy Bathgate,	10	5	2
		Chevy)			
11/30	Hunting Dog	Colts, (Lincoln, Desoto,	10	5	3
		Coke, Triumph)			
12/07	College BKB	John Brodie, C. Connerly	20	10	2
	Issue				
12/14	Tom Watson/Family	Colts/Giants,	10	5	2
	ski	Skiing (Volvo, Porsche, Imperial)	+100(d)		
12/21	Holiday Issue	Bowl Preview, Football's	14	7	2
		Babe Ruth, Wilt Chamberlain, Silver			
		Anniversary, (Mercedes, Volvo)			

1960

DATE	COVER/Sport/Team	FEATURES //(ADS)	MT	EM	VG
1/04	Ingemar Johansson Boxer (SOY)	Sportsman, Colts/Giants Bobby Hull, Snead	40 +30	20	2
1/11	Jerry Lucas Ohio State Basketball		40 +20	20	1
1/18	Art Wall Golfer	Golf Preview (Plymouth, Desoto)	15 +15	5	1
1/25	Russian Boys	AFL (Bing Crosby, T-Bird)	10	5	1
2/01	Betsy Snite US Skier	Royals, Oscar Robertson (Lincoln, Mercury)	10 +10	5	1
2/08	Bedlington Dog	Richard Nixon, Willie Mays (Corvette, Pan Am, Olds 60)	10	5	4
2/15	Gennady Voronia Speedskater	Olympics (Dodge, Ford, Chevy, Imperial)	10 +20	5	1
2/22	Elliot Burch/ Sword Dancer Horse Trainer	Chamberlain vs Russell (Corvair, VW, Coke)	10 +50(d)	5	3
2/29	Squaw Valley Skiing	Yankees, Olympics (Chevy, Plymouth, Continental)	10	5	2
3/07	Phillies Cartoon Baseball	Winter Olympics (Corvette, Oldsmobile, Imperial)	15	10	5
3/14	Family Bowling	NCAA Tourney, (Coke, Sprite, 7-up, VW, Corvair)	10	5	3
3/21	Maurice Richard Montreal Canadiens	Cardinals, NCAA Tourney (Dart, A.Palmer, Lincoln)	40 +15	20	3
3/28	James Leisenring Fisherman	NCAA Tourney, Dodgers (Desoto, Chevy, T-bird, Ford, Rambler)	10	5	3
4/04	Masters Golf	The Masters, W. Chamberlain, (Coke, A.Palmer, Corvette, S.Snead, Oldsmobile)	15	10	5
4/11	60 Baseball	E.Banks, N.Fox, Olympics,Giants (Harmon Killebrew, White Sox, Pontiac)	40	20	10
4/18	Carin Cone Swimmer	Arnold Palmer-Masters, (Indians, Mercedes, Corvair, Chrysler)	10 +10	5	3
4/25	Dallas Long Shotputter	Giants, Stanley Cup Finals (Gene Sarazen, Porsche, Chrysler, Lincoln)	10 +10	5	3
5/02	Jockey	Kentucky Derby, Ted Williams (Thunderbird)	10	5	2
5/09	Boating	Luis Aparicio Dodge Dart, Corvette, Ambassador V-8)	10	5	5
5/16	Australian Sport	Kentucky Derby (Corvair, Coke, 7-Up, Pontiac)	10	5	4
5/23	Charles Goren Bridge	Indians, Orlando Cepeda (Sam Snead, Chevy, Contential)	10 +100(d)	5	1
5/30	Herb Elliott* Running	Indy 500-Watson, Senators (Valient) (* Cover includes Dyrol Burleson)	10 +15	5	1
6/06	Red Schoendienst Braves	(Chevy, Coke, VW Van)	50 +15	25	3
6/13	Arnold Palmer* Golfers (FC)	US Open Golf (Corvair, Volvo, Chrysler) (* Cover also includes Ken Venturi, Don Finsterwald)	100 +40/+15	40	10
6/20	Ingemar Johansson Boxing	Indians (Corvette, Thunderbird)	25 +25	12	5
6/27	Glen Davis Track	Floyd Patterson, US Open (Campbell, Chevy, Rambler)	10 +10	5	2

1960

DATE	COVER/Sport/Team	FEATURES /(ADS)	MT	EM	VG
7/04	Comiskey Park Baseball	Maris/Mantle, Archie Moore White Sox (Campbell)	30	15	1
7/11	Jim Beatty Track	A's, Arnold Palmer (Corvair, Lincoln, Ambassador)	10 +10	5	1
7/18	Candlestick Park Baseball	Arnold Palmer - British Open (7-Up, Chevy)	35	20	1
7/25	Yachting -Art	All Star Game, John Kennedy Stan Musial,(Coke, Corvette)	12	7	5
8/01	Mike Troy Swimmer	PGA	10 +10	5	1
8/08	Dick Groat* Pirates	(Campbell Soup, Coke) (* Cover includes Phillies #20)	40 +10	25	2
8/15	Olympics Flag Olympics	Olympics, Dodgers	10	5	1
8/22	Barbara McIntire Golfer	Cardinals	10 +10	5	1
8/29	Mountain Climber (VW)	Roth	10	5	1
9/05	Olympic Team Olympics	*Olympics Rafer Johnson Mantle/Maris	10	5	3
9/12	Jack Nicklaus Golf (1st Cover)	Olympics, Stan Musial	125 +50	45	10
9/19	Lois Goetz Cheerleader-Syracuse	College Football Preview	10 +10	5	1
9/26	Jim Brown Browns	Pro Football Preview Giants, Orioles (Frank Gifford)	110 +25	40	2
10/03	Bob Schloredt Washington	Pirates, World Series (VW Valient)	30 +10	15	1
10/10	Vernon Law Pirates	Jack Nicklaus, Thompson Home Run Bob Clemente (Corvair, Oldsmobile, Falcon, Plymouth)	45 +10	20	2
10/17	Model Fashion Model	Swimsuits, World Series, Pro Basketball Preview (Corvette, VW)	15	7	5
10/24	Football Players Football	World Series, Hawks	10	5	2
10/31	Jack Brabham Car Racing	Casey Stengel (Coke, Chevy, Pontiac)	10 +15	5	3
11/07	James Thurber Cartoon	Bobby Jones Series #1 (Bob Hope, VW, Buick, Ford)	10 +15	5	3
11/14	Bobby Hull Blackhawks	Oscar Robertson, Bobby Jones Series #2 (T-bird)	50 +15	25	2
11/21	Skiers	(Cadillac, Mercedes, Chrysler)	10	5	3
11/28	Joe Bellino Navy	Norm Van Brocklin	15 +10	8	1
12/05	Sam Snead Golf	Eagles, Sam Snead (Corvette, Bud)	50 +25	25	4
12/12	Basketball Issue		10	5	3
12/19	Norm Van Brocklin Eagles	Hockey (Coke, T-Bird)	45 +100(d)	20	5
12/26	John Kennedy/ Jackie Kennedy	Rose Bowl, Bowl Preview Bear Bryant, (Huff)	75 +1000(d)/+500(d)	40	5

1961

DATE	COVER/Sport/Team	FEATURES /(ADS)	VALUE GUIDE MT	EM	VG
1/09	**Arnold Palmer** Golf (SOY)	Sportsman, Bowl Review, Eagles, (61 Buick)	110 +40	40	5
1/16	**Bob Cousy** Celtics	Bill Russell, Tom Heinshon	100 +40	40	2
1/23	**Golfers**	Crosby Pro Am, Bobby Fisher (61 Chevy, Dart)	10	5	1
1/30	**Safe Driving** Cars	Crosby, Thunderbirds (Corvette)	10	5	5
2/06	**Track Runners**	(Lincoln, Pontiac, VW)	10	5	1
2/13	**Laurence Owen** Figure Skater	Yogi Berra (Corvette, MG)	10 +10	5	5
2/20	**Billy Casper** Golf	(Buick)	15 +10	10	1
2/27	**Bobsledders**	Duke (T-Bird, Lincoln, Cadillac, Chrysler)	10	5	1
3/06	**Raul Sanchez Miquel Cueller** Reds	Spring Training, Dodgers Yankees (Maris, Colovito, Palmer Ads)	12 +10/+10	6	5
3/13	**Floyd Patterson** Boxer	Yankees, NCAA Tournament (Arnold Palmer)	15 +15	10	1
3/20	**Lynn Pyland** Sky Diver	Floyd Patterson, Celtics (Corvette, George Mikan)	10 +10	5	5
3/27	**Jerry Lucas John Havlicek** Ohio State	NCAA Tournament, (Dodge, T-bird, Rambler, Lincoln)	25 +20	10	3
4/03	**The Masters** Golfer	NCAA, Marlyn Monroe Joe Dimaggio, Carl Yaz (Chevy, A.Palmer)	40	15	5
4/10	**Cardinal Player** Cardinals	1961 Baseball Issue, B. Robinson, R.Maris, M. Mantle, N.Fox	25	20	10
4/17	**Fishing - Art**	Masters, Mickey Mantle, Orioles,(Dodge, Corvette)	10	5	5
4/24	**Hot Rodders**	Angels, Senators (VW, Dodge, Continental)	10	5	1
5/01	**Kentucky Derby**	Yankees (Pontiac, T-Bird)	10	5	1
5/08	**Gary Player** Golfer (FC)	Warren Spahn (Corvair)	30 +15	15	1
5/15	**Cookie Lavagetto** Twins	Kentucky Derby, Sam Snead (VW)	30 +50(d)	15	1
5/22	**Snorkling**	Giants, Tigers, Swimsuits (Porsche, Corvette, VW, Pontiac)	10	5	5
5/29	**Indy 500 Racer**	Orioles (Skylark, VW, T-Bird)	10	5	1
6/05	**Sailing Racing**	Charlie Finley-A's (VW, Cadillac, Chrysler)	10	5	1
6/12	**Golfers**	U.S. Open Golf, Reds (T-Bird, VW)	10	5	1
6/19	**Earl Young** Track	Indians (Skylark, Lincoln, VW)	10 +10	5	1
6/26	**Ernie Broglio*** Cardinals	US Open Golf Results (VW) (* Cover includes Willie Mays)	20 +15	10	1

1961

1962

VALUE GUIDE

DATE	COVER/Sport/Team	FEATURES //(ADS)	MT	EM	VG
1/87	**Jerry Lucas**	Sportsman, Packers Champs	50	25	2
	Ohio State (SOY)	(Bart Starr, Buick-Skylark)	+20		
1/15	**Don Heal**	A. Palmer, J. Nicklaus	12	7	2
	Bruins	(Rambler, T-Bird, Imperial, Pontiac)	+10		
1/22	**Mr./Mrs.D.Sanders**	Knicks	10	5	5
	Golfer	(Corvette, Dodge, Lincoln, Cutlass)	+15/+50(d)		
1/29	**Chet Jastremski**	Swimsuit Issue	10	5	5
	Swimmer	(Studenbaker, Ford, Buick)	+10		
2/05	**Joan Hanah**	Wilt Chamberlain	10	5	2
	Skiing	(Cadillac, T-bird)	+10		
2/12	**Sonny Liston (FC)**	Figure Skating	20	15	2
	Boxing	(62 Chevy)	+300(d)		
2/19	**Mickey Wright**		10	5	5
	Golfer	(VW Ghia, Corvette)	+10		
2/26	**John Uelses**		10	5	1
	Pole Vault	(Valiant)	+10		
3/05	**Casey Stengel**		20	15	2
	Mets	(Don Drysdale, Ted Williams, VW)	+200(d)		
3/12	**Horses Racing**	Jack Nicklaus	15	8	1
		Kentucky Derby (Grand Prix)			
3/19	**Gary Cunningham & John Green***		30	15	2
	UCLA/USC	(UCLA), * also John Rudometkin(USC)	+10		
3/26	**Ricardo Rodriguez** NCAA Tournament		15	7	2
	Race Car Driver	(Imperial, T-bird, Pontiac)	+50(d)		
4/02	**Arnold Palmer**	Masters,Spring Training,	60	30	4
	Golf	NCAA Finals, Mantle/Maris Movie	+40		
		(Babe Ruth, (Mantle/Maris/Ford)			
4/09	**Frank Lary**	Baseball Issue, W.Mays	60	30	5
	Tigers	S.Koufax, E.Banks	+15		
		(Babe Ruth, Mantle/Maris/Ford)			
4/16	**Donna DeVarona**	Arnold Palmer	10	5	5
	Swimmer	(Buick, Corvette, Chrysler)	+10		
4/23	**Jerry Schmidt**	Dodger Stadium	10	5	1
	Lacrosse	(Casey Stengel, Whitey Ford)	+10		
4/30	**Luis Aparico**	Celtics Champs,Stanley Cup Finals,	50	25	5
	White Sox	Willie Mays, Stan Mikita	+20		
		(VW Van, Casey Stengel,			
		Corvette, Valient)			
5/07	**Horses Racing**	Sonny Liston, Hoston Colts	12	8	1
	Kentucky Derby	(Buick, VW)			
5/14	**Gene Littler**		80	40	2
	Golfer	(Sam Snead, Avanti, VW Van)	+20		
5/21	**Water Skiing**	E. Hemingway, Reds, Twins	10	5	5
		(Roger Maris, Don Drysdale)			
5/28	**Floyd Patterson**	Yankees-Mantle	30	15	1
	Boxing	(Chevy II)	+20		
6/04	**Willie Mays**	Floyd Patterson, J.Nicklaus	100	40	5
	Giants	(VW, Mercedes, Corvette, Cadillac)	+35		
6/11	**US Open**	US Open Preview,	40	20	5
	Golf Course	(Ben Hogan, Bob Hope)			
6/18	**Crew Team***	[*includes John Beeman/ William Stowe/	10	5	2
	Cornell	Michael McGuirk/ Richard Thackaberry			
		/John Abele/ Victor Erickson/ Donald			
		Light/ David Nisbet/ Gary Brayshaw.]			
		Nicklaus, (T-Bird, Triumph, VW)			
6/25	**Jack Nicklaus**	U.S. Open	60	35	5
	Golfer		+50		

1962

VALUE GUIDE

DATE	COVER/Sport/Team	FEATURES //(ADS)	MT	EM	VG
7/02	**Mickey Mantle**	Yankees, J. Nicklaus	190	85	20
	Yankees	(Imperial)	+200(d)		
7/09	**Gretel- Yacht**	Angels, Yankees	10	5	1
	American Cup	(Lincoln)			
7/16	**Igor Ter-Ovanesyan**		10	5	1
	Long Jump	(Triumph, Chevy, VW, Sunbean)	+25		
7/23	**Barbara McAlister**	Arnold Palmer, Braves	10	5	1
	Diving	(VW)	+10		
7/30	**Ken Boyer**	Gary Player	20	12	5
	Cardinals		+100(d)		
8/06	**Paul Runyan**	Cubs	20	10	1
	Golfer	(VW)	+10		
8/13	**Dick Fortenberry**	Wilt Chamberlain, Mets	10	5	1
	Sky Diving	(Bart Starr)	+10		
8/20	**Don Drysdale (FC)**		45	25	5
	Dodgers	(Porsche, Corvair)	+100(d)		
8/27	**Helga Schultze**	Nicklaus	10	5	1
	Tennis	(Triumph)	+10		
9/03	**California Beaches**		10	5	1
	Art Drawing	(P. Hornung, B. Cousy, K. Venturi, Triumph, VW)			
9/10	**Jim Taylor(FC)/ Forrest Gregg*** Packers	Pro Football Issue, Yankees (*Also includes Packers/49ers Players)	50 +20	25	2
9/17	**Sonny Liston**	Giants,Palmer/Nicklaus	30	15	4
	Boxer	(Maris/Mantle/Ford ad, Crazy Leg Hirsh)	+300(d)		
9/24	**Flag Girls**	College Football Issue	25	12	5
	Texas	J. Nicklaus, S.Liston (Ted Williams, Whitey Ford)			
10/01	**Baseballs**	World Series, Yankees,	30	15	5
	62 World Series	Frank Gifford (Corvette, T-Bird, Chevy, Ted Williams, Sunbeam)			
10/08	**Tommy McDonald**	Willie Mays	30	15	2
	Eagles		+15		
10/15	**Sonny Gibbs**	World Series, Whitey Ford	15	7	1
	TCU	(Jack Nicklaus)	+10		
10/22	**Hunter**	World Series	10	5	5
	Art	(Corvette)			
10/29	**Fran Tarkenton**	Pro Basketball Issue, J. West	40	25	5
	Vikings(FC)	(VW Van, Sunbean, Rambler, Ford)	+25		
11/05	**Mary Anderson**	Dallas Texans	10	5	1
	Skin Diving	(Lincoln, Pontiac, Dodge)			
11/12	**Sam Snead/Arnold Palmer**		50	30	1
	Golfer		+25/+40		
11/19	**Nick Pietrosante**	Lions,Giants, A.Palmer, S.Snead	12	8	2
	Lions	(Dart, VW, Lincoln, Chrysler, Rambler)	+10		
11/26	**Paul Dietzel**	Clay	10	5	5
	Army	(Corvette, VW, Triumph, Skylark)	+10		
12/03	**Skier**	Detroit/Packers, Celtics	10	5	2
	Montana	Jack Nicklaus (Cadillac, Lincoln)			
12/10	**Cotton Nash**	Basketball issue,	30	15	5
	Kentucky	Tom/Dick Van Arsdales	+10		
12/17	**Frank Gifford**	Bill Bradley	50	25	3
	Giants	(Ford, 7-Up, T-Bird, Pontiac)	+25		
12/24	**Bold Americans**	Swimsuits, John Kennedy	10	5	2
	Sky Diving	(Lincoln)			

1963

DATE	COVER/Sport/Team	FEATURES /(ADS)	MT	EM	VG
1/07	Terry Baker	Packer Champs	50	25	3
	Oregon (SOY)		+10		
1/14	Phil Rodgers		20	10	2
	Golfer	(A.Palmer/G.Player)	+10		
1/21	Vacationer	Arnold Palmer	10	6	2
		(Chrysler, Cadillac, Rambler, Bob Cousy)			
1/28	Howie Young		20	10	3
	Red Wings	(7-Up)	+10		
2/04	Valeri Brumel	Jack Nicklaus	10	6	2
	High Jump	(Chrsyler, Chevy, Volvo)	+25		
2/11	Cathy Nagel	Jack Nicklaus	10	6	3
	Skier	(VW, Pontiac, Dodge, Mercedes)	+10		
2/18	Jerry Barber	Leo Durocher	20	10	1
	Golfer	(VW)	+50(d)		
2/25	Rex Ellsworth	Celtics vs Lakers	10	6	1
	Horseracing	(Triumph, Volvo)	+25(d)		
3/04	Sandy Koufax (FC)	Spring Training	65	30	10
	Dodgers	(Ted Williams, Stan Musial,	+40		
		Ralph Kiner)			
3/11	Chuck Ferries	Cassius Clay,	10	6	1
	Skier	(VW, Corvair, Rambler)	+10		
3/18	Larry Singleton	Jack Nicklaus, NCAA Basketball	20	10	5
	Cincinati-Basketball	(Ted Williams, Ford, MG,	+10		
		Cadillac, Sam Snead)			
3/25	Sonny Liston	Cassius Clay	30	15	3
	Boxer	(VW, GM, Triumph, Casey Stengel)	+750(d)		
4/01	Ken Venturi	NCAA-Finals, Masters	25	10	3
	Golfer	Ben Hogan	+15		
		(Jack Nicklaus/Arnold Palmer)			
4/08	Harmon Killebrew	Baseball Preview, N. Fox	75	30	5
	Twins	Walt Alston, Arthur Ashe(FACES)	+20		
		(Ted Williams, Barbara Streisand)			
4/15	Bill Talbert		10	6	5
	Tennis	(Corvette, Jaquar, Studenbaker)			
4/22	Fishing	Bob Cousy,	10	6	4
	Fishing	J. Nicklaus, Masters			
		(Mercedes, GM, Ford, Yankees)			
4/29	Art Mahaffey	Stanley Cup Finals	40	20	5
	Phillies	(Sam Snead, Arnold Palmer,	+10		
		T-Bird, Chrysler)			
5/06	Candy Spot	Kentucky Derby, Celtics,	10	6	5
	Horse	Mets (Stan Musial, S.Snead, VW,			
		Corvair, T-Bird)			
5/13	Boat	W.Alston, Yankees, J.Nicklaus	10	6	5
		Masters, (Corvette, Rambler, 7-Up, Cadillac)			
5/20	Paul Hornung	Ernie Davis, Roger Maris	50	25	5
	Packers	(Golf Ball History, Jaquar, J.Nicklaus)	+10		
5/27	Dan Gurney	Indy 500,Roger Maris,Angels	10	6	2
	Car Racing	(Chevy, Ford)	+10		
6/03	Bob Hope	Arnold Palmer	60	25	2
	Indians Owner	(Chevy, Nicklaus)	+40		
6/10	Cassius Clay		150	75	25
	Boxer (FC)	(Corvette, Bud)	+90 (ali)	+120 (clay)	
6/17	Jack Nicklaus	US Open/Golf	50	25	5
	Golfer		+50		
6/24	Roy Face	A.Palmer, J. Nicklaus	30	15	5
	Pirates	(Corvette, J. Nicklaus, Rambler)	+15		

1963

DATE	COVER/Sport/Team	FEATURES //(ADS)	MT	EM	VG
7/01	Julius Boros Golfer	US Open Golf, Twins, W.McCovey, C. Clay (S.Musial, Chevy)	30 +50(d)	15	3
7/08	Jon Tarantino Fisherman	Mickey Mantle (Cadillac)	10 +10	6	3
7/15	Arnold Palmer Golfer	Wimbledon, White Sox (Corvette, Volvo, GM, VW)	50 +40	25	5
7/22	Dick Groat Cardinals	A. Palmer (Ted Williams)	40 +15	20	3
7/29	Sonny Liston Boxing	J. Nicklaus, S. Koufax A. Palmer, (Ford, VW, MG)	30 +750(d)	15	2
8/05	Nancy Vonderheide Archery	(Bing Crosby)	10 +10	6	1
8/12	Alfred Vanderbilt Horseracing	Red Sox, Arnold Palmer (7-Up, VW)	10 +10	6	2
8/19	Ron Vanderkelen Vikings	Phillies	10 +10	6	1
8/26	Dennis Ralston Tennis	Alvin Dark, Mickey Mantle	10 +10	6	2
9/02	Ron Fairly Dodgers	(Schwinn) (Sam Huff, Bob Cousy, Bob Feller)	30 +10	15	3
9/09	Dallas Cowboys*	Pro Football Preview [*Cover includes George Andrie/ Chuck Howley/ Bob Lilly/ Lee Roy Jordan]	50 +10/auto	25	2
9/16	Yachting	S. Koufax, J. Nicklaus A. Palmer, Ron Mix (Koufax, VW)	10 +10	6	2
9/23	George Mira Dolphins	Dodger, Cardinals (Bart Starr)	20 +10	10	2
9/30	Whitey Ford* Yankees	Bear Bryant, World Series (T-Bird, M. Mantle, Corvette, B.Feller) (* Also Al Downing on fold)	60 +20	25	5
10/07	Deer Hunter	Jim Brown, Stan Musial (Ford Fairlaine, Dodge, Sam Huff)	10 +10	6	3
10/14	Ronnie Bull Bears	Sandy Koufax, World Series (Dodge Dart, VW Ghia, Chevy, Comet)	30 +10	15	2
10/21	Duke Carlisle Texas	(Mercury, GM Rambler, Cadillac)	10 +10	6	1
10/28	Jerry Lucas* Royals	Pro Basketball Preview (Pontiac, Chrysler, Honda, Dodge) (* includes Art Heyman Knicks)	25 +15	10	2
11/04	Jack Cvercko Northwestern	Raiders, 49ers, YA Title (Comet, Corvair)	10 +10	6	2
11/11	Referee	Texas Football (64 Rambler, Chevy Dodge 880,Spitfire, 7-Up, Galaxia, Riveria)	10 +10	6	1
11/18	Cindy Hollingworth Skier	C. Clay, S. Liston, Bill Russell, YA Title (Cadillac, Ford, T-Bird)	10 +10	6	2
11/25	Willie Galimore Bears	J. Nicklaus (Studenbacker, Squirt, YA Title) (VW Ghia, Falcon)	25 +120(d)	10	2
12/02	Roger Staubach Navy (FC)	Army/Navy (Chevy II, Schwinn, Stan Musial, VW)	75 +35	35	10
12/09	Frank Ramsey Celtics	Basketball Preview (Corvette, Ford, Skylark, LeMans, Cadillac)	50 +15	25	5
12/18	Tobin Rote Paul Lowe Chargers	Bob Cousy, AFL/NFL (VW, 7-Up, Squirt, Ford)	25 +10	10	5
12/23	C.K. Yang Decathalon	YA Title, Bowl Preview, (T-Bird, Squirt)	10 +30	6	2

1964

DATE	COVER/Sport/Team	FEATURES //(ADS)	MT	EM	VG
1/06	**Pete Rozelle** Commissioner	Championship NFL Commissioner (SOY)	50 +30	25	5
1/13	**Jack Dempsey**+ Boxing	AFL Champs (* Cover includes Willard)	40	25	
1/20	**Babette March** Model	First Swimsuit Issue (Corvette, VW)	120 +30	50	15
1/27	**Buddy Werner** Skiing	A. Palmer, Winter Olympics (Chevy, Dodge, Chrysler, Wilt Chamberlain)	10 +50(d)	6	3
2/03	**Bobby Hull** Blackhawks	Olympics (Corvair, Ford)	40 +20	25	5
2/10	**Egon Zimmermann** Skier	Olympics, Sonny Liston (Sam Snead,7-Up, Chevy, Porsche)	10 +10	6	3
2/17	**Charles Goren** Bridge Card	Olympics, Cassius Clay (Corvette, Chrysler, Mercury)	10 +50(d)	6	5
2/24	**Cassius Clay** Boxing	(Covair, GM, Imperial, Triumph, Imperial)	60 +90	45	5
3/02	**Casey Stengel Yogi Berra** Mets/Yankees	Wilt Chamberlain (Waren Spahn, VW Van)	40 +200(d)/+25	20	5
3/09	**Cassius Clay Sonny Liston** Boxing	Cassius Clay, Jerry West (Bobby Hull, Stan Musial, 7-Up, Cadillac)	80 +90/+750(d)	40	5
3/16	**Gordon Howe** Red wings	NCAA Basketball Tourney	50 +20	25	5
3/23	**Tony Lema** Golf	(Grand Prix, Triumph, Chevy, Dart)	30 +50(d)	15	2
3/30	**Walt Hazard**/* **Jeff Mullins** UCLA	UCLA NCAA Champs (Corvair, VW Ghia) *(Cover includes Duke)	30 +10	15	2
4/07	**Jack Nicklaus** Golf	Masters, Senators (7-Up)	50 +50	25	2
4/13	**Sandy Koufax** Dodgers	Baseball Issue (Schwinn, Corvette Riveria, LeMans, Whitey Ford)	75 +40	35	5
4/20	**Janis Rinchlott** Texas Sprinters	A.Palmer-Masters, Richie Allen (64 Mustang, Stan Musial, YA Title, Corvair)	10 +10	6	5
4/27	**Claude Harmon** Golf	Willie Mays Lew Alcindor [fic]	15 +10	10	1
5/04	**Kentucky Derby** Horseracing	Celtics NBA Champs (Triumph, 7-Up)	10	7	1
5/11	**Al Kaline (FSC)** Tigers	Kentucky Derby, Jack Nicklaus (Corvette, Chevy)	75 +20	30	5
5/18	**Joey Giardello** Boxing	Twins, Juan Marichal (64 Mustang, J.Nicklaus, Buick, YA Title)	10 +10	6	5
5/25	**Frank Howard** Dodgers	Nothern Dancer (Mercury, Jaquar, Barracuda, Chevy, VW)	30 +10	15	2
6/01	**AJ Foyt** Car Racing	Indy 500, Cassius Clay, Jim Fregosi (T-Bird, 7-Up, Jack Nicklaus)	20 +15	10	3
6/08	**Bill Hartack** Horseracing	Robin Roberts, AJ Foyt (VW, Warren Spahn, Chrysler, Bob Cousy)	10 +10	6	5
6/15	**Arnold Palmer** Golf	US Open, Roberto Clemente (Stan Musial)	50 +40	25	3
6/22	**Tom O'Hara** Loyola	Cassius Clay, Mickey Mantle, Brooks Robinson (VW, Chrysler)	10 +10	6	3
6/29	**Ken Venturi** Golf	U.S. Open Golf, White Sox (7-Up, Volvo)	40 +15	20	5

1964

DATE	COVER/Sport/Team	FEATURES /(ADS)	MT	EM	VG
7/06	Alvin Dark	Giants, Angels, Floyd Patterson	30	15	5
	Giants		+10		
7/13	Bill Talbert	Orioles, Brooks Robinson	10	6	2
	Tennis	F.Patterson	+10		
		(Jack Nicklaus, Buick)			
7/20	Shirley Maclaine	Angels	25	15	1
	Actress		+20		
7/27	Tommy McDonald	Yogi Berra	25	12	2
	Cowboys	(Cadillac, 7-Up)	+10		
8/03	Betsy Rawls	Tony Congiliaro	20	10	2
	Golf		+10		
8/10	Johnny Callison	Chi Chi Rodriquez	40	20	2
	Phillies	Astrodome	+15		
8/17	Don Trull	10 Years of SI, Swimsuit	20	10	5
	Oilers	Frank Robinson (Mustang)	+10		
8/24	Sovereign*	American Cup, Yogi Berra,	10	6	3
	Yachting	Reds (Paul Hornung)	+10		
		(*Cover includes Yachting Team)			
8/31	Brooks Robinson*	[* also Gerry McNerty (White Sox)/	40	25	5
	Orioles	Earl Robinson (Orioles)]	+20		
		(VW Van)			
9/07	YA Title	Pro Football Preview	30	15	5
	Browns		+15		
9/14	Jim Ryun	Rollie Fingers(FIC)	10	6	5
	Track	(VW)	+15		
9/21	Jimmy Sidle	College Football Preview	20	10	2
	Auburn		+10		
9/28	Tommy Mason	Yankees,	15	8	2
	Vikings	(Corvair, Grand Prix, Rambler, Riveria)	+10		
10/05	Tokyo Olympics*	*Dyrol Burleson, Marie Walther, Donna	10	6	5
		DeVarona, Don Schollander, Henry Carr,	+10		
		Fred Hansen. (Mustang, Mercury,			
		Packers, Pontiac, Comet, Buick, Cadillac)			
10/12	Dick Butkus (FC)		80	40	5
	Illinois	(Corvair, VW, Yogi Berra)	+20		
10/19	Yoshinori Sakai	Floyd Patterson,	10	6	1
	Olympics	Cardinals World Series (7-Up)	+10		
10/26	Tommy Heinsohn	Pro Basketball Issue,	50	25	5
	Celtics	Olympic Games, World Series	+20		
11/02	John Huarte	Olympics	50	25	4
	Notre Dame	(Green Bay Packers - Schick, Corvette)	+15		
11/09	John David Crow	Bill Russell-Celtics, Bear Bryant	20	10	5
	Cardinals	(Micky Mantle, Ford Galaxie, YA Title)	+10		
11/16	Cassius Clay*		60	30	5
	Boxer	(Comet, Bud, Impala, Gene Sarazen,	+90/+200(d)		
		(* Also Sonny Liston), VW, Grand Prix)			
11/23	Helmut Falch	Muhammad Ali (Saab, VW,	10	6	5
	Skier	Mustang, Rambler, Dart, Corvair)	+15		
11/30	Alex Karras	Jack Nicklaus, Arnold Palmer	20	10	3
	Lions	(T-Bird, Jerry West, Pontiac)	+15		
12/07	Bill Bradley	College Basketball Issue (Squirt,	60	30	10
	Princeton	Corvette, Gordie Howe, Mickey Mantle)	+40		
12/14	Charley Johnson	Arnold Palmer, Jack Nicklaus	25	12	4
	Cardinals	(7-Up, Comet, Gordie Howe, Cadillac)	+10		
12/21	Ken Venturi	Bowl Preview, Sportsman	50	25	2
	Golf (SOY)				

1965

1965

DATE	COVER/Sport/Team	FEATURES /(ADS)	MT	EM	VG
7/05	Bill Talbert	Jim Ryun, Sam Snead	10	5	1
	Tennis	(VW, Sprite)	+15		
7/12	Maury Wills	Atlanta Stadium	35	15	5
	Dodgers		+10		
7/19	Joe Namath (FC)		60	30	5
	Jets	(Sprite)	+40		
7/26	Arnold Palmer		40	20	5
	Golf	(Coke)	+40		
8/02	Powerboating	Sandy Koufax	10	5	1
	Fishing	(Sprite)			
8/09	Juan Marichal	Arthur Ashe	75	30	3
	Giants	(Coke)	+20		
8/16	YA Title	Pro Football Quarterback	50	20	2
	Giants Football		+20		
8/23	Tony Oliva	YA Title, Arnold Palmer	40	15	2
	Twins	(Budweiser, Ford)	+10		
8/30	Michel Jazy	Juan Marichal bat hit SF/LA,	10	5	3
	Track	YA Title (Sprite)	+10		
9/06	Sugar Ray Robinson	Don Drysdale	20	9	3
	Stan Harrington	(Coke, Zsa Zsa Gabor)	+175(d)		
	Boxing				
9/13	Fran Tarkenton	Tommy Mason, Pro Football Issue	40	20	4
	Vikings	(Ed Mathews, Bart Starr,Lance Alworth)	+20		
9/20	Frank Solich	College Football Issue	10	5	1
	Nebraska	Arthur Ashe	+10		
9/27	Frank Ryan	Green Bay, Giants,	20	10	2
	Browns	Willie Mays (Coke)	+10		
10/04	Zoilo Versailles	World Series	20	10	4
	Twins	(Ford Mustang, Bob Hope,	+50(d)		
		Porsche, Mercury Comet)			
10/11	Ken Willard	Alabama	20	10	5
	49er's	(Bill Russell, Corvette,	+10		
		Plymouth, Impalla)			
10/18	Tommy Nobis	World Series	40	20	5
	Texas	(T-Bird)	+10		
10/25	Bill Russell(FC)	Pro Basketball Issue	30	15	3
	Celtics	Sandy Koufax, World Series	+195		
		(Bronko Nagurski, SS Chevy, Dart)			
11/01	Sonny Randle/Charley Johnson		20	10	2
	Cardinals	Satchel Paige	+10/+10		
11/08	Harry Jones	Gale Sayers	20	10	3
	Arkansas Football	(Barracuda, T-Bird, Mercury, Chevy SS)	+10		
11/15	Ted Johnson	Cassius Clay, Wilt Chamberlain,	7	5	5
	Skiing	B.Russell (Corvette, TV, Bonneville,			
		Maurice Richard)			
11/22	Cassius Clay/		50	20	7
	Floyd Patterson	(Mustang, Squirt, Corvette, Sprite)	+90		
	Boxing				
11/29	Dennis Gaubatz	Cassius Clay	10	5	1
	Colts	(Buick, T-Bird, Dart)	+10		
12/06	UCLA	College Basketball Issue	20	15	5
	Basketball	G.Sayers, C.Clay, L.Alcindor, Rick Mount(FIC)			
		(Coke, GTO, Sprite)			
12/13	Lance Alworth	(Squirt)	95	40	6
	Chargers	(Willie Mays Coke Ad, Budweiser,	+20		
12/20	Sandy Koufax	Sportsman, Paul Hornung,	95	35	5
	Dodgers (SOY)	(Squirt)	+40		

1966

DATE	COVER/Sport/Team	FEATURES /(ADS)	MT	EM	VG
1/03	**Bowls Preview**	AFL Championship	30	15	1
		(GT Fairlane)			
1/10	**Jim Taylor**	Bowl Games (Coke, Galaxie,	60	30	5
	Packers	Wilt Chamberlain,VW, Jim Brown)	+20		
1/17	**Sunny Bippus**	Swimsuit Issue, Arnold Palmer	100	40	10
	Model		+20		
1/24	**George Peeples**	Golf Courses	20	10	3
	Iowa Basketball	(Bob Cousy, Dodge Charger, VW Van)	+15		
1/31	**Stan Mikita(FC)**	George Halas, Jo Jo White	40	20	6
	Black Hawks	Calvin Murphy(FIC)	+20		
		(Corvette, Jerry West, Ford Galaxie)			
2/07	**Billy Casper**	Royals, Bill Bradley, Peggy Fleming	20	10	4
	Golf	(Bob Hope, Mustang, Malibu, A.Palmer)	+10		
2/14	**Rick Mount**		30	15	2
	Basketball	(Mustang)	+10		
2/21	**Jean-Claude Killy**	Joe Frazier	12	9	5
	Skier	(Pan Am, T-Bird, Corvette, Toranado)	+10		
2/28	**Leo Durocher/Eddie Stanky**		30	15	2
	Cubs / White Sox		+100(d)/25		
3/07	**Adolph Rupp**	R. Clemente, M. Ali, P.Riley	15	12	3
	Kentucky	R. Petty,(Mustang, Porsche)	+200(d)		
3/14	**Richmond Flowers**	Dodgers, B.Bradley	10	5	4
	Tennessee -Track	(VW Bug, Pam Am, Mustang)	+10		
3/21	**Gary Player**	Bobby Hull	40	20	5
	Golf	(Polara, Porsche, Corvette, T-Bird)	+15		
3/28	**Hem Flournou/**	NCAA Championship, Ted Turner	40	20	4
	Pat Riley	(Mustang, Chevy SS, Lincoln)	+10/+25		
	Texas Western/Kentucky				
4/04	**Jack Nicklaus/**	Masters, Drysdale/Koufax	50	25	2
	Arnold Palmer	(VW, Tony Lema, Gary Player)	+50		
	Golf				
4/11	**George Chuado/**	Celtics, M. Ali (Corvette, Starfire,	40	20	6
	Muhammad Ali	Whitey Ford, T-bird)	+90/+10		
4/18	**Dick Groat**	Baseball Issue, Masters, C. Clay	40	20	3
	Phillies	(T-Bird, VW, Bob Hope, Bing Crosby)	+15		
4/25	**Bill Gadsby/**	Jack Nicklaus, Cassius Clay, Lakers	20	10	2
	Stan Mikita	L.Durocher, (T-bird, Impalla, Schwinn)	+10		
	Chicago/Detroit				
5/02	**Peggy Fleming**	Cassius Clay	30	15	3
	Figure Skater	(Sprite, Mustang, Russell)	+15		
5/09	**John Havlicek**	Muhammad Ali	30	15	3
	Celtics (FC)	(Volvo, Buick, Palmer)	+15		
5/16	Don Brunfield/Kauai King	Kentucky Derby, Yankee	10	5	3
	Horseracing	(Budweiser, Ford, Coke, Charger)	+10		
5/23	**Sam McDowell**	Giants, Willie Mays, Gary Player	20	10	2
	Indians	(Falcon, Schwinn)	+10		
5/30	**John Boyd**	Brooks/Frank Robinson	10	5	3
	Indy 500	Cassius Clay, Mario Andretti	+10		
		(Sam Snead, Comet, Coke)			
6/06	**Joe Morgan/**	Indy 500, Jack Nicklaus	30	15	5
	Sonny Jackson	(J. Brown, B. Cousy,	+20/+15		
	Astros	F. Gifford, B. Hull)			
6/13	**Ken Venturi**	Indy 500, US Open	40	20	5
	Golfer	(VW, Coke)	+15		
6/20	**Jim Ryun**	Dodgers, Sandy Koufax, Yankees	20	10	2
	Kansas	(Le Mans)	+20		
6/27	**Billy Casper**	Mets, Rick Mount	30	15	2
	Golf	US Open Golf (Coke)	+10		

1966

DATE	COVER/Sport/Team	FEATURES /(ADS)	MT	EM	VG
7/04	Ocean Sailors	Warren Spahn	10	5	2
		(VW Van)			
7/11	Andy Etchebarren	Tony Oliva, Denny McLain	20	10	2
	Orioles	(Coke)	+10		
7/18	Phil Edwards	Jack Nicklaus	15	9	2
	Surfer	(Sprite)	+20		
7/25	Otto Graham/	Jim Brown, Jack Nicklaus	12	9	2
	Edward Williams	(Coke)	+20/+50(d)		
	Redskins				
8/01	Jim Ryun	Orioles, Hank Aaron, Brooks Robinson	20	10	2
	Track		+15		
8/08	Frank Emanual	Casey Stengel/Ted Williams to HOF,	20	10	2
	Dolphins	Steve McQueen	+10		
8/15	Paul Bryant (FC)	Cassius Clay, Bear Bryant #1	75	35	3
	Alabama Football	(VW,Coke)	+200(d)		
8/22	Paul Hornung/*	Bryant Series #2 (Coke)	70	35	2
	Jim Taylor		+20/+15		
	Packers	[* Flap has Jim Grabowski/Donny Anderson]			
8/29	Arthur Ashe	U.S. Open Tennis, John Brodie	30	15	2
	Tennis	Bear Bryant #3, Don Drysdale	+100(d)		
9/05	Harry Walker	Bear Bryant #4	20	10	1
	Pirates	(Jack Kemp, Joe Namath)	+15		
9/12	Gale Sayers/	Pro Football Issue Jack Kemp,	60	35	2
	Randy Bukuich	John Unitas, Bart Starr,	+20/+10		
	Bears Football	Paul Hornung (VW)			
9/19	Gary Beban	College Football Issue	20	10	5
	UCLA	Packers, Dodgers, Cassius Clay	+10		
		(Paul Hornung, Sean Connerly, Sam Huff)			
9/26	Gaylord Perry (FC)	Giants, Dallas, D.Reeves	45	25	2
	Giants	(Lance Alworth, Bob Cousy)	+15		
10/03	Roman Gabriel	(Rams) Orioles,	20	10	2
	Tommy McDonald	(Pontiac GTO, Camaro, Dart, Delta 88)	+10		
	Rams Team				
10/10	Brooks Robinson/	World Series	80	35	2
	Frank Robinson/	(Willie Mays)	+20/+20		
	Hank Bauer - Flap				
10/17	Joe Namath	World Series, Bobby Orr	50	25	4
	Jets	(Camero, Mustang)	+40		
10/24	Elgin Baylor	Pro Basketball Issue, Pele,W.S.	40	20	2
	Lakers	(Sprite, Dart, Cadillac)	+15		
10/31	Bart Starr		40	20	2
	Packers	(Chevy SS, 67 Olds, T-Bird)	+20		
11/07	Terry Hanratty		30	15	2
	Notre Dame		+15		
11/14	Skier		10	5	2
		(Corvette, T-Bird)			
11/21	Ross Fichtner	C. Clay (SI, Sean Connery,	15	7	5
	Browns	Mustang GT, Squirt)	+10		
11/28	Football Players	Billy Casper, Koufax Retires	40	20	5
	Notre Dame vs Mich State				
12/05	Lew Alcindor (FC)	College Basketball Issue	50	25	2
	UCLA	Cowboys	+40 "Jabbar"		
12/12	Jim Nance*		12	6	2
	Patriots/Buffalo	(T-Bird, Squirt, Bob Hope)	+10		
		(* Cover includes Buffalo players)			
12/19	Jim Ryun	F.Robinson	50	25	2
	Track (SOY)	Bobby Hull, Lew Alcindor	+20		
		(Sean Connery, Squirt)			

1967

DATE	COVER/Sport/Team	FEATURES / (ADS)	MT	EM	VG
1/02	**Kitty McManus** Nebraska Cheerleader	Bowls, Jack Kemp (Mustang, Buick)	20 +10	10	3
1/09	**Bart Starr** Packers	Playoffs, Bowls (Coke)	40 +15	20	2
1/16	**Marilyn Tindall** Model	Swimsuit Issue, Vince Lombardi	60 +30	30	5
1/23	**Max McGee** Packers	Superbowl #1, Len Dawson (Chevy SS, Mercury)	60 +10	30	2
1/30	**Rod Gilbert** Rangers	(Frank Sinatra, Bud, Corvair, Mustang)	20 +10	10	5
2/06	**Cassius Clay** Boxing	(Bob Hope)	40 +90	20	3
2/13	**Rick Barry(FC)** Warriors	Cassius Clay (Olds, Mustang, Corvette, Sammy Davis Jr.)	20 +15	10	6
2/20	**Bob Seagren** USC Pole Vaulter	(Ken Venturi, T-Bird, VW Ghia, Coronet)	10 +10	6	2
2/27	**George Walters/Chris Thomforde** Princeton	(67 Chevy)	10 +10	6	2
3/06	**Mr/Mrs. Arnold Palmer** Golf	(Corvair, Firebird)	30 +40/+10	15	
3/13	**Jim Nash** A's	A.Palmer, Peggy Fleming (T-Bird, Corvette, Cougar)	20 +10	10	5
3/20	**Stan Mikita/ Kenny Wharram/ Doug Mohns** Blackhawks	NCAA, Bobby Hull (Ford Galaxia)	30 +15	15	1
3/27	**Jean-Claude Killy** Skiing	Lew Alcindor, A.Palmer (Camero, Elgin Baylor, Brooks Robinson, Fairlane)	10 +15	6	3
4/03	**Lew Alcindor** UCLA	Muhammad Ali, NCAA Champs (Firebird, VW Van)	30 +35	15	1
4/10	**Jack Nicklaus** Golf	Masters, M. Ali, Orioles (G Player, Galaxia, Corvair, A. Palmer)	30 +50	15	2
4/17	**Maury Wills** Pirates	Baseball Issue, Chamberlain Masters, Maris (Chevy SS, Golf Dress)	30 +15	12	2
4/24	**Rick Barry** Warriors	Roger Maris (GT)	20 +15	10	1
5/01	**Jim Hall** Car Racing	(Firebird, Shelby GT, Mantle, Galixie)	10 +10	6	4
5/08	**Ken Berry/ Mickey Mantle** White Sox/Yankees	M.Ali, W. Chamberlain (White Sox, Palmer, Sam Snead, VW Van)	40 +10	20	5
5/15	**Sandy Koufax/Maury Wills Walt Alston Don Drysdale**	(Cadillac), Stanley Cup Finals	30 +40/+100(d)/ +100(d)/+10	15	1
5/22	**Tommie Smith** San Jose -Track	(Plymouth, B. Hull, P.Hornung, B.Cousy)	10 +20	6	2
5/29	**Indy 500 - Art**	(Bud, Coke, Red Ruffing, Mustang)	10	6	4
6/05	**Al Kaline** Tigers	(Volvo, GM, Hull)	40 +20	20	2
6/12	**Billy Casper/ Arnold Palmer**	U.S. Open	30 +10	15	1
6/19	**Joe Harris** Boxing	Bill Russell	10 +10	6	1
6/26	**Jack Nicklaus** Golf	U.S. Open, Tom Seaver Ronald Reagan (Camaro) Ralph Garr(FIC)	30 +50	15	5

1967

DATE	COVER/Sport/Team	FEATURES /(ADS)	MT	EM	VG
7/03	Roberto Clemente		150	35	3
	Pirates (FC)		+500(d)		
7/10	Muhammad Ali	[*George Chivalo, Ernie Terrell,	30	15	1
	& Challengers*	Karl Mildenberger, Joe Frazier.]	+90/+15		
	Boxing	Baseball Stadiums			
7/17	Fran Tarkenton	Orioles, Swimsuits	40	20	4
	Giants		+25		
7/24	Surfer Girls	Fran Tarkenton, Orlando Cepeda	10	6	2
	Hawaii	Hall of Fame			
7/31	Spitball	Fran Tarkenton	20	10	2
8/07	Gay Brewer	Willie Mays, F. Tarkenton	20	10	2
	Golf	Masters	+50(d)		
8/14	Jim Taylor/	Muhammad Ali, Rick Barry, Swaps	30	15	2
	Gary Cuozzo		+15/+10		
	Saints				
8/21	Carl Yastrzemski	Muhammad Ali, Ted Williams	75	35	5
	Red Sox		+25		
8/28	Intrepid	Muhammad Ali	10	6	2
	Yachting	(Paul Hornung)			
9/04	Tim McCarver		30	15	2
	Cardinals		+15		
9/11	Terry Hanratty*	Colleges Football Issue	30	15	2
	Notre Dame	(* Also includes Bill	+20		
		Bradley,Ted Henricks, Kirby Moore)			
9/18	Tommy Mason	Pro Football Issue, G.Sayers, Killebrew	15	8	4
	Rams	Leroy Kelly, Ed Mathews	+10		
9/25	Nino Benvenuti		10	6	5
	Boxing	(Corvette)	+10		
10/01	John McKay	John Unitas	10	6	2
	USC Coach	(Chrysler, GTO, T-Bird, Buick)	+20		
10/08	Mike Phipps	W.Shoemaker, Red Sox, Cards	10	6	2
	Purdue Football	(Toronado, River, SI)	+10		
10/15	Lou Brock (FC)	World Series, Joe Namath	30	15	7
	Cardinals	(Mustang, Star Trek)	+25		
10/22	Pro Basketball	Pro Basketball Issue, OJ Simpson	15	8	3
	Knicks names	World Series (Shelby Cobra GT)	+10/+40/+10		
10/29	Dennis Homan/		30	15	2
	Jimmy Weatherford				
	Alabama/Tenn. Football				
11/06	Dan Reeves	Pro Hockey Issue	20	10	5
	Cowboys	(Toronado, Star Trek)	+10		
11/13	Ski Fashions		10	5	1
	France	(VW, Chrysler, Cadillac)			
11/20	OJ Simpson,Gary Beban		40	20	2
	USC/UCLA		+40/+10		
11/27	Jim Hart	OJ Simpson	15	7	1
	Cardinals	(VW Van, Mercury, Buick)	+10		
12/02	Basketball Art	College Basketball Issue	20	10	2
		(Coke, VW Gia, Firebird, Rivera)			
12/09	Bobby Orr (FC)	Raiders, R. Mount, C. Murphy	30	15	2
	Bruins		+30		
12/18	Roman Gabriel/Willie Davis		20	10	1
	Rams/Packers	Bill Bradley, Vince Lombardi	+15		
12/25	Carl Yastrzemski	Holiday	75	30	2
	Red Sox (SOY)	(Cadillac, Torino)	+25		

1968

VALUE GUIDE

DATE	COVER/Sport/Team	FEATURES //(ADS)	MT	EM	VG
1/08	Chuck Mercein/ Hewitt Dixon Packers/Raiders	George Blanda, Bowl Games (Cadillac, Coke)	30 +10/+15	15	2
1/15	Turia Mau Swimsuit Model	Swimsuit Issue	40 +25	20	2
1/22	Vince Lombardi/ Jerry Kramer Packers	Superbowl II (Chevy, Bud)	60 +300(d)/+15	30	1
1/29	Lew Alcindor/ Elvin Hayes UCLA/Houston	Olympics	30 +40	15	1
2/05	Billy Kidd/ Jimmy Heuga Skier	Winter Olympics (GTO, Fury III)	10 +10	6	1
2/12	Bobby Hull Bruins	Olympics (Camaro, Corvette)	30 +15	15	5
2/18	Peggy Fleming Ice Skating	Muhammad Ali, Olympics (Cadillac, Toronado, Bonneville)	20 +15	10	1
2/26	Curtis Turner NASCAR	(Corvette) John Havlicek, Olds, Camaro)	10 +10	5	5
3/04	Pete Maravich* LSU	Joe Frazier (Corvette) (* Also includes Pete's Dad)	75 +200(d)/+50(d)	35	5
3/11	Johnny Bench* Reds	(*Cover includes Alan Foster, Mike Torrez, Don Pepper, Cisco Carlos)	60 +25/10 each others	30	3
3/18	Bill Bradley Knicks	NCAA, Joe Frazier (Camaro, Mustang)	50 +40	25	4
3/25	Julius Boros Golfer	NCAA, Carl Yaz (GTO, Toronado)	10 +50(d)	5	1
4/01	Lew Alcindor/ Elvin Hayes UCLA/Houston	NCAA final (T-Bird, Camaro)	20 +40	10	2
4/08	Goalie LA Kings	Stanley Cup, Masters, Pete Maravich (AMX, Cougar, Arnold Palmer, Bonneville)	10	5	2
4/15	Lou Brock Cardinals	1968 Baseball Issue, Pete Rose (Corvette, Palmer, Carl Yaz, YA Title)	20 +20	10	5
4/22	B.Goalby/R.DeVicenzo Golf	Masters (Satellite, Firebird)	10 +15/+15	6	1
4/29	Elgin Baylor/ Jerry West Lakers	Harmon Killebrew, Reggie Jackson Bill Russell (Chevy SS 396)	30 +15 each	15	2
5/07	Ron Swoboda Mets	Nolan Ryan, Tom Seaver (Chrysler, Harmon Killebrew, Schwinn)	20 +10	9	2
5/13	Graham Hill Car Racing	Indy 500, Kentucky Derby, Celtics Champs (Corvette, Cadillac, Brooks Robinson)	10 +10	6	5
5/20	Dancer Image Horse	Kentucky Derby (Charger, Plymouth, T-Bird)	10	6	1
5/27	Pete Rose Reds (FC)	VW, Chevy SS) (Palmer, Torino, Harmon Killebrew)	70 +25	30	5
6/02	Dave Patrick	Villanova- Track	10 +10	5	1
6/10	Arnold Palmer/ Jack Nicklaus Golf	U.S. Open Preview, Willie Mays Ted Williams (Corvette, Campaneris, Unser)	40 +40/+50	15	5
6/17	Don Drysdale Dodgers	Ted Williams	40 +100(d)	20	2
6/24	Lee Trevino (FC) Golf	U.S. Open, Ted Williams (Cadillac, Chevy SS)	30 +25	15	2

1968

VALUE GUIDE

DATE	COVER/Sport/Team	FEATURES /(ADS)	MT	EM	VG
7/01	Black Athlete	Ted Williams (Gatorade)	10	5	1
7/08	Ted Williams	'The Science of Hitting'	30	15	2
	Red Sox		+150		
7/15	Ray Nitschke	Olympics (Harmon Killebrew,	50	25	3
	Packers	VW Ghia, Bud, Johnny Bench)	+20		
7/22	Mark Spitz		10	5	1
	Swimmer		+15		
7/29	Denny McLain(FC)		40	20	1
	Tigers	(VW Van)	+10		
8/05	Nevele Pride	Orioles	10	5	1
	Harness racing	(Roman Gabrial)			
8/12	Paul Brown	Jack Nicklaus	12	7	1
	Bengals		+100(d)		
8/19	Curt Flood		20	10	2
	Cardinals	(Coke)	+10		
8/26	Rod Laver	U.S. Open, Joe Namath	15	6	1
	Tennis		+10		
9/02	Ken Harrelson	Bobby Orr	24	12	1
	Red Sox		+10		
9/09	Leroy Keyes	College Football Issue	15	7	2
	Purdue Football	John Riggens	+10		
		(Charley Taylor, Dan Reeves, Frank Ryan)			
9/16	Don Meredith	Pro Football Issue, Carl Yaz. Arthur	40	20	5
	Cowboys	Ashe,(FB Hall of Fame, H. Killebrew)	+20		
9/23	Denny McLain/	McLain's 30th Victory, Bobby Jones	50	25	2
	Al Kaline	(Charger, Chrysler)	+10/+20		
	Tigers				
9/30	Jim Ryun*/	World Series. (Cadillac, Chevy)	20	10	1
	Kip Keino	(*Also Harry Edwards/Avery Brundage)	+15		
	Olympics Preview				
10/07	Roger Maris/Lou Brock/Tim McCarver		60	30	5
	Bill Shannon/Orlando Cepeda, Curt Flood		+200(d)/+20/+10/+10		
	Julius Javiar, Bill Maxwill, Red Schoendiest		+10/+10/+10/+10		
	Cardinals		+20		
10/14	OJ Simpson	Hockey Preview, World Series	30	15	2
	USC	(Ray Nitschke, LeMans, SS)	+40		
10/21	Sotela Basilio/	Pro Basketball Preview, Olympics	10	6	3
	Norma Enriqueta	(Unitas, Crosby, Cougar)			
	Olympic Torchbearers	World Series			
10/28	F.Gregg/Bob Brown	Olympics	20	9	1
	Packers	(VW Ghia, Toronado, Nova, Dart)	+15/+10		
11/04	Earl Monroe	Olympics	20	10	1
	Bullets	(Coronet, Bud)	+20		
11/11	Bruce Jankowski	Peggy Fleming	10	5	1
	Ohio State	(Pontiac, Charger, Buick GS)	+15		
11/18	Jean-Claude Killy	OJ Simpson	10	5	2
	Skiing	(VW Van, Unitas, Camaro, Palmer)	+15		
11/25	Earl Morrall		40	20	1
	Colts	(Charger, Squirt, Nicklaus)	+20		
12/02	Mike Casey*	College Basketball Issue (J.Havilek,	20	10	3
	Kentucky	J. Unitas, J. West) (*Cover includes	+10		
		Charlie Scott-NC, Mike Malloy-Davidson)			
12/09	Joe Namath	OJ Simpson, Notre Dame, Gordie. Howe,	30	15	2
	Jets	Royals (Delta, Squirt)	+40		
12/16	Rick Volks/	Bart Starr, Connie Hawkins	20	9	1
	Donny Anderson	(Coronet, Imperial)	+15 each		
	Colts/ Packers	(*Cover includes Dennis Gabatz)			
12/21	Bill Russell(SOY)	Colts, J. Kelly, Bowls	40	20	2
	Celtics	(Squirt, J. Unitas)	+200		

1969

DATE	COVER/Sport/Team	FEATURES /(ADS)	MT	EM	VG
1/06	**Tom Matte***	John Wooden, Joe Namath	24	12	1
	Colts	(*also shows Charley Talyor)	+10		
1/13	**Jamee Becker**	1969 Swimsuit Issue	50	25	1
	Swimsuit Model	(GTO)	+40		
1/20	**Joe Namath**	Superbowl III	100	45	2
	Jets	(Wilt Chamberlain, Don Maynard)	+50		
1/27	**Wilt Chamberlain**		30	15	2
	Lakers	(Imperial, Bob Hope, John Havlicek)	+80		
2/03	**Bobby Orr**	Frank Robinson	40	20	1
	Bruins		+40		
2/10	**Bud Ogden**	(Bob Hope,	10	5	2
	Santa Clara	John Havlicek, Wilt Chamberlain, GTO)	+15		
2/17	**Bob Lunn**	Jack Nicklaus	10	5	1
	Golf	(Chrysler, Bud, T-Bird)	+15		
2/24	**Willis Reed/**	Ted Williams, Earl Monroe	15	6	1
	Billy Cunningham	(Bonnyville, W.Chamberlain)	+15		
	Knicks/ 76ers				
3/03	**Vince Lombardi**	Tom McMillen(FIC)	25	10	1
	Redskins	(Nicklaus, Toronado, Nova)	+300(d)		
3/10	**Puma's & Adidas**		10	5	3
	Shoe Scandal	(Elgin Baylor, Wilt Chamberlain,			
		Jack Nicklaus, T-Bird)			
3/17	**Ted Williams**	Lew Alcindor	30	15	2
	Senators	(Bud, Playboy Club, Camaro,	+150		
		Opel GT, Grand Prix)			
3/24	**Richie Guerin/**	Charlie Scott,Dan Gable	10	5	1
	Jeff Mullins	(Chamberlain, Dodge, Imperial)	+15/+15		
	Hawks/ Warriors				
3/31	**Lew Alcindor**	NCAA Champ, Johnny Bench	30	15	3
	UCLA	George McGinnis (fic)	+40		
		(T-Bird, Al Kaline, Charger, G.Howe)			
4/07	**Red Berenson**	Tony Conigliaro, Masters	25	12	3
	Blues	(Arnold Palmer, Wilt Chamberlain, Volvo)		+15	
4/14	**Bill Freeham**	Baseball Issue, John Havlicek, T.Seaver	30	15	3
	Tigers	(P.Rose, J.Nicklaus, A.Kaline, Bud)	+15		
4/21	**George Archer**	Willie Mays, Masters	20	10	1
	Golf		+10		
4/28	**Bill Russell**	Bobby Orr, Bobby Murcer	30	15	1
	Celtics	(Camaro)	+200		
5/05	**Muhammad Ali**		30	15	3
	Boxing	(Maverick, Lee Trevino, Mercedes)	+90		
5/12	**John Havlicek**	Kentucky Derby	30	15	3
	Celtics	(Chevelle SS, Roy Campanella, Pepsi)	+20		
5/19	**Walt Alston***	(*Cover shows: Ted Sizemore, Bill	30	15	1
	Dodgers	Sudakis, Bill Grabarkewitz.)	+200(d)/+15 each		
		Jack Nicklaus, (VW, Casper)			
5/26	**Grizzly Bear**		10	5	2
		(Mercedes, Pete Rose)			
6/02	**Water Scooter**	Frank Robinson,	10	5	2
		Lee Trevino, Billy Casper)			
		Steve Prefontaine (fic)			
6/09	**Lee Trevino**	Indy 500-Mario Andretti	30	15	
	Golf	OJ, US Open	+25		
6/16	**Joe Namath**	Arnold Palmer	30	15	1
	Jets	(Opel GT)	+40		
6/23	**Drugs**	US Open Golf	10	5	2
		(Fresca, Olympic Beer, Arnold Palmer, MG)			
6/30	**Ron Santo**		30	15	1
	Cubs	(Mercedes)	+15		

1969

VALUE GUIDE

DATE	COVER/Sport/Team	FEATURES / (ADS)	MT	EM	VG
7/07	**Reggie Jackson**(FC) A's		70 +40	30	1
7/14	**O.J. Simpson** Bills	Billy Casper (VW)	30 +40	15	1
7/21	**Billy Martin** Twins	(VW)	30 +50(d)	15	1
7/28	**Sonny Jurgensen/Vince Lombardi** Redskins	(Pete Rose)	20 +15/+350(d)	10	2
8/04	**Bill Russell** Celtics	All Star Game, Willie McCovey (Olympic Beer, Pepsi, Gatorade)	30 +200	15	2
8/11	**Joe Namath** Jets		30 +40	15	1
8/18	**Henry Aaron**(FC) Braves		40 +25	20	1
8/25	**O.J. Simpson** Bills	Luis Aparicio (Gatorade, OJ Simpson)	30 +40	15	1
9/01	**Arnold Palmer** Golfer		30 +40	15	1
9/08	**Pete Rose/Ernie Banks** Reds / Cubs		50 +25/+25	25	1
9/15	**Woody Hayes/ Rex Kern** Ohio State Football	College Football Issue Willie McCovey, Nancy Lopez (FIC) (Bear Bryant, Ernie Banks)	30 +200(d)	15	3
9/22	**Jim Turner** Jets	Pro Football Issue (Vince Lombardi, Cutlass, Gale Sayers, GTO, Budweiser)	30 +15	15	3
9/29	**Jimmy Jones** USC	Willie Mays, Ernie Banks (Mustang, Pete Rose, SS)	20 +15	10	2
10/05	**Frank Robinson/ Boog Powell**(Flap) Orioles	(G.Howe, Cyclone, Monte Carlo, Pee Wee Reese)	30 +20/+15	15	4
10/12	**Bruce Kemp** Georgia	Pro Hockey Issue (Impalla, John Havlicek, Charger, Toronado)	20 +15	9	2
10/20	**Brooks Robinson*** Orioles	Connie Hawkins, Lew Alcindor (Arnold Palmer, Buick) (* Cover includes: Paul Hendricks)	40 +15/+10	20	1
10/27	**Lew Alcindor** Bucks	Pro Basketball Issue World Series	30 +40	15	1
11/03	**Alan Page/Roy Winston** Carl Eller Vikings Football	Lew Alcindor, Joe Kapp (Imperial, J.Kramer)	15 +15	6	1
11/10	**Steve Owens** Oklahoma Football	Archie Manning, Joe Namath L. Alcindor (John Wayne, Mach 1 Mustang)	10 +15	5	2
11/17	**Beredette Barzini** Ski Model	Jerry Lucas, Jack Nicklaus (Porsche, Mustang)	10 +25	5	1
11/24	**Len Dawson*** Chiefs	Joe Namath (Olympic, G. Sayers, P. Rose, Squirt) (* Cover includes Chiefs 45,21,55,84)	30 +25	15	5
12/01	**Pete Maravich** LSU Basketball	College Basketball Issue (Gale Sayers, Joe Montana)	90 +200(d)	35	1
12/08	**Walt Frazier/ Bob Weiss** Knicks/ Bulls	Jack Nicklaus (Bud, Willis Reed, Duster)	30 +15	15	2
12/15	**James Street** Texas Football		30 +15	15	1
12/22	**Tom Seaver*** Mets (SOY)	Notre Dame, Stadium (Torino, R. Gabrial, Rose Bowl) (*flap cover includes Joe Namath, Muhammad Ali)	75 +25	35	1

1970

DATE	COVER/Sport/Team	FEATURES /(ADS)	MT	EM	VG
1/05	Dave Osborn/		15	7	1
	Deacon Jones	(Lee Trevino, Joe Kapp,	+15		
	Vikings/ Rams	Darryl Lamonica, Craig Morton)			
1/13	Cheryl Tiegs(FC)	Swimsuit Issue	60	30	2
	Model	Playoffs, D.Lamonica	+25		
1/19	Len Dawson	Superbowl IV	60	30	1
	Chiefs	(Bud)	+20		
1/26	Bob Cousy	Ted Williams [Bill Walton (FIC)]	30	15	1
	Royals	(Don Maynard)	+30		
2/02	Environment	(AMX)	10	5	1
2/08	Terry Bradshaw		40	20	2
	La Tech	(Bob Hope, VW, Lee Trevino)	+30		
2/16	Tom McMillen	Joe Frazier	15	7	1
	HS Basketball	(Jerry West)	+12		
2/23	Denny McLain		20	10	1
	Tigers	(Toronado)	+15		
3/02	Eddie Giacomin	Spring Training	10	7	3
	Rangers	(Mustang, Camaro)	+10		
3/09	Lew Alcindor		30	15	1
	Bucks		+40		
3/16	Dan Issel*	(* Includes Bob Lanier-St. Bonaventure,	10	5	1
	Kentucky	Jim Collins New Mexico, J. Vallely-UCLA)	+15		
3/23	Richie Allen	Steve Carlton, Bob Gibson	30	15	2
	Cardinals	(Sam Snead, Stan Mikita)	+15		
3/30	Sidney Wicks/	Basketball Final Four	24	12	3
	Art Gilmore	Pete Maravich	+15		
	UCLA/Jacksonville				
4/06	Keith Magnuson	Pete Maravich, Masters,	10	6	4
	Black Hawks	(Williams/Hodges,Koosman,	+15		
		Ben Hogan, Sam Snead)			
4/13	Jerry Koosman	Baseball Issue, W.McCovey, Rod Carew	15	8	3
	Mets	(J. Wayne, Bud, Lou Brock,	+15		
		Arnold Palmer, Jack Nicklaus)			
4/20	Billy Casper	Master	24	12	2
	Golf	(Pepsi)	+15		
4/27	Lew Alcindor/	Wilt Chamberlain	20	10	1
	Willis Reed	(Peggy Fleming)	+40/+15		
	Bucks/Knicks				
5/04	Bobby Orr		40	20	1
	Bruins		+40		
5/11	David Smith	Mario Andretti	10	5	2
	Peace Pentathlon	(Camaro, Gil Hodges, Earl Weaver)	+15		
5/18	Dave Debusschere	NBA Champs, Ben Hogan	20	10	1
	Knicks	(Datzun 280z, Brooks Robinson)	+15		
5/25	Hank Aaron		40	20	1
	Braves	(Firebird, Arnold Palmer)	+25		
6/01	Jack Nicklaus/	Bob Griese, Tom Seaver	30	15	1
	Arnold Palmer		+50/+40		
	Golf				
6/08	Al Unser	Bill Russell	10	6	1
	Indy 500	(Cary Middlecoff)	+15		
6/15	Steve Prefontaine	Jack Nicklaus	40	15	1
	Oregon-Track	(Bud)	+200(d)		
6/20	Tony Conigliaro		40	15	1
	Red Sox		+200(d)		
6/29	Tony Jacklin	US Open, Denny Mclain, Pele	24	12	1
	Golf	Tony Conigliaro (Lee Trevino)	+50(d)		

1970

DATE	COVER/Sport/Team	FEATURES /(ADS)	MT	EM	VG
7/06	**George Frenn**	Frank/Brooks Robinson	10	4	2
	Hammer throw	Willie Mays, Luis Aparico,	+15		
		(Pepsi), Orlando Cepeda			
7/13	**Johnny Bench**	Tony Perez	40	20	1
	Reds	(Jerry Koosman)	+25		
7/20	**Joe Kapp**	Jack Nicklaus	15	7	1
	Vikings		+15		
7/27	**Willie Mays**	Joe Kapp	40	20	1
	Giants		+35		
8/03	**Frank Shorter***		10	4	1
	Track	(* Also Mikitenko)	+15		
8/10	**Mike Garrett**		10	6	1
	Chiefs		+15		
8/17	**Joe Namath**	George Foreman, Tony Oliva	20	10	1
	Jets		+40		
8/24	**Rick Barry**	PGA	10	6	1
	Squires - ABA		+15		
8/31	**Les Sly**	Roger Staubach	15	6	2
	Cowboys	(Gale Sayers)	+15		
9/07	**Bud Harrelson***	(* cover include Pete Rose)	20	10	1
	Mets		+15		
9/14	**Archie Manning**	College Football Issue, Muhammad Ali	40	20	2
	Mississippi	(Joe Namath)	+20		
9/21	**Dick Butkus**	Pro Football Issue	60	30	2
	Bears		+20		
9/29	**Danny Murtaugh***	Roberto Clemente	15	10	4
	Pirates	(Mustang)	+100(d)/+100(d)/200(d)		
		(* Also Leo Durocher- Cubs & Gil Hodges - Mets)			
10/05	**Football players**	Willie Stargell,	10	7	2
	Colorado/Penn State	Frank/Brooks Robinson			
10/12	**Alex Karras**		15	7	1
	Lions		+15		
10/19	**Brooks Robinson***	World Series	20	9	1
	Orioles	(Mickey Mantle, Camaro, Joe Namath)	+15/+10each		
	(* Cover includes P. Hendricks, Boog Powell, C.Carbo, L. May, T.Perez)				
10/26	**Oscar Robertson**	NBA Pro Basketball,	30	12	2
	Bucks	Joe Theisman, Pete Maravich	+40		
		(Challenger)			
11/02	**Monday Football**	Muhammad Ali	10	4	1
		(Jaquar)			
11/09	**Joe Theismann***		24	12	1
	Notre Dame		+15		
	(*Cover includes Jack Tatum - Ohio State, Steve Worster - Texas)				
11/16	**Calvin Murphy**		30	12	1
	Rockets	(Joe Namath)	+15		
11/23	**George Blanda /**		30	12	1
	Daryl Lamonica		+20		
	Raiders				
11/31	**Sidney Wicks**	College Basketball Issue	24	12	1
	UCLA	Stadium	+15		
12/07	**Roman Gabriel**	Jack Kemp	20	10	1
	Rams		+15		
12/14	**Steve Worster**	Muhammad Ali, Notre Dame	10	5	1
	Texas		+15		
12/30	**Bobby Orr**	Raiders, Muhammad Ali	50	25	3
	Bruins (SOY)		+40		

1971

DATE	COVER/Sport/Team	FEATURES /(ADS)	MT	EM	VG
1/04	**John Roche**	49ers, Bowl Games	30	15	–
	South Carolina		+15		
1/11	**Joe Theismann**		30	15	–
	Notre Dame		+15		
1/18	**Craig Morton**		30	15	1
	Cowboys		+15		
1/25	**Jim O'Brien/**	Superbowl V	40	20	1
	Earl Morrell				
	Cowboys		+15		
2/01	**Tannia Rubiano**	Swimsuit Issue, Muhammad Ali	40	20	3
	Model		+40		
2/08	**Willis Reed/**	Tony Conigliaro	15	7	–
	Lew Alcindor		+15/+40		
	Knicks				
2/15	**Jim Plunkett**	Muhammad Ali	15	7	–
	Stanford		+15		
2/22	**Del Meriwether**	Joe Frazier	10	4	–
	Track		+30		
3/05	**Joe Frazier/Muhammad Ali**		50	22	2
	Boxing		+25/+90		
3/08	**Jack Nicklaus**	PGA, Pete Maravich	30	12	1
	Golf	Spring Training	+50		
3/15	**Joe Frazier/Muhammad Ali**		50	22	2
	Boxing		+25/+90		
3/22	**Wes Parker**		20	10	1
	Dodgers		+15		
3/29	**Phil & Tony Esposito**		40	20	–
	Bruins/Blackhawks		+15/+15		
4/05	**Steve Patterson**	NCAA Championship	10	5	–
	UCLA		+15		
4/12	**Boog Powell**	Baseball Issue	20	10	3
	Orioles	(SI, Lou Brock, Pete Rose, Corvette)	+15		
4/19	**Willis Reed/**	Lew Alcindor, Bobby Orr	10	6	1
	Abdul-Jabbar	(Johnny Carson, Porsche)			
	Knicks/Bucks				
4/26	**Derek Sanderson**		10	5	–
	Bruins				
5/03	**Dave Duncan/**	Jack Nicklaus, A's, Derby	15	7	2
	Jim Fregosi	Chris Evert(FACES) (Mustang)	+15/15		
	A's/Angels				
5/10	**Oscar Robertson***	NBA Title	15	7	2
	Bucks	(Porsche, Jerry Lucas, Ted Williams)	+30		
		*Cover also shows Wes Unseld/Gus Johnson			
5/17	**James McAlister**	Giants	10	4	2
	UCLA	(Mustang, Phil Esposito)	+10		
5/24	**Liquori/Jim Ryun**	Kentucky Derby, Red Sox	6	4	–
	Villanova Track	(VW Ghia)	+15/+15		
5/31	**Vida Blue**	Pete Maravich	30	12	1
	A's		+15		
6/07	Al Unser/Pete Revson	All Star Game, Jack Nicklaus	20	10	3
	Indy 500	(Porsche, All Star Ballot-Gilette,Foyt)	+10		
6/14	**Canonero II**	Bobby Jones	7	4	1
	Horseracing				
6/21	**Jerry Grote**		15	7	–
	Mets		+15		
6/28	**Lee Trevino**	US Open	30	12	3
	Golf	(Corvette)	+25		

1971

|------|------------------|------------------|------|------|------|
7/05	**Alex Johnson** Angels	(Brooks Robinson)	15 +15	6	1
7/12	**Evonne Goolagong** Tennis	Wimbledon, Vida Blue	10 +15	4	-
7/19	**George Blanda** Raiders	Tony Conigliaro, Boug Powell (Brooks Robinson)	25 +15	10	2
7/29	**Muhammad Ali** Boxing	George Blanda (Porsche)	30 +80	12	1
8/02	**Willie Stargell** Pirates (FC)	Muhammad Ali, Lee Trevino, George Blanda, Roberto Clemente	30 +15	15	1
8/09	**Mike Peterson** Kansas		10 +15	6	-
8/16	**Calvin Hill** Cowboys	(Porsche)	12 +15	6	-
8/23	**Steve McQueen** Actor		20 +200(d)	5	-
8/30	**Ferguson Jenkins** (FC) Cubs	(Ferrari)	30 +15	15	1
9/06	**Jackie Stewart** Auto Racing	OJ Simpson	15 +20	4	-
9/13	**Tommy Casanova** LSU	College Football Issue Bear Bryant	15 +15	6	1
9/20	**John Brodie** 49ers	Pro Football Issue	25 +20	10	1
9/27	**Maury Wills** Dodgers	Giants/Dodgers	25 +15	10	1
10/04	**Sonny Sixkiller** Washington	(Gale Sayers, Porsche)	20 +15	12	1
10/11	**Joe Greene** Steelers	(Willie Mays)	30 +20	15	-
10/18	**Frank Robinson** Orioles	Willie Stargell (Alex Karras, Bob Griese, Bart Starr)	30 +20	15	1
10/25	**Gus Johnson*** **Dave Debuschere** Bullets/Knicks	Pro Basketball Issue	15 +15/+15	6	1
11/01	**Ed Marinaro** Cornell		15 +15	6	-
11/08	**Norm Bulaich** Colts		12 +15	6	-
11/15	**Ski Jumper** Olympics Sapporo	Olympics (Bob Griese)	12	4	-
11/22	**Football Players** Oklahoma/Nebraska	(Johnny Unitas)	20	10	1
11/29	**Tom Burleson** North Carolina State	College Basketball	15 +15	6	1
12/06	**Johnny Musso** Alabama		15 +15	5	-
12/13	**Gail Goodrich** Lakers		15 +15	7	-
12/20	**Lee Trevino** Golf (SOY)	Sportsman (Gale Sayers)	40 +30	20	1

1972

DATE	COVER/Sport/Team	FEATURES /(ADS)	MT	EM	VG
1/03	**Garo Yepremian** Dolphins	Playoffs, Bruins	15 +20	7	1
1/10	**Janssen/Terrio** Nebraska Football	Bowl Games, Bill Walton, UCLA Basketball	20 +15 each	10	1
1/17	**Sheila Roscoe** Swimsuit	Swimsuit Issue, Cheryl Tiegs, Lakers	40 +25	20	2
1/24	**Duane Thomas** Dallas Cowboys	Super Bowl VI: Cowboys Beat Dolphins Jack Nicklaus, (Mustang)	30 +20	15	2
1/31	**Annie Henning** Speedskating	Nolan Ryan, George McGinnis, Olympics	8 +15	4	2
2/07	**Cowens/Frazier** Celtics/Knicks	Jerry West, John Havlicek, Fran Tarkenton	14 +15 each	7	1
2/14	**Ken Dryden (FC)** Canadiens	Olympics, (Bob Hope)	12 +15	6	-
2/21	**Al McGuire** Marquette Basketball	Olympics, (Mustang)	8 +15	4	1
2/28	**AJ Foyt** Autoracing	Daytona 500	10 +15	5	-
3/06	**Bill Walton(FC)** UCLA Basketball	NCAA Basketball	14 +20	7	1
3/13	**Johnny Bench** Reds	Pete Rose	30 +20	15	1
3/20	**College Basketball**	NCAA Final 4, (Pinto, Mustang, Porsche)	10	5	2
3/27	**Vida Blue** A's	UCLA Basketball	20 +15	10	1
4/03	**Bill Walton** UCLA Basketball		20 +20	10	1
4/10	**Joe Torre** Cardinals	Baseball Issue, Brooks Robinson, Tom Seaver, Carl Yaz, (Jesse Owens)	20 +15	10	3
4/17	**Jack Nicklaus** Golf	Masters	20 +60	8	-
4/24	**Lew Alcindor*** Bucks	[*Cover also shows Jim McMillan/Dave Meyers/Flynn Robinson (Bucks/Lakers).] Steve Carlton, Juan Marichal, (Hank Aaron)	20 +60	10	-
5/01	**Willie Davis** Dodgers		12 +15	6	1
5/08	**Phil Esposito/Bobby Orr** Bruins		25 +20/+35	12	1
5/15	**Wilt Chamberlain** Lakers	Kentucky Derby, (Porsche)	30 +65	15	1
5/22	**Willie Mays** Mets	Stanley Cup, Orr, Indy 500	30 +40	15	1
5/29	**Louie Jacobs**	Pacers ABA Champs	10 +15	4	-
6/05	**Mark Donohue** Car Racing	Indy 500, Astros, Jim Palmer, (SI/Goudeys)	12 +15	6	-
6/12	**Dick Allen** White Sox	US Open Golf, (Hogan)	18 +15	8	1
6/19	**Bobby Hull** Black Hawks		25 +20	10	1
6/26	**Jack Nicklaus** Golf	US Open Golf, (Boog Powell) Johnny Unitas	18 +60	9	1

1972

DATE	COVER/Sport/Team	FEATURES /(ADS)	MT	EM	VG
7/03	Steve Blass Pirates	Roberto Clemente	12	6	–
7/10	Johnny Unitas Colts	Muhammad Ali	30 +20	15	1
7/17	Jim Ryun Track		10 +15	4	–
7/24	Tommy Prothro Rams	Lee Trevino, (Hank Aaron)	12 +10	6	–
7/31	Robyn Smith Jockey	A's, (Porsche)	10 +10	4	–
8/07	Larry Csonka Jim Kiick Dolphins		20 +20/+10	9	1
8/14	Bobby Fischer Chess	Joe Morgan, (SI)	10 +10	4	–
8/21	Sparky Lyle Yankees		12 +10	6	–
8/28	Olympics Preview	Cathy Rigby	10	4	–
9/04	Mark Spitz Swimmer	Jack Nicklaus, Olympics, (Porsche)	10 +20	6	–
9/11	Bob Devaney Nebraska	College Football Issue, (Joe Namath, SI)	16 +20	8	1
9/18	Walt Garrison Cowboys	Pro Football Issue, Mark Harmon, Tom Landry, Olympics, (Bob Griese, SI)	20 +20	10	1
9/25	Carlton Fisk Red Sox		30 +20	15	2
10/02	Greg Pruitt Oklahoma Football	Orioles, Muhammad Ali	8 +10	4	–
10/09	Joe Namath Jets	World Series	20 +60	10	1
10/16	Wilt Chamberlain Lakers	World Series, (Brooks Robinson), Pro Basketball Issue,	20 +60	10	1
10/23	Jim Hunter A's	World Series, (Bart Starr)	20 +20	10	1
10/30	Dave/Don Buckey NC State Football	World Series, (Johnny Carson, Porsche)	10 +10 each	4	–
11/06	Larry Brown Redskins		10 +20	5	–
11/13	John Havlicek* Celtics	[*Cover also shows Mike Riodar.] Sugar Ray Robinson	18 +25	9	1
11/20	Terry Davis Alabama Football		12 +20	6	–
11/27	Walter Luckett Ohio State Basketball	College Basketball, Dolphins	12 +10	6	–
12/04	Steve Spurrier 49ers	(Jack Nicklaus)	12 +15	7	1
12/11	Campy Russell Michigan Basketball	Franco Harris, Dr. J, Oscar Robertson, (Roger Staubach) Pete Maravich,	10 +15	5	–
12/18	Lee Roy Jordan Cowboys	Colts, (Roger Staubach)	20 +15	10	1
12/25	John Wooden (SOY) Billie Jean King (SOY) UCLA Basketball/Tennis		40 +20 each	15	1

1973

DATE	COVER/Sport/Team	FEATURES //(ADS)	MT	EM	VG
1/08	Mercury Morris Dolphins	Playoffs, Dolphins, Bowls, (Opel GT, Roger Staubach)	12 +20	6	1
1/15	Doug Collins Illinois State	Sam Snead, Redskins,George Foreman, Stan Mikita,(John Wooden)	12 +15	6	-
1/22	Bob Griese Dolphins	Super Bowl VII: Dolphins Beat Redskins	30 +30	15	2
1/29	Dayle Haddon Swimsuit Model	Swimsuit Issue	40 +40	20	2
2/05	Bill Walton* UCLA Basketball	[*Cover also shows Keith Wilkes, Larry Hollyfield, John Schumate (UCLA/Oregon)] George Foreman, (Bob Hope, Jack Nicklaus)	14 +20	7	1
2/12	Steve Smith Pole Vault	Notre Dame, (Bobby Orr)	10 +10	4	1
2/19	Kareem Abdul-Jabbar Wilt Chamberlain Bucks/Lakers	Bobby Knight, Jack Nicklaus	12 +40/+95	6	-
2/26	Gil Perreault Sabres	Muhammad Ali, (Mustang, SI)	12 +15	6	1
3/05	Broadway Actors	Lee Trevino	8	4	
3/12	Bill Melton White Sox	Chris Evert, (Willie Mays, VW, Schwinn)	10 +15	6	1
3/19	Olga Korbut Gymnastics	Pirates, NCAA Tournament	30 +20	15	-
3/26	Bill Walton*	[*Cover also shows Marvin Barnes-(Providence), Steve Downs (Indiana), Larry Keron (Memphis State).] Secretariat, (Mustang)	12 +20	6	-
4/02	Henry Richard Canadiens	UCLA NCAA Champs, Masters, Cowens, (Gale Sayers)	20 +15	10	1
4/09	Steve Carlton Phillies	Baseball Issue, Joe Morgan,(Bobby Hull, J. Garagiola, M.Ali, J. Nicklaus)	20 +20	10	1
4/16	Earl Monroe* Knicks	[*shows Phil Chenier/Walt Frazier.] Masters, (Nicklaus, Palmer, SI Posters)	12 +20	6	-
4/23	Muhammad Ali Boxing		20 +95	9	1
4/30	Chris Speier Giants	49ers, Kentucky Derby	20 +15	9	1
5/07	Frazier/West Knicks/Lakers	Bill Russell (VW Bug, Corvette, SI Posters)	20 +20/+20	10	2
5/14	Spitz/Weiner Swimmers	Kentucky Derby, Nolan Ryan, (Mustang, Johnny Bench)	12 +10 each	6	1
5/21	Bobby Riggs Tennis	Knicks NBA Champs, Pacers ABA Champs, Stanley Cup, (Toyota, Johnny Miller)	10 +50(d)	5	-
5/28	Women in Sports	Secretariat, Hank Aaron, (Fergie Jenkins	6	3	-
6/04	Wilbur Wood White Sox	(J.Nicklaus, SI, Porsche, Tom Seaver)	14	7	1
6/11	Secretariat Penny Tweedy Horseracing		30	15	2
6/18	George Foreman Boxing	Secretariat, A's	14 +30	7	1
6/25	Johnny Miller Golf	US Open Golf, Reds, (Arnold Palmer, Len Dawson, Mustang, Porsche)	15 +20	8	1

1973

DATE	COVER/Sport/Team	FEATURES /(ADS)	MT	EM	VG
7/02	Bobby Murcer Ron Blomberg Yankees	Bob Hayes	18 +15each	9	1
7/09	George Allen Redskins	Secretariat, Willie Mays	12 +20	6	1
7/16	Billie Jean King Tennis	Wimbledon, Gaylord Perry	20 +20	10	-
7/23	Tom Weiskopf Golf	Don Maynard, (Fergie Jenkins) British Open	12 +20	6	1
7/30	Carlton Fisk Red Sox	(Pinto)	20 +25	10	1
8/06	John Matuszak Houston Football	(SI)	12 +15	6	-
8/13	Children Motorcross	Secretariat, B. Williams, L. Durocher	12	4	-
8/20	Claude Osteen Bill Russell Dodgers	Nicklaus, Steelers, Negro Baseball	12 +20each	6	-
8/27	Duane Thomas Redskins	(Fergie Jenkins)	12 +15	6	-
9/03	Bob Rigby Soccer	Orioles, Bubba Smith	10 +15	5	-
9/10	Texas Football	College Football Issue	12	6	1
9/17	Larry Csonka/ Bob Griese Dolphins	Pro Football Issue	20 +30each	10	1
9/24	Danny Murtaugh Pirates		12 +50(d)	6	-
10/01	Anthony Davis USC Football	Mets	12 +15	6	-
10/08	Fran Tarkenton Vikings	Jerry Lucas	30 +30	15	1
10/15	Tiny Archibald Rick Adleman Kings/Trailblazers	Pro Basketball Issue, Tracy Austin [FIC] (Walt Frazier, Joe Namath, Bill Bradley)	12 +15each	6	1
10/22	Campaneris/Milner A's/Mets	Hockey Issue, World Series	14 +15each	7	1
10/29	OJ Simpson Bills	Reggie Jackson, World Series Bill Russell	18 +50	9	1
11/05	Anthony Davis USC	(Johnny Carson, Porsche, Camaro) Secretariat	18 +20	6	1
11/12	Pete Maravich* Hawks	*Cover shows Garfield Heard (Suns) & Lou Hudson (Hawks). (SI Posters)	15 +200(d)	10	-
11/19	Phil Esposito Bruins	(Camaro, Porsche, Bob Griese)	18 +20	7	1
11/26	David Thompson NC State Basketball	College Basketball Issue	20 +20	9	1
12/03	Paul Bear Bryant Gary Rutledge Alabama Football	Harlem Globetrotters, OJ Simpson, (Schwinn)	20 +100(d)/+15	10	1
12/10	Bill Walton/ Len Elmore UCLA/Maryland Basketball		12 +30/+20	6	-
12/17	Marv Hubbard Raiders	Warriors, (Jack Nicklaus, Johnny Bench, Dick Butkus)	15 +15	6	-
12/24	Jackie Stewart Autoracing (SOY)	OJ Simpson, Walt Frazier, George Foreman	25 +40	10	-

1974

DATE	COVER/Sport/Team	FEATURES //(ADS)	MT	EM	VG
1/07	Fran Tarkenton*	Playoffs, Bowls	30	15	1
	Vikings	[*Grady Alderman (Vikings)]	+25		
1/14	Julius Erving	Bob Griese, Fran Tarkenton	40	20	1
	Nets(FC)	(SI Poster)	+25		
1/21	Larry Csonka	Superbowl VIII Issue, M. Ali	30	15	1
	Dolphins	(Joe Namath, Sonny/Cher)	+25		
1/28	Ann Simonton	Swimsuit Issue	50	25	2
	Model	Cheryl Tiegs	+50		
2/04	Muhammad Ali/	Bill Cartwright (FIC)	30	15	2
	Joe Frazier	(Corvette, Bob Hope)	+80		
	Boxing				
2/11	Ben Crenshaw		24	12	-
	Golf	(Pete Maravich-SI Ad)	+15		
2/18	John Havlicek		30	12	1
	Celtics	(Porsche, Bart Starr)	+15		
2/25	Bill Walton/Gerald Lillett		15	8	1
	UCLA/Oregon	(Walt Frazier, Reggie Jackson)	+15		
3/04	Jimmy Connors(FC)	A's	20	10	-
	Tennis	(Sam Snead)	+15		
3/11	Gordie Howe	Elvin Hayes, Walt Alston	30	12	1
	WHA Houston Aeros	(Sean Connery, Jack Nicklaus)	+20		
3/18	Babe Ruth	Babe Ruth	15	7	1
	Yankees	(Camaro, Porsche)			
3/25	Bill Walton	Babe Ruth	25	10	-
	UCLA	(Johnny Carson)	+15		
		(* Cover includes Tom Burleson/NC state)			
4/01	Bill Walton*	Babe Ruth	25	10	-
	UCLA	(* Cover includes Thompson, Burleson NC State)			
4/08	Pete Rose	Baseball Issue, Bobby Bonds,	30	15	2
	Reds	Jim Palmer, Reggie Jackson, Hank Aaron	+25		
		(Hank Aaron)			
4/15	Henry Aaron #715	Home Run #715, Masters	50	25	2
	Braves	(Porsche, Jack Nicklaus)	+30		
4/22	Gary Player	Masters, Hank Aaron	30	12	1
	Golf	(Jack Nicklaus)	+15		
4/29	Bruce Hardy	Kentucky Derby	7	3	-
	Utah Football	Dick Allen, Bart Conners(FIC)	+15		
5/06	Bobby Clarke(FC)	(Brooks Robinson)	10	4	-
	Fliers	(* Cover includes Pete Stenkowski/NY)	+15		
5/13	Cannonade/	Kentucky Derby, Dave Cowens	7	3	-
	Angel Cordero	Jack Nicklaus	+15		
	Horse	(Arthur Ashe, Hank Aaron-SI ad)			
5/20	John Havlicek	A's, Celtics NBA Champs	20	9	-
	Lew Alcindor	(Porsche) Nets ABA Champs	+15/+40		
	Celtics/Bucks				
5/27	Jim Wynn	Stanley Cup, Steve Garvey	15	6	-
	Dodgers		+15		
6/03	John Rutherford	Indy 500	12	6	-
	Car racer		+15		
6/10	Johnny Miller	US Open	15	6	1
	Golf	(Bill Russell, Porsche, Camaro,			
		Hank Aaron, Mercedes 450 SL)	+15		
6/17	Reggie Jackson		20	9	1
	A's	(Car foldout - Goodyear)	+35		
6/24	Hale Irwin	US Open, Reds, Bjon Borg	12	4	1
	Golf	(Hank Aaron, SI Poster ad)	+15		

1974

DATE	COVER/Sport/Team	FEATURES /(ADS)	MT	EM	VG
7/01	**Rod Carew (FC)** Twins	Moses Malone, Arnold Palmer, Braves	30 +15	12	1
7/08	**Gerald Ford** Vice President	(Don Schula, Porsche, Camaro)	40 +40	15	1
7/15	**Jimmy Connors/** **Chris Evert** Tennis	Wimbledon (Willie Mays)	20 +25	10	1
7/22	**Lou Brock** Cardinals	Superdome, Gary Player (Willie Mays, AJ Foyt)	24 +25	12	1
7/29	**Terry Bradshaw** Steelers	Indians	30 +25	12	-
8/05	**Football Strike**	Dodger, Golf Hall of Fame (Porsche, Bill Russell, SI Poster)	5	3	-
8/12	**Mike Marshall** Dodgers		15 +15	6	-
8/19	**Lee Trevino** Golf	PGA, Reds, OJ (Sean Connery, Willie Mays, SI Poster)	30 +25	12	1
8/26	**John Newcombe** Golf	Red Sox	15 +15	5	
9/02	**Evel Knievel** Stuntman	Browns, A's	25 +20	10	-
9/06	**Archie Griffin** Ohio State	College Football Issue	30 +15	12	1
9/16	**OJ Simpson** Bills	Pro Football Issue (AJ Foyt, Lee Roy Jordan, VW)	30 +40	15	1
9/23	**Joe Gilliam** Steelers	Yankees, 49ers	15 +15	5	-
9/30	**Tom Clements** Notre Dame		20 +15	10	-
10/07	**Jim Hunter** A's	World Series , Wilt Chamberlain (Don Schula, Terry Bradshaw)	30 +15	12	1
10/14	**Bill Walton/** **K.Abdul-Jabbar** Trailblazers/ Lakers	Jim Plunkett, Playoffs Arnold Schwarzenegger	20 +15/+40	10	-
10/21	**Rollie Finger*** A's / Dodgers	Arnold Schwarzenegger Frank Robinson (Phil Esposito)	30 +15each	12	1
	(* Also includes Steve Garvey, Steve Yeager, Bill Butler)				
10/28	**Muhammad Ali** Boxing	Pro Basketball Issue Secretariat, A's, Sunny Jurgensen (Wilt Chamberlain Poster ad for Spalding)	25 +90	15	1
11/04	**Joe Washington** Oklahoma	Moses Malone (Don Schula)	15 +15	6	-
11/11	**Muhammad Ali/** **George Foreman** Boxing	Muhammad Ali (Corvette, Sports Poster ad, Johnny Carson)	25 +90	12	2
11/18	**Woody Green** Chiefs	(Porsche)	12 +15	6	-
11/25	**Ken Dryden** Canadiens	(Tyco Trains, Hank Aaron)	12 +15	6	1
12/02	**Louisville*** Basketball Mascots	College Basketball Preview Raiders, C. Murphy (Jack Nicklaus) (*includes Marquette, UCLA, NC State, Indiana, Alabama, Maryland, S.Carolina)	15 +7	7	1
12/09	**Anthony Davis** USC Football	Kareem Abdul Jabbar	20 +15	9	-
12/16	**Rick Barry*** Warriors	(* Also Keith Erickson(suns)) (Porsche)	30 +15	12	-
12/23	**Muhammad Ali** Boxing (SOY)		50 +100	25	1

1975

DATE	COVER/Sport/Team	FEATURES /(ADS)	MT	EM	VG
1/06	**Franco Harris/ Bubba Smith**	Playoffs, Bobby Orr (Superbowl, Don Schula) Steelers/ Raiders	20 +15	10	1
1/13	**Bill Tilden** Tennis	Fran Tarkenton, Bowls Terry Bradshaw	10	4	1
1/20	**Terry Bradshaw** Steelers	Superbowl IX	30 +25	15	2
1/27	**Cheryl Tiegs** Model	Swimsuit Issue, C. Brinkley, B. Walton (Bear Bryant)	50 +25	25	2
2/03	**John Laskowski** Indiana-Basketball	(Bob Hope, Telly Salvas)	10 +15	5	-
2/10	**Rogie Vachon** Kings	Walt Frazier (SI Poster ad - Dr. J)	10 +15	5	
2/17	**Dave Meyers** UCLA	Pete Maravich (OJ Simpson, Arthur Ashe)	10 +15	5	1
2/24	**Sheep dog**		10	3	-
3/03	**Cincinnati Reds*** Reds	Spring Training, Celtics, Tom Seaver [*also shows Clay Kirby/ Gary Nolan/ Clay Carroll/ Jack Billingham/ Don Gullett]	20 +15 each	10	-
3/10	**Lee Elder** Golf	Dr. J, Arthur Ashe Foolish Pleasure (OJ Simpson)	16 +15	8	-
3/17	**Phil Ford/ Mo Rivers** UNC/ NC State Basketball		20 +15	10	-
3/24	**Chuck Wepner** Boxing	Frank Robinson (Johnny Carson, Terry Salvas)	20 +40(d)	6	
3/31	**Mike Flynn/Benson** Kentucky	Final Four, Sam Snead (Jack Nicklaus)	10 +15	4	-
4/07	**Steve Garvey (FC)** Dodgers	Baseball Issue, Carlton Fisk NCAA Champions (Mercury, Corvette, OJ Simpson)	45 +15	20	2
4/14	**Vasili Alexeyev**	Weightlifting (Bear Bryant)	10 +35	5	
4/21	**Jack Nicklaus** Golf	Masters, Giants (Terry Salvas)	30 +50	10	-
4/28	**Garfield Heard*** Braves	(* also includes Bob McAdoo, Smith)	10 +15	5	-
5/05	**Jimmy Conners** Tennis	(Jack Nicklaus)	12 +20	5	
5/12	**Foolish Pleasure*** Horse	Kentucky Derby (* Also Jaciata Vasquez) (NBA Players -John Havlicek, SI Poster Ad)	10	5	1
5/19	**A.J. Foyt** Car racing	Indy 500, A's	10 +15	5	-
5/26	**Filbert Bayi** Track	Cubs	10 +15	5	-
6/02	**Billy Martin** Rangers	Indy 500, Warriors-Champs Stanley Cup	15 +60(d)	7	-
6/09	**Rocky Bleier** Steelers	Reds, Pete Rose Steve Prefontaine (Budweiser)	20 +15	10	-
6/16	**Nolan Ryan** Angels	(Bill Russell)	75 +25	30	5
6/23	**Pele** Soccer	(OJ Simpson)	16 +40	8	-
6/30	**Lou Graham** Golf	US Open	20 +15	10	-

1975

DATE	COVER/Sport/Team	FEATURES //(ADS)	MT	EM	VG
7/07	**Fred Lynn (FC)**	Carlton Fisk, Thurmon Munson	30	15	-
	Red Sox	Orioles	+15		
7/14	**Arthur Ashe**	Wimbledon	30	15	1
	Tennis	(Willie Mays, Bear Bryant)	+100(d)		
7/21	**Jim Palmer/**	Arthur Ashe	30	10	-
	Tom Seaver		+20/+25		
	Orioles/Mets				
7/28	**Paul Warfield/Larry Csonka/Jim Kiick**		40	15	-
	Memphis Grizzlies		+15each		
8/04	**Tim Shaw**		10	3	-
	Swimming		+15		
8/11	**Baseball Boom**	Fans	5	3	-
8/18	**Jack Nicklaus**	Bruce Jenner, PGA	20	10	-
	Golf	(SI Poster ad, Johnny Miller)	+50		
8/25	**Bart Starr**		20	10	-
	Packers		+20		
9/01	**Brian Oldfield**		10	3	-
	Track		+15		
9/08	**Terry Davis**	College Football Issue,	15	6	1
	Barry Switzer	Nolan Ryan, A's, Archie Griffin			
	Joe Washington				
	Oklahoma				
9/15	**Muhammad Ali/Don King/Joe Frazier**		20	10	-
	Boxing		+80		
9/22	**Joe Greene**	Pro Football Issue	30	15	-
	Steelers	(Baseball Card Ad- Duke Snider)	+15		
9/29	**Rick Slager/Dan Devine**	Joe Namath, Muhammad Ali,	20	10	-
	Notre Dame	Pete Rose, Reds Stadium	+15/+15		
10/06	**Reggie Jackson**	Red Sox, A's, Pirates, World Series	12	9	1
	A's	(Jack Nicklaus, Terry Bradshaw)	+30		
		Babe Dickerson			
10/13	**Muhammad Ali/**	Manilia fight, OJ,	12	9	-
	Joe Frazier	Babe Dickerson	+80/+25		
	Boxing				
10/20	**Luis Tiant/**	Pro Hockey Preview	25	12	1
	Johnny Bench	Babe Dickerson, World Series	+15/+25		
	Red Sox/Reds				
10/27	**George McGinnis**	Pro Basketball Issue,	12	6	1
	76ers	World Series	+15		
11/03	**Will Mceenaney/**	World Series	15	7	-
	Johnny Bench	(Frank Gifford)	+15/+20		
	Reds				
11/10	**Fran Tarkenton***	Pete Maravich	25	12	1
	Vikings	(Tom Selleck, Willie Mays)	+25		
		[*Cover also shows Ed Marinaro (Vikings)]			
11/17	**Hockey Players**	Violence, Terry Bradshaw	12	5	-
			+15		
11/24	**Chuck Muncie**	Tony Dorsett	12	7	-
	Cal Bears	(Yul Bryner ad)	+15		
12/01	**Kent Benson**	College Basketball	12	6	1
	Indiana		+15		
12/08	**Bubba Bean**	Indiana	10	5	-
	Texas A & M		+15		
12/15	**George Foreman/Muhammad Ali**		15	7	-
	Boxing		+25/+80		
12/22	**Pete Rose**		60	25	3
	Reds (SOY)		+25		

1976

DATE	COVER/Sport/Team	FEATURES /(ADS)	MT	EM	VG
1/05	**Preston Pearson** Cowboys	[*Cover also shows Wally Hilgenberg (Vikings)]	30 +15	15	1
1/12	**Franco Harris*** Steelers	Cowboys, Cav's, Bowls [*Cover also shows Gerry Mullens/Otis Sistrunk]	20 +20	10	1
1/19	**Sylvander Twins** Models	Swimsuit Issue, Dorthy Hamill Christy Brinkley, Cheryl Tiegs (* Model names are Yvette & Yuonne)	40 +25each	20	2
1/26	**Lynn Swann** Steelers	Superbowl X (Giants/Yankees)	30 +15	15	1
2/02	**Sheila Young** Speedskating	Olympic Issue, Bulls (Johnny Miller)	8 +15	4	-
2/09	**Ernie Grunfield*** Tennessee	Olympics (Teamster, Datsun 280z) (* Cover includes Bernard King)	30 +10/+15	12	-
2/16	**Franz Klammer** Skier	UCLA, Warriors (Tom Seaver, Bud History)	8 +25	4	1
2/23	**Bobby Clarke** Fliers	UNLV, Dorthy Hamell, Sonics	10 +15	5	-
3/01	**Muhammad Ali** Boxing	(SI Poster ad- Pete Maravich) (* Cover includes Jean Piere Coopman)	25 +80/+20	10	-
3/08	**Bob McAdoo** Buffalo		10 +15	5	-
3/15	**Bill Veeck** Owner	Dr J, ABA Championship	10 +100(d)	5	-
3/22	**Tracy Austin** Tennis		10 +15	5	-
3/29	**Kent Benson** Indiana	Nuggets, Spring Training	10 +15	5	-
4/05	**Scott May** Indiana	NCAA Final (Johnny Carson, Merc. 450sl)	15 +15	5	1
4/12	**Joe Morgan** Reds	Baseball Issue,Jerry Rice, Fred Lynn, J.Jensen, (Tom Seaver, Bob Griese) (SI poster ad, Jim Hunter, Nolan Ryan)	40 +20	20	1
4/19	**Raymond Floyd** Golf	Masters,Giants (Johnny Miller)	20 +15	10	-
4/26	**Evonne Goolagong** Tennis	Yankees Stadium, Tom Landry, Dr J.	10 +25	4	-
5/03	**Mike Schmidt** Phillies		30 +30	15	-
5/10	**Angel Cordero/ Bold** Jockey	Kentucky Derby, Muhammad Ali, Arnold Palmer, Jim Palmer (Gale Sayers, Bob Griese)	10 +15	4	1
5/17	**Julius Erving*** Nets	[* Cover includes Chuck Williams] (SI ad)	40 +25	20	-
5/24	**Larry Robinson** Montreal	Stanley Cup, Suns (Carlton Fisk)	10 +15	5	-
5/31	**Carlton Fisk Lou Pinella** Red Sox/Yankees	Larry Holmes (Arnold Palmer)	30 +25	12	-
6/07	**Alvan Adams/ Dave Cowens** Suns/Celtics	Indy 500, Giants	20 +15/+15	10	-
6/14	**Dwight Stones** High Jump Track	Bobby Jones, Boston Celtics Phillies	12 +15	4	-
6/21	**George Brett** Royals	Bobby Orr Joe Namath	30 +25	15	-
6/28	**Bowie Kuhn** Baseball		15 +50(d)	4	-

1976

VALUE GUIDE

DATE	COVER/Sport/Team	FEATURES /(ADS)	MT	EM	VG
7/05	Frank Shorter Track		10 +15	4	-
7/12	Randy Jones Padres		10 +15	5	-
7/19	Frank Shorter Track	Olympic Issue, Braves (Datsun 280z, Heineken) (* Cover includes Shirley Babashoff, Scott May)	10 +15	4	
7/26	Torch Carriers Olympics	OJ Simpson, Jim Palmer	10	4	-
8/02	Nadia Comaneci Gymnastics	Olympic, Oklahoma (SI Poster ad)	20 +15	10	-
8/09	Bruce Jenner Track	Olympics	20 +15	10	-
8/16	Calvin Hill Redskins	(Heineken)	10 +15	5	-
8/23	Steve Spurrier Tampa Bay	Stan Musial, Bernard King (Bill Cosby, Johnny Miller)	20 +15	5	-
8/30	Reggie Jackson Orioles	Tennis US Open, Chris Evert	30 +30	15	-
9/06	Rick Leach Michigan	College Football Issue Reds,Tony Dorsett	10 +15	4	-
9/13	Bert Jones Colts	Pro Football Issue, Thurmon Munson	15 +15	6	-
9/20	Jimmy Connors Tennis	A's, Tony Dorsett (Bill Cosby, Ben Hogan, SI Poster)	15 +15	4	-
9/27	Ken Norton Boxing	OJ Simpson, Muhammad Ali	12 +15	4	-
10/04	Mark Manges Maryland	Raiders (Ben Hogan)	12 +15	4	-
10/11	George Foster Reds	Reds, M. Ali,World Series (Lou Brock/Steve Garvey, MG)	30 +15	12	1
10/18	Chuck Foreman Vikings	Playoffs, Reds, Bobby Orr (Gail Goodrich) Hockey Issues	12 +15	5	-
10/25	Dave Cowens/Dr J Boston	Pro Basketball Issue World Series	30 +15/+25	10	1
11/01	Johnny Bench Reds	World Series, Dr J, 49ers Steve Cauthen(FIC) (SI Poster ad, Jack Nicklaus)	30 +25	15	1
11/08	Tony Dorsett Pirates	Pete Maravich John McEnroe(FIC)	20 +20	10	1
11/15	David Thompson Nuggets	Michigan, Dr J	20 +20	8	-
11/22	Walter Payton Bears	Dave Cowens (Porsche, Dave Cowens)	40 +30	20	-
11/29	Rickey Green Michigan	College Basketball Issue USC,Cav's (Dave Cowens, Schwinn)	10 +15	5	-
12/06	Rocky Bleier/ Sam Davis Steelers	Bruins (Dave Cowens)	20 +20	7	-
12/13	Bill Walton Trail Blaziers	Raiders, Reggie Jackson Oklahoma	10 +15	5	-
12/20	Chris Evert Tennis (SOY)	Muhammad Ali, Tony Dorsett (Squirt)	30 +15	15	2
	Year In Sports	Muhammad Ali, Reggie Jackson	10	6	1

1977

DATE	COVER/Sport/Team	FEATURES /(ADS)	VALUE GUIDE MT	EM	VG
1/03	**Clarence Davis/Mel Blout/Glen Edwards**		15	6	1
	Raiders/ Steelers	(TR7)	+15		
1/10	**Tony Dorsett**	Playoff, Bowls	30	10	1
	Pittsburgh		+20		
1/17	**Ken Stabler**	Superbowl XI, Moses Malone	35	15	1
	Raiders		+15		
1/24	**Lena Kansbod**	Swimsuit Issue, Bobby Orr	24	12	1
	Model	Dave Cowen, Cheryl Tiegs	+20		
1/31	**Bill Cartwright**		10	6	-
	USF		+10		
2/07	**Guy Lafleur**	Bernard King (Camaro,	15	7	1
	Montreal	Walt Frazier, Gale Sayers, Tom Selleck)	+15		
2/14	**Kareem Abdul-Jabbar**		12	5	-
	Lakers		+40		
2/21	**NBC TV Deal**	UNLV	10	4	-
	Olympics	(Tom Selleck, Mustang, SI Poster)			
2/28	**Carl Yarborough**	Daytona 500	20	8	1
	Car Racer-Nascar	(Joe Morgan, SI Ad, Pinto)	+15		
3/07	**Steve Cauthen**		12	5	-
	Jockey		+15		
3/14	**Tom Lasorda**	(Mariners-Tickets)	12	5	-
	Dodgers	(SI poster- Pete Maravich, Camaro)	+15		
3/21	**George McGinnis/**	Dr J, Atlanta Stadium	12	5	1
	Paul Silas	(Tom Selleck,Dr J-Converse,Bob Griese)	+15		
	76'ers/Nuggets				
3/28	**Bump Wills**		12	5	4
	Rangers	(McDonalds Basketball - Magic Johnson)	+15		
4/04	**Butch Lee/**	Seattle Slew, NCAA 4	10	4	1
	Walt Davis	(Dr J-Converse)	+15		
	Marquette/NC				
4/11	**Joe Rudi**	Baseball Issue,	10	5	1
	Angels	(Lou Brock-Converse, Jack Nicklaus)	+15		
4/18	**Tom Watson**	Masters (Kareem Abdul-Jabbar,	15	5	1
	Golf	BMW, Ford, Tom Seaver)	+15		
4/25	**Sidney Wicks***	Joe Namath	15	6	1
	Celtics	(SI Poster-Dr J., Pete Rose, Roger	+15		
		Staubach,[* also C.Scott/Billy Paultz]			
5/02	**Reggie Jackson**	Thurmon Munson, Willie McCovey	20	8	1
	Yankees	(Arthur Ashe, Horseracing,	+15		
		Roger Staubach Tom Selleck, Ford)			
5/09	**Brad Park***	(Johnny Bench RC Can ad	10	3	2
	Bruins	(SI poster ad- Dr J, Ben Hogan)	+15		
		(* Also Garry Cheevers)			
5/16	**Seattle Slew/**	Kentucky Derby	15	5	-
	J Cruguet	(Arthur Ashe)	+15		
	Horse				
5/23	**Bill Walton***	[*also shows Lanny, K. Abdul-Jabbar,	12	8	6
		Steelers (Blazers)]. Magic Johnson[FIC]			
	Trailblazers/Lakers	Stanley Cup, (McDonalds-/Magic Johnson)			
5/30	**Dave Parker**	Roger Staubach, Budweiser Ad)	20	8	2
	Pirates	Pirates, Busch Stadium,	+15		
6/06	**Mark Fidrych**	AJ Foyt, Dr J	20	8	2
	Tigers	(SI poster - Dr J, The Deep poster)			
6/13	**Bill Walton***	[* Cover includes Joe Bryant/76ers]	15	5	1
	Trailblazers	(SI poster-C.Evert, Dave Cowens-YMCA)	+15		
6/20	**Seattle Slew***	Triple Crown, Roger Maris	20	5	1
	Horse	(* Also Jean Cruguet)	+15		
6/27	**Tom Seaver**		20	10	1
	Reds		+20		

1977

DATE	COVER/Sport/Team	FEATURES /(ADS)	MT	EM	VG
7/04	Ted Turner	American Cup, Indians	12	5	-
	Yachting		+15		
7/11	Bjorn Borg(FC)	Wimbledon, Dave Winfield	15	5	-
	Tennis		+15		
7/18	Rod Carew/Ted Williams		15	5	-
	Twins	(Joe Namath, Danny White)	+20/+150		
7/25	Conrad Dobler	Cubs	10	4	-
	Cardinals		+15		
8/01	Colorado Rapids		6	3	-
8/08	Carlos Monzom*	Orioles	10	5	-
	Boxing	(* Cover includes Rodrigo Valdes)	+50(d)		
8/15	Sadaharu Oh		30	15	2
	Tokoyo Giants		+45		
8/22	Lanny Wadkins	PGA, Reds, Lou Brock	8	4	-
	Golf		+15		
8/29	Greg Luzinski	Archie Manning, Mike Schmidt	10	5	-
	Phillies	(Tom Selleck,US Open)Jackie Joyner(FIC)	+15		
9/05	Ross Browner	College Football Issue	10	5	1
	Notre Dame	Pele (Mickey Mantle -AMC)	+15		
9/12	Alberto Juantoren	Meadows Stadium	10	4	-
	Track	(* Cover include Boit)	+25/+15		
9/19	Kenny Stabler	Pro Football Issue	30	15	1
	Raiders		+15		
9/26	Robert Duran/	Cowboys, Yankees (Tom Selleck)	20	10	1
	Edwin Viruet	(Lite Beer Fold Out 15 Jocks)	+25/+10		
	Boxing				
10/03	Billy Sims	Raiders	10	5	-
	Oklahoma	(Jack Nicklaus, Arnold Palmer)	+15		
10/10	Muhammad Ali/	Pele, Yankee Stadium	15	7	-
	Ernie Shavers	(World Series, Jack Nicklaus)	+80/+15		
	Boxing				
10/17	Rubin Carter	Pro Hockey Preview	10	4	-
	Denver	Dodgers, Raiders	+15		
10/24	Thurmon Munson/	World Series	40	15	
	Bill Russell	(Rowin/Martin-Laugh in)	+200(d)/+10		
	Yankees/Dodgers				
10/31	Maurice Lucas	Pro Basketball Issue Reggie Jackson,	15	7	1
	Blaziers	Joe Montana, Bill Bradley	+15		
11/07	Burt Reynolds*	Oakland, Indians	10	5	-
	Movie Star	(Danny White, Camaro)	+25/+20/+10		
		(* Also Kris Kristofferson, Jill Clayburn)			
11/14	Belmont Swindle		10	4	1
	Crime	(Chuck Munice, BMW, Joe Namath)			
11/21	Dave Casper*		15	5	-
	Raiders	(Tom Selleck)	+10each		
		(* Also Pruitt, Cunningham, Lambert, Jones)			
11/28	Larry Bird (FC)	First Issue	100	40	10
	Indiana State	College Basketball Issue	+50		
12/05	Earl Campbell		25	10	-
	Texas		+15		
12/12	Bryan Trottier	Lyle Alzado	15	5	-
	Islanders	(Chuck Munice)	+15		
12/19	Steve Cauthen	Sportsman	40	15	1
	Horseracing	(Danny White, Champion plug)	+15		
	Year In Sports	Joe Montana, Munson, Dr J	20	10	2
	1977	(Mickey Mantle -AMF, Roger Staubach, SI Poster)			

1978

DATE	COVER/Sport/Team	FEATURES //(ADS)	MT	EM	VG
1/02	**Mark Van Eeghan** Raiders	NFL Playoffs	20 +15	10	–
1/09	**Terry Eurick** Notre Dame	Bowls, Playoffs (Superbowl)	20 +15	10	1
1/16	**Maria Joao** Model	Swimsuit Issue	40 +25	20	2
1/23	**Randy White/ Harvey Martin** Cowboys	Dallas Superbowl (Magic Johnson)	30 +15/+15	15	2
1/30	**Robert Duran*** Boxing	(Corvette, Ken Stabler) (* Cover includes Esteban DeJesus)	20 +20/+15	7	1
2/06	**Dick Buerkle/Filbert Bayi** Miler	Carl Lewis(FIC),(Reggie Jackson)	15 +15	5	1
2/13	**Sidney Moncrief** Arkansas Basketball		20 +15	7	–
2/20	**Walter Davis** Suns		15 +15	7	–
2/27	**Leon Spinks** Boxing		12 +15	5	–
3/06	**Houston McTear** Track	Spring Training (Ferrari, Dr. J, Jack Nicklaus, Walt Frazier)	12 +15	5	1
3/13	**Gene Banks** Duke Basketball	White Sox, Leon Spinks (Dr. J)	12 +15	5	1
3/20	**Clint Hurdle** Royals	UCLA	12 +15	5	
3/27	**Jack Nicklaus** Golf	TPC, NCAA final four	20 +50	10	–
4/03	**Goose Givens/ Duke-Gene Banks** Kentucky Basketball	NCAA Finals, (Red Holtman)	10 +15	5	–
4/10	**George Foster/ Rod Carew** Reds/Twins	Baseball Issue John Havlicek (Reggie Jackson, Lou Brock)	16 +15/+20	8	2
4/17	**Gary Player** Golf	Bill Walton, Masters (Meadowlark Lemon, John Bench)	15 +15	8	1
4/24	**Mark Fidrych** Tigers	Bucks (Dr. J)	20 +15	10	–
5/01	**Gary Player** Golf	Red Sox, Bill Walton	20 +15	10	–
5/08	**Elvin Hayes/Mike Green** Bullets		10 +15/+10	5	–
5/15	**Steve Cauthen/ Affirmed** Jockey	Kentucky Derby,76ers Pete Rose, (Terry Bradshaw)	15 +15	7	–
5/22	**Marvin Webster/Jack Silema** Sonics		10 +15/+10	5	–
5/29	**Leroy Robinson/Ken Dryden** Canadiens	(Jim Palmer, Corvette)	10 +10/+10	5	1
6/05	**Al Unser** Car racing	Indy 500, Sonics, Stanley Cup	10 +15	5	–
6/12	**Kenny Norton** Boxing	Sonics	10 +15	5	–
6/19	**Affirmed/Alydar** Horse	Belmont	10 +15	4	–
6/26	**Andy North** Golf	US Open Golf	10 +15	4	–

1978

DATE	COVER/Sport/Team	FEATURES /(ADS)	MT	EM	VG
7/03	Daniel Passarella	World Cup	10	4	-
	Argentiana Soccer		+40		
7/10	Nancy Lopez		10	4	-
	Golf		+15		
7/17	Money & Sports	Wimbeldon, Celtics	10	3	-
7/24	Jack Nicklaus	British Open, Orioles	15	8	-
	Golf		+50		
7/31	Billy Martin		20	8	-
	Yankees		+50(d)		
8/07	Pete Rose	Giants/Dodgers	30	15	-
	Reds	(Tom Selleck)	+20		
8/14	Brutality/Football	Giants/Dodgers	10	4	-
8/21	Bill Walton	Tigers	15	5	-
	Trail Blazers		+15		
8/28	Maxie Anderson, Ben Abruzzo		10	5	
	Larry Newman -				
	Ballooning	US Open,	+10each		
9/04	Roger Staubach	Pro football Issue	40	20	1
	Cowboys	(Jim Palmer)	+25		
9/11	Lou Holtz*	College Football Issue, M. Ali	15	5	1
	Arkansas	(Lite Miller Jock Foldout)	+15 each		
		(* Cover includes Calcagni, D. Cowins)			
9/18	Jimmy Conners	US Open, Red Sox	15	5	-
	Tennis	White Sox-Harry Carey	+25		
9/25	Muhammad Ali*	(* Cover includes Michael Spinks)	20	10	-
	Boxing		+80/+15		
10/02	Charles White	Dodger -Reggie Smith	20	8	1
	USC	(Corvette, Camaro-fold out)	+15		
10/09	Terry Bradshaw	Yankee/Red Sox	30	15	-
	Steelers	(World Series)	+25		
10/16	Marvin Webster	Pro Basketball Issue	10	5	1
	Knicks	Elvin Hayes	+15		
		(Camero, World Series, Willis Reed)			
10/23	Lee Lacy/	World Series, Hockey Issue	15	6	-
	Brian Doyle	(Ben Crenshaw, Terry Bradshaw)	+15		
	Dodgers/ Yankees				
10/30	Bill Rogers	NY Marathon,World Series	10	4	1
	Runner	(Sylvester Stalone Movie, Dr.J)	+15		
11/06	Race Fixer	Pete Rose, Larry Holmes,	5	4	-
		Dr. J, (Tom Selleck)			
11/13	Chuck Fusina	Sonics, Cowboys	15	8	1
	Penn State	(Tom Selleck, Roger Staubach, SI Poster)	+15		
11/20	Rick Berns*	Nebraska, Rams, Charlie White	15	5	-
	Nebraska	(Tom Selleck, Willis Reed)	+15		
		(* Cover includes Oklahoma #85)			
11/27	Magic Johnson(FC)	College Basketball Issue	100	30	10
	Michigan State	Celtics, Magic foldout, Tom Selleck)	+60		
12/04	Earl Campbell*	[*Cover includes Ross	15	5	-
	Houston	Browner (Bengals)]	+15		
12/11	Jeff Love		10	3	-
	Mountain Climber		+15		
12/18	John McEnroe	Davis Cup, Indiana	8	5	-
	Tennis	Terry Bradshaw, Jimmy Carter	+15		
12/25	Jack Nicklaus	Sportsman	50	25	-
	Golf (SOY)		+50		
	Year In Sports	Terry Bradshaw, Muhammad Ali	20	10	-
	1978	(Willis Reed)			

1979

DATE	COVER/Sport/Team	FEATURES /(ADS)	MT	EM	VG
1/08	Alabama/Penn St	Bowls Games, Pro Playoffs	20	8	1
1/15	Terry Bradshaw	Tony Dorsett	20	12	1
	Steelers	(SI Poster ad)	+25		
1/22	Herb Willie		10	4	-
	Ohio State		+15		
1/29	Rocky Bleier	Superbowl, Ron Guidrey	30	15	1
	Steelers	Roger Staubach	+20		
		Sam Bowie (FIC)			
2/05	Christie Brinkley	Swimsuit Issue, Larry Bird	50	25	3
	Model	(SI Poster Ad)	+30		
2/12	Danny Lopez		12	4	-
	Boxing		+15		
2/19	Moses Malone (FC)*	[*Cover also shows Mike	20	10	-
	Rockets	Dunleavey/Rick Barry/Rudy	+20		
		Tomjanovich (Rockets) and			
		Leon Douglas/ML Carr (Pistons)]			
2/26	Eamonn Coghlan	Eric Heiden	10	3	-
	Runner		+15		
3/05	#42 -art	Baseball Spring Training	20	10	-
	Reds				
3/12	Dudley Bradley	Rod Carew, Arnold Palmer	10	5	-
	North Carolina		+15		
3/19	Harry Chappas		10	5	-
	White Sox	(Roger Staubach)	+15		
3/26	Larry Bird		50	25	2
	Indiana State		+50		
4/02	Magic Johnson		40	20	2
	Michigan State	NCAA Basketball/	+50		
4/09	Jim Rice	Pro Baseball Issue,	20	10	2
	Red Sox	Trailblaziers,Q.Dailey(FACES)	+15each		
		[(* Cover includes Dave Parker/Pirates)]			
4/16	Denis Potvin		10	4	-
	Islanders		+15		
4/23	Fuzzy Zoeller	Masters, Ken Stabler, K.Jabbar	10	5	1
	Golf	(Roger Staubach, Tom Watson)	+15		
4/30	George Bamberger	Magic Johnson	15	5	1
	Brewers	(SI Poster ad)	+15		
5/07	Elvin Hayes*	Bryon Nelson	10	5	-
	Bullets		+15		
		(* Cover includes Ray Dandridge)			
5/14	Spectacular Bid*	Kentucky Derby	8	5	-
	Horse	(Si Poster)	+15		
		(* Also Ronnie Franklin)			
5/21	Giorgio Chinaglia	Sonics, A's	10	4	-
	Cosmos		+30		
5/28	Pete Rose		20	10	-
	Phillies		+25		
6/04	Tom Watson		10	5	-
	Golf		+15		
6/11	Gus Williams*	[*Cover also shows Wes	10	5	-
	Sonics	Unseld/Bob Dandridge	+15		
		(Bullets)]. Sonics NBA Champs.			
6/18	Earl Weaver	Edwin Moses	10	5	-
	Orioles		+15		
6/25	Hale Irwin	US Open	10	4	-
	Golf		+15		

1979

DATE	COVER/Sport/Team	FEATURES /(ADS)	MT	EM	VG
7/02	Robert Duran/Palomino		6	3	-
	Boxing		+20/+15		
7/09	Eamonn Coghlan	Dave Winfield,Jack Nicklaus	6	3	
	Track	(SI Poster Ad)	+20		
7/16	Bjorn Borg	Alan Page	20	10	5
	Tennis	Don Mattingly(FACES)	+20		
7/23	Nolan Ryan	Pan Am Games	50	20	5
	Angels		+30		
7/30	Sebastian Coe	Boston Red Sox	15	3	-
	Track		+15		
8/06	Kenny Stabler		30	15	
	Raiders		+15		
8/13	25th Anniversery	Year of Photos, Orioles,Russell/Cousy	12	6	-
		(Wilt Chamberlain/Rick Barry) PGA			
8/20	John Jefferson		20	10	-
	Chargers	(US Open)	+15		
8/27	Baseball's	[*Cover shows Rose,Yastrzemski,Stargell,	15	7	-
	Oldies*	P. Nieckro,G.Perry, M.Mota.L. Brock]	+15 each		
9/03	Earl Campbell	Pro Football Issue, Reds	15	5	3
	Oilers	(Steelers, Joe Greene, T. Bradshaw)	+15		
		Hershel Walker (FIC)			
9/10	Charle White/	Col Football Issue	15	7	2
	Billy Simms	(Muhammad Ali)	+15		
	USC/Oklahoma				
9/17	Tracy Austin	US Open Tennis	10	5	-
	Tennis		+15		
9/24	Vagas Ferguson		10	5	-
	Notre Dame		+15		
10/01	Dewey Selmon		10	5	-
	Buc's	(SI Poster Ad)	+15		
10/08	Larry Holmes/	Pro Hockey Issue	10	5	-
	Ernie Shavers	(World Series insert)	+15 each		
	Boxing				
10/15	Bill Walton	Pro Basketball Issue	10	6	1
	Clippers	Larry Bird	+15		
10/22	Doug Decinces/	World Series	15	7	-
	Phil Garner		+15		
	Orioles/Pirates				
10/29	Bill Rogers	World Series	10	4	-
	Runner		+15		
11/05	Franco Harris		20	8	-
	Steelers		+15		
11/12	Jarvis Redwine	College Football Issue	12	6	1
	Nebraska	Greg Lemond(FACES) , Mark Spitz	+15		
		(Cover includes Jimmy Jordan- Florida St., Steadman Shealy,			
		Alabama, Art Schlichter -Ohio S., Delrick Browner- Houston)			
11/19	Magic Johnson/George McGinnis		25	15	5
	Lakers/Denver		+60/+10		
11/26	Art Schlichter	Sugar Ray Robinson	10	3	-
	Ohio State	OJ Simpson	+15		
12/03	Indiana Jersey	College Basketball Issue	7	5	2
	Indiana	(Bruce Jenner-Boy Scout)	+15 (Knight)		
12/10	Sugar Ray Leonard	Lynn Swann	10	4	
	Boxing (FC)	(Paul Newman)	+15		
12/17	Ralph Sampson		15	5	-
	Virgina		+15		
12/24	Willie Stargell/Terry Bradshaw Sportsman		30	15	2
	Pirates/Steelers(SOY)	Bowl Preview	+15/+25		
	Year In Sports		15	7	-

1980

DATE	COVER/Sport/Team FEATURES /(ADS)	MT	EM	VG
1/07	**Ricky Bell** Bowl	10	5	-
	Bucs	+15		
1/14	**L.C. Greenwood/Don Pasorini**	10	5	-
	Steelers/Oilers	+15		
1/21	**Gordie Howe**	15	6	-
	Whalers	+15		
1/28	**John Stallworth** Superbowl XIV	20	10	1
	Steelers	+15		
	(* Cover includes Rams player)			
2/04	**Christie Brinkley** Swimsuit	50	25	5
	Model	+40		
2/11	**Mary Decker** Olympic	10	4	-
	Speed Skating	+15		
2/25	**Eric Heiden** Winter Olympics	10	4	-
	Speed Skating	+15		
3/03	**USA Hockey Team**	50	25	2
	Olympic Hockey	+10 each		
3/10	**Jim Craig**	10	3	-
	Flame	+15		
3/17	**Albert King*** NCAA Tournament	10	4	-
	Maryland [*Cover includes	+15		
	Steve Johnson (Tennessee)]			
3/24	**Kirk Gibson**	12	6	-
	Tigers	+15		
3/31	**Darrell Griffith** NCAA Finals	10	4	-
	Lousiville Basketball	+15		
4/07	**Keith Hernandez** Baseball Issue	10	6	-
	Cardinals	+15		
4/14	**Muhammand Ali**	28	10	-
	Boxing	+15		
4/21	**Steve Ballesteros** Masters	10	5	-
	Golf	+15		
4/28	**Larry Bird/Dr J*** [*Cover includes Darryl Hawkins]	30	15	2
	Celtics/76ers	+50		
5/05	**Kareem Abdul-Jabbar***	10	5	-
	Lakers (* Also Sonics Dennis Johnson, other)	+35		
5/12	**Geniune Risk** Kentucky Derby	5	3	-
	Horse			
5/19	**Athlete Hoax**	6	3	-
5/26	**Magic Johnson** Lakers NBA Champs	30	15	-
	Lakers	+50		
6/02	**John Rutherford** Indy 500, Stanley Cup - Islanders	10	4	-
	Car Racing	+15		
6/09	**Darrell Porter**	15	5	-
	Royals	+15		
6/16	**Roberto Duran**	20	10	-
	Boxing	+25		
6/23	**Jack Nicklaus** US Open	20	10	-
	Golf	+50		
6/30	**Roberto Duran/**	20	10	-
	Sugar Ray Leonard	+25 each		
	Boxing			

1980

DATE	COVER/Sport/Team FEATURES //(ADS)	MT	EM	VG
7/07	**Steve Scott**	10	3	-
	Track	+15		
7/14	**Bjorn Borg** Wimbledon	10	3	-
	Tennis	+15		
7/21	**Steve Carlton**	30	15	-
	Phillies	+15		
7/28	**Olympics - Moscow**	5	3	-
8/04	**Reggie Jackson**	20	10	-
	Yankees	+35		
8/11	**Sebastian Coe**	10	3	-
	Track	+15		
8/18	**J.R. Richard**	30	12	-
	Astros	+20		
8/25	**Yankees/Orioles*** [*Cover shows Bucky Dent/	25	10	
	Fred Stanley(Yankees) &	+25		
	Al Bumbry (Orioles)]			
9/01	**Hugh Green** College Football Issue	7	3	-
	Pittsburgh Football	+15		
9/08	**Dave Logan** Pro Football Issue	8	6	-
	Browns			
9/15	**John McEnroe** US Open	7	5	-
	Tennis	+15		
9/22	**Billy Sims**	7	5	-
	Lions	+15		
9/29	**Muhammad Ali**	15	7	-
	Boxing	+80		
10/06	**Gary Carter (FC)**	20	10	-
	Expos	+15		
10/13	**Muhammad Ali** Pro Hockey Issue	20	10	-
	Boxing	+80		
10/20	**Paul Westphal** Pro Basketball Issue	15	6	1
	Sonics	+15		
10/27	**Mike Schmidt(FC)** World Series	15	7	-
	Darrell Porter	+25/+10		
	Phillies/Royals			
11/03	**Alberto Salazar**	10	5	-
	Track	+15		
11/10	**L.C. Greenwood**	7	5	-
	Steelers	+15		
11/17	**Herschel Walker (FC)**	20	10	-
	Georgia	+15		
11/24	**Sugar Ray Leonard**	20	10	-
	Boxing	+15		
12/01	**Ralph Sampson** College Basketball Issue	7	3	-
	Virignia	+15each		
	(* Cover includes Bernard King-Maryland, Mark Aquirre-DePaul)			
12/08	**Vince Ferragamo**	10	5	-
	Rams	+15		
12/15	**Loyld Free*** [*Cover shows Kareem	7	3	-
	Warriors Abdul-Jabbar/Lakers]	+15		
12/22	**USA Hockey Team*** [*Team: Bill Bake/Neil Broton/	40	20	1
	Hockey (SOY) Dave Christian/Steve Christoff/	+10each		
	Jim Craig/Mike Eruzione/JohnHarrington/Steve Janaszak/			
	Mark Johnson/Rob McClanahan/Ken Morrow/John O'Callahan/			
	Mark Pavelich/Mike Ramsey/BuzzSchneider/Dave Silk/Erik Strobel			
	Bob Suter/Phil Verchota/Mark Wells/ Herb Brooks.]			
	Year in Sports	15	5	-

1981

DATE	COVER/Sport/Team	FEATURES //(ADS)	MT	EM	VG
1/05	Dave Winfield(FC)		20	10	1
	Yankees		+20		
1/12	Chuck Muncie*	[*Cover also shows Rod	20	10	-
	Chargers	Kush/Steve Freeman (Bills)]	+15		
1/19	Mark Van Eeghan		20	10	-
	Raiders		+15		
1/26	Bobby Knight		15	5	-
	Indiana		+15		
2/02	Rod Martin	Superbowl XV	20	10	1
	Raiders		+15		
2/09	Christie Brinkley	Swimsuit Issue	50	25	5
	Model		+25		
2/16	Point Shaving Scheme		5	3	-
2/23	Bobby Carpenter		10	3	-
	Hockey		+15		
3/02	J.R. Richard		20	10	
	Astros		+20		
3/09	Magic Johnson		20	10	1
	Lakers		+50		
3/16	Rollie Fingers		12	6	-
	Brewers		+15		
3/23	Rolando Blackman*	[*Cover also shows Mark	10	5	-
	Kansas State	Radford/Ray Blume(Oregon State).]	+15		
3/30	Ralph Sampson*	[*Cover also shows Danny	10	3	-
	Virginia	Ainge (BYU)]	+15		
4/06	Isaiah Thomas	Indiana NCAA Champs	20	10	1
	Indiana (FC)		+15		
4/13	George Brett/	Baseball issue	25	12	1
	Mike Schmidt		+25each		
	Royals/Phillies				
4/20	Tom Watson	Masters	10	5	-
	Golf		+15		
4/27	Oakland A's	[**Cover Shows Brian Kingman	10	5	-
	Pitchers*	Mike Norris, Matt Keogh,	+10each		
		Rick Langford, Steve McCantey]			
5/04	Gerry Cooney		10	5	-
	Boxing		+15		
5/11	Larry Bird/Kevin McHale*		30	15	1
	Celtics		+50/+15		
		(* Cover includes Maurice Cheeks-76ers)			
5/18	Fernando Valenzuela		10	5	-
	Dodgers		+15		
5/25	A.J. Foyt	Indy 500, Celtic Champs	10	5	-
	Car Racing		+15		
6/01	Joe/Marvis Frazier		10	5	-
	Boxing		+20/+10		
6/08	Greg Luzinski		10	4	-
	Phillies		+15		
6/15	Bjorn Borg		10	4	-
	Tennis		+15		
6/22	Baseball Strike		5	3	-
6/29	David Graham	US Open	10	4	-
	Golf		+15		

1981

DATE	COVER/Sport/Team	FEATURES //(ADS)	MT	EM	VG
7/06	Sugar Ray Leonard*	(* Cover includes Ayub Kalule)	15	7	-
	Boxing		+15		
7/13	John McEnroe	Wimbledon	10	4	-
	Tennis		+15		
7/20	Vince Ferragano		10	5	-
	Rams		+15		
7/27	Tom Seaver		20	10	1
	Reds		+20		
8/03	John Hannah		10	4	-
	Patriots		+15		
8/10	George Brett	Baseball issue	20	10	1
	Mike Schmidt				
	Royals/Phillies		+25 each		
8/17	Gary Carter/Dick Williams		15	7	-
	Expos		+15		
8/24	Wendell Tyler*	[*Cover also shows Kent Hill	10	5	-
	Rams	(Rams) and Randy White/	+15		
		Bill Gregory/Bob Breunig(Cowboys)]			
8/31	Herschel Walker	College Football Issue	20	7	-
	Georgia		+15		
9/07	Jim Plunkett	Pro Football Issue	20	7	-
	Raiders		+15		
9/14	Thomas Hearns		10	7	-
	Boxing		+15		
9/21	John McEnroe	US Open	10	5	-
	Tennis		+15		
9/28	Sugar Ray Leonard/		10	5	-
	Thomas Hearns		+15 each		
	Boxing				
10/05	Marcus Allen (FC)		10	5	-
	USC		+15		
10/12	Wayne Gretzky	Pro Hockey Issue	50	25	5
	Oilers (FC)		+35		
10/19	Texas Players		10	5	-
	Texas				
10/26	Graig Nettles	World Series	10	5	-
	Yankees		+15		
11/02	Dave Lopes	World Series	10	5	-
	Dodgers		+15		
11/09	Larry Bird	Pro Basketball Issue	30	15	2
	Celtics	World Series	+50		
11/16	Larry Holmes*		10	5	-
	Boxing	(* Cover includes Renaldo Snipes)	+15 each		
11/23	Bear Bryant		20	10	-
	Alabama		+200(d)		
11/30	Dean Smith/James Worthy/Sam Perkins		20	10	-
	Jimmy Black/Matt Doherty		+15 each		
	North Carolina	College Basketball Issue			
12/07	Tony Dorsett		20	10	-
	Cowboys		+15		
12/14	Cris Collinsworth		10	5	-
	Bengals		+15		
12/21	Earl Cooper		15	7	1
	49ers		+15		
12/28	Sugar Ray Leonard		30	15	-
	Boxing (SOY)		+25		
	Year in Sports		10	6	-

1982

DATE	COVER/Sport/Team	FEATURES /(ADS)	VALUE GUIDE		
			MT	EM	VG
1/11	**Perry Tuttle**	Bowl Games	20	10	–
	Clemson		+15		
1/18	**Dave Clark**	"The Catch"	60	25	3
	49ers		+15		
1/25	**Joe Montana (FC)**		25	12	1
	49ers		+50		
2/01	**Earl Cooper**	Superbowl XVI	20	10	–
	49ers		+15		
2/08	**Carol Alt**	Swimsuit Issue	40	20	2
	Model		+30		
2/15	**Wayne Gretzky**		30	15	3
	Oilers		+30		
2/22	**Sidney Moncrief**		12	6	–
	Bucks		+15		
3/01	**Herschel Walker**		10	5	–
	Georgia		+15		
3/08	**The Banzai Pipeline**		5	3	–
	Surfer				
3/15	**Reggie Jackson**		20	10	–
	Angels		+35		
3/22	**Patrick Ewing(FC)**		15	5	–
	Georgetown		+25		
3/29	**Sam Perkins***	(* Cover includes James Worthy)	20	10	2
	North Carolina		+15/+20		
4/05	**James Worthy***	(* Cover includes NC Brust, #45;	20	10	2
	North Carolina	Georgetown Ewing, 50)	+20		
4/12	**Steve Garvey**	Baseball Issue	20	10	–
	Dodgers		+15		
4/19	**Craig Stadler**		10	5	–
	Golfer		+15		
4/26	**Renaldo Nehemiah**		10	4	–
	49ers		+15		
5/03	**Moses Malone/Jack Skima**		10	5	–
	Rockets/Sonics		+20/+10		
5/10	**Georgia Frontier/Bert Jones**		10	3	–
	Rams		+15 each		
5/17	**Gaylord Perry**		15	5	–
	Mariners		+15		
5/24	**Magic Johnson***		24	12	–
	Lakers	(* Cover includes Michael Cooper)	+50		
5/31	**Julius Erving**		20	10	1
	76ers	(* Cover includes Parrish, Ford,Cheeks)	+25/+15		
6/07	**Gerry Cooney**		10	4	–
	Boxing		+15		
6/14	**Don Reese**		5	3	–
	Special Report "Cocaine"				
6/21	**Larry Holmes/Gerry Cooney***		10	3	–
	Boxing		+15 each		
6/28	**Tom Watson**	US Open Golf	10	5	–
	Golf		+15		

1982

DATE	COVER/Sport/Team	FEATURES /(ADS)	MT	EM	VG
7/05	Kent Hrbek		15	7	-
	Twins		+15		
7/12	Jimmy Conners	Wimbeledon	10	3	-
	Tennis		+15		
7/19	Pete Rose/Carl Yastrezemski		15	7	-
	Reds		+20		
7/26	Mary Decker Tabb		10	3	-
	Track		+15		
8/02	Ray Mancini/Ernesto Espana		10	3	-
	Boxing		+15		
8/09	Dale Murphy		15	6	-
	Braves		+15		
8/16	Walter Payton (FC)		20	10	-
	Bears		+35		
8/23	Franco Harris		15	6	-
	Steelers		+15		
8/30	Tom Cousineau		10	4	-
	Browns		+15		
9/01	Football	Pro & College Football	10	5	-
9/06	Rickey Henderson (FC)		20	10	-
	A's		+15		
9/13	Wayne Peace		10	3	-
	Florida		+15		
9/20	Jimmy Conners	US Open	10	3	-
	Tennis		+15		
9/27	NFL Strike		5	3	-
10/04	Todd Blackledge		10	3	-
	Penn State		+15		
10/11	Robin Yount (FC)	Pro Hockey Issue	20	10	2
	Brewers		+20		
10/18	Marvin Hagler		10	5	-
	Boxer		+15		
10/25	Robin Yount/Lonnie Smith		20	10	2
	Brewers/Cards	World Series	+15		
11/01	Moses Malone	Pro Basketball Issue	10	5	-
	76ers	World Series	+25		
11/08	John Elway (FC)		20	10	1
	Stanford		+25		
11/15	Sugar Ray Leonard		10	3	-
	Boxing		+15		
11/22	Ray Mancini/Duke Koo Kim		10	3	-
	Boxing		(Does not sign)/(d)		
11/29	Ralph Sampson/	College Basketball Issue	10	6	-
	Patrick Ewing		+15		
	Virginia/Georgetown				
12/06	Lyto Kaab		10	3	-
	Eagles				
12/14	Marcus Allen*		10	6	-
	Raiders	(*also Keith Butler (Seahawks)	+15		
12/20	Ralph Sampson		10	5	-
	Virginia		+15		
12/27	Wayne Gretzky	Sportsman	50	25	1
	Oilers	Bear Bryant Retires	+35		
	Year In Sports		10	6	-

1983

DATE	COVER/Sport/Team	FEATURES /(ADS)	MT	EM	VG
1/10	**Greg Garrity** Penn State	Bowls	10 +15	5	-
1/17	**Chuck Muncie*** Chargers	(*also Jack Lambart/Donnie Shild)	10 +15	4	-
1/24	**Andra Franklin** Dolphins		10 +15	5	-
1/31	**Darrell Grant** Redskins		10 +15	4	-
2/07	**John Riggins** Redskins	Superbowl XVII Issue	15 +15	6	-
2/14	**Cheryl Tiegs** Model	Swimsuit Issue	40 +20	20	1
2/21	**Terry Cummings** Clippers		15 +15	6	-
2/28	**Julius Erving** 76ers	(*also Andrew Tomey (76ers)) (*also Moses Malone/Marc Iavaroni)	24 +20	12	1
3/07	**Hershel Walker** Generals		15 +15	8	-
3/14	**Pete Rose/Joe Morgan/Tony Perez** Reds		30 +20/+15/+15	12	1
3/21	**Billy Goodwin** St. John's		10 +10	3	-
3/28	**Michael Spinks** Boxing	(* Cover includes Dwight Braxton)	10 +15	3	-
4/04	**Gary Carter** Mets	Baseball Issue	15 +15	6	-
4/11	**Thurmon Bailey*** NC State	NCAA Champs (* Cover includes Sidney Lowe, Derrick Whittenburg)	10 +15	3	-
4/18	**Tom Seaver** NY Mets	Masters	15 +20	6	-
4/25	**Steve Garvey** Padres		15 +15	6	-
5/02	**Larry Bird** (* Cover includes Robert Parrish, Danny Ainge; Celtics	Hawks-Tree Rollins, Johnny Davis)	30 +50	15	2
5/09	**Kareem Abdul-Jabbar** Lakers		12 +35	6	-
5/16	**Sunny Halo** Horse	Kentucky Derby	5	3	-
5/23	**Billy Smith** Islanders	Stanley Cup	10 +15	3	-
5/30	**Larry Holmes** Boxing		10 +15	6	-
6/06	**Moses Malone/Jamaal Wilkes** 76ers/Lakers		10 +20	6	-
6/13	**Rod Carew** Angels	76ers NBA Champs	16 +20	8	-
6/20	**Marcus Dupree** Oklahoma		12 +15	5	-
6/27	**Robert Duran** Boxing	(* Cover incldues Davey Moore)	20 +20	8	-
7/04	**Dale Murphy** Braves		20 +15	8	-

1983

DATE	COVER/Sport/Team	FEATURES /(ADS)	MT	EM	VG
7/11	John McEnroe	Wimbledon	10	3	-
	Tennis		+15		
7/18	Andre Dawson/Dave Steib		15	8	-
	Expos/Blue Jays		+15		
7/25	Tom Watson	British Open Golf	10	5	-
	Golf		+15		
8/01	Richard Todd		10	4	-
	Jets		+15		
8/08	Howard Cosell		10	3	-
			+100(d)		
8/15	John Elway		15	6	1
	Bronco's		+25		
8/22	Carl Lewis (FC)		10	3	-
	Track		+15		
8/29	Tony Dorsett	College/Pro Football Issue	15	6	-
	Cowboys		+15		
9/05	Mike Rozier		10	5	-
	Nebraska Football		+15		
9/12	Edwin Moses		10	3	-
	Track		+15		
9/19	Martina Navratilova(FC)		10	3	-
	Tennis		+30		
9/26	Doug Flutie(FC)		10	8	-
	Boston College		+15		
10/03	Steve Carlton		20	10	-
	Phillies		+20		
10/10	Joe Washington	Pro Hockey Issue	10	3	-
	Redskins		+15		
10/17	Eric Dickerson		10	5	-
	Rams		+15		
10/24	Rick Dempsey	World Series	10	3	-
	Orioles		+15		
10/31	Ralph Sampson	Pro Basketball Issue	10	3	-
	Rockets		+15		
11/07	Marvin Hagler/Roberto Duran		10	3	-
	Boxing		+15		
11/14	Dan Marino (FC)		30	15	1
	Dolphins		+15		
11/21	Marvin Hagler/Robert Duran		10	3	-
	Boxing		+15		
11/28	Michael Jordan (FC)/Sam Perkins		150	70	5
	North Carolina		+75/+15		
12/05	Sam Bowie		6	3	-
	Kentucky		+15		
12/12	Jim Brown		10	5	-
	Raiders		+25		
12/19	John Riggins*		10	4	-
	Redskins	(also George Strake (Redskins))	+15		
12/26	Mary Decker		30	15	-
	Track (SOY)		+15		
	Year In Sports		10	5	-

1984

DATE	COVER/Sport/Team	FEATURES /(ADS)	MT	EM	VG
1/09	**Keith Griffith**		10	5	-
	Dolphins	Bowl Games	+15		
1/16	**Joe Theismann**		10	5	-
	Redskins	(* Cover includes Tucker-49ers)	+15		
1/23	**Wayne Gretzky**		20	10	-
	Oilers		+35		
1/30	**Jack Squirek**	Superbowl XVIII	20	10	-
	Raiders		+15		
2/06	**Scott Hamilton/Tamara McKinney**		10	3	-
	Rosalynn Summers/Phil Mahre		+15 each		
	Olympic Americans				
2/14	**Paulina Porizkova** Swimsuit		30	15	2
	Model		+25		
2/20	**Debbie Armstrong** Olympics		10	3	-
	Skier		+15		
2/27	**Bill Johnson**	Olympics	10	3	-
	Skier		+15		
3/05	**Magic Johnson***	(*also Mo Cheeks,	20	10	1
	Lakers	Dr J, Clint Richardson)	+50		
3/12	**George Brett**		20	10	-
	Royals		+25		
3/19	**Patrick Ewing**		15	6	-
	Georgetown		+25		
3/26	**Sam Perkins**		20	10	1
	North Carolina		+15		
4/02	**Yogi Berra**	Baseball Issue	20	10	1
	Yankees		+20		
4/09	**Michael Graham**	NCAA Finals	10	3	-
	Georgetown	(*also Winslow & Anderson)	+15		
4/16	**Graig Nettles/Rich Gossage**		10	5	-
	Padres		+15		
4/23	**Darryl Strawberry(FC)**		10	6	-
	Mets		+15		
4/30	**Bull Cyclones Coach**		6	3	-
5/07	**Bernard King***		10	5	-
	Knicks	(*Kelly Tripuka/Len Robinson)	+15		
5/14	**Mike Bossy**		20	10	-
	Islanders		+15		
5/21	**Soviet Boycott**		6	3	-
5/28	**Alan Trammell (FC)**		20	9	-
	Tigers	Stankley Cup	+15		
6/04	**Magic Johnson***	(* cover includes Kurt	15	7	-
	Lakers	Rambis/Dennis Johnson)	+50/+10		
6/11	**Leon Durham**		10	3	-
	Cubs		+15		
6/18	**Martina Navartilova**		10	3	-
	Tennis	French Open	+30		
6/25	**Carl Lewis**		10	3	-
	Track	Celtics NBA Champs	+15		
7/02	**Dwight Stone**		10	3	-
	High Jump		+15		

1984

DATE	COVER/Sport/Team	FEATURES /(ADS)	MT	EM	VG
7/09	**Jeff Float**		10	3	-
	Swimming		+10		
7/16	**John McEnroe**	Wimbledon	10	3	-
	Tennis		+10		
		Preview of Summer Olympic Issue	10	5	-
7/23	**Michael Jordan**		100	40	5
	US Olympic Team		+60		
7/30	**Jack Lambert**		10	5	-
	Steelers		+15		
8/06	**Rafer Johnson**		10	3	-
	Olympics	Olympics	+25		
8/13	**Mary Lou Retton**		10	3	-
	Gymnastics	Olympics	+10		
8/20	**Carl Lewis**		10	3	-
	Track	Olympics	+10		
8/27	**Pete Rose**		12	6	-
	Reds		+20		
9/03	**Joe Theismann**		10	5	-
	Redskins		+10		
9/09	**Clayton/Green**		5	2	-
	Dolphins/Redskins		+10		
	Dan Marino/Bernie Kosar		30	15	-
	Dolphins	Col/Pro Football Issue	+35		
9/17	**John McEnroe**	US Open Tennis	10	3	-
	Tennis		+15		
9/24	**Dwight Gooden/Rick Sutcliffe**		10	3	-
	Mets/Cubs		+15		
10/01	**Jeff Smith**		10	2	-
	Nebraska		+15		
10/08	**Sammy Winder**		10	3	-
	Broncos		+15		
10/15	**Walter Payton**	Payton Breaks Record	30	12	-
	Bears	Pro Hockey Issue	+30		
10/22	**Alan Trammell**	World Series	20	9	1
	Tigers		+15		
10/29	**Larry Bird/Bill Russell**		25	12	2
	Celtics	Pro Basketball Issue	+50/+200		
11/05	**Gerry Faust**		12	5	-
	Notre Dame		+15		
11/12	**NFL Issue/Trouble**		5	3	-
11/19	**Mark Duper**		10	3	-
	Dolphins		+15		
11/26	**Patrick Ewing/John Thompson/Ronald Reagan**		10	3	-
	Georgetown	College Basketball Issue	+25/+15/+150		
12/03	**Doug Flutie**		10	3	-
	Boston College		+15		
12/10	**Michael Jordan***		100	40	10
	Bulls	(*also Mike Dunleavy/Sidney Moncrief)	+40		
12/17	**Eric Dickerson**		10	5	-
	Rams		+15		
12/24	**Mary Lou Retton/Edwin Moses**		30	15	-
	Gymnastics (SOY)		+15/+20		
	The Year In Sports		15	5	-

1985

DATE	COVER/Sport/Team FEATURES /(ADS)	MT	EM	VG
1/07	**Walter Abercrombie**	10	5	-
	Steelers Bowls	+15		
1/14	**Dan Marino**	30	15	1
	Dolphins	+30		
1/21	**Dan Marino/Joe Montana**	30	15	-
	Dolphins/49ers	+30/+40		
1/28	**Roger Craig** Superbowl XIX	20	10	1
	49ers	+15		
2/04	**Walter Berry***	10	5	-
	St John (*Mike Gminski (St John))	+15		
2/11	**Paulina Porizkova** Swimsuit Issue	40	15	2
	Model	+30		
2/18	**Wayne Gretzky**	20	10	1
	Oilers	+35		
2/25	**Doug Flutie**	10	5	-
	Generals	+15		
3/04	**Mike Schmidt**	20	10	
	Phillies	+25		
3/11	**Jack/Gary Nicklaus**	6	3	-
	Golf	+50/+15		
3/18	**Fred Lynn**	10	5	-
	Red Sox	+15		
3/25	**Peter Ueberroth/Willie Mays/Mickey Mantle**	10	5	-
	Commissioner	+15/+40/+150(d)		
4/01	**Patrick Ewing/Chris Mullin/Dwayne McClain**	10	5	-
	Georgetown/St John's/Villonava	+25/+15/+10		
4/08	**Ed Pinckney** NCAA Finals	10	5	-
	Villanovia	+15		
4/15	**Dwight Gooden** Baseball Issue	10	5	-
	Mets	+15		
4/22	**Marvin Hagler**	10	3	-
	Thomas Hearns	+15 each		
	Boxing			
4/29	**Hulk Hogan**	16	8	-
	Wrestling	+15		
5/06	**Billy Martin**	15	5	-
	Yankees	+60(d)		
5/13	**Magic Johnson**	15	7	-
	Lakers	+50		
5/20	**Patrick Ewing**	10	5	-
	Knicks	+25		
5/27	**Herschel Walker**	16	8	-
	Generals	+15		
6/03	**Danny Sullivan** Indy 500, Stanley Cup	10	3	-
	Car racing	+15		
6/10	**Kareem Abdul-Jabbar***	10	5	-
	Lakers (* Larry Bird)	+35		
6/17	**Kareem Abdul-Jabbar/Michael Cooper**	10	4	-
	Danny Ainge (Cover Inset Chris Evert)			
	Lakers/Celtics Lakers NBA Champs	+35		
	(* Cover includes Danny Ainge/Celtics)			
6/24	**Andy North** US Open Golf	10	3	-
	Golf	+15		
	(* Corner inset Earl Weaver/Orioles)			
7/01	**Larry Holmes**	10	3	-
	Boxing	+15		

1985

DATE	COVER/Sport/Team FEATURES /(ADS)	MT	EM	VG
7/08	**Fernando Valenzuela**	10	5	-
	Dodgers	+15		
7/15	**Boris Becker**	10	3	-
	Tennis	+15		
7/22	**Howie Long**	10	5	-
	Raiders	+15		
7/29	**Mary Decker Slaney/Zola Budd**	10	3	-
	Track	+15		
8/05	**Pedro Guerrero**	10	5	-
	Dodgers	+15		
8/12	**Tony Dorsett**	10	6	-
	Cowboys	+15		
8/19	**Pete Rose**	15	9	1
	Reds	+20		
8/26	**Bernie Kosar**	16	8	
	Browns	+15		
9/02	**Dwight Gooden**	12	6	
	Mets	+15		
9/04	**Eric Dickerson** College & Pro Football	10	6	-
	Rams	+15		
	(* Cover includes McCullin-Navy)			
9/09	**Bill Elliott**	30	15	-
	Car Racing	+15		
9/16	**Joe Louis**	10	3	-
	Boxing			
9/23	**Ozzie Smith (FC)**	16	10	
	Cardinals	+15		
9/30	**Michael Spinks**	10	3	-
	Boxing	+15 each		
	(* Cover includes Larry Holmes)			
10/07	**Tony Robinson**	10	3	-
	Tennessee	+15		
10/14	**Eddie Robinson** (*Robinson Breaks Bryant Record)	10	3	-
	Grambling	+15		
10/21	**Jim McMahon**	10	5	-
	Bears	+15		
10/28	**Ozzie Smith** World Series	15	8	-
	Cardinals Pro Basketball Issue	+15		
11/04	**Royals Players** World Series	8	6	-
	Royals	+10 each		
11/11	**Roy McDonald/DJ Dozier**	10	3	-
	Florida/Penn State	+15		
11/18	**Dale Brown**	10	3	-
	LSU	+15		
11/20	**Cheryl Miller/Mark Price/Bruce Dalrymple**	10	6	-
	USC/Georgia Tech	+15		
11/25	**Danny White*** (*Cover also shows Dave	10	6	-
	Cowboys Dureson/Otis Wilson)	+15		
12/02	**Bo Jackson/Chuck Long/Joe Dudek**	15	7	-
	Auburn/Iowa/Plymouth State	+25/+10 each		
12/10	**Kirk Gibson**	15	6	-
	Tigers	+15		
12/17	**Marcus Allen**	12	5	-
	Raiders	+15		
12/23	**Kareem Abdul-Jabbar**	30	15	1
	Lakers (SOY) Sportsman	+35		
	The Year In Sports	12	6	-

1986

DATE	COVER/Sport/Team	FEATURES / (ADS)	MT	EM	VG
1/06	**Mike Tyson (FC)**		15	6	-
	Boxing		+25		
1/13	**Craig James**		10	5	-
	Patriots	[Corner Oklahoma Player]	+15		
1/20	**Jim McMahon***		10	5	-
	Bears	[Cover shows Jerry Gray-Rams]	+15		
1/27	**Mike Singletary**		10	5	-
	Bears		+15		
2/03	**Hampton/Eason**	Superbowl XX	12	6	-
	Bears		+15		
2/10	**Elle Macpherson**	Swimsuit issue	30	15	2
	Model (fc)		+25		
2/17	**Danny Manning**		10	5	-
	Kansas		+15		
2/24	**Networks**		10	3	-
3/03	**Larry Bird**		20	10	1
	Celtics		+50		
3/10	**Gambling**		4	3	-
3/17	**Mark Alarie**		10	4	-
	Duke		+15		
3/24	**Marvin Hagler**		10	4	-
	Boxing	(* Cover includes John Mugabi)	+15		
3/31	**LSU #44***		10	5	-
	LSU	(* also Louisville/Duke/Kansas)			
4/07	**Pervis Ellison**		10	4	-
	Louisville	NCAA Finals	+15		
4/14	**Wade Boggs (FC)**	Baseball 86	10	5	-
	Red Sox		+15		
4/21	**Jack Nicklaus**		10	5	-
	Golf		+50		
4/28	**Dominique Wilkins**		10	5	-
	Hawks		+15		
5/05	**Ernest Hemingway**		10	3	-
5/12	**Roger Clemens**		10	5	-
	Red Sox		+15		
5/19	**James Worthy***		10	6	1
	Lakers	(*Cover shows Rodney McCray)	+15		
5/26	**Akeem Olajuwan (FC)/Kareem Abdul-Jabbar**		30	15	
	Rockets/Lakers	[* Corner is Naratovia/Evert]	+25		
6/02	**Montreal Canadiens**		10	5	-
	Candadiens				
6/09	**Larry Bird**		20	10	1
	Celtics		+50		
6/16	**Kevin McHale**		10	5	-
	Celtics		+15		
6/23	**Christine/Raymond Floyd**		10	3	-
	Golf		+10/+15		
6/30	**Len Bias**		10	5	-
	Cocaine				
7/07	**Diego Maradona**		10	4	-
	Argentina Soccer		+40		

1986

VALUE GUIDE

DATE	COVER/Sport/Team FEATURES /(ADS)	MT	EM	VG
7/14	**Bo Jackson**	20	10	-
	Chicks	+15		
7/21	**Jim Kelly (FC)** Generals	20	10	
	Generals	+15		
7/28	**Rickey Henderson**	10	5	-
	Yankees	+15		
8/04	**"Oil Can" Boyd**	12	5	-
	Red Sox	+15		
8/11	**William Perry/Too Tall Jones**	10	5	-
	Bears/Cowboys	+15 each		
8/18	**Herschel Walker**	10	5	-
	Cowboys	+15		
8/25	**Ron Darling**	10	5	-
	Mets	+15		
9/01	**Kristie Phillips**	10	3	-
	US Gymnaists	+15		
9/08	**Sugar Ray Leonard**	10	5	-
	Boxer	+15		
9/15	**Ivan Lendl**	10	3	-
	Tennis	+15		
9/22	**Football Players**	10	5	-
	Michigan/Notre Dame			
9/22	**Jim McMahon/Brian Bosworth**	10	5	-
	Bears/Oklahoma Col/Pro Football 86	+15 each		
9/29	**Mark Gastneau/Lawrence Taylor**	10	5	-
	Jets	+15 each		
10/06	**Darryl Strawberry**	10	5	-
	Mets	+15		
10/13	**John Elway**	10	5	-
	Broncos Pro Hockey Issue	+25		
10/20	**Bobby Grich/Doug Decinces**	10	6	-
	Angels	+15 each		
10/27	**Gary Carter/Jim Rice**	10	6	-
	Mets/Red Sox	+15 each		
11/03	**Ray Knight** World Series	10	5	-
	Mets Pro Basketball Issue	+15		
11/10	**Injuries**	4	3	-
11/17	**Michael Jordan** (* Cover includes M. Thompson/Alvin	40	20	2
	Bulls Robertson- San Antonio)	+40		
	Dave Robinson Basketball Issue	20	10	-
	Navy	+20		
11/24	**Vinny Testaverde**	10	5	-
	Miami	+15		
12/01	**Mike Tyson/Trevor Berbick**	10	5	-
	Boxing	+15		
12/08	**Walter Payton**	15	6	-
	Bears	+30		
12/15	**Mark Bavaro**	10	6	-
	Giants	+10		
12/22	**Joe Patereno** Sportsman	24	12	-
	Penn State (SOY)	+15		
	Year In Sports	12	6	-

1987

VALUE GUIDE

DATE	COVER/Sport/Team	FEATURES /(ADS)	MT	EM	VG
1/05	**Brian Bosworth**		10	5	-
	Oklahoma	[Corner Kentucky-Rex Chapman]	+15		
1/12	**Ozzie Newsome***		10	5	-
	Browns	[Corner Penn State]	+15		
1/19	**Rich Karlis***		10	5	-
	Broncos	[*also Gary Kubiak]	+15		
1/26	**Lawrence Taylor**		10	5	-
	Giants		+20		
2/02	**Phil Simms/Simon Fletcher**		10	5	-
	Giants/Denver	Superbowl XXI	+15 each		
2/09	**Elle Macpherson**	Swimsuit issue	30	15	1
	Model		+25		
2/16	**Ronald Reagan/Dennis Conner**		20	10	-
	President/Yachting		+200/+15		
2/23	**Magic Johnson/Dennis Johnson**		20	10	-
	Lakers/Celtics		+50/+15		
		[Corner Bill Elliott- Daytona]			
3/02	**JR Reid**		10	6	-
	North Carolina		+15		
3/09	**Ripken's (Carl, Jr, Billy)**		30	15	1
	Orioles		+15/+35/+10		
		[Corner Variations #1 Notre Dame; #2 SMU]			
3/16	**Gary McLain**		10	3	-
	Cocaine		+10		
3/23	**Bobby Knight**		10	5	-
	Indiana		+10		
		[Corner variations #1 Wyoming, #2 Rebels, #3 DePaul]			
3/30	**Marvin Hagler/Sugar Ray Leonard**		10	3	-
	Boxing	[Corner variation #1 Indiana #12]	+15		
4/06	**Cory Snyder/Joe Carter** Baseball Issue		10	4	-
	Indians	(* Cover includes Joe Carter)	+10/+15		
		[Corner - Indiana #12]			
4/13	**Sugar Ray Leonard/Marvin Hagler**		10	4	-
	Boxing		+20		
4/20	**Baseball Players** (Cover has 43 players)		10	4	-
	Salaries	(*Puckett,Mattingley,Schmidt,Brett,Smith,Jackson,etc)			
4/27	**Rob Deer**		10	5	-
	Brewers	[Corner - Hockey Thriller]	+15		
5/04	**Julius Erving**		20	10	-
	76ers		+25		
5/11	**Reggie Jackson**		20	10	-
	A's	[Corner -Alysheba- Horse Race]	+30		
5/18	**Isaiah Thomas**		20	7	-
	Pistons	[Corner - Indy 500]	+15		
5/25	**Eric Davis**		10	5	-
	Reds	[Corner - Larry Bird]	+15		
6/01	**Wayne Gretzky**		20	10	1
	Oilers	[Corner - Wayne Gretzky]	+35		
6/08	**Larry Bird**		20	10	1
	Celtics	[Corner - Wayne Gretzky]	+50		
6/15	**Byron Scott***	(*also McHale/Roberts-Celtics)	10	5	-
	Lakers	(*also Kurt Rambus-Kalers)	+10 each		
6/22	**Kareem Abdul-Jabbar**		10	5	-
	Lakers		+35		
6/29	**Scott Simpson** US Open		10	5	-
	Golf		+15		
	(Cover includes Tom Watson)				
7/06	**One Day in Baseball**		10	5	-

1987

DATE	COVER/Sport/Team	FEATURES /(ADS)	MT	EM	VG
		VALUE GUIDE			
7/13	Don Mattingly/Darrell Strawberry		10	5	-
	Yankees	[Corner - Martina Navratilova]	+15 each		
7/20	Andre Dawson		10	5	-
	Cubs		+15		
7/27	Pit Bull Terrier		5	4	-
	Dog	[Corner includes Don Mattingly]			
8/03	Vinny Testaverde		10	4	-
	Tampa Bay		+15		
8/10	Mike Tyson		10	4	-
	Boxing	[Corner - Pete Rose]	+20		
8/17	Alan Trammell		10	5	-
	Tigers	[Corner - 49er player]	+15		
8/24	Jim McMahon		10	5	-
	Bears		+15		
8/31	Tim Brown	College Football Issue	10	5	-
	Notre Dame	[Corner-Oklahoma Football Insert]	+15		
9/07	Surfs Up		4	3	
9/14	Mark Bavaro	Pro Football Issue	10	5	-
	Giants		+15		
9/14	Jackie Joyner Kersee		14	7	-
	Track	[Corner var. #1LSU,#2Wash,#3 Kirby Puckett]	+15		
9/21	John Elway		15	7	-
	Broncos		+25		
9/27	Ozzie Smith		15	7	-
	Cardinals	(* Cover includes Ray Collins - Reds)	+15		
10/05	Lloyd Moseby		10	5	-
	Blue Jay	[*Corner variations #1 Strike, #2 SEC]	+15		
10/12	Steve Walsh	Pro Hockey Issuey	10	5	-
	Florida State	[* Corner is Alan Trammell]	+15		
10/19	Greg Gagne		10	5	-
	Twins	(* Cover includes Darrell Evans- Tigers)	+15		
10/26	Dan Gladden	World Series	10	5	-
	Twins		+15		
11/02	Twins Team	World Series	20	9	-
			+10 each		
11/09	Eric Dickerson*	Pro Basletball Issue	10	5	-
	Colts	(*Michael Jordan Inset)	+15		
11/16	Rotnei Anderson		10	4	-
	Oklahoma		+15		
11/23	Feennis Dembo	College Basketball Issue	10	4	-
	Wyoming	[Corner Indiana variation]	+15		
11/23	Dexter Manley		10	4	-
	Redskins		+15		
11/30	Oklahoma/Nebraska		10	4	-
		[Corner variations #1 North Carolina, #2 USC]			
12/07	Arnold Schwarzenegger		12	6	-
	Movie Star		+40		
		[Corner variations #1 Saints, #2 Lee Trevino]			
12/14	Bo Jackson		12	6	-
	Royals/Raiders		+20		
12/21	Dale Murphy*	Sportsman	20	10	1
	Braves		+10 each		
	(* Also Rory Sparrow, Patty Sheeham, Reggie Williams, Chip Rives, Bobby Bourne, Judy Brown King, Kip Keino)				
	Michael Jordan Year In Pictures		10	8	-
	Bulls				

1988

DATE	COVER/Sport/Team	FEATURES /(ADS)	MT	EM	VG
1/11	Miami	Bowls	10	5	-
1/18	Anthony Carter		10	5	-
	Vikings		+15		
1/25	John Elway		10	5	-
	Broncos		+25		
1/27	Winter Olympics		5	3	-
2/01	Mike Tyson		10	4	-
	Boxing		+20		
2/08	Doug Williams	Superbowl	20	10	-
	Redskins		+15		
2/15	Elle Macpherson	Swimsuit Issue	30	15	1
	Model		+25		
2/22	Wilt Chamberlain/Bill Russell		30	10	-
	Warriors/Celtics		+75/+200		
2/29	Brian Boitano	Ice Skating	10	5	-
	Ice Skating		+15		
3/07	Kirk Gibson		10	5	-
	Dodgers	[Corner Kathy Witt/Ice Skating]	+15		
3/14	Pam Postema	Woman Ump	10	3	-
			+15		
3/21	Larry Bird		20	10	1
	Celtics		+50		
3/28	Mark Macon/Mark Tillmon	[Corner var.#1 Arizona,	10	5	-
	Temple/Georgetown	#2 Oklahoma, #3 Michigan,#4 RI]	+15		
4/04	Will Clark/Mark McGwire		20	10	1
	Giants/A's	Baseball 88	+15 each		
4/11	Danny Manning	NCAA Champs	.10	4	-
	Kansas		+15		
4/18	Lakers Team (Players/Coaches)		15	7	1
	Basketball	+10 each/+35 Kareem/+50 Magic/+200 all			
4/25	Muhammad Ali		10	5	-
	Boxing		+95		
5/02	Billy Ripken		10	5	-
	Orioles	[Corner - Wayne Gretzky]	+15		
5/09	Pete Rose		14	7	-
	Reds		+20		
5/16	Michael Jordan/Scotty Pippen*		30	15	1
	Bulls	[Lady - Horseracing]	+50/+25		
		(*also Brad Daugherty/Cavs)			
5/23	Magic Johnson/Karl Malone		15	7	-
	Lakers/Jazz		+50		
5/30	Wayne Gretzky		20	10	1
	Oilers		+35		
6/06	Bill Russell*	(* Cover includes C. Ripken Sr.,	8	4	-
		Chuck Tanner, Larry Bowa	+200/15 each		
		John Wetzel, Larry Keenan)			
6/13	Mike Tyson/Robin Givens		10	5	-
	Boxing		+50/+15		
6/20	Michael Spinks		10	5	-
	Boxing	[Corner AC Green - Lakers]	+15		
6/27	Magic Johnson/Bill Lambeer		15	6	-
	Lakers/Pistons	[Corner - Curtis Strange/Golf]	+50/+15		

1988

DATE	COVER/Sport/Team	FEATURES //(ADS)	MT	EM	VG
7/04	Mike Tyson/Michael Spinks		10	3	-
	Boxing		+25/+15		
7/11	Darryl Strawberry		10	5	
	Mets		+15		
7/18	Actor Mike Regan		10	5	-
		"Casey at the Bat"			
7/25	Florence Griffith Joyner		10	5	-
	Track		+15		
8/01	Tony Dorsett		10	5	-
	Bronco's	[Corner Wade Boggs- Red Sox]	+15		
8/06	Beer		5	3	-
8/14	China Kids		5	3	-
8/22	Wayne Gretzky/Magic Johnson		30	15	-
	Kings/Lakers		+35/+50		
8/29	Bernie Kosar	NFL Preview	14	7	-
	Browns		+15		
9/05	Florida	College Football Issue	10	4	-
9/12	Jim McMahon		10	5	-
	Bears	[Corner - Jose Canseco]	+15		
9/12	Matt Biondi		10	3	-
	Olympics	Summer Olympic Preview	+15		
9/19	Steffi Graf		10	3	-
	Tennis		+15		
9/26	Dwight Evans		15	7	-
	Red Sox	Olympics	+15		
10/03	Ben Johnson		10	3	-
	Track	Olympics	+20		
10/10	Florence Griffith Joyner/Jackie Joyner Kersee		15	6	-
	Track		+15 each		
10/17	Jose Canseco (FC)		15	6	-
	Athletics		+15		
10/24	Tony Rice*	(Also Aussell Maryland/Miami)	15	6	-
	Notre Dame	[Corner - Kirk Gibson/Dodger]	+15		
10/31	Orel Hershiser/Rick Dempsey		15	6	-
	Dodgers		+15		
11/07	Karl Malone*	Pro Basketball Issue	10	6	-
	Utah	(*Rod Higgens (Warriors))	+15		
11/14	Tom Landry/Chuck Knoll		10	6	-
	Cowboys/Steelers		+15		
	Billy Owens	College Basketball Issue	10	5	-
	Syracuse		+15		
11/21	Saints/Rams		10	5	-
		(*shows Greg Bell (Rams))			
11/28	Rodney Peete		10	4	-
	USC		+15		
12/05	Tony Rice		10	4	-
	Notre Dame		+15		
12/12	Charles Barkley(FC)		15	7	1
	76ers		+20		
12/19	Orel Hershiser	Sportsman	38	10	1
	Dodgers		+15		
	Flo Joyner Keerse	Pictures - 1988	10	5	
	Track		+15		

1989

DATE	COVER/Sport/Team	FEATURES /(ADS)	MT	EM	VG
1/09	**Tony Rice**	Bowls	10	4	-
	Notre Dame		+15		
1/16	**Ickey Woods**		10	4	-
	Bengels		+10		
1/23	**Kareem Abdul-Jabbar**		10	5	-
	Lakers		+35		
1/30	**Jerry Rice**	Superbowl XXIII	15	10	1
	49ers		+35		
2/07	**Kathy Ireland**	Swimsuit Issue	25	15	1
	Model (FC)		+25		
2/06	**Mario Lemieux**		20	10	-
	Penquins (FC)		+25		
2/13	**Patrick Ewing**		10	4	-
	Knicks		+25		
2/20	**Chris Jackson**		10	4	-
	LSU		+25(islamic)		
2/27	**Charles Thompson/Barry Switzer**		10	4	-
	Sooners		+10 each		
3/06	**Wade Boggs**		10	5	-
	Red Sox	[Corner - Mike Tyson]	+15		
3/13	**Michael Jordan**		24	12	1
	Bulls		+45		
3/20	**Jimmy Johnson**		10	5	-
	Cowboys		+10		
3/27	**Steffi Graf**		10	4	-
	Tennis	[Corner - NC State]	+15		
4/01	**Benito Santiago**	Baseball Issue	10	5	-
	Padres		+15		
4/03	**Pete Rose**		10	5	-
	Reds	[Corner -Danny Ferry- Duke]	+20		
4/10	**Rumeal Robinson**		10	5	-
	Glen Rice	NCAA Champs	+15 each		
	Michigan				
4/17	**Nick Faldo** - Golf Masters		10	5	-
	Golf	[Corner-Magic Johnson/Lakers]	+15		
4/24	**Tony Mandarich**		10	4	-
	Football Player		+10		
5/01	**Nolan Ryan**		25	10	1
	Texas		+25		
5/08	**Jon Peters** -	high school pitcher	10	4	-
	Baseball	[Corner - Chris Mullin/Warriors]	+10		
5/15	**Michael Jordan**		25	12	1
	Bulls		+45		
5/22	**Julie Krone**		10	3	-
	Woman Jockey		+15		
5/29	**Kentucky Basketball**		10	3	-
6/05	**James Worthy**	Stanley Cup Final	10	6	-
	Lakers		+20		
6/12	**Bo Jackson**		10	5	-
	Royals		+20		
6/19	**Sugar Ray Leonard/Thomas Hearns**		10	5	-
	Boxing	[Corner- Michael Chang Tennis]	+20		
6/26	**Curtis Strange**	US Open	10	4	-
	Golf	NBA Finals	+15		

1989

DATE	COVER/Sport/Team	FEATURES /(ADS)	MT	EM	VG
7/03	Pete Rose		10	5	-
	Reds		+20		
7/10	Rick Reuschel		10	5	-
	Giants		+15		
7/17	George Foreman		15	7	-
	Boxing		+20		
7/24	Greg Jefferies		12	6	-
	Mets		+15		
7/31	Greg Lemond	Tour De France	10	5	-
	Cycling		+15		
8/07	Boomer Esiason		12	6	-
	Bengels		+15		
8/14	Michael Jordan		20	12	-
	Golf		+45		
8/21	Troy Aikman (FC)		20	10	-
	Cowboys		+20		
8/27	Chris Evert		10	5	-
	Tennis	[Corner - Pete Rose]	+15		
9/04	Lou Holtz	Col Football Issue	5	3	-
	Notre Dame	(*Ernie Davis/Lafeyette/Pete Rose)			
9/11	Randell Cunningham		10	5	-
	Eagles	Pro Football Issue	+15		
9/18	Boris Becker	U S Open Tennis	10	4	-
	Tennis		+15		
9/25	Raghib Ismail		10	4	-
	Notre Dame		+15		
10/02	Joe Montana		20	10	-
	49ers		+30		
10/09	Sergiei Starikov	Pro Hockey Issue	10	5	-
	Viacheslav Fetisov		+15		
10/16	Rickey Henderson*		10	6	-
	A's	(*also Kelly Gruber (Jays))	+15		
10/23	Herschel Walker		12	6	-
	Vikings		+15		
		[Corner Dave Stewart, Wayne Gretzky]			
10/30	Kelly Downs	Earthquake	12	5	-
	Giants				
11/06	Joe Dumars		24	12	-
	Michael Jordan		+15		
	Pistons/Bulls				
11/13	Deion Sanders		20	10	-
	Atlanta		+20		
11/15	Muhammad Ali	35th Anniversary	20	10	-
	Boxing		+95		
11/20	Rumeal Robinson	College Basketball Issue	12	6	-
	Michigan		+15		
11/27	Harris/Rice/Smith/Thompson/Ware		10	4	-
	UWV/N.Dame/FL/In/Hoston		+10 each		
12/04	Steve McGuire		10	4	-
	Miami		+15		
12/11	Larry Bird	(Cover shows Randolph Keys(Cavs)	20	10	-
	Celtics	[Corner Nadi Comaneci, Mark Langston]	+50		
12/18	Joe Montana- 49ers		30	15	-
	Magic Johnson - Lakers		+30/+50/+35		
	Wayne Gretzky - Kings				
12/31	Greg Lemond - Sportsman*		24	12	-
	Cycling		+20		
	The Year In Photo's		10	7	-

1990

DATE	COVER/Sport/Team	FEATURES /(ADS)	MT	EM	VG
1/08	**Craig Erickson** Miami	Bowls	8 +20	4	-
1/15	**Jerry Rice** 49ers		15 +60	9	-
1/22	**John Elway** Bronco's		8 +30	4	-
1/29	**Dave Robinson** Spurs		10 +30	5	-
2/05	**Joe Montana/ McIntyre** - 49ers	49ers Superbowl XXIV	10 +40	4	-
2/12	**Judit Mascow** Model	Swimsuit issue	20 +45	12	1
2/19	**Mike Tyson** Boxing		5 +40	3	-
2/26	**Buster Douglas** Boxing	(Michael Jordan)	5 +20	3	-
3/05	**Gary Payton** Oregon State	College Basketball Issue	5 +15	3	
3/12	**Tony Larussa** Athletics		5 +15	3	
3/19	**Jennifer Capriati** Tennis		5 +15	3	-
3/26	**Bo Kimble** Loyola Marymount		5 +15	3	-
4/02	**Stacey Augmon/Chris Knight** UNLV/LOYOLA	NCAA Basketball	5 +10/+10	3	
4/09	**Rod Scurry/Brian Davis** UNLV/Duke	NCAA Finals	5 +15/+10	3	-
4/16	**Ted Williams** Red Sox	Baseball Issue, Masters	20 +150	10	-
4/23	**Thomas Sandstrom** LA Kings	[Corner Bo Jackson, Steffi Graf]	5 +15	3	
4/30	**Jeff George** Colts		5 +15	3	-
5/07	**Ken Griffey(FC)** Mariners		20 +40	10	-
5/14	**Sneakers**		5	3	-
5/21	**Michael Jordan** Bulls		20 +50	10	-
5/28	**Will Clark (FSC)** Giants		10 +15	5	-
6/04	**Lenny Dykstra** Phillies		10 +15	5	-
6/11	**Isaiah Thomas** Pistons		8 +15	4	-
6/18	**Jack Nicklaus/Monica Seles/George Steinbrenner** Golf/Tennis/Baseball		8 +40/+15/+10	4	-
6/25	**Hale Irwin** Golf	US Open	6 +20	4	-
7/02	**Marvin Hagler** Boxer		4 +25	3	-

1990

DATE	COVER/Sport/Team	FEATURES /(ADS)	MT	EM	VG
7/09	Darryl Strawberry		10	4	-
	Mets		+15		
7/16	Martina Navratilova		5	2	-
	Tennis	NBA Finals	+25		
7/23	Narciso Elrira	Minor Baseball Teams	5	1	-
	Dodgers	Pistons NBA Champs			
7/30	Greg Lemond		5	3	-
	Cycling		+15		
8/06	Joe Montana		10	4	-
	49ers		+30		
8/13	Autograph Madness		5	1	-
8/20	Jose Canseco		10	5	-
	A's		+15		
8/27	Troy Aikman*		15	5	1
	Cowboys	[*Also Mike Wise - Raiders]	+35		
9/03	Todd Marinovich	College Football Issue	5	2	-
	USC		+10		
9/10	Barry Sanders (FC)		10	5	-
	Lions		+25		
9/17	Peter Sampras		5	2	-
	Tennis		+15		
9/24	Rick Mirer		10	4	-
	Notre Dame		+15		
10/01	Bobby Bonilla		10	4	-
	Pirates		+15		
10/08	OJ Simpson	Pro Hockey Issue	10	5	-
	Bills		+40		
10/15	Burt Grossman	Pro Football Issue	10	5	-
	Chargers		+15		
10/22	Dennis Eckersley		10	4	-
	A's	World Series	+10		
10/29	Chris Sabo	World Series	10	4	-
	Reds		+15		
11/05	Bill Laimbeer	Pro Basketball Issue	5	3	-
	Pistons		+15		
11/12	William Bell		5	3	-
	Georgia Tech		+15		
11/19	Stacey Augmon/Larry Johnson		10	5	-
	UNLV	College Basketball Issue	+15/+20		
11/26	Notre Dame/Penn State		4	3	-
12/03	Magic Johnson		10	5	-
	Lakers		+50		
12/10	Ty Detmer		8	4	-
	BYU		+15		
12/17	Michael Jordan*		20	10	1
	Bulls	[*also Kevin Duckworth-Blazers]	+40		
12/24	Joe Montana	Sportsman	30	15	1
	49ers		+40		
12/31	Chiefs Player	Pictures of 1990	5	4	-

1991

DATE	COVER/Sport/Team	FEATURES /(ADS)	MT	EM	VG
1/14	**Dan Marino**	Bowls	20	10	-
	Dolphins		+35		
1/21	**Shaquille O'Neal (FC)**		20	10	2
	LSU		+35		
1/28	**Otis Anderson**		5	3	-
	Giants		+15		
2/04	**Everson Walls**	Superbowl XXV	5	5	-
	Giants		+15		
2/11	**Robert Parrish**		10	5	-
	Celtics		+15		
2/18	**Michael Jordan/Charles Barkley/Patrick Ewing**		40	15	2
	Karl Malone/Magic Johnson		+40 Jordan/		
	Olympic Team	Johnson/Ewing	+15 for others		
2/25	**Rocket Ismail**		5	3	-
	Notre Dame		+15		
3/04	**Darryl Strawberry**		10	3	-
	Dodgers		+15		
3/11	**Ashley Montana**	Swimsuit Issue	6	5	1
	Model		+15		
3/18	**Brett Hull**		10	5	-
	Blues		+15		
3/25	**Mike Tyson/**		10	4	-
	Razor Ruddock		+20		
	Boxing				
4/01	**Mark Randall**	NCAA	10	4	-
	Kansas		+15		
4/08	**Grant Hill**	Duke NCAA Champs	20	10	-
	Duke		+15		
4/15	**Nolan Ryan**	Baseball Issue	30	15	1
	Rangers		+25		
4/22	**Ian Woosnam**	Masters	10	4	-
	Golf		+10		
4/29	**Evander Holyfield**		10	4	-
	George Foreman		+15 each		
	Boxing				
5/06	**Bjorn Borg**		10	4	-
	Tennis		+15		
5/13	**Roger Clemens***		8	4	-
	Red Sox	[*Corner Nolan Ryan]	+15		
5/20	**Michael Johnson**		5	3	-
	Track		+15		
5/27	**Mickey Mantle**		20	10	1
	Roger Maris		+200(d)		
	Yankees				
6/03	**Michael Jordan**	Stanley Cup	20	10	1
	Bulls		+45		
6/10	**Magic Johnson/Michael Jordan**		20	10	1
	Lakers/Bulls	NBA Finals	+40 each		
6/17	**Michael Jordan**		20	10	1
	Bulls	NBA Finals	+40		
6/24	**Mike Tyson**		10	5	-
	Boxing	[* Corner inset -Michael Jordan]	+20		
7/01	**Orel Hershiser**		10	5	-
	Dodgers		+15		
7/08	**Lyle Alzado**		4	1	-
	Football		+40(d)		
7/15	**Steffi Graf**		5	3	-
	Tennis		+15		

1991

VALUE GUIDE

DATE	COVER/Sport/Team	FEATURES /(ADS)	MT	EM	VG
7/22	Fans World		2	1	-
7/29	Cal Ripken Jr (FSC)		24	12	1
	Orioles		+40		
8/05	Black Athlete (Jordan)		20	10	-
		[Michael Jordan]	+40		
8/12	Eric Dickerson		5	2	-
	Colts		+15		
8/19	John Daly		20	7	-
	Golf	[Corner inset George Bush]	+15		
8/26	David Klingler	College Football Issue	5	3	-
	Houston		+15		
9/02	Bruce Smith	Pro Football Issue	5	3	-
	Bills		+15		
9/09	Mike Powell		5	3	-
	Long Jump		+15		
9/16	Jimmy Connors	US open Tennis	5	3	-
	Tennis		+15		
9/23	Desmond Howard		5	2	-
	Michigan		+15		
9/30	Ramon Martinez		5	3	
	Dodgers		+15		
10/07	Bobby Hebert	Pro Hockey Issue	5	3	-
	Saints		+15		
10/14	Gary Clark		5	3	-
	Redskins		+15		
10/21	Kirby Puckett(FC)		15	7	-
	Twins		+25		
10/28	Dan Gladden	World Series	10	5	-
	Gregg Olson		+10 each		
	Twins				
11/04	Twins	World Series	10	3	-
			+10 each		
11/11	Michael Jordan	Pro Basketball Issue	24	12	1
	Phil Jackson/		+40		
	Scotty Pippen				
	Bulls				
11/18	Magic Johnson		12	6	1
	Lakers		+40		
11/25	Christian Laettner		5	2	-
	Duke	College Basketball Issue	+15		
12/02	Jim McMahon	100 yrs of Basketball	5	2	-
	Eagles		+15		
12/09	Desmond Howard		5	2	-
	Michigan		+15		
12/16	Buffalo Bills		4	3	-
			+15		
12/23	Michael Jordan	Sportsman of the Year	25	15	2
	Bulls (SOY)		+50		
12/30	Pictures of 1991 (Discus Thrower)		10	4	-
F1/91	Red Grange	Classic SI	10	5	-

1992

DATE	COVER/Sport/Team	FEATURES /(ADS)	MT	EM	VG
1/13	**Muhammad Ali** Boxing	Bowl Games	6 +95	3	–
1/20	**Thurman Thomas** Bills		6 +15	3	–
1/27	**AJ Kitt** Skier	Olympics	4 +15	2	–
2/03	**Mark Rypien** Redskins	Redskins Win Super Bowl XXVI	6 +15	3	–
2/10	**Patrick Ewing Chris Mullin** Knicks/Warriors		4 +40/+20	2	–
2/17	**Mike Tyson** Boxing	Olympics	4 +40	2	–
2/24	**Bonnie Blair** Speedskating	Olympics	8 +15	4	–
3/02	**Kristi Yamaguchi** Figure Skating	Olympics	8 +15	4	–
3/09	**Kathy Ireland** Model	Swimsuit Issue	15 +25	10	1
3/16	**Ryne Sandberg** Cubs		10 +25	5	–
3/23	**Larry Bird** Celtics		8 +40	4	–
3/30	**Malcolm Mackey** Georgia Tech	NCAA Basketball	4 +15	2	–
4/06	**Kirby Puckett** Twins	Baseball Issue	10 +25	5	–
4/13	**Bobby Hurley** Duke	Duke NCAA Basketball Champs	6 +15	4	–
4/20	**Fred Couples** Masters	Masters	6 +15	3	–
4/27	**Deion Sanders** Braves		8 +20	4	–
5/04	**Barry Bonds (FC)** Pirates		12 +40	6	1
5/11	**Michael Jordan Clyde Drexler** Bulls/Trailblazers		14 +40/+25	7	1
5/18	**Baseball Errors**		4	2	
5/25	**Michael Jordan* Patrick Ewing** Bulls/Knicks	[*also Gerald Wilkens(Knicks)] (also Scottie Pippen (Bulls))	12 +40	6	–
6/01	**Mark McGwire (FSC)** A's		4 +15	3	–
6/08	**Mario Lemieux** Penguins	Stanley Cup	5 +20	4	–
6/15	**Michael Jordan** Bulls		9 +40	7	1
6/22	**Michael Jordan** Bulls	NBA Finals	9 +40	7	1
6/29	**Tom Kite** Golf		4 +15	2	–

1992

DATE	COVER/Sport/Team	FEATURES /(ADS)	MT	EM	VG
		VALUE GUIDE			
7/06	**Steve Palermo**		4	2	-
	Baseball Umpire		+10		
7/13	**Andre Agassi**		4	2	-
	Tennis		+20		
7/20	**Jackie Joyner Kersee**		10	5	-
	Track	Summer Olympic Preview	+20		
7/27	**Joe Montana**	Olympics	6	3	-
	49ers		+35		
8/03	**Nelson Diebel**	Olympics	4	2	-
	Swimmer		+10		
8/10	**Gail Devers**	Olympics	4	2	-
	Track		+10		
8/17	**Carl Lewis**	Olympics	8	4	-
	Dennis Mitchell		+10 each		
	Track				
8/24	**Deion Sanders**		8	4	-
	Braves/Falcons		+20		
8/31	**Miami Football**	College Football Issue	4	2	-
9/07	**Jerry Rice**	Pro Football Issue	10	5	-
	49ers		+50		
9/14	**Jim Harbaugh**		4	2	-
	Bears		+10		
9/21	**Stefan Edberg**		4	2	-
	Tennis		+10		
9/28	**Tony Mandarich**		4	2	-
	Packers		+10		
10/05	**George Brett**		10	5	-
	Royals		+30		
10/12	**Randall Cunningham**		8	4	-
	Eagles	Pro Hockey Issue	+10		
10/19	**Dave Winfield**		10	5	-
	Walt Weiss		+20/+10		
	Blue Jays/A's				
10/26	**John Smoltz***	[*also Roberto Alomar (Jays)/	20	8	-
	Braves	Mike Reilly (Ump)] World Series,	+20/+10		
		SI FIRST Sideways Cover	+20		
11/02	**Blue Jays Team**	Blue Jays Win Series	8	4	-
11/09	**Charles Barkley**	Pro Basketball Issue	10	5	-
	Suns		+25		
11/16	**Everett/Norton**		10	5	-
	Cowboys		+20 each		
11/23	**Riddick Bowe**	College Basketball Issue	4	2	-
	Evander Holyfield		+15/+20		
	Boxing				
11/30	**Shaquille O'Neal**		10	5	-
	Magic		+50		
12/07	**Campten/Blackmon**		4	2	-
	Packers		+10		
12/14	**Larry Bird**		20	10	1
	Magic Johnson		+40 each		
	Celtics/Lakers				
12/21	**Arthur Ashe (SOY)**		16	8	-
	Tennis		+200(d)		
12/28	**Year In Pictures**		12	6	1
Fall/92	**Willie Mays**	(Classic SI)	20	10	2
	Giants		+40		

1993

DATE	COVER/Sport/Team	FEATURES /(ADS)	MT	EM	VG
1/11	Jim Valvano Coach	Bowl Games	8 +100(d)	4	-
1/11	Derric Lassic Alabama	(Regional Issue-Alabama state)	30	15	5
1/18	Steve Young (FC) 49ers		24 +40	12	-
1/25	Emmitt Smith (FC) Cowboys		24 +50	12	-
2/01	Dr Z on Football	(Eastern US) "bad news Buffalo" (Western US) 'Good News Dallas'	8 8	4 4	- -
2/08	Troy Aikman Cowboys	Cowboys Win Super Bowl XXVII	10 +40	5	-
2/15	Arthur Ashe Tennis		6 (Deaceased)	3	-
2/22	Ingrid Seynhare Ashley Richardson	Swimsuit Issue	16 +40 each	8	1
3/01	George Steinbrenner Yankees		6 +15	3	-
3/08	Brian Reese North Carolina		6 +10	3	-
3/15	Reggie White Football		8 +15	4	-
3/22	Dwight Gooden Mets		6 +15	3	-
3/29	Kidd/Hurley California/Duke BKB	NCAA Basketball	6 +15 each	3	-
4/05	David Cone Royals	Baseball Issue	6 +15	3	-
4/12	Eric Montross* UNC Basketball	*Cover also shows George Lynch (UNC)/ Chris Webber/Juwan Howard (Michigan)	6 +10	3	-
4/19	Mario Lemieux Penquins	Masters	10 +20	5	-
4/26	Joe Montana 49ers		6 +40	3	-
5/03	Joe Dimaggio (FC) Yankees		16 +180	8	-
5/10	Monica Seles Tennis		6 +15	3	-
5/17	Hakeem Olajuwon Rockets		6 +40	4	-
5/24	Barry Bonds Giants		6 +40	4	-
5/31	Patrick Ewing Bill Cartwright Knicks/Bulls		6 +40/+10	3	-
6/07	Michael Jordan Bulls		8 +40	4	-
6/14	Mathieu Schneider Tomas Sandstrom Canadiens/Kings	Stanley Cup	6 +10 each	3	-
6/21	Michael Jordan Charles Barkley Bulls/Suns		12 +40/+30	6	1
6/28	Michael Jordan Scottie Pippen Bulls	Bulls NBA Champs	12 +40/+30	6	1
7/05	Mike Piazza (FC) Dodgers		8 +25	4	-

1993

DATE	COVER/Sport/Team	FEATURES /(ADS)	MT	EM	VG
7/12	Laurie Crews		4	2	-
	Patti Olin		+15 each		
	Indians' Wives				
7/19	Bob Gibson		10	5	-
	Denny McLain		+15 each		
	Cardinals/Tigers				
7/26	Greg Norman(FC)	British Open	6	3	-
	Golf		+15		
8/02	John Elway		6	3	-
	Dan Reeves		+40/+10		
	Broncos				
8/09	Reggie Lewis		6	3	-
	Celtics		+100(d)		
8/16	Nike's Phil Knight		4	2	-
			+10		
8/23	Mary Pierce		4	2	-
	Tennis		+10		
8/30	Scott Bentley	College Football Issue	4	2	-
	Florida State Football		+10		
9/06	Junior Seau	Pro Football Issue	8	4	-
	Chargers		+15		
9/13	Joe Montana		8	4	-
	Chiefs		+40		
9/20	Pernell Whitaker		6	3	-
	Julio Cesar Chavez		+20 each		
	Boxing				
9/27	Ron Gant		5	3	-
	Braves		+15		
10/04	Boomer/Gunnar Esiason		6	3	-
	Jets		+15		
10/11	Chuck Cecil	Hockey Preview	6	3	-
	Cardinals Football		+10		
10/18	Michael Jordan	Jordan Retires ("Why?")	12	6	-
	Bulls		+40		
10/25	Michael Irvin	World Series	12	6	-
	Cowboys		+40		
11/01	Joe Carter	Blue Jays Win World Series	10	5	-
	Blue Jays		+30		
11/08	Alonzo Mourning(FC)		8	4	-
	Bill Russell	Pro Basketball Issue	+30/+200		
	Hornets/Celtics				
11/15	Evander Holyfield		8	4	-
	Boxing		+15		
11/22	Jim Flanigan		6	3	-
	Notre Dame Football		+10		
11/29	BC/Notre Dame FB	College Basketball Issue	6	3	-
12/06	Football Player		4	2	-
12/13	Damon Bailey		4	2	-
	Indiana Basketball		+15		
12/20	Don Shula (SOY)		3	2	-
	Dolphins		+30		
12/27	Uniforms	Year In Pictures	10	5	1

1994

DATE	COVER/Sport/Team	FEATURES /(ADS)	MT	EM	VG
1/10	**Florida State**	#1 Bowl Games	6	4	-
1/17	**Nancy Kerrigan**		6	4	-
	Ice Skating		+15		
1/24	**Joe Montana**		8	6	-
	Kansas City Chiefs		+40		
1/31	**Emmitt Smith**		8	6	-
	Cowboys		+50		
2/07	**Emmitt Smith**	Superbowl	8	6	-
	Cowboys		+50		
2/14	**Kathy Ireland/Rachel Hunter**		20	12	-
	Swimsuit Issue		+40 each		
2/21	**Tommy Moe**	Olympics	6	4	-
	Skier		+10		
2/28	**Dan Jansen/**	Olympics	8	6	-
	Bonnie Blair				
	Skaters		+10 each		
3/07	**David Robinson**		8	5	-
	Spurs		+20		
3/14	**Michael Jordan**		14	7	-
	Whitesox		+50		
3/21	**Bill Clinton**		8	4	-
	President		+100		
3/28	**Boston College**	Basketball Players	6	4	-
	Basketball		+10 each		
4/04	**Ken Griffey Jr/**	Baseball Issue	10	7	-
	Mike Piazza		+50/+30		
	Mariners/Dodgers				
4/04	**Ken Griffey Jr**	(Canadian Issue)	40	25	10
	Mariners		+50		
4/11	**Corliss Williamson**		6	4	-
	Arkansas	NCAA Finals	+10		
4/18	**Mickey Mantle**		14	7	-
	Yankees		+200(d)		
4/25	**Dan Wilkinson**		6	4	-
	Ohio State		+10		
5/02	**Gary Payton**		6	4	-
	Sonics		+20		
5/09	**Tennis in Crisis**		5	3	-
5/16	**Florida**	State Football	6	4	-
5/23	**Atlanta vs Mets**		6	4	-
5/30	**John Starks**		6	4	-
	Knicks		+10		
6/06	**Ken Griffey Jr**		14	7	-
	Seattle		+35		
6/13	**Mark Messier**		6	4	-
	Rangers		+20		
6/21	**Mike Richter/Pat Ewing**		6	4	-
	Rangers/Knicks		+20		
6/20	**Mike Richter -**	Regional Cover	25	15	-
	Rangers		+20		
6/27	**OJ Simpson -**	Murder	6	4	-
			+50		

1994

1995

DATE	COVER/Sport/Team FEATURES /(ADS)	MT	EM	VG
1/09	**Tom Osborne**	10	6	-
	Nebraska	+10		
1/16	**Steve Young/Troy Aikman**	10	6	-
	49ers/Cowboys	+40 each		
1/23	**Steve Young**	10	6	-
	49ers	+40		
1/30	**Derric Coleman**	6	3	-
	Nets	+10		
2/06	**Steve Young**	10	6	-
	49ers NFL Champs	+40		
2/13	**Penny Hardaway**	10	6	-
	Magic	+40		
2/20	**Daniela Glisten** Swimsuit Issue	15	10	-
	Swimsuit Issue	+40		
2/27	**Darryl Strawberry/Dwight Gooden**	6	3	-
	Mets	+10/+10		
3/06	**Jerry Stackhouse**	6	3	-
	NC	+10		
3/13	**Andre Aggasi**	6	3	-
	Tennis	+20		
3/20	**Michael Jordan**	10	5	-
	Bulls	+40		
3/27	**Michael Jordan**	10	5	-
	Bulls	+40		
4/03	**Arkansas Basketball**	6	3	-
4/10	**Ed O'Bannon** UCLA Champs	6	3	-
	UCLA	+15		
4/10	**Jennifer Rizzotti**	20	10	2
	Univ. Of Conn. (Conneticut Regional)	+15		
4/17	**Ben Crenshaw**	6	3	-
	Golf Masters	+15		
4/24	**Joe Montana**	10	5	-
	Chiefs	+40		
5/01	**Cal Ripken Jr**	10	5	-
	Orioles	+40		
5/08	**Vlade Divac**	6	3	-
	Lakers	+15		
5/15	**Erickson, Moeller, Cox**	6	3	-
	Coaches	+10 each		
5/22	**Michael Jordan/Shaq**	10	5	-
	Bulls/Magic	+40 each		
5/29	**Dennis Rodman**	20	10	-
	Spurs	+35		
6/05	**Matt Williams**	6	3	-
	Giants	+20		
6/05	**Serqei Fedorov** (Canadian Only)	30	20	-
	Redwings	+15		
6/12	**University of Miami**	6	3	-
6/19	**Clyde Drexler**	6	3	-
	Rockets	+20		
6/26	**Kevin Garnett**	6	3	-
	High School	+20		
7/03	**Mike Tyson**	6	3	-
	Boxing	+40		
7/10	**Hideo Nomo**	10	5	-
	Dodgers	+30		

1995

DATE	COVER/Sport/Team FEATURES /(ADS)	MT	EM	VG
7/17	Monica Seles	6	3	-
	Tennis	+10		
7/24	Car Racing	6	3	-
7/31	John Daily	6	3	-
	Golf	+20		
8/07	Cal Ripken Jr	15	8	-
	Orioles	+40		
8/14	Greg Maddux	20	10	-
	Braves	+40		
8/14	Gene Stallings (Southeast Region)	25	15	1
	Alabama	+15		
8/21	Mickey Mantle Yankees (Special Story)	15	7	-
8/28	Keyshawn Johnson	6	3	-
	USC	+10		
9/04	Dan Marino	10	5	-
	Dolphins	+40		
9/11	Cal Ripken Jr	10	5	-
	Orioles	+40		
9/18	Emmitt Smith	10	5	-
	Cowboys	+40		
9/25	Danny Wuerfel	6	4	-
	Gators	+10		
10/02	Mo Vaughn	6	4	-
	Red Sox	+20		
10/09	Deon Sanders	6	4	-
	Cowboys	+25		
10/09	Eric Lindros (Canadian Only)	30	20	-
		+20		
F1/95	Bobby Layne	6	4	-
	Lions Sports History	(d)		
10/16	Ken Griffey Jr	10	5	-
	Mariners	+30		
10/23	Michael Jordan/Dennis Rodman	10	5	-
	Bulls	+40/+30		
10/30	Bo Jackson	6	4	-
		+30		
11/06	Greg Maddux & Team	10	5	-
	Braves World Series Champs	+40		
11/13	Northwestern	6	4	-
11/20	Elvis	6	4	-
	49ers	+15		
11/27	Jacque Vaughn	6	4	-
	Kansas	+10		
11/27	Mike Keenan (Canadian Issue)	30	20	-
	Blues	+15		
12/11	Pat Riley/Don Shula	6	4	-
	Heat/Dolphins	+20 each		
12/19	Cal Ripken Jr Sportsman	15	10	-
	Orioles	+40		
12/25	Shaq (National)	20	10	-
	Magic	+40		
12/25	Steve Spurrier (South East Issue)	20	10	-
	Florida	+10		
12/25	Steve Tasker (Eastern Cover)	20	10	-
	Bills	+10		
12/25	Barry Sanders (Central Michigan Area)	30	20	-
	Lions	+15		
12/25	Tommy Frazier (Central Nebraska Area)	30	20	-
	Nebraska	+15		

1996

DATE	COVER/Sport/Team	FEATURES /(ADS)	MT	EM	VG
1/08	**Billy Payne** Olympics	Playoff & Bowl	5 +10	3	-
1/15	**Brett Favre** Packers	Playoff, Wade Boggs	5 +20	3	-
1/22	**Emmitt Smith** Cowboys`	Playoff, Mario Lemieux	5 +40	3	-
1/29	**Valeria Mazza/Tyra Banks** Swimsuit Models		15 +40 each	6	1
2/05	**Emmitt Smith** Cowboys	Superbowl	7 +40	4	
2/12	**Magic Johnson** Lakers	Magic Johnson Returns	7 +40	4	
2/19	**Marcus Stroud** Georgia Basketball		5 +10	2	-
2/26	**Rick Pitino** Kentucky		5 +20	2	-
3/04	**Dennis Rodman** Bulls		10 +20	5	
3/11	**Wayne Gretzky/Neil O'Donnell** Blues/Steelers		5 +40/+10	2	-
3/18	**Jay Buhner/Son** Mariners		5 +10	2	-
3/25	**#20 Texas Tech** Texas Tech	Final 16 NCAA	5 +10	2	-
4/01	**Manny Ramirez** Indians	Baseball Issue	5 +10	3	-
4/08	**Antoine Walker** Kentucky	NCAA Finals	5 +10	3	-
4/15	**Christy Martin** Boxing	Female Boxer	5 +10	2	-
4/22	**Greg Norman** Golfer	Masters	5 +25	3	-
4/29	**Dave Robinson** Spurs	Bulls	5 +25	3	-
5/06	**Albert Belle** Indians		5 +20	3	-
5/13	**Dan Marino/Jimmy Johnson** Dolphins		5 +40/+10	3	-
5/20	**Marge Schott** Reds	Shaq	5 +10	3	-
5/27	**Phil Jackson/Michael Jordan** Bulls		6 +10/+40	4	-
6/03	**Michael Jordan** Bulls	Playoffs	6 +40	4	-
6/10	**Gary Payton** Sonics		5 +10	3	-
6/17	**Michael Jordan** Bulls	NBA Playoffs/NHL Finals	6 +40	4	-
6/17	**Patrick Roy** Avalanche	[Regional Cover] NHL Championship	20 +15	7	-
6/24	**Richie Parker** Basketball Scandal		6 +10	2	-

SI PRESENTS/SPECIAL ISSUES

In addition to its regular issues, *Sports Illustrated* has published a number of special or commemorative issues over the years. The best-known special issues are the annuals that feature photos of the preceding sport year. There seems to be a misconception in the hobby that these issues are rare or especially valuable. As this price guide indicates, most "Year in Sports" and "Pictures" were released with the regular issues and go for slightly more than a regular issue. The most collectible of the special issues is the 1978 "25th Anniversary" magazine, which was distributed to advertisers and has a low circulation. Like the later "35th Anniversary" issue (also desirable, largely as a reference, among *SI* collectors), this issue is comprised largely of color images of covers and was sold on the newsstand.

Sports Illustrated did not begin to produce commemorative covers until 1989 when it started with a test issue 'Sports Illustrated Presents the Superbowl' (Life magazine size) with the 1968 Superbowl cover of Vince Lombardi. A second test issue occurred in 1990 with a Life size magazine format with Joe Montana which covered 25 years of Superbowls. However, it was in 1993 when they began using the 1993 Sports Illustrated Presents as an official commerative issue. On January 11 of that year, after Alabama had won college football's National Championship *SI* ran a cover of NC State basketball coach Jim Valvano. This decision incensed Alabama fans, who communicated their ire in a barrage of letters and phone calls to Time, Inc. *SI* responded to the outcry with their first commemorative issue, which featured Crimson Tide star Derek Lassic on its cover. The commercial success of that effort prompted a series of commemorative issues, which *SI* continues to produce to this day. Rumor has it that *Sports Illustrated* had a commemorative issue ready to go to celebrate the New York Knicks' victory in the 1994 NBA Finals, but had to hold it back when Olajuwon and the Rockets snatched the title away from Ewing and the Knicks. SI Presents also handles special advertiser commemorative issues that are done with a specific advertiser (Kelloggs, etc). These issues are only obtained through the particular product promotion and not through Sports Illustrated. These are footnoted in the list below.

SPECIAL & PROMOTIONAL ISSUES

1978   25TH ANN.   *Depicts SI Covers 54-78 ($75-100) Distributed to Advertisers only. Multiple covers of SI shown

1977-1984   Hardbound version of the 'Year in Sports' and 'Sportsman of the Year' were also used as sales promotion tools. These books are worth two times the regular cover (approximately $30 each).

SPORTS ILLUSTRATED AUSTRALIA

In 1992, SI tried to make a go of it in Australia. Six issues were released all with Cricket and Rugby players. The issues were never released in the United States. I value the issues around $25 each. The magazine covered both local and international sports.

"YEAR IN SPORTS" SERIES

DATE	COVER	FEATURES	MT	EM
1976	Year In Sports		15	10
		*Cover shows M.Ali/D.Hamill/R.Jackson/ NASTASE/ALEXEYEV/PAYTON.		
1977	The Year in Sports		15	6
1978	The Year in Sports		15	6
		Cover shows Navratilova/Yarborough/Staubach/ Elvin Hayes/Passarella/Spinks/Affirmed/Lopez/ Lafleur.		
1979	The Year in Sports		15	6
		**Cover shows Rose/McEnroe/Heiden/Maravich.		
1980	The Year in Sports		15	6
1981	The Year in Sports		15	6
		**Cover shows Bird/Erving/McEnroe/Borg/ Leonard/Valenzuela/Montana/Gretzky/Austin		
1982	The Year in Sports		15	7
		*Cover shows Evert/Holmes/Dorsett/Yount Parish/Gretzky/Nicklaus/Connors/Walker/ Ricky Henderson/Billy Smith.		
1983	The Year in Sports		15	6
		*Cover shows: Marino/NC State BKB/McEnroe/ Riggins/Moses/Holmes/Cosell/Tiegs/Carlton /Billy Smith/Watson/ Bowie/Andra Franklin/ Navratilova/Walker/Lewis/Carew/Rozier/Hagler/ Sunny's Halo/Cummings/Dickerson/Murphy/Abdul-Jabbar.		
1984	The Year In Sports		15	6
1985	The Year In Sports		15	6

The concept "The Year in Sports" shifted to "Pictures of'. These issues were given at the end of the year instead of a month or two later in 'The Year of Sports". In 1994 "The Year In Pictures" life magazine format was introduced and is given out as a promotional subscription offer and therefore more scarce.

"PICTURES OF"

DATE	COVER	FEATURES	MT	EM
1987	Michael Jordan Bulls	Pictures '87	20 +50	10
1988	Florence Joyner Track	Pictures '88	20 +20	10
1990	Stephone Paige Chiefs	Pictures '90	15 +15	7
1991	Christian Schenk	Pictures '91	10 +15	5
1992	Carl Lewis Track	Pictures '92	20 +20	10
1993	Uniforms	Pictures '93	10	5
1994	Troy Aikman Cowboys	Year In Pictures (Life Magazine Size)	20 +40	10
1995	Michael Jordan Bulls	Year In Pictures (Life Magazine Size)	25 +40	15
1995	Bret Fahre Packers	The year In Pictures NFL & College Football		
1996	Jerry Rice 49ers	Pictures of the Year	20 +40	6

SPORTS ILLUSTRATED PRESENTS SERIES

'Sports Illustrated Presents is a separate division within the Sports Illustrated family. The group develops the Football, Baseball, and Basketball Annuals as well as special commemorative issues for both sport championships and marketing promotionals. 'SI Present' issues are not available through subscriptions and are sometimes only available in very local markets. The scarcity and demand for the issue influences the value of the magazine.

DATE	COVER	FEATURES	MT	EM
1989	Vince Lombardi Jerry Kramer	"Dr Z's Great Moments in Super Bowl History"	35 +15	25
1990	Joe Montana 49ers	Super Bowl History (Test Issue)	35 +40	25
1990		35 Years of Covers 1954-1989 (Newstands Only)	25	15
1991	Eric Heiden	Golden Winter Olympic Moments' (Kelloggs Premium)	35	15
F 91		SI's 25 Unforgettable Moments	15	7
F 93		Baseball Greatest Teams (Kelloggs Premium)	25	15
1993	Gene Stalling Alabama	Alabama Championship Commerative Issue	25 +20	10
1993	Ace Atkins Auburn	Auburn Championship Commerative Issue	25 +15	10
1993	Michael Jordan Phil Jackson Bulls	Bulls NBA Champions Commemorative Issue	20 +25/+10	10
1993	Dean Smith UNC	North Carolina NCAA Champs Commerative Issue	25 +15	10
1993	Michael Irvin Cowboys	Cowboys NFL Champs Commerative Issue	15 +20	10
1994	Shaq* Magic	NBA Hot Shots Gatorade Promotional (*also Barkley, Pippen, Hardaway, Mourning)	25	15
1994	Emmitt Smith Cowboys	Cowboys NFL Champs Commerative Issue	15 +20	7
1994	N.Richardson Arkansas	Arkansas NCAA Champs Commerative Issue	25 +15	10
1994	Mike Richter Rangers	Rangers NHL Champs Commerative Issue	35 +20	15
1995	Kathy Ireland Model	'Best of the Swimsuit Models'	40 +25	20

SI PRESENTS COMMEMORATIVE ISSUES

DATE	COVER	FEATURES	MT	EM
1995	Penn State	NCAA Championship Issue	25	10
		Commerative Issue		
1995	Lawrence Phillips	NCAA Championship Issue	25	10
	Nebraska	College Football Champs		
1995	Steve Young	49ers Commemorative Issue	25	10
	49ers	NFL Champs	+30	
1995	Cal Ripken Jr.	Breaks Lou Gehrig Record	25	15
	Orioles	Commemorative Issue	+40	
1995		200 Moments to Remember	20	10
		Life Magazine Size		
		Jim Beam Promotional		
1995		NFL Classics (Ford)	20	10
		Ford Promotional		
1995	Dave Justice	World Series Issue	15	7
	Braves	Commemorative Issue	+15	
1995	Mantle Remembered (hard-cover book)		20	10
		First book in series		
1996	Tom Frazier	Nebraska Commemorative Issue	25	10
		College Football Champs		
1996	Emmitt Smith	Cowboys Commemorative Issue	15	7
		NFL Champs		
1996	Kentucky	Kentucky Commemorative Issue	15	7
		NCAA Basketball Champs		
1996	Michael Jordan	Bulls NBA Champions	15	7

95 SI PRESENTS COLLEGE FOOTBALL ANNUAL ISSUE

Cover/Team	Mt	Em	Cover/Team	Mt	Em
Lawrence Phillips	20	10	Bobby Engram	30	15
Nebraska(National)	+10		Penn State	+10	
Peyton Manning	30	15	Shawn Walters	30	15
Tennessee	+10		USC	+10	
S.Davis/Bryan Bufgdorf	30	15	J. Brown/L. McElroy	30	15
Auburn/Alabama	+10		Texas/Texas A&M	+10	
Wuerffel/Kanell/Collins	30	15	D.Huard/C. McLemore	30	15
Florida/Fl.St/Miami]	+10		Washington/Oregon	+10	
Ron Poulus	30	15	Pete Kendall	30	15
Notre Dame	+10		Boston College	+10	
Tshimanga Biakabutuka	30	15	Brice Hunter	30	15
Michigan	+10		Georgia	+10	

96 SI PRESENTS COLLEGE FOOTBALL ANNUAL ISSUE

Cover/Team	Mt	Em	Cover/Team	Mt	Em
Almon Green	10	5	Ron Polwlus	10	5
Nebraska (National)	+10		Notre Dame	+10	
Jarrett Irons	10	5	Heines Ward	10	5
Michigan	+10		Georgia	+10	
Todd Pollack	10	5	Donovan McNabb	10	5
Boston College	+10		Syracuse	+10	
Mike Vrable	10	5	Clay Etmer	10	5
Ohio State	+10		Colorado	+10	
Kevin Falk	10	5	Danny Weurffel	10	5
LSU	+10		Florida	+10	
Payton Manning	15	5	James Brown	10	5
Tennessee	+20		Texas	+10	
Dennis Riddle	10	5	Tony Graziana	10	5
Alabama	+10		Oregon	+10	
Brad Ohon	10	5	W. Dunn/Ferguson	10	5
USC	+10		Florida State	+10 each	

95 SI PRESENTS PRO FOOTBALL ANNUAL ISSUE

Cover/Team	Mt	Em	Cover/Team	Mt	Em
Troy Aikman/Steve Young	7	3	Tim Brown	15	10
Cowboys/49ers(Nat)	+40ea		Raiders	+20	
Drew Bledsoe	15	10	Bruce Smith	20	10
Patriots	+15		Bills	+20	
Brett Farve	20	10	Carry Collins	20	10
Packers	+15		Carolina	+10	
Jerome Bettis	20	10	James Stewart	20	10
Rams	+15		Jacksonville	+10	
Ricky Watters	15	10	Kevin Green	15	10
Eagles	+15		Steelers	+10	

96 SI PRESENTS PRO FOOTBALL ANNUAL ISSUE

Cover/Team	Mt	Em	Cover/Team	Mt	Em
Troy Aikman	5	2	Cordell Stewart	10	5
Cowboys (National)	+40		Steelers	+10	
Steve Young	10	5	Brian Cox	10	5
49ers	+40		Bears	+10	
Thurmon Thomas	10	5	John Elway	10	5
Bills	+10		Broncos	+25	
Derrick Thomas	10	5	Jim Harbaugh	10	5
Chiefs	+20		Colts	+10	
Dan Marino	15	5	Rodney Peete	10	5
Dolphins	+35		Eagles	+10	
Neal O'Donnell	10	5	Barry Sanders	10	5
Jets	+10		Lions	+10	
Brett Farve	15	5	Kerry Collins	10	5
Packers	+20		Panthers	+10	
Drew Bledstoe	10	5	Vinny Testaverde	10	5
Patriots	+10		Ravens	+10	

95 SI PRESENTS COLLEGE BASKETBALL ANNUAL ISSUE

COVER/Team	Area/Team	MT	EM
Tony Delak	National Issue	15	10
University of Kentucky		+10	
Keyana Garris	Illinois Aera	15	10
University of Il.		+10	
Ray Allen	Connecticut Region	15	10
University of Ct.		+10	
Marice Taylor	Michigan Area	15	10
Michigan		+10	
Marcus Comby	Massachusetts	15	10
Univ. Of Mass		+25	
Don Te Calabria	North Carolina	15	10
North Carolina		+10	
Marvin Organe	Alabama Area	15	10
Univ. of Alabama		+10	
Allen Iverson	Washington DC Area	15	10
Georgetown		+10	
Bryan Evans	Indiana Region	15	10
Indiana University		+10	
Jacque Vaughn	Kansas Region	15	10
Univ. Of Kansas		+10	

95 SI PRESENTS PRO BASKETBALL ANNUAL ISSUE

COVER/Team	(Area)/Team	MT	EM
Eric Montross	(Boston Area)	25	10
Celtics		+10	
Michael Jordan	(National Issue)	25	10
Bulls		+40	
J. Gill	(Charlotte Area)	25	15
Heat		+15	
Grant Hill	(Detroit Region)	25	15
Pistons		+25	
Hakeem Olajuwon	(Texas Area)	25	15
Rockets		+30	
Reggie Miller	(Indianapolis Area)	25	15
Pacers		+25	
Nick Van Excel	(LA Region)	25	10
Lakers		+15	
Patrick Ewing	(New York Area)	25	10
Knicks		+30	
Shaq O'Neal	(Florida Area)	25	15
Magic		+40	
Chris Webber	(Philadelphia Area)	25	15
Sixers		+20	
Damon Stoudamire	(Toronto Area)	30	15
Raptors		+10	
Byron Reeves	(Vancouver Area)	25	15
Grizzlies		+10	
Juwan Howard	(Washington D.C. Area)	25	15
Bullets		+10	

To get the National issue of the SI annual you can contact **Sports** Illustrated at 1-800-528-5000.

96 SI PRESENTS PRO BASEBALL ANNUAL ISSUE

COVER/Team	MT	EM	COVER/Team	MT	EM
Greg Maddux	10	5	Jack McDowell	10	5
Braves (National Issue)	+25		Indians	+10	
Cal Ripken Jr.	10	5	Mo Vaugh	10	5
Orioles	+40		Red Sox	+15	
Ryan Sandberg	10	5	Barry Larkin	10	5
Cubs	+20		Reds	+10	
Dante Bichette	10	5	Gary Shepfield	10	5
Rockies	+10		Marlins	+10	
Mike Piazza	10	5	Dennis Eckersley	10	5
Dodgers	+25		Blue Jays	+15	
Dave Cone	10	5	Greg Jefferies	10	5
Yankees	+15		Phillies	+15	
Ken Griffey Jr.	10	5			
Mariners	+30				

SPORTS ILLUSTRATED 1996 OLYMPIC DAILY

In 1996, Sports Illustrated became the official 1996 Atlanta games olympic magazine. Over 16 daily issues were released which captured the daily games. This was a first for a daily magazine (not a newspaper). You can order the complete set through Sports Illustrated (1-800-274-5200). Approximately 250,000 were printed.

July 19, 1996	The Olympic Torch	$ 5
July 20, 1996	The Olympic Stadium	$ 5
July 21, 1996	Toni Kukoc (Croatia) vs Lithuania #12	$ 7
July 22, 1996	Tom Dolan - US Swimmer wins Gold	$ 5
July 23, 1996	Naim Suleymanoglu - Weight Lifting	$ 5
July 24, 1996	Dominique Dawes - US Gymanist Gold!	$ 5
July 25, 1996	Australia - Equestrian Champs	$ 5
July 26, 1996	Brooke Bennett - Swimming Champion!	$ 5
July 27, 1996	Randy Barnes - Shot Putter Champion!	$ 5
July 28, 1996	Donovan Bailey - 100 Champion	$ 5
July 29, 1996	Shannon MacMillian - US Soccer	$ 5
July 30, 1996	Carl Lewis - Long Jump Champion	$ 5
July 31, 1996	Fidel Castro & Primo Nebiolo - Cuba	$ 5
Aug. 1, 1996	Lisa Leslie - US Basketball	$ 5
Aug. 2, 1996	Michael Johnson - Track	$ 5
Aug. 3, 1996	Omar Linares - Cuba Baseball	$ 5
Aug. 4, 1996	John Stockton - USA Basketball	$20
Aug. 5, 1996	Woman Basketball Players - Win Gold	$ 5

CHAPTER SIX:

SPORTS ILLUSTRATED FOR KIDS

Sports Illustrated for Kids started in 1989 and is produced every month. The issues are unique in the *Sports Illustrated* family because of the cards, ads, features and posters that are in each issue. The *SI for Kids* is the last of the magazines that continue with a card insert tradition. Many of these cards are of the current great stars (Jordan, Ripken, Ryan, for example) however, they do have older stars (Ruth) as well. Just as important, the *SI for Kids* card set is now the most diverse and well represented card set ever developed. More sports and more athletes are represented in this series than any other card set ever issued. Many of these cards are sought after by player and sport collectors. Many times the price of the magazine is driven by a highly collectable card included inside.

However, the ads, features and posters should not be neglected. Some of the most unique ads only seem to appear in the *SI for Kids* magazine (then again, I don't read every kid magazine). The features ask players questions reporters normally don't seem interested to ask about, like the game and favorite food (innocent stuff).

The magazine is geared toward kids and will have a lack of adult collecting appeal, except for those who collect players on the cover, ads, articles, and cards. Yet, it is exactly that reason why these magazines may be great sleepers in the years to come. Many of these issues are already becoming popular in the hobby because collectors of favorite players never seem to be able to find enough of their favorite player's cover (or cards).

Many *SI for Kids* issues are cut up for the cards and therefore the number of mint issues left in the market will be continually shrinking. Currently *SI for Kids* has a circulation of 1.1 million issues a month. The autograph value is more subjective since very few of the issues have been traded after they have been signed.

SI for Kids has produced their own series of extras'. A few books and magazines have appeared and are offered through *SI for Kids*. In 1995 *SI* released a special magazine called "Michael" on Michael Jordan, and a paperback called Emmitt Smith/Barry Sanders. Two magazines were released in 1996 called "Amazing Sports Photo's I" with Michael Jordan and "Amazing Sports Photo's II" with Barry Sanders. A third mailed packet focused on the Olympics called "The Kids' Guide to the 1996 Summer Olympics" with Carl Lewis, Scotty Pippen and others appearing on the cover, and two paperback books "Frank Thomas and Ken Griffey Jr" and "The Everything you want to know about Sports Encyclopedia" with Michael Jordan on the cover. There is also a list of 'SI For Kids' for Parents. This add on magazine comes with subscriptions about two to three times a year.

The Price guide is similar to *Sports Illustrated* with the exception that every card and their number is listed (*listed in italics*). The *SI for Kids* did start the numbering cards twice (1989 & 1992). They also had Olympic cards issued in 1996. Ads, articles, and posters are not listed. Since this is a recent magazine, a collectible condition magazine is in mint or exmt condition.

SPORTS ILLUSTRATED FOR KIDS

Date	Cover - Team /Cards	MT	EM	+Auto
1/89	Michael Jordan - Bulls	$40	$30	+$50
	#1-9 Howie Long, Steffi Graf, Mario Lemieux, Isaiah Thomas, Orel Hershiser, Larry Bird, Florence Griffith Joyner, Tom Curren, Doug Williams			
2/89	Wayne Gretzky - Oilers	$40	$30	+$30
	#10-18 Mark Jackson, Jose Canseco, Katrarina Witt, Dante Muse, Alberta Tomba, Joe Nieuwendyk, Michael Jordan, Herschel Walker, Jackie Joyner-Kersee			
3/89	Spud Webb -Hawks	$30	$20	+$10
	#19-27 Wayne Gretzky, Darryl Strawberry, Janet Evans, Martina Navratilova, Dominique Wilkens, Maria Walliser, Steve Yzerman, Carl Lewis, Magic Johnson			
4/89	Tony Gwynn - Padres	$35	$20	+$15
	#28-36 Sean Burke, Charles Barkley, Keba Phipps, Tony Gwynn, Camille Duvall, Mike Greenwell, Mary Decker Slaney, Frank Viola, Alex English			
5/89	Kenny Walker - Knicks	$30	$20	+$10
	# 37-45 Mike King, Louise Ritter, Don Mattingly, Kareem Abdul-Jabbar, Mario Andretti, Zina Garrison, Nancy Lopez, Akeem Olajuwon, Ozzie Smith			
6/89	Janet Evans - Swimmer	$25	$20	+$10
	#46-54 Chris Sabo, Andre Agassi, Rickey Henderson, Evelyn Ashford, Curtis Strange, Connie Young, Lyn St. James, Roger Kingdom, Andrew Dawson			
7/89	Jessee Roach - Skateboarder	$20	$10	-
	#55-63 Kirsten Hanssen, Alan Trammell, Kristin Otto, Roger Clemens, Jerry Rice, Ricky Davis, Andres Galarraga, Gabriela Sabatini, Butch Reynolds			
8/89	Little League	$35	$20	-
	#64-72 Kim Gallagher, Al Toon, John Franco, Cal Ripken Jr, Ivan Lendl, Mike McGill, Patty Sheehan, Karch Kiraly, Will Clark			
9/89	Boomer Esiason - Bengals	$20	$10	+$10
	#73-81 Frida Zamba, Inerid Kristiansen, Bo Jackson, Boomer Esiason, Patrick Ewing, Mike Singletary, Brandy Johnson, Tab Ramos, Nolan Ryan			
10/89	Hershal Walker - Vikings	$25	$15	+$15
	# 82-90 Al Macinnis, Sandra Farmer-Patrick, Dan Marino, Mike Stewart, Eric Dickerson, Said Aouita, Chris Evert, Karl Malone, Mike Schmidt			
11/89	Karl Malone - Utah Jazz	$25	$15	+$20
	#91-99 Chris Mullin, Kristi Yamaguchi, Joe Dumars, Pat LaFontaine, Greg Lemond, Reggie Roby, Ruth Lawanson, Bobby Hebert, Rbidgette Gordon			
12/89	Magic Johnson - Lakers	$30	$20	+$40
	#100-108 Tamara McKinney, Nancy Liberman-Cline, Mark Messier, Mike Rozier, John Stockton, John Elway, HugoPerez, Michael Cooper, Lynnette Love			
1/90	Buzz to the Future	$15	$10	-
	#109- 117 Christy Henrich, Randall Cunningham, Midori Ito, Jon Lugbill, James Worthy, Kevin Mitchell, Jack Sikma, Brian Leetch, Lori McNeil			
2/90	Snowboarding	$15	$10	-
	#118-126 Preki, Sandra Hodge, Denis Savard, Brad Daugherty, Paula Ivan, Ryne Sandberg, Kale Hawerchuk, Wendy Bruce, Dale Ellis			
3/90	Jackie Joyner Kersee - Track	$20	$10	+$15
	# 127-135 Robin Yount, Kent Desormeaux, Bill Laimbeer, Aranhxa, Sanchez Vicario, David Robinson, Diane Dixon, Dave Stewart, Ray Bourque, Jeannie Loneo			
4/90	Dave Stewart - A's	$15	$10	+$10
	#136-144 Cathy Hearn, Moses Malone, Vicki Huber, Charla Hartness, Eric Davis, JR Reid, Mike Scott, Grant Fuhr, Paul Caligiuri			
5/90	Ed and Tony George - kid car racers	$10	$5	+$10
	#145-153 Merlene Ottey, Mark McGwire, Reggie Miller, Rex Chapman, Boris Becker, Wendy Williams, Sheryl Johnson, Tony Hawk, Dwight Gooden,			
6/90	Paul Caligiuri - Soccer	$10	$5	+$10
	#154-162 Monica Seles, Steve Ballesteros, Rosa Mota, Tony Meola, Ken Griffey Jr., Mike Barrowman, George Brett, Michelle Gilman, Scottie Pippen			
7/90	Eric Davis - Reds	$15	$10	+$10
	#163-171 Ruben Sierra, Jennifer Azzi, Diego Maradona, Joe Montana, Kirby Puckett, Inga Thompson, Carlton Fisk, Jolanda Jones, Robby Naish			
8/90	Martina Navratilova - Tennis	$10	$5	+$15
	#172-180 John Tomac, Joetta Clark, Fred McGriff, Lynn Jennings, Wade Boggs, Michael Chang, Bobby Humphrey, Kris Karlson, Tim Raines			

SPORTS ILLUSTRATED FOR KIDS

Date	Cover - Team /Cards	MT	EM	+Auto
9/90	Dan Marino - Miami Dolphins	$25	$20	+$40
	#181-189 Shannon Higgin, Jack Nicklaus, Bobby Bonnilla, Jimmy Connors, Ronnie Lott, Sinjin Smith, Kelly Gruber, Ana Quirot, Danny Sullivan also Jackie Joyner Kersee McDonalds Cards			
10/90	Dave Robinson - San Antonio Spurs	$20	$10	+$20
	#190-198 Dennis Rodman, Tatu, Pam Shriver, Paula Newby Fraser, Bernie Kosar, Brett Hull, Bo Jackson, Dennis Eckersley, Lori Johns Michael Jordan McDonalds cards			
11/90	D'Shaun Crockett - football player kid	$10	$5	+$5
	#199-207 Kim Zmeskal, Terry Cummings, Lynettte Woodard, Kevin Johnson, Patti Sue Plumer, Barry Sanders, Randy Barnes, Willie Anderson, Cecil Fielder			
12/90	Kevin Johnson - Phoenix Suns	$20	$10	+$10
	#208-216 Billie Jean King, Jesse Owens, Wilt Chamberlain, Pele, Jackie Robinson, Babe Didrikson, Babe Ruth, Wilma Rudolph, Gordie Howe: Michael Jordan McDonalds			
1/91	Bobsledder kids Brian Shimer, Kyle Beach	$10	$5	-
	#217-225 Anita Wachter, Don Majkowski, Tom Chambers, Betty Okino, Clyde Drexler, Christopher Bowman, Lawrence Taylor, Ron Hextall, Teresa Edwards			
2/91	Charlie Barkley - Sixers	$15	$10	+$20
	#226-234 Bernie Nicholls, Lori Norwood, Ricky Pierce, Suzy Favor, Bernard King, Barry Bonds, Karl Mecklenburg, Jill Trenary, Warren Moon			
3/91	Monica Seles - Tennis	$10	$5	+$15
	#235-243 Rochelle Stevens, Christian Hosoi, Kevin McHale, Jose Rijo, Charles Smith, Chris Chelios, Jennifer Capriati, John Smith, Donna Weinbrecht			
4/91	Cecil Fielder - Tigers	$15	$10	+$15
	#244-252 Vlade Divac, Maureen Mendoza, Rolando Blackman, Beth Daniel, Sandy Alomar, Erin Baker, Joe Mullen, Ron Gant, Mike Liut			
5/91	Robert Parrish - Celtics	$15	$10	+$10
	#253-261 Kevin Duckworth, Steve Larmer, Michael Johson, Mary Joe Fernandez, Al Unser Jr, April Heinrichs, Bob Welch, Angela Cochran, Dave Justice.			
6/91	Kids of Famous Fathers	$10	$5	
	#262-270 Desmond Armstrong, Alvin Robertson, Michelle Finn, Bunki Davis, Doug Drabek, Todd Holland, Leroy Burrell, Deena Mapple, Rafael Palmeiro			
7/91	BMX Champs Gary and Rich Houseman	$10	$5	-
	#271-279 Sergei Bubka, Kim Jones, Paul Molitor, Ned Overend, Bobby Thigpen, Daedra Charles, Edgar Martinez, Summer Sanders, OJ Anderson			
8/91	Darryl Strawberry - Dodgers	$15	$10	+$5
	#280-288 Dave Winfield, Sonja Henning, Terry Schroeder, Betsy King, Thurmon Thomas, Mark Grace, Dwight Evans, Anne Marden, Mark Allen			
9/91	Nolan Ryan - Rangers	$30	$20	+$25
	#289-297 Dave Henderson, Rick Mears, Derrick Thomas, Carey Kemnex, Victor Nogueira, Lee Smith, Emmitt Smith, Shannon Miller, Jennifer Leachman			
10/91	Barry Sanders - Lions	$20	$10	+$20
	#298-306 Paul Coffey, Michelle Stahl, Art Monk, Ramon Martinez, Tim Hardaway, Sanna Neilson, Mark Carrier, Lance Ringnald, Gwen Torrence			
11/91	Chris Mullin/Manute Bol - Warriors	$20	$10	+$5 each
	#307-315 Hersey Hawkins, Gail Roberts, Chuck Person, Karolyn Kirby, Keith Jackson, Venus Lacy, Morten Andersen, Javier Gaspar, Mark Gonzales			
12/91	Reggie White - Eagles	$20	$10	+$15
	#316-324 Wyomia Tyus, Bobby Orr, Joe Louis, Ty Cobb, Jim Thorpe, Althea Gibson, Sonja Henie, Bill Russell, Red Grange			
1/92	Bo Jackson - WhiteSox/Raiders	$20	$10	+$15
	#1-9 Jim Kelly, Monica Seles, Mike Powell, Bonnie Blair, Christian Okoye, Michael Jordan, Tom Barrasso, Dee Brown, Kerri Strug			
2/92	Mogul Skiing star Donna Weinbrecht	$10	$5	+$5
	#10-18 Matti Nykanen, Eric Heiden, Mike Eruzione, Toni Sailer, Paul Hildgartner, Scott Hamilton, Dorthy Hamill, Wolfgang Hoppe, Hannie Wenzel			
3/92	Isaiah Thomas - Pistons	$20	$10	+$20
	#19-27 Pam Burridge, Brian Bellows, Dominique Wilkins, Terry Pendleton, Mark Rypien, Meg Mallon, Roswitha Raudaschl, Fernando Clavijo, Derrick Coleman			
4/92	Sandy Alomar Jr./Roberto Almor	$20	$10	+$10 each
	#28-36 Greg Barton, Kirby Puckett, Francie Larrieu Smith, Mitch Richmond, Martina Navratilova, Ed Belfour, Angela Rock, David Robinson, Roger Clemens			

SPORTS ILLUSTRATED FOR KIDS

Date	Cover - Team /Cards	MT	EM	+Auto
5/92	Michael Jordan - Bulls	$25	$20	+$40
	#37-45 Jim Courier, Pat Bradley, Robert Parish, Mark Messier, D. Mutombo, Tom Glavine, Frank Thomas, J. Eickhoff, Liz McColgan			
6/92	Cal Ripken Jr - Orioles	$25	$20	+$30
	#46-54 D. Waltrip, J. Driscoll, Shawn Kemp, N. Morceli, Jim Abbott, W. Botha, Roberto Alomar, C. Guidry, John Daly			
7/92	Janet Evans & Matt Biondi - Divers	$10	$5	+$10 each
	#55-63 Al Oerter, T. Stevenson, D. Fraser, N.Comaneci, G.Louganis, A. Bilkila, M. Spitz, F. Koen, V. Alexeyev			
8/92	Kirby Puckett - Twins	$25	$15	+$20
	#64-72 Richard Petty, Anita Nall, Matt Williams, Deion Sanders, Bobby Bonilla, Dawn Staley, Chuck Finley, Mia Hamm, Fred Couples			
9/92	Michelle Akers - Stahl - Soccer Player	$10	$5	+$5
	#73-81 Danny Tartabull, Troy Aikman, T. Larsen, B Murray, J Krone, Marcus Allen, Jack Morris, S.Edberg, K. Smyers			
10/92	Warren Moon - Oilers	$20	$10	+$10
	#82-90 K. Steffes, C. Burnsside, L. Russell, C. Jennings, Will Clark, Larry Johnson, Tom Kite, Anthony Carter, Karen Neville			
11/92	Patrick Ewing - Knicks	$20	$10	+$20
	#91-108 Patrick Roy, Michael Adams, Gao Min, Lori Endicott, Q.Watts, Haywood Jeffires, Bruce Smith, K.Yamaguchi, Detlef Schrempf			
12/92	Jerry Rice - 49ers	$25	$15	+$25
	#109-#117 Sugar Ray Robinson, R. Laver, W White, Olga Korbut, Julius Erving, R. Bannister, L. Gehrig, M. Wright, J. Brown			
1/93	Buzz Beamer - Maniac Sports	$20	$10	
	#118-126 M.Washington, E. Mataya, D. Petrovic, N. Mansell, Dan Marino, H. Boulmerka, J. Jagr, K Sprague, A. Munoz			
2/93	Clyde Drexler - Trailblazers	$25	$15	+$15
	#127-135 S. Billmeier, Steve Young, N. Kerrigan, A. Rison, Karl Malone, J. Gonzalez, M.Maleeva, M. Lemieux, Horace Grant			
3/93	Kevin Johnson, Tony Gwynn, Troy Aikman	$25	$15	Varies
	#136-#144 D. Mochrie, Pete Sampras, C. Mullin, Cal Ripken Jr., Shaquille O'Neal, D. Steirotter, Eric Lindros, K. Lende, Rod Woodson			
4/93	Ken Griffey Jr. - Seattle	$20	$10	+$20
	#145-153 Junior Seau, Maria Mutola, Jack McDowell, K. Oden, Charles Barkley, J. Furtado, Marquis, Grissom, M. Balboa, N.Diebel			
5/93	Scottie Pippen - Bulls	$20	$10	+$15
	#154-162 Spud Webb, J. Thompson, Andy Van Slyke, L. Fernandez,K Young, Andre Agassi,Wayne Gretzky, Dennis Eckersley, Tish Johnson			
6/93	Karl Malone - Jazz	$20	$10	+$15
	#163-171 Dana Chladek, Cliff Robinson, A. Mogilny, S.Scott, Steffi Graf, Barry Bonds, Greg Maddux, Matt Hoffman, Amy Alcott			
7/93	Frank Thomas -White Sox	$20	$10	+$15
	#172-180 M. Indurain, Val Whitting, B. Becker, Nolan Ryan, L. Maskayan, Patrick Ewing, Dan O'Brien, Dave Winfield, J. Cooper			
8/93	Barry Bonds - Giants	$20	$10	+$20
	#181-189 R. Erbesfield, Ken Griffey Jr., O. Markova, A. Medvedev, D. Dawes, K. Slater, S. Sharpe, Nick Faldo, Wade Boggs			
9/93	Girls in Sports	$10	$5	-
	#190-198 N. Lowery, S. Webber, R. Scarpa, T. Dees, Kirk Gibson, S. Swoopes, M. Gould, Randal Cunningham, Albert Belle			
10/93	John Elway - Broncos	$20	$10	+$15
	#199-207 C. Kennedy, Manon Rheaume, John Burkett, K. Grissom, Barry Foster, C. Laettner, John Harkes, Holli Hyche, John Kruk			
11/93	Steve Young - 49ers	$20	$10	+$15
	#208-216 J. Parisien, T. Selanne, Randy Johnson, Lou Whitaker, Brett Favre, Barbara Marois, Tony Meola, Lisa Ondieki, Clye Simmons			
12/93	Mario Lemieux - Pittsburgh	$20	$10	+$15
	#217-225 Johnny Unitas, M.Ali, Helen Wills, Oscar Robertson, Yogi Berra, Bobby Hull, K. Whitworth, Jim Ryun, K. Ender			
2/94	Oksana Baiul - Ice Skater	$10	$5	+$5
	#226 -234 Katarina Witt, Gustav Weder, Donna Wenbrecht, Cathy Turner, T. Nieminen, Tovill & Dean, A. Tomba, Bonnie Blair, V. Ulvang			

SPORTS ILLUSTRATED FOR KIDS

Date	Cover - Team /Cards	MT	EM	+Auto
3/94	Bryce Jordan - Snow Boarding	$10	$5	-
	#235-243 W. Wnia, L. Dykstra, T. Dooley, P. Simms, Breinalda, Hakeem Olajuwon, R. Twigg, Dennis Rodman, U. Robitaille			
4/94	Juan Gonzalez - Rangers	$10	$5	-
	#244-252 Mike Gartner, J. Rodriquez, Caros Baerga, Alonzo Mourning, Tim Brown, M. Jones, H. McPeak, James Briggs, John Starks			
5/94	Charles Barkley - Suns	$15	$5	+$20
	#253-261 Joe Amato, Joe Carter, L. Butler, T. Martin, K. Quance, Emmitt Smith, L. Hill, Chris Webber, Sergei Fedorov			
6/94	Cobi Jones & Alexi Lalas - Soccer	$10	$5	+$7
	#262-270 Danny Manning, Ricky Watters, Derek Ho, S. Gunnell, Chuck Carr, Cam Neely, Michael Jordan, L. Leslie, J. Croteau			
7/94	Pets Pals	$10	$5	-
	#271-279 L. French, J. Bettis, Greg Norman, L. Armstrong, Gwen Torrence, Andres Galarraga, Anfernee Hardaway, Jeff Bagwell, Janet Evans			
8/94	Deion Sanders - Reds	$10	$5	+$15
	#280-288 Brandi Hunt, John Olerud, K. Lilly, B. Kempainen, Mike Richter, Reggie White, Tony Gwynn, M. Clark, Mark Price			
9/94	Jim Abbott - Yankees	$10	$5	+$10
	#289-297 Drew Bledsoe, M. Giove, L. Davies, B. Miller, S. Bruguera, G. Jefferies, Mo Vaughn, John Taylor, L. Sprewell			
10/94	Emmitt Smith, Troy Aikman - Dallas Cowboys	$10	$5	+30 each
	#298-306 U. Pippig, Dikembe Mutombo, M. Alou, Pavel Bure, Joe Montana, C. Martinez, T. Zorn, J. Key, R. Turnbull			
11/94	Junior Seau - Chargers	$10	$5	+$10
	#307-315 D. Gilmour, BJ Armstrong, J. Golay, Amy Feng, M.Mussina, Eric Metcalf, S. Joyner, A.Marsh, Mike Piazza			
12/94	Shawn Kemp - Sonics	$10	$5	+$10
	#316-324 M. Connolly, Phil Esposito, Ann Meyers, Walter Payton, Stan Musial, Bobby Jones, S. Gould, Rafer Johnson, Bill Bradley			
1/95	Jeanie Thompson & Dominique Moceanu - Gymnasts	$10	$5	+$5
	#325-333 Matt Williams, G. Tamega, Kim Batten, H. Alfredsson, Mugsy Bougues, T. Dolan, J.Roenick, J. Foudy, Mel Gray			
2/95	Greed!!	$5	$3	-
	#334-342 Reggie Miller, B. Lancer, G. Bodine, C. Hearn, J. Vanbiesbrouck, D. Meggett, N. Price, Shaquille O'Neal, Liz Mcintyre			
3/95	Shaq - Magic	$5	$3	+$20
	#343-351 Karl Malone, Steffi Graf, Frank Thomas, Janet Evans, Mike Messier, Scottie Pippen, Dan Marino, Joyner Kersee, Michael Jordan			
4/95	Grant Hill - Pistons	$5	$3	+$20
	#352-360 Mary Price, David Robinson, R. Wegerle, Barry Sanders, Felix Potvin, T.Loroupe, H. Lindh, Kenny Lofton, Pat Smith			
5/95	Ken Griffey Jr. - Mariners	$5	$3	+$20
	#361-369 R. Lobo, R. Mondesi, Grant Hill, S. Stevens, T. Hughes, N. Means, S. Persons, J. Mashburn, M. Smith			
6/95	Mike Piazza - Dodgers	$5	$3	+$10
	#370-378 Ben Coates, Lisa Andersen, Larry Johnson, T. Roberts, Michael Jordan, L. Davenport, John Stockton, P. Kariya, Colin Jackson			
7/95	Buzz Beamer	$5	$3	-
	#379-387 David Cone, S. Bonaly, Dana Barros, M. Faulk, Gary Payton, Jim Carey, C.Teuscher, Brady Anderson, Cindy Blodgett			
	Olympic Cards #1-4: Tommy Kno, Tracy Caulkins, Jesse Owens, Ulrike Meyfarth			
8/95	Cal Ripken Jr - Orioles	$5	$3	+$25
	#388-396 Tisha Nenturini, Cosmas Ndeti, Eric Karros, Paul O'Neill, Bruce Baumgartner, Nicole Bobek, Bev Odenn, Jason Kidd, Chris Carter			
	Olympic Cards #5-8 Lis Hartel, Mark Spitz, Abebe Bikila, Mary Lou Retton			
9/95	Emmitt Smith - Cowboys	$5	$3	+$30
	#397-405 Eric Lindros, Eddie Murray, M. Moses, Barry Larkin, T. Muster, S. Slone, Picabo Street, Horace Grant, K. Greene,			
	Olympic cards #9-12 Wilma Rudolph, Matt Biondi, Vera Caslavska, Rafer Johnson			

SPORTS ILLUSTRATED FOR KIDS

Date	Cover - Team / Cards	MT	EM	+Auto
10/95	Dan Marino - Dolphins	$5	$3	+$20
	#406-414 M.Stewart, Edgar Martinez, Nikki McCray, Clyde Drexler, J. Benedict, Rodney Hampton, J Facett, M.Brodeur, Mark McGwire			
11/95	Shaq - Magic	$5	$3	+$20
	#415-423 Vin Baker, Albert Belle, Jerry Rice, P. Coffey, Shaq O'Neal, Grant Hill, V. Williams, Chris Webbe			
	Olympic Card 13-16 Babe Didrikson Zaharias, Karoly Takacs, Olga Korbut, Billy Mills			
12/95	Penny Hardaway - Magic	$5	$3	+$20
	#424-432 B. Bennett, P. Forsberg, N. Exel, J. Seau, Glen Robinson, D. Moceani, K. Bye, Steve Young, Mark Grace			
	Olympic Cards #17-20 Fanny Blankers-Koen, Dawn Fraser, Paavo Nurmi, Jeff Blatnick			
1/96	Hakeem Olajiuwon - Rockets	$5	$3	+$20
	#433-441 Peter. Bondra, Meredith Rainey, Chuck Knolauch, Trica Saunders, John Elway, John Roethlisberger, Terance Mathis, Glen Rice, Dot Richardson			
	Olympic Cards #21-24 Shun Fujimoto, Patricia McCormick, Jim Thorpe, Mary Meagher			
2/96	Gheorghe Muresan - Washington Bullets	$5	$3	+$10
	#442-450 Katrina McClain, Cammy Potter, Dominik Hasek, Chipper Jones, Alexi Lalas, Deion Sanders, Brett Favre, Alonzo Mourning, Nancy Reno			
	Olympic Cards #25-28 Nadia Comaneci, Edwin Moses, Naim Suleymanoglu, Wyomia Tyus			
3/96	Michael Jordan - Bulls	$5	$3	+$40
	#451-459 Mario Lemieux, Teresa Edwards, Tom Glavine, Mia Hamm, Cal Ripken, Jr., Barry Sanders, Troy Aikman, David Robinson, Gabriela Sabatini			
4/96	Ken Griffey Jr. - Seattle Mariners	$5	$3	+$40
	#460-468 Jeff Conine, Mahmoud Abdul-Rauf, Amy Van Dyken, Brendan Skanahan, Kristin Folk, Jonathan Edwards, Rik Smits, Kordell Stewart, Annika Sorenstam			
	Olympic Cards #29-32 Cassius Clay, Gabriela Andersen, Alice Coachman, Pablo Morales			
5/96	Shaquille O'Neal - Magic	$5	$3	+$40
	#469-477 Michelle Kawn, Hideo Nomo, Juwan Howard, Steve Yzerman, Magic Johnson, Monica Seles, Jenny Spangler, Jim Harbaugh, Bernie Williams			
	Olympic Cards #33-36 Al Oerter, Gao Min, Carl Lewis, Lyudmila Tourischeva			
6/96	Kenny Lofton - Cleveland Indians	$5	$3	+$20
	#478-486 Dale Jarrett, Jeannie Longo, Craig Biggio, Darrell Green, Dennis Rodman, Karrie Webb, Loretta Claiborne, Jose Meza, Clifford Robinson			
	Olympic Cards 37-40 Shane Gould, Teofilo Stevenson, Dan Gable, Joan Benoit			

CHAPTER SEVEN:

SPORT MAGAZINE

Sport Magazine is the oldest running continous sports magazine and is best remembered for being the greatest magazine during the Golden Era of Sports Publications. The Golden era occurs between 1946 - 1959. This is when the primary information was radio and publications. *Sport* magazine was the primary magazine that focused on major sports, used glossy covers on the cover and had color photo's inside. The combination of great sports stories and great photographs made *Sport* magazine the leader until the late 1950's when *Sports Illustrated* changed its marketing style to focus only on major sports.

Sport magazine articles, ads, photo's are some of the best during this era. The color pages are the most remembered (and most removed from magazines). These pages are still photo's taken for the magazine stories. The photograph fills the entire page and is known for being cut up and made into pin ups on walls. Many of the pages were used for autograph pieces for collectors.

Many of the articles in *Sport* magazine were written by the leading sports writers of that era. The features range from the greatest athletes to unknown rookies. It is important to note that the golden era and silver era (1960's) had many classic feature articles as well. The Corvette giveaway and the College girl section were classics of an innocent era long gone.

The ads in *Sport* magazine feature many sports celebreties in color pushing every product under the sun. If you are a collector of a particular player, pay attention to the ads mentioned. Ads range from underwear to cars. Ads are in paranthesis (). Color ads are underlined.

Finally, the covers are just photo pic awsome. Some of the best, if not the best, covers were found during the golden era on *Sport* Magazine. These pictures are remembered by every elder sports fan that has ever read *Sport* magazine. The 1960's brought us Television and the faster pace of gathering information. This lead to changes in the marketing of sports information and *Sports Illustrated* took the powerful lead in providing information quickly. This force *Sport* magazine to change its style to appeal to a broader audience. The marketing of *Sport* magazine in recent years has shifted to key proven superstars, key events, preseason issues and swimsuits. Marketing efforts have shown multiple covers (store verse mail) and (east verse west) versions.

The *Sport* magazine price guide section is similar to *Sports Illustrated* with the Date, Cover, Articles and prices. However, the price guide underlines key color pictures and ads that are featured in the magazine. That is because so many collectors ask about the color photographs when they are collecting *Sport* magazine.

The prices for *Sport* magazine have an extreme wide range based on condition. The magazine is so easily damaged that it is rather rare to find the 'popular' *Sport* magazines in top condition. The NM means near mint to mint condition magazines. The EM means excellent to mint and this usually means there is some flaw in the

magazine. Most quality *Sport* magazines have a flaw in the spin and/or
the cover and usually fall in this collectable condition However,
most *Sport* magazines that exist are usually in excellent condition or
very good condition. Excellent condition means that it has at least
one serious flaw (spin is splitting over an inch or a creased corner).
Very good condition magazines have two serious flaws. Either magazine
is not used at all for autographing but mostly for research and
content. The value for Ex grade *Sport* Magazines is 50% of the EM
price. VG is 25% of the EM price.

The autograph value of *Sport* magazine is less than *Sport Illustrated*
or *Time* but it is collected at times for players who do not appear on
any other magazine. Autographed magazine of deceased players still
can command a premium when found in quality condition.

SPORT

DATE	COVER/Team	MAJOR FEATURE STORIES (Ads)	Value Guide NM	EM	AUTO
09/46	Joe Dimaggio &Son	Joe Dimaggio, Joe Lewis, Bob Feller, Mel Ott/John McGraw, Ben Hogan.	700	450	+200
10/46	Glenn Davis /Doc Blanchard Army	Stan Musial, Joe Cronin, Bob Waterfield, Bobby Doer Doc Blanchard, Hal Newhouser, Eddie Arcaro	200	100	+ 10 each
11/46	Johnny Lujack Frank Leahy* Notre Dame	Charley Trippi, Bobby Riggs, Babe Didrikson (*also Wedemeyer-St Mary's, Bechtol-Texas, Davis-Army, Trippi-Georgia)	150	75	+ 20 each
12/46	Tom Harmon Rams	Harry Gilmer, Green Bay Packers, Tom Harmon, Ace Parker, Jack Kramer	150	75	+ 50 (d)
01/47	Andy Phillips Illinois	Jackie Robinson, Babe Ruth, Bill Veeck Frank Brimsek	60	40	+ 20
02/47	Doug/Max Bentley Blackhawks	Ted Williams, Jack Dempsey, Bentley Brothers, Bucky Harris	50	30	+ 25 each
03/47	Alex Groza Kentucky	Joe Dimaggio, Maurice Richard/Toe Blake 1927 Yankees	50	30	+ 50 (d)
04/47	Leo Durocher* Dodgers	Happy Chandler, Leo Durocher, Howie Pollet, Walter Johnson History, National League (*also Bob Feller, Stan Musial, Howie Pollet, Ted Williams)	63	36	+ 50 (d)
05/47	Horse Racing	Reese/Reiser, Bonnie Baker, American League History, Johnny Pesky	40	20	
06/47	Bob Feller Indians	Hank Greenberg, Bob Feller, Ben Hogan, Enos Slaughter, Charley Keller, Dixie Walker	70	40	+ 20
07/47	Joe Cronin /Ed Dyer Cardinals/Red Sox	Joe Cronin, Eddie Dyer, Lou Boudreau Graziano/Zale, Larry McPhail	40	24	+100(d) each
08/47	Ted Williams Red Sox	Pittsburgh Pirates, Clint Hartung, Tommy Henrich Bill Nicholson, Ted Williams	150	75	+100
09/47	Joe Dimaggio Dom Dimaggio Red Sox/Yankees	Joe Dimaggio, Knute Rockne, Jackie Robinson, John Mize, Billy Southworth	150	75	+100/20
10/47	Harry Gilmer Alabama	Leo Durocher, Lujack, Leahy & Notre Dame, World Series Thrills Johnny Jorgensen, Charley Justice, Harry Brecheen, Sugar Ray Robinson, George McQuinn, Babe Didrikson (Rita Hayworth)	42	24	+ 20
11/47	Johnny Lujack Notre Dame	Jersey Joe Walcott, Branch Rickey, Notre Dame/Army	40	24	+ 25
12/47	Charley Trippi Cards	Joe Louis, Chicago Sports Teams, George Weiss, Red Grange	35	20	+ 25
01/48	Ralph Beard* Kentucky	Joe Dimaggio, Bill Klem, Rocky Graziano, Joe McCarthy Bobby Layne (Gary Cooper - Chesterfield) (*also Arnold Ferrin - Utah)	35	20	+ 20
02/48	Frank Brimsek Bruins	Maurice Richard, Walter Hagen, Primo Carnera	35	20	+ 15
03/48	George Kaftan Holy Cross	Joe Louis, Connie Mack, Ralph Kiner, Syl Apps, Red Barber	35	20	+ 20

SPORT

DATE	COVER/Team	MAJOR FEATURE STORIES (Ads)	NM	EM	AUTO
04/48	Ted Williams Red Sox	Leo Durocher, Ted Williams, Ewell Blackwell, Howie Morenz, Stanley Ketchel	88	50	+100
05/48	Babe Ruth* Yankees	Bob Elliott, Dizzy Dean, Joe Page/Hugh Casey (*also Johnny Mize, Ralph Kiner, Ted Williams)	112	60	
06/48	Joe Louis Boxing	Bob Feller, Mel Ott, Joe Louis, George Kell, Babe Didrikson, Luke Appling, Vern Stephens	56	36	+300(d)
07/48	Ewell Blackwell Reds	Baseball HOF, Lou Boudreau, Charley Grimm, Art Houtteman, Carl Hubbell/'34 All Star game, Harry Walker	42	24	+ 20
08/48	Stan Musial Cardinals	Stan Musial, Hal Newhouser, Eddie Stanky, Eddie Joost, (Gregory Peck -Beer, William Bendix 'Babe Ruth Story')	88	50	+ 20
09/48	Ted Williams/ Joe Dimaggio Red Sox/Yankees	Babe Ruth, Bill Veeck, Walker Cooper, Hank Greenberg, Sammy Baugh, Richie Ashburn, (Indian Motorcycle)	300	150	+100/80
10/48	Lou Gehrig Yankees	Dom Dimaggio, Lou Gehrig, Joe Gordon, Jackie Robinson Marty Marton, Frank Leahy, World Series (Jane Wyman - Chesterfield)	112	64	
11/48	Doak Walker SMU	Turk Broda, Alvin Dark, Ty Cobb, Doak Walker	49	25	+ 25
12/48	Johnny Lujack Bears Blackhawks	Branch Rickey, George Halas, Satchel Paige, Casey Stengel (Bob Hope - Beer)	42	25	+ 25
01/49	Ed Macauley* St Louis	Lou Boudreau, John McGraw, Ed Macauley, Johnny Sain, Jim Conacher, George Mikan (Harley Davidson) (*also Jim Conacher-Redwings, Lou Boudreau, , Rod Franz)	35	20	+ 20
02/49	Lou Boudreau* Indians	Clark Griffith, The Celtics, Max Bentley, Gene Bearden (*also Jim McIntyre, Sandy Saddler, Buddy O'Connor)	42	20	+ 20
03/49	Ralph Beard* Kentucky	Joe Louis, Stan Musial, Ralph Beard, Larry Dolby, Ted Lindsay (*also Larry Doby-Indians, Ted Atkinson-Jockey, Ted Lindsay-Redwings)	35	20	+ 20
04/49	Bob Feller* Indians	Happy Chandler, Ewell Blackwell, Bob Feller, Babe Herman, Pete Reiser, Jim Thorpe (*Also Bob Mathias-track, John Palmer-Golf, Victor Seixas-Tennis)	70	40	+ 20
05/49	Enos Slaughter* Cardinals	Ted Williams, Willie Pep, Pee Wee Reese, Veeck/Boudreau, Dempsey/Tunney, Eddie Arcaro, Sam Snead, Enos Slaughter (NY Yankees -Jock Strap, Joe Dimaggio- Vitallas) (Also Beverly Baker-Tennis, Jimmy Demaret-Golf, Eddie Arcaro-Jockey)	49	25	+ 20
06/49	Hal Newhouser* Tigers	Joe McCarthy, Honus Wagner, Hal Newhouser, Joe Louis, Tinker/Evers/Chance, Birdie Tebbetts (Bob Hope - Chesterfield) (Also Birdie Tebbits-Redsox, Joe Louis-Boxing, Don Gehrmann-Track)	42	24	+ 20
07/49	Lou Boudreau Joe Gordon Indians	Joe Gordon, Bill Dickey, Phil Marchildon, Ralph Kiner, Rogers Hornsby & Joe Gordon	42	24	+ 20
08/49	Jackie Robinson Dodgers	Vern Stephens & Bobby Jones, Babe Ruth, Rocky Graziano, Jackie Robinson, Yogi Berra	88	50	+200 (d)
09/49	Joe Dimaggio Yankees	Ben Hogan, Joe DiMaggio & Mickey Walker, Dale Mitchell , George Stallings, Mel Parnell, Red Schoendienst	140	70	+100
10/49	Christy Mathewson NY Giants	Shoeless Joe Jackson, Christy Mathewson & Tommy Henrich, Billy Goodman	56	30	-
11/49	Charlie Justice North Carolina	Bob Dillinger, Frank Leahy & Francis Ouimet, Charlie Justice, Dempsey/Rickard, Bill Durnan, Eddie LeBaron	35	20	+ 20
12/49	Johnny Lujack/ Sid Luckman Bears	Maurice McDermott, Jim Thorpe & Sid Luckman, Roland LaStarza	42	24	+ 20 each
01/50	Don Lofgran /Rene Herrerias USF	Phil Rizzuto, Walter Johnson & Bing Crosby, Lofgren/Herrerias Roy Conacher (Bing Crosby - Chesterfield)	30	12	+ 15 each
02/50	Tommy Henrich Yankees	Tommy Henrich, Jake LaMotta & Eddie Shore, Preacher Roe	40	24	+ 15
03/50	George Mikan Lakers	Kenny Reardon, Joe Page & John L. Sullivan, Joe Louis, George Mikan, Bill Veeck	40	20	+ 20
04/50	Casey Stengel Yankees	Leo Durocher, Casey Stengel & Grover Alexander, Eddie Waitkus, Sam Snead, Bill Veeck, Sid Abel, Andy Pafko(Kirk Douglas - Chesterfield)	40	20	+100 (d)
05/50	Ralph Kiner Pirates	Gene Tunney & Dom Dimaggio, Ralph Kiner, Virgil Trucks, Bobby Thomson, Glenn Davis, Bill Veeck	40	20	+ 10

SPORT

DATE	COVER/Team	MAJOR FEATURE STORIES (Ads)	NM	EM	AUTO
06/50	Bob Lemon Indians	Ted Williams, Bob Lemon & Kenesaw M. Landis, Ezzard Charles Whiz Kids, Connie Mack, Charley Faust, Carl Furillo	40	20	+ 10
07/50	Stan Musial Cardinals	Happy Chandler, Jerry Priddy, Stan Musial, Luke Easter, Warren Spahn, Earl Sande & Sugar Ray Robinson	75	45	+ 20
08/50	Art Houtteman Tigers	Art Houtteman, Max Baer & Joe McCarthy, Roy Campanella, Willie Jones	33	20	+ 10
09/50	Don Newcombe Dodgers	Don Newcombe, Baseball Club History series Chicago Cubs, Ben Hogan, Vic Wertz, Walt Dropo, Allie Reynolds	40	24	+ 10
10/50	World Series Painting	Brooklyn Dodgers, Bob Williams, Hoot Evers, Bronko Nagurski Chico Carrasquel, Dick Sisler	33	20	
11/50	Harry Aganis Boston Col.	Detroit Tigers, Earl Blaik, Joe Dimaggio, Harry Agganis, Ruth/Wagner/Cobb	33	20	+250 (d)
12/50	Football Painting	Boston Red Sox, Red Grange, Ted Kluszewski	30	15	-
01/51	Basketball painting	St. Louis Cardinals, Ezzard Charles, '50 Phillies, Jerry Coleman,	25	15	-
02/51	Nat Holman Basketball	Philadelphia Athletics, Bill Tilden, Ted Williams, Jake Lamotta, Sugar Ray Robinson, Branch Rickey	25	15	+ 50 (d)
03/51	George Mikan Lakers*	Boston Braves, Hank Greenberg, Eddie Stanky (*the cover is art with other athletes)	25	15	+ 20
04/51	Baseball Art	Lee Durocher, St. Louis Browns, Andy Seminick ("Follow The Sun"-Ben Hogan)	33	20	-
05/51	Joe Dimaggio Stan Musial*	Reds, 1927 Yankees, Jim Konstanty, Ty Cobb, Rabbitt Maranville (Ben Hogan) Baseball Jubilee issue (*the cover is art with many deceased HOF, Ruth etc)	50	30	+90/+20
06/51	Sugar Ray Robinson Boxing	Chicago White Sox, Pee Wee Reese, Sugar Ray Robinson Early Wynn, Sam Jethroe, Mickey Mantle	40	24	+150 (d)
07/51	Ewell Blackwell Reds	Ewell Blackwell, New York Giants, Chico Carrasquel, Duke Snider, Lou Boudreau, Basketball Fix (Harly Davidson)	25	15	+ 15
08/51	Yogi Berra Yankees	Philadelphia Phillies, Ezzard Charles, Larry Jansen, Bob Feller, Ferris Fain, Kid Gavilan, Bob Mathias, (Ted Williams Car Wax)	50	30	+ 20
09/51	Ted Williams Red Sox	New York Yankees, Otto Graham, Richie Ashburn, Enos Slaughter Gil Hodges, Eddie Robinson, Ted Williams, Sal Maglie	75	45	+100
10/51	Jackie Robinson Dodgers	Pittsburgh Pirates, Jackie Robinson, Wally Westlake, Vic Raschi, Bobby Doerr, Joe Walcott, Doak Walker, Bob Feller, Luis Firpo, Rocky Marciano (Marlyn Monroe)	75	45	+250 (d)
11/51	Bill McColl Stanford	Bob Waterfield, Cleveland Indians, Willie Mays, Charley Gehringer, Nelson Fox	25	15	+ 10
12/51	Johnny Lujack Bears	Johnny Lujack, Washington Senators, Gordie Howe, Mike Garcia, Mickey Mantle, Maureen Connolly	30	12	+ 20
01/52	No Issue Published				
02/52	Sugar Ray Robinson Boxing	Minnie Minoso, Maurice Richard, Jim Corbett, Larry Doby Leo Durocher, Joe Dimaggio, Ted Williams	30	15	+250 (d)
03/52	Gil McDougald Yankees	Rocky Marciano, Gil McDougald, Dick Groat, Willie Shoemaker, Art Houtteman, Roy Campanella, Roger Hornsby, Rocky Graziano, Jimmie Foxx, Babe Ruth ((Liz Taylor Pin up ad)	30	15	+ 15
04/52	Chico Carrasquel Reds	Terry Sawchuk, Bobby Thomson, Gus Zernial, Chicago White Sox Ellis Kinder, Marty Marion, (Joe Dimaggio -Spalding)	25	15	+ 20
05/52	Alvin Dark Giants	Eddie Stanky, Earl Torgeson, Al Rosen, Ralph Branca, Murry Dickson, Alvin Dark ("The Story of Dizy Dean" Pride of St Louis)	25	15	+ 10
06/52	Ralph Kiner Pirates	Ralph Kiner, Johnny Pesky, Robin Roberts, Hal Newhouser, Jim Rivera, Billy Cox, Dizzy Dean, Eddie Lopat, Ben Hogan	33	20	+ 10
07/52	Stan Musial Cardinals	Tris Speaker, Bobby Shantz, Ted Williams, Sugar Ray Robinson Stan Musial, Whitey Ford, Jeck Dempsey, Chuck Connors	65	40	+ 20
08/52	Allie Reynolds Yogi Berra Yankees	Allie Reynolds, Red Schoendienst, Del Ennis, Leo Durocher, Bob Feller, Jim Piersall, Marty Marion	30	12	+ 50 (d) + 15
09/52	Mike Garcia Indians	Sal Maglie, Gran Hamner, Andy Pafko, Tommy Byrne, Ewell Blackwell, Augie Donatelli, Football Club history- L.A. Rams, Dixie Walker, Ballpark series- Fenway Park (Otto Graham -Batteries)	25	15	+ 15

138

SPORT

DATE	COVER/Team	MAJOR FEATURE STORIES (Ads)	NM	EM	AUTO
10/52	Jackie Robinson/ Pee Wee Reese Dodgers	Curt Simmons, Jim Hegan, George Kell, Gerry Staley, Monte Irvin, Charlie Dren, Joe Walcott, Hank Sauer, Billy Martin, Chicago Bears	100	60	+250 (d) + 40
11/52	J. Robinson* Dodgers	Archie Moore, Doak Walker, Joe DiMaggio, Satchel Paige, Whitney Lockman, Cleveland Browns, Henry Armstrong (*also Allie Reynolds, Harry Agganis, Doak Walker)	33	20	Varies
12/52	Johnny Olszewski Cal Bears	Harry Agganis, Jackie Jensen, Johnny Olszewski, Green Bay Packers, Bill Veeck, Russ Myer	25	15	+ 20
01/53	Rocky Marciano Boxing	Rocky Marciano, Joe Black, Johnny Mize, Clint Courtney, S.F. 49ers, Boom Boom Geoffrion	40	25	+400(d)
02/53	Bobby Shantz A'S	Jimmie Dykes, Gene Woodling, Milt Schmidt, Jackie Robinson, Florence Chadwick	30	15	+ 20
03/53	Bob Cousy Celtics	Frank Frisch, Red Kelley, Frank Shea, Bob Cousy, Duke Snider, Ralph Kiner, Ten Greatest Fights, Stanley Ketchel, Bob Pettit	30	15	+ 25
04/53	Mickey Mantle Yankees	Mickey Mantle, Larry Doby, Branch Rickey, Ford Frick, Roger Hornsby	150	90	+200 (d)
05/53	Bob Lemon Indians	Roy McMillan, Bob Lemon, Carl Hubbell, Ewell Blackwell, Jim Piersall, (Phil Rizzuto - Spalding)	25	15	+ 15
06/53	Hank Sauer Cubs	Hank Sauer, Luke Easter, Bucky Harris, Bill Veeck, Bobby Thomson, Pepper Martin, Billy Loes, (Joe Dimaggio-Reach, Mantle-Camels)	25	15	+ 10
07/53	Ferris Fain White Sox	Gil Hodges, Sid Gordon, Ferris Fain, Charley Gehringer, Ted Williams, Solly Hemus, Vic Wertz	25	15	+ 10
08/53	Warren Spahn Braves	Warren Spahn, Ted Klu, Walt Dropo, Jim Braddock, Ezzard Charles, Ed Yost, Don Zimmer (George Mikan -Sports Star Shoes)	33	20	+ 20
09/53	Robin Roberts Phillies	Kid Gavilan, Bobby Avila, Ed Mathews, Johnny Mize, Robin Roberts, Babe Didrikson, Detroit Lions, (Bobby Layne - Batteries)	33	20	+ 15
10/53	Roy Campanella Dodgers	Charlie Grimm, Whitey Ford, Billy Pierce, Rocky Marciano, Roy Campanella, Gus Bell, Mickey Vernon, Pittsburgh Steelers, Peanuts Lowery	50	30	+150 (d)
11/53	Phil Rizzuto/ Johnny Lattner Yankees/Notre Dame	Willie Pep, Enos Slaughter, Knute Rockne, Phil Rizzuto, Carl Furillo, Washington Redskins, Three-Finger Brown	33	20	+ 30 each
12/53	Michigan State Football Issue	Ben Hogan, Norm Van Brocklin, Elmer Lach, Michigan State Football, Benny Leonard, Ralph Kiner, Philadelphia Eagles, Virgil Trucks	20	12	Varies
01/54	Eddie Le Baron Redskins	Eddie Le Baron, Mickey Mantle, Ted Williams, N.Y. Giants	20	12	+ 10
02/54	Ed Mathews Braves	1953 N.Y. Yankees, Danny O'Connell, Bob Porterfield, Charlie Dressen, Robin Roberts, Jean Beliveau	40	24	+ 15
03/54	Casey Stengel Yankees	Harlem Globetrotters, Jim Piersall, Willie Shoemaker, George Mikan, Walter Alston, Harvey Kuenn (Goose Tatum - Globetrotters)	33	20	+100 (d)
04/54	Don Newcombe Dodgers	Jesse Owens, Lew Burdette, Al Rosen, Ted Williams, Don Newcombe, Eddie Stanky, Floyd Patterson, Joe McGinnity (Yogi Berra - Spalding)	30	12	+ 15
05/54	Ted Kluszewski Reds	Mel Parnell, Harvey Haddix, Billy Martin, Joe Black, Bill Terry, Bobby Bragan, Germany Schafer (Milky Way Candy Bar Phil Rizzuto-Spalding)	30	12	+ 50 (d)
06/54	Rocky Marciano Boxing	Andy Pafko, Carl Erskine, Chico Carrasquel, Terry Brennan, Rocky Marciano, Branch Rickey, Bill Dickey (Ted Kluzenski - MacGregor)	33	20	+400 (d)
07/54	Stan Musial Cardinals	Eddie Matthews, Rocky Marciano, Casey Stengel, Ray Boone, Stan Musial	60	36	+ 20
08/54	Minnie Minoso White Sox	Ted Williams, Leo Durocher, Jim Busby, Vic Raschi, Minnie Minoso (John Wayne - Camels)	30	12	+ 15
09/54	Duke Snider Dodgers	Birdie Tebbetts, Bob Turley, Bear Bryant, Sal Maglie, Bobo Olson, George Strickland, Vic Power, Rudy York	50	30	+ 20
10/54	Al Rosen Indians	Babe Ruth, Willie Mays, Al Rosen, Mickey McDermott	30	12	+ 15
11/54	Larry Morris* Georgia Tech	Bronko Nagurski, Stan Musial, Art Houtteman, Josh Gibson (*also Stan Musial, Crazy Legs Hirsch, Roy Campanella)	20	12	+ 15
12/54	Pete Vann Army	Paul Brown, Charlie Justice, Phil Rizzuto, Pete Vann, Baltimore Colts	20	12	+ 15
01/55	Pete Philos* Eagles	Henry Armstrong, Pete Philos, Wally Moon, Lester Patrick, Chicago Cardinals (George Mikan - Keds, Corvette) (*also Don Schlundt-Basketball, Cisco Andrade, Art Houtteman)	16	10	+ 15

SPORT

DATE	COVER/Team	MAJOR FEATURE STORIES (Ads)	NM	EM	AUTO
02/55	Alvin Dark Giants	Alvin Dark, Eddie Stankey, Jackie Jensen, (Coke, Rock Hudson - Camel) (*Also Nino Valdes Boxing, Bob McKeen Cal bears, Terry Sawchuk -Redwings)	20	12	+ 10
03/55	Rocky Marciano Boxing	Bob Cousy, Leo Durocher, Frank Thomas, Vic Wertz, Wilt Chamberlain	25	15	+400 (d)
04/55	Bob Turley Yankees	Montreal Canadiens, Dusty Rhodes, Floyd Patterson, Ralph Kiner, Gene Conley, Bob Turley, (Wilson Gloves) (*also Joe Norris-Bowling, Ralph Kiner-Indian, Maurice Richard-Hockey)	20	12	+ 15
05/55	Bobby Thomson Braves	Bobby Thomson, Walter Alston, Jack Harshman, Ray Jablonski, Carmen Basilio	20	12	+ 15
06/55	Johnny Antonelli Giants	Johnny Antonelli, Ed Mathews, Yogi Berra, Joe Louis Schoendiest/Musial, Hal Smith, (Ted Kluszenski - MacGrego)r	20	12	+ 15
07/55	Ned Garver Orioles	Pepper Martin, Minnie Minoso, Ned Garver, Pee Wee Reese, Fred Hutchinson (Musial - Rawlings)	16	10	+ 10
08/55	Paul Richards	Paul Richards, Rogers Hornsby, Herb Score, Joe Adcock Don Mueller, Don Newcombe, Al Kaline, Sammy White	20	12	+ 10
09/55	Duke Snider Dodgers	Duke Snider, Jim Hegan, Nellie Fox, Roger Hornsby Curt Simmons, Hank Bauer	60	35	+ 20
10/55	Yogi Berra Yankees	Archie Moore, Jackie Robinson, Jim Rivera, Jim Finigan, Pete Reiser, Yogi Berra (Corvette)	40	24	+ 15
11/55	Eddie Erdelatz* Navy	Eddie Erdaletz, Carmen Basilio, Johnny Podres, Lefty O'Doul,(*also Johnny Podres, Carmen, Basilio, Whitey Rouviere)	16	10	+ 10
12/55	Hugh McElhenny 49ers	Glenn Davis/Doc Blanchard, Robin Roberts, The Heavyweight Champs, Hugh McElhenny, Mickey Cochrane	20	12	+ 10
01/56	Doak Walker Lions	Rocky Graziano, Doak Walker, Tommy Byrne, Willie Mosconi	16	10	+ 15
02/56	Sihugo Green* Basketball	Howie Morenz, Dick Donovan, Mickey Mantle, '55 Dodgers (Coke, Rock Hudson)(*also Mickey Mantle, Marcino, Boffoon)	16	10	+ 10
03/56	Walter Alston Dodgers	Early Wynn, Floyd Patterson, Frank Lane, Maurice Stokes	20	12	+150 (d)
04/56	Larry Doby White Sox	Larry Doby, Wally Post, Jean Beliveau, Larry MacPhall (Chevy 56', Robin Roberts - MacGregor, Harlem Globetrotters)	20	12	+ 15
05/56	Bob Lemon Indians	Marty Marion, Bob Lemon, Del Ennis, Sugar Ray Robinson Larry MacPhail, Horace Stoneham, Bob Friend (Rock Hudson - Camels)	20	12	+ 15
06/56	Willie Mays Giants	Willie Mays, Johnny Logan, Bill Hoeft, Mickey Vernon Willie Pep (Ted Williams - Wilson)	50	30	+ 30
07/56	Ted Williams Red Sox	Ted Kluszewski, Ted Williams, Ernie Banks, Ray Boone	60	36	+100
08/56	Vinegar Minell Cardinals	Robin Roberts, Bob Feller, Vinegar Bend Mizell, Vic Power Ford Frick, Archie Moore (Al Kaline - Wilson)	16	10	+ 15
09/56	10th Anniversary Issue	Joe DiMaggio, Curt Simmons, Gus Bell, Al Smith, Top Performer of the Decade	33	20	-
10/56	Mickey Mantle Yankees	'56 Brooklyn Dodgers, Mantle/Martin, Floyd Patterson, Hank Aaron (500 photo's, Van Broklin - Spalding, Corvette)	100	60	+150(d)
11/56	Paul Hornung Notre Dame	Bud Wilkinson, Jackie Robinson, Paul Hornung, Whitey Ford (George Mikan - Keds, Ted Williams, Wilson, 56 Chevy, Yogi Berra NSC, Howard Cassady -Wilson)	16	10	+ 20
12/56	Bobby Morrow Track	Rocky Marciano, Casey Stengel	16	10	+ 10
01/57	Wilt Chamberlain Kansas	Alan Ameche, Don Larsen, Bobo Olson, Ted Williams, Doug Harvey, Frank Lane, Harvey Kuenn	25	15	+ 75
02/57	Jacques Plante* Canadiens	'56 Cincinnati Reds, Sal Maglie, Al Rosen, Hockey's Goalie's (Herb Score - Wilson, 57 Pontiac) (*also Sal Maglie, Art Aragon, Jack George)	20	12	+ 15
03/57	Mickey Mantle Yankees	Gene Conley, Don Newcombe, Detroit Red Wings, Al Lopez, Dale Long	85	50	+150 (d)
04/57	Ed Mathews Braves	Don Larson, Bob Pettit, Gene Fullmer, Tony Galento,(Corvette)	25	15	+ 15
05/57	Robin Roberts/ Roy Campanella/ Warren Spahn/ Ted Kluzewski/ Phillies/Reds/Dodgers/Braves	Lou Boudreau, Floyd Patterson, Hank Greenberg	25	15	Varies
06/57	Early Wynn Indians	Pee Wee Reese, Leo Durocher, Gil McDongald, Early Wynn (Corvette, Ted Williams -Wislon, Musial - Rawling)	25	15	+ 10

Value Guide

SPORT

DATE	COVER/Team	MAJOR FEATURE STORIES (Ads)	NM	EM	AUTO
				Value Guide	
07/57	Al Kaline Tigers	Walter O'Malley, Ralph Kiner, Vic Raschi, Sam Jones (Ford 57, Spalding)	40	25	+ 15
08/57	Joe Adcock Braves	Mickey Mantle, Joe Adcock, Score/Colavito, Willie Mays, Roberto Clemente, Joe Garagiola (Corvette)	25	15	+ 10
09/57	Duke Snider Dodgers	Fred Haney, Duke Snider, Sugar Ray Robinson, Ed Bailey, Sherm Lollar, Joe DiMaggio (Ford 57)	50	30	+ 20
10/57	Billy Pierce White Sox	Carmen Basilio, Mantle/Ford/Martin, Frank Robinson, Gil Hodges, Billy Pierce (John Wayne - Movie)	20	12	+ 10
11/57	Don Stephenson* Georgia Tech	Berra/Newcombe, Floyd Patterson, Jackie Robinson, Ted Lindsay (Bob Pettitt-Rawlings; Frank Gifford - Wilson) (*also includes Yogi Berra and Don Newcombe)	16	10	+ 10
12/57	Chicago Bears	Chicago Bears, Mickey Mantle/Willie Mays, Henri Richard) (Herb Score-Wilson, Pontiac)	16	10	Varies
01/58	Snider/Reese/ Robinson/Mays/* Durocher/ Dodgers/Giants	Lew Burdette, Ted Williams, Norm Van Brocklin Don Hoak, Chuck Stobbs , Sugar Ray Robinson Giants/Dodgers Feud (Geroge Mikan - Keds, Chevy 57) (*also Johnny Antonelli)	25	15	Varies
02/58	Carmen Basilio Boxing	Stan Musial, Carmen Basilio, Terry Sawchuk, Robin Roberts, Ted Klu	20	12	+ 15
03/58	Lew Burdette Braves	Lew Burdette, Cousy/Sharman/Russell & Co., Wilt Chamberlain, Hockey's All-Time All-Star Team (Lew Burdette - Rawlings, Corvette)	20	12	+ 10
04/58	Nellie Fox White Sox	Nellie Fox, Don Drysdale, Rocky Marciano, Harvey Kuenn) Dick Groat - Shoes, Ted Williams - Wilson, Stan Musial - Rawlings)	40	24	+150 (d)
05/58	Yogi Berra Yankees	Larry Doby, Wes Covington, Duke Snider, Joe Louis, Don Blasingame, Bear Bryant	30	12	+ 20
06/58	Willie Mays Giants	Warren Spahn, Ted Williams, Billy Loes, S.F. Giants (Nellie Fox - Wilson)	33	20	+ 30
07/58	Herb Score* Indians	Herb Score, Chicago White Sox, Alvin Dark, Ken Venturi (Al Dark - Wilson) (*also Hot Rod Rodriquez, Duke Snider, Ken Venturi)	20	12	+ 10
08/58	Billy Martin Tigers	Ted Klu, Enos Slaughter, Gene Littler, Frank Leahy, Minnie Minoso, Eddie Arcaro	20	12	+ 75
09/58	Ed Mathews Braves	Sports Hall of Fame series begins: Ed Mathews, Lou Gehrig, Roy Campanella, Jackie Jensen, Arnold Palmer	25	15	+ 15
10/58	Bob Turley* Yankees	Sam Snead, Jim Thorpe, Bob Turley, Hank Aaron, Orlando Cepeda, Bill Mazeroski (Corvette) (* also Mel Allen, Hank Aaron, Sam Snead)	16	10	+ 10
11/58	Bob Anderson Army	Lou Groza, Ty Cobb, Bob Anderson, World Series Heroes (Bob Pettit - Rawlings)	16	10	+ 10
12/58	John Unitas* Colts	Whitey Ford, S.F. Giants, Red Grange, Ernie Banks, John Unitas (Mantle - Rawlings) (* Willie Mays, Bob Pettit, Tom Bolt)	20	12	+ 20
01/59	Maurice Richard	Bill Sharman, Richie Ashburn, Jack Dempsey, Maurice Richard Jack Twyman, Tony Kubeck	25	15	+ 15
02/59	Rafer Johnson Track	Lew Burdette, Eddie Shore, '59 Yankees, Maurice Stokes, Bob Cerv	20	12	+ 25
03/59	Al Kaline* Tigers	Adolph Rupp, L.A. Dodgers, Al Kaline, Sugar Ray Robinson, George Mikan, Andy Bathgate, Oscar Robertson (* also Oscar Robertson, Ron Delany, Floyd Patterson)	33	20	+ 15
04/59	Rocky Colavito Indians	Rocky Colavito, Bob Skinner, Elgin Baylor, Elston Howard, Ed Litzenberger, Solly Hemus, Wilt Chamberlain, Elston Howard (Harvey Kuenn-Wilson, Bill Mazeroski, Mays, Aaron, F. Robinson, -MacGregor, Johnny Unitas - Corvette)	40	24	+ 25
05/59	Hank Bauer/* Gil Hodges Yankees/Dodgers	Willie Mays, Archie Moore, Gil Hodges, Roger Hornsby, Billy O'Dell (Corvette, Hodges, Mays, Bauer-Bats, Nellie Fox - Wilson, Mickey Mantle -Rawlings), (*Also Terry Brennan-ND)	20	12	+ 10/ +100 (d)
06/59	MickeyMantle/* Ted Williams Yankees/Red Sox	Floyd Patterson, Mickey Mantle, Duke Snider, Walter Hagen Nellie Fox, Billy Martin, (Corvette, Harley Davidson) (*Also Floyd Patterson), Ted Williams	65 +150	40	+150 (d)
07/59	Don Newcombe/ Jimmy Piersall Reds/Indians	Don Newcombe, Jim Piersall, Fred Haney, Sal Maglie Bill Skowron, Ken Boyer (Harvey Kuenn-Wilson, Harley Davidson)	16	10	+ 10 + 10

DATE	COVER/Team	MAJOR FEATURE STORIES (Ads)	NM	EM	AUTO
		Value Guide			
08/59	Mantle/Mays/ Matthews /Colavito	Rocky Colavito, Joe Dimaggio, Bill Rigney & Giants, Bill Veeck Vic Power, Del Crandall (Nellie Fox-Wilson)	40	24	varies
09/59	Ted Williams/ Stan Musial Red Sox/Cards	Hank Aaron, Williams/Musial, John McGraw, Dick Stuart, Hoyt Wilhelm, Cal McLish	60	36	+150 + 20
10/59	Warren Spahn/ World Series Braves	Casey Stengel, Warren Spahn, Dizzy Dean, Bob Feller, Ten Greatest World Series Games, Chicago Black Sox Harmon Killebrew	33	20	+ 20
11/59	Coach Dietzel Billy Cannon* LSU	Basilio/Sugar Ray Robinson, Luis Aparicio, Don Meredith, Sam Baugh, Orlando Cepeda (Corvette, Nellie Fox-AMF, Corvair) (Nellie Fox-Wilson)(*also Roger Maris, Harmon Killebrew, Milt Pappas, Vada Pinson)	16	10	+ 15
12/59	Johnny Unitas Colts	Johnny Unitas, Ingemar Johansson, Johnny Antonelli, Red Schoendienst, Sam Huff, Early Wynn Babe Didrikson	20	12	+ 25
01/60	Bob Cousy Celtics	Bob Cousy, Floyd Patterson, Honus Wagner, Tito Francona, Johnny Temple	15	10	+ 35
02/60	Ingemar Johansson* Boxing	L.A. Dodgers, Ingemar Johansson, Ted Kluzewski, Don Budge Enos Slaughter, Joe Gordon, Gordie Howe, Sonny Liston, Gene Conley (Stan Musial - Rawlings) (*Also Larry Sherry - Dodgers)	12	8	
03/60	J. Robinson Willie Mays Chamberlain Althea Gibson	Jackie Robinson, Bob Pettit, Joe Louis, Dickie Moore, Ernie Banks, Chamberlain/Russell (Corvette, John Taylor, Ken Boyer)	24	16	varies
04/60	Duke Snider Dodgers	Duke Snider, Willie Mays, Mickey Cochrane, Roy Face, Gene Fullmer (Banks, Nellie Fox-Wilson, Corvette, Bill Sharman-Spalding, George Mikan-Keds, Stan Musial-Spalding)	24	16	+ 20
05/60	Willie McCovey/ Har. Killebrew Giants/Senators	Al Kaline, Johnny Temple, Willie McCovey, Bobby Jones, Roger Maris, Harmon Killebrew, Stan Musial, Sugar Ray Robinson, White Sox (Corvette)	30	20	+ 15 each
06/60	Don Drysdale Dodgers	Sam Jones, Don Drysdale, Gene Woodling, Casey Stengel Hank Greenberg, Jim Lemon, (Corvette, Nellie Fox - BB Guns)	18	12	+100 (d)
07/60	Luis Aparicio/ Frank Howard WhiteSox/Dodgers	Ingemar Johansson, Frank Howard, Vada Pinson, Johnny Weismuller, Bob Shaw (Corvette, Nellie Fox -BB Guns) (*also Ingemar Johansson)	15	10	+15/+10
08/60	Mickey Mantle Yankees	Gil Hodges, Mickey Mantle, Wilt Chamberlain, Tris Speaker Jim Landis	45	30	+150 (d)
09/60	Colavito/ Mays/Fox	Bill Skowron, Rocky Colavito, Bob Mathias, Vern Law, Bill White	30	20	Varies
10/60	Babe Ruth/ Larry Sherry	Harvey Kuenn, Larry Sherry, Roberto Clemente, Floyd Patterson Babe Ruth, Stan Musial, Jack Nicklaus	24	16	+ 15
11/60	Roger Maris* Yankees	Roger Maris, Floyd Patterson, Ernie Davis, Paul Hornung, Jim Gentle, Davis/Blanchard, Joe Adcock (Also Ernie Davis - Syracuse)	45	30	+250 (d)
12/60	Johnny Unitas Colts	Baltimore Colts, Willie Mays, Bobby Hull, Bronko Nagurski Sonny Liston, Jim Brown (Corvette)	12	8	+ 25
01/61	Bobby Lane Steelers	Bobby Lane, Herb Score, Norm Larker, Bill Russell, Joe Garagiola, Benny Leonard	12	8	+ 10
02/61	Danny Murtaugh* Pirates	Ted Williams, Danny Murtaugh, N.Y. Yankees, Jackie Jensen, Vinegar Bend Mizell, John L. Sullivan, Gordie Howe, Jerry Lucas (*also Ted Williams, Jerry Lucas, Bobby Richardson)	15	10	+ 50 (d)
03/61	Jack Twyman/ Oscar Robertson Royals	Wilt Chamberlain, Jimmy Piersall, Twyman/Robertson Henri Richard, Spahn/Wynn, Stengel/Martin, Wilma Rudolph Gene Tunney, Brooks Robinson	15	10	+ 10 + 20
04/61	Frank Howard Dodgers	Frank Howard, Bill Mazeroski, Elgin Baylor, Floyd Patterson, Ron Hansen, Carl Yastrzemski, Frank Mahovlich (Stan Musial/Ken Boyer Rawlings)	12	8	+ 10
05/61	Dick Groat/ Mickey Mantle Pirates/Yankees	Dick Groat, Gene Fullmer, Ernie Broglio, Mickey Mantle Jim Brosnan, Minnie Minoso, Mel Ott (Ken Boyer Rawlings, Corvair, Yogi Berra - Spalding)	50	25	+ 20 +150 (d)

SPORT

DATE	COVER/Team	MAJOR FEATURE STORIES (Ads)	NM	EM	AUTO
06/61	Willie Mays* Giants	Willie Mays, Frank Robinson, Leo Durocher, Yogi Berra Johnny Longden, Jim Bunning (*also Yogi Berra/Roy Face) (Roger Maris-Spalding, Mickey Mantle -Rawlings)	24	16	+ 35
07/61	Rocky Colavito* Tigers	Arnold Palmer, Rocky Colavito, Jim Perry, Bob Allison, Orlando Cepeda, Bill Dickey, L.A. Dodgers (Yogi Berra - Spalding)(*Also Orlando Cepeda/Arnold Palmer)	30	20	+ 20
08/61	Warren Spahn* Braves	Ken Boyer, Warren Spahn, Woodie Held, Frank Lary, Strangler Lewis, Maury Wills, Frank Malzone (*also Ken Boyer, John Thomas)	18	12	+ 15
09/61	Joe DiMaggio/ Mickey Mantle Yankees	Bob Friend, Top Performers of 1946-1961 - Sport's Special 15th Anniversary Issue (Musial -Rawlings)	60	40	+100 each +150(d)
10/61	Wally Moon Dodgers	Ed Mathews, John Romano, Wally Moon, Hoyt Wilhelm Al Dark, Norm Cash (Norm Van Broklin-Spalding)	12	8	+ 10
11/61	Paul Hornung Packers	Paul Hornung, Sandy Koufax, Gene Freese, Walter Johnson	12	8	+ 20
12/61	Sam Huff Giants	Sam Huff, Frank Robinson, Glen Hall, Elston Howard (Harley Davidson)	12	8	+ 15
01/62	Jim Brown Browns	Jim Brown, Mickey Mantle, Roger Maris, Don Mossi, Frank Thomas, Boom Boom Geoffrion (Corvette)	15	10	+ 25
02/62	Roger Maris Yankees	Jerry Lucas, Bob Cousy, Roger Maris, Gordon Coleman, Steve Barber, Ty Cobb (Bob Cousy-Seamless, Roger Maris-Spalding)	45	30	+350 (d)
03/62	Wilt Chamberlain Warriors	Floyd Patterson, Wilt Chamberlain, Frank Lary, Jim Gentle (Don Drysdale-Vitalis(2pg)	15	10	+ 75
04/62	Vada Pinson/ Norm Cash Reds/Tigers	Orlando Cepeda, Pinson/Cash, Vern Law, John Blanchard (Stan Musial-Rawlings)	12	8	+ 40 (d) + 20
05/62	Baseball Sluggers	Harmon Killebrew, Roberto Clemente, Branch Rickey, Robin Roberts, Mantle/Maris, (Mickey Mantle-Rawlings, Bobby Richardson-Vitalis, Harly Davidson)	18	12	varies
06/62	Hank Aaron Braves	Luis Aparicio, Sport's Greatest Team series- '55 Dodgers, Whitey Ford, Floyd Patterson, Hank Aaron, Roy Sievers (Galexie, Ken Boyer-Spalding) (*also Whitey Ford, Floyd Patterson, Luis Aparicio)	21	14	+ 25
07/62	Mickey Mantle Yankees	Mickey Mantle, Sonny Liston, Early Wynn, Ron Santo Milt Pappas, Al Kaline, Pie Traynor	45	30	+150 (d)
08/62	Rocky Colavito/ Harvey Kuenn Giants/Tigers	Colavito/Kuenn, Dick Stuart, Roger Maris, '34 Cards (Don Drydale - Vitalis)	24	16	+ 20 + 50 (d)
09/62	Stan Musial/ Ken Boyer Cardinals	Don Drysdale, Felipe/Matty Alou, Bobby Richardson, Charlie Finley, Arnold Palmer, Bo Belinsky, Paavo Nurmi (Mantle & Maris - Big Yank, Bob Cousy, Frank Gifford, Ken Venturi, Mike Ditka, RogerMaris-Camel, 63 Crovalr, Bob Pettit-Rawlings)	24	16	+20/50(d)
10/62	Willie Mays Giants	Maury Wills, Willie Mays, Liston/Patterson, Rich Rollins Chuck Essegian, '27 Yankees	18	12	+ 30
11/62	Tommy Davis Jim Taylor Dodgers/Packers	Tommy Davis & Jim Taylor, Ralph Houk, Jim Davenport, '24 Notre Dame, Dick Donovan, Curt Flood	12	8	+ 10 each
12/62	Johnny Unitas/ Jim Brown Colts/Browns	Y.A. Tittle, Stan Mikita, Clete Boyer, Casey Stengel, Willie Davis, Cassius Clay	15	10	+ 25 each
1/63	Paul Hornung Packers	Packers Sonny Liston, Mickey Mantle, Paul Hornung Leon Wagner, Dave Keon, Jim Gilliam	12	8	+ 20
2/63	Maury Wills* Dodgers	Dodger, Bill Russell, Willie Mays, Maury Wills, Jim Piersall Marcel Cerdan, Tom Tresh (*Bill Russell, Jim Perisall)	15	10	+ 10
3/63	Bob Cousy Celtics	Celtics, Elgin Baylor, Bob Cousy, Jack Sanford, Jim Brown Jerry Lucas, George Sisler (Chevy II)	12	8	+ 25
4/63	Stan Musial/ Wilt Chamberlain Cardinals/Warriors	Ernie Banks, Wilt Chamberlain, Stan Musial, Ed Mathews, Hank Aguirre (Stan Musial Rawlings, Boby Cousy Seamless Maris, Mantle, Ford - Big Yaks, B. Robinson- Rawlings, Bob Cousy -Jentzen)	15	10	varies
5/63	Mickey Mantle/ Yogi Berra Yankees	Vic Power, Berra/Mantle, Arnold Palmer, Bart Starr, Bill Mazeroski, Boston Bruins	45	30	+150 (d) + 20

SPORT

DATE	COVER/Team	MAJOR FEATURE STORIES (Ads)	NM	EM	AUTO
6/63	Maury Wills Dodgers	Frank Robinson , Maury Wills , Henry Armstrong Dick Stuart , Luis Aparicio , Juan Marichal	15	10	+ 10
7/63	Rocky Colavito/ Al Kaline Tigers	Jack Nicklaus , Colavito/Kaline, Willie McCovey , '42 cards , Ralph Terry (Arnold Palmer - Ford)	30	20	+ 15 each
8/63	Willie Mays Giants	Joey Jay , Willie Mays , John Unitas Boog Powell , HOF , Johnny Podres , Ted Williams	18	12	+ 30
9/63	Sandy Koufax Dodgers	Sandy Koufax & Babe Ruth, Special Babe Ruth section , Paul Hornung , Yaz	30	20	+ 30
10/63	Mickey Mantle Yankees	Brooks Robinson , Cassius Clay , Mickey Mantle , Dick Groat , Casey Stengel , Ernie Davis , '05 Giants , Ron Fairly (Paul Hornung, Bob Cousy - Jantzen)	36	24	+150 (d)
11/63	Whitey Ford Yankees	Fred Hutchinson , Ford/Musial , Felipe Alou , Nellie Fox , Lefty Grove	15	10	+ 20
12/63	Del Shofner Giants	Bobby Mitchell , Sonny Liston , Jerry Kramer , Jerry Lucas , Jim Maloney , Dick Ellsworth , Joe Pepitone	12	8	+ 10
1/64	Jim Taylor Packers	Allie Sherman , Stan Musial , Pierre Pilote , Elston Howard , Gary Peters	15	10	+ 10
2/64	Sandy Koufax Dodgers	Gordie Howe , Yogi Berra, Wilt Chamberlain , Al Kaline , Curt Simmons , Floyd Patterson , '40 Chicago Bears , Zoilo Versalles , Bill Bradley , John Callison	30	15	+ 30
3/64	Cassius Clay Boxing	Frank Howard , Bob Cousy , Jim Bouton , Frank Frisch	30	16	+ 75
4/64	Oscar Robertson Royals	Elgin Baylor, Bobby Hull , Rocky Colavito , Joe Torre (Al Kaline-Wilson) (YA Title, Rocky Colavito)	15	10	+ 15
5/64	Warren Spahn Braves	Steve Barber , Alex Karras , Jean Beliveau , Vada Pinson , Warren Spahn	15	10	+ 15
6/64	Dick Stuart* Red Sox	Dick Stuart , Cassius Clay , Willie Mays , Pete Rose , Tommy Davis , The Whiz Kids , Jerry Lumpe (*Also M. Ali) (Ford Mustang, Al Lopez-MacGregor)	15	10	+ 10
7/64	Tommy Davis/ Tom Tresh/Yaz Dodgers/Yankees/Red Sox	Bill White , Vic Davalillo , Orlando Cepeda , Tony Lema ,	15	10	varies
8/64	Joe DiMaggio/ Willie Mays Yankees/Giants	Joe Nuxhall , Bill Skowron , Luke Appling , Hank Aaron , Jim Brown , Billy Williams	50	30	Varies
9/64	Mickey Mantle Yankees	Juan Marichal , Mickey Mantle , Jim Taylor , Ted Williams , Richie Allen , Casey Stengel , Bob Allison , John Roseboro (Bart Starr-MacGregor)	45	25	+150 (d)
10/64	Willie Mays Giants	Bobby Richardson , Willie Mays, Tony Oliva , Willie Stargell , Jesse Owens , Norm Siebern	20	12	+ 25
11/64	Harmon Killibrew* Twins	Jim Bunning , Harmon Killebrew, Paul Hornung , Sandy Koufax , '14 Boston Braves , Dusty Rhodes , Jackie Brandt , Dick Butkus (Oscar Roberson-Macgregor) (*also Paul Hornung)	25	12	+ 15
12/64	Jim Brown Browns	Mike Ditka, Mickey Mantle , Brooks Robinson , '64 Phillies Roger Staubach , Deron Johnson, Juan Pizzaro (Oscar Roberson- Macgregor, Mickey Mantle-Rawlings)	15	10	+ 20
1/65	Johnny Unitas Colts	Cookie Gilchrist , Johnny Unitas,Dean Chance , Richie Allen , Eric Nesterenko , Pedro Ramos	15	10	+ 20
2/65	Fred Hutchinson Reds	Bob Pettit , Bob Pulford , Warren Spahn , Bill Sharman Ray Sadecki , Bill Freehan (* also Oscar Robertson-Royals/Lenny Moore)	10	6	+ 10
3/65	Jerry West* Lakers	Red Auerbach , Jerry West, Bobby Hull , Curt Flood , Phil Linz , Bob Bailey , Mickey Lolich (*also Brooks Robinson)	20	10	+ 15
4/65	Dean Chance Angels	Jerry Lucas , Dean Chance , Ron Hunt , Tony Conigliaro , Cassius Clay , Jack Nicklaus , Bill Bradley , Rico Carty (Corvette, 7-up, Stan Musial-Macgregor, Ron Santo - Rawlings)	12	6	+ 10
5/65	Sandy Koufax Dodgers	Roberto Clemente , Elston Howard , Floyd Patterson , Lou Brock , Bill Terry (Stan Musial - Macgregor, Ron Santo - Rawlings)	30	15	+ 25
6/65	Willie Mays Giants	Willie Mays , Tim McCarver , Ed Mathews , ' 48 Indians , Wally Bunke, Arnold Palmer	25	12	+ 25
7/65	Johnny Callison* Phillies	Johnny Callison , Rocky Colavito , Bob Gibson , Larry Jackson , Don Zimmer, (Ford Auora Model) (*also Rocky Colavito)	15	10	+ 10

SPORT

DATE	COVER/Team	MAJOR FEATURE STORIES (Ads)	NM	EM	AUTO
8/65	Mickey Mantle — Yankees	Mickey Mantle , Joe Namath , Max Alvis, Hank Bauer , Ron Santo, Sam Ellis (7-up)	40	25	+150 (d)
9/65	Gehrig/Dimaggio, Frank Robinson — Yankees/Orioles	Pete Ward , Frank Robinson ,Willie Horton , Mudcat Grant , Charlie O. Finley , Jim Ryun , Ron Swoboda , Jesus Alou (7-up)	30	16	varies
10/65	Sandy Koufax/ Maury Wills — Dodgers	Vada Pinson , Hank Aaron ,Wilt Chamberlain , Al Kaline , Jim Taylor , Al Lopez , Sam McDowell (Babe Ruth-Aurora Model, 7-up)	25	12	+ 30/+10
11/65	Johnny Unitas/ Tommy Mason — Colts/Vikings	Ray Nitschke , Jack Kemp , Harmon Killebrew , LuJack , Leahy & Notre Dame , Ron Fairly , Roseboro/Marichal , Norm Ullman (Ford Mustang)	15	10	+ 20/+10
12/65	Fran Tarkenton/ Sonny Jurgensen — Vikings/Redskins	Sonny Jurgensen , Willie Mays , Sid Luckman , Hank Thompson , Pete Rose , John Havlicek (7-up)	12	8	+ 15 each
1/66	Charley Johnson — Cardinals	Charley Johnson , Don Drysdale , Yaz , Brooks Robinson (Coke)	12	8	+ 10
2/66	Sandy Koufax — Dodgers	Bobby Hull , Sandy Koufax, , Gale Sayers , Special Ted Williams section (Dodger-Chargers, Cyclone GT)	30	12	+ 25
3/66	Bill Russell — Celtics	Zollo Versalles , Bill Russell, Tony Zale , Gordie Howe , Lou Johnson , Judge Landis , Rick Barry (Wilt Chamberlain-Spalding, Coke, Pontiac GTO)	20	10	+200
4/66	Willie Mays/ Paul Hornung — Giants/Packers	Jerry West , Bobby Rousseau , Roger Maris , Vern Law , Willie Mays , Paul Hornung , Sam Mele (Bob Hope-Chrysler)	20	10	+25/+10
5/66	Maury Wills — Dodgers	Maury Wills , Arthur Ashe , Richie Allen , Denny McLain , 55-'56 Montreal Canadiens , Bert Campaneris (Harmon Killebrew-shoes, Dr. Pepper, Paul Hornung Jantzen, Coke)	15	10	+ 10
6/66	Joe Namath — Jets	Joe Torre , Joe Namath , Frank Howard Juan Marichal , Special Lou Gehrig section (55 Chevy, Coke, [Juan Marichal fights back]	25	16	+ 30
7/66	Mickey Mantle — Yankees	Deron Johnson , Mickey Mantle, Orlando Cepeda , Arnold Palmer , Bobby Hull , Don Buford , Bob Feller (Coke)	30	20	+150(d)
8/66	Frank Robinson — Orioles	Tony Oliva , Frank Robinson , Ed Mathews , Dick Butkus , Jim Pagliaroni, (Coke)	15	10	+ 20
9/66	Willie Mays — Giants	Sam McDowell , Top Performers of 1946-1966 (Sports Special 20th Anniversary Issue)	25	15	+ 25
10/66	Sandy Koufax — Dodgers	Alex Karras , Sandy Koufax , Brooks / Frank Robinson Thompson/Branca , George Scott , Dick McAuliffe (Coke)	25	12	+ 25
11/66	John Brodie — 49ers	John Brodie , Jim Brown , Boog Powell (Corvette) Steve Spurrier , Leo Durocher , Roger Crozier , Gaylord Perry	12	8	+ 15
12/66	Gale Sayers — Bears	Gale Sayers , Jim Kaat , Jim Thorpe , Ralph Kiner , Bears (Mickey Mantle-Rawlings)	20	10	+ 15
1/67	Don Meredith — Cowboys	Don Meredith & Lance Alworth, Joe Morgan , Mickey Mantle , Phil Regan , Ted Green ,	20	10	+ 15
2/67	Frank Robinson — Orioles	Rick Barry , Frank Robinson , Babe Ruth , Earl Wilson , Tommy Helms (Camero)	15	10	+ 15
3/67	Wilt Chamberlain — Warriors	Wilt Chamberlain , Bart Starr, Sandy Koufax , Bobby Hull Warriors , Knute Rockne , Dave DeBusschere , Jim Nash (Supremes - Coke, GTO,Charger)	15	10	+ 75
4/67	Lew Alcindor — UCLA	Lew Alcindor , Willie Davis , Bill Russell , Tommie Agee Walter Johnson , Rod Gilbert , Sam McDowell , (Ford Mustang, Corvette, Moody Blues-Coke)	15	10	+ 35
5/67	Mickey Mantle — Yankees	Ron Santo , Mickey Mantle , Jack Nicklaus , Dave Boswell Jim Lefebvre Barney Ross , Ken Wharram (Firebird, Rawling Gold Glove)	40	25	+150 (d)
6/67	Willie Mays — Giants	Felipe Alou , Willie Mays', Bear Bryan, Roy Campanella (The Fortunes - Coke)	20	10	+ 30
7/67	Richie Allen/ Jim Ryan — Phillies/Runner	Richie Allen & Jim Ryan , Sandy Koufax , Sonny Siebert Bill Tilden , Lee May , Bobby Orr	15	10	+ 10
8/67	Roberto Clemente — Pirates	Frank Robinson , Dean Chance , Ernie Banks , Joe McGinnity , Jim Northrup (Vaudeville Band - Coke)	40	25	+350 (d)
9/67	Pete Rose — Reds	Pete Rose , Juan Marichal , Rico Petrocelli , Lou Brock , Joe Horlen	30	20	+ 20

145

DATE	COVER/Team	MAJOR FEATURE STORIES (Ads)	Value Guide		
			NM	EM	AUTO
10/67	Orlando Cepeda/ Johnny Unitas Cards/Colts	Eddie Stanky , Orlando Cepeda , Johnny Unitus, Lew Alcindor Tony Perez , Harmon Killebrew (Ray Charles - Coke, Dodge Charger)	15	10	+10/20
11/67	Joe Namath Jets	Joe Namath , Tim McCarver, Yaz, Elgin Baylor , Jimmy Wynn , Colavito/K. Boyer '47-'49 Toronto Maple Leafs , Rod Carew	15	10	+ 30
12/67	Bart Starr Packers	Bart Starr , '67 Red Sox , Ed Glacomin , Musial/Schoendienst Oscar Robertson , Mike McCormick , Rusty Staub, (Bob Hope-Chrysler, Firebird)	15	8	+ 15
1/68	Mike Garrett Chiefs	Mike Garrett , Rick Barry , Julian Javier , Mickey Mantle, (Coke)	15	8	+ 10
2/68	Carl Yastrzemski Red Sox	Stan Mikita & Wilt Chamberlain , Yaz , Ferguson Jenkins Joe Frazier , Elvin Hayes (Sandy Posey - Coke, Ford Torino)	20	12	+ 15
3/68	Lew Alcindor UCLA	Nate Thurmond , Lew Alcindor , Roberto Clemente , Tom Seaver Maurice Stokes , Johnny Unitas	15	10	+ 40
4/68	Bobby Hull Black Hawks	Vince Lombardi , Bobby Hull , Jim Bouton, Bill Bradley , Reggie Smith , Paul/Lloyd Waner , Juan Marichal (Bobby Hull-Black hawks)	20	12	+ 10
5/68	Willie Mays Giants	Bob Gibson , Al Kaline , Baseball '68 Special section, (Roberto Clemente - Louisville Slugger, GTO, Corvette, Coke Camaro)	15	10	+ 35
6/68	Carl Yastrzemski Red Sox	Carl Yastrzemski, Jim Bunning , Jim Beliveau , '31 A's Cesar Tovar (Coke)	20	10	+ 20
7/68	Hank Aaron Braves	St. Louis Cardinals , Tony Conigliaro , Tommy Davis , Hank Aaron (Coke)	20	10	+ 20
8/68	Pete Rose Reds	Bill Freehan , Pete Rose , Joe DiMaggio , Johnny Unitas, Dal Maxvill , Curt Blefary (Coke)	24	10	+ 20
9/68	Don Drysdale Dodgers	Frank Howard , Don Drysdale , Luis Tiant , Alex Johnson (Harmon Killebrew-Head Shoulders, Jim Ryan Olympics)	15	10	+100 (d)
10/68	Fran Tarkenton Giants	Curt Flood & Randy Matson , Denny McLain , Matty Alou (Bob Hope Chrysler, Harmon Killebrew Head Shoulders)	15	6	+ 15
11/68	Don Meredith Cowboys	Leroy Kelly , Don Meredith , Lew Alcindor, Willie Horton Lou Brock , Hoyt Wilhelm (Johnny Unitas -Head & Shoulders)	15	6	+ 15
12/68	O.J. Simpson USC	Bob Hayes , O.J. Simpson , Denny McLain , Bert Campaneris , Arnold Palmer , Phil Esposito	30	20	+ 30
1/69	Deacon Jones Rams	Deacon Jones , Mike Shannon , Boom Boom Geoffrion Joe Namath , Tommy John , Satchel Paige , Johnny Bench (Bob Hope - Chrysler)	12	6	+ 10
2/69	John Havlicek/ O.J. Simpson Celtics/USC	John Havlicek , O.J. Simpson , Glenn Beckert , Celtics/Bills Maravich , Stan Musial, Lee Trevino (Camaro/Corvette, Wilt Chamberlain Head & Shoulders, Coke)	15	6	+ 10
3/69	Chamberlain/ West/Baylor Lakers	Chamberlain , West , Baylor , Bobby Hull , Mickey Stanley Rick Barry , Felix Millan , Frank Robinson , Jerry Koosman , Camaro)	20	12	Varies
4/69	Mickey Mantle Yankees	Bobby Orr , Joe Namath , Mickey Mantle John Unitas , Charlie Gehringer , Bill Mazeroski	60	40	+150 (d)
5/69	Babe Ruth/ Willie Mays/ Ty Cobb/ Sandy Koufax/ Joe Dimaggio	Babe Ruth , Special Issue: 100 Years of Baseball	24	16	Varies
6/69	Ted Williams Senators	Willie McCovey , Ted Williams , Sonny Liston , Dave McNally Pele , Bo Belinsky , Ernie Banks , Willie Shoemaker	25	15	+125
7/69	Tony Conigliaro Red Sox	Lou Brock , Tony Conigliaro , Reggie Jackson Sugar Ray Robinson , Elgin Baylor	20	12	+200(d)
8/69	O.J. Simpson Bills	Willie Mays , O.J. Simpson , Wilt Chamberlain , Bobby Murcer Don Kessinger , Phil Niekro , Jim Palmer	24	16	+ 20
9/69	Durocher/Banks Santo/B. Williams Cubs	Durocher & '69 Cubs , Joe Namath , Graziano/Zale Chico Cardenas , Paul Blair , Blue Moon Odom	36	24	Varies

SPORT

DATE	COVER/Team	MAJOR FEATURE STORIES (Ads)	NM	EM	AUTO
10/69	Sonny Jurgensen Redskins	Rod Carew & Notre Dame , Randy Hundley , Cleon Jones , Doak Walker	10	6	+ 10
11/69	Gale Sayers Bears	Roman Gabriel , Gale Sayers , Maurice Richard , Jim Maloney , Killebrew/Powell , Bill Russell Vada Pinson , Sal Bando	12	8	+ 20
12/69	O.J./McLain Orr/Unseld Bills/Tigers/Bruins/Bullets	Johnny Bench & Morton/Staubach , '69 Mets , Richie Hebner 10 Greatest Sporting Events of the 60's	15	8	Varies
1/70	Calvin Hill Cowboys	Viking Front Four , Calvin Hill , '69 World Series , Joe Namath Bobby Bonds, Mike Cuellar	12	6	+ 10
2/70	Lew Alcindor/ Gil Hodges Bucks/Mets	Lew Alcindor , Gil Hodges , Rico Carty	12	6	+ 35/ +100 (d)
3/70	Jerry West Lakers	Pete Maravich , Curt Flood , Ted Williams , Tommie Agee (Mustang Mach 1)	12	6	+ 20
4/70	Willis Reed Knicks	Willis Reed , Joe Pepitone , Ernie Banks/ Ron Santo	10	6	+ 10
5/70	Tom Seaver Mets	Tom Seaver , Bill Freehan , Walt Alston , Tony/Phil Esposito (Paper Flap - Camaro)	15	10	+ 25
6/70	Harmon Killebrew Twins	Rico Petrocelli , Harmon Killebrew , Denny McLain Bobby Tolan , Carlos May (Paper Flap - Camaro , Paul Hornung/Roger Maris - Champion Spark plug)	15	10	+ 15
7/70	Johnny Unitas/ Bart Starr Colts/Packers	Richie Allen , Wilt Chamberlain , Starr/Unitas , Jim Bouton , Andy Messersmith	12	10	Varies
8/70	Hank Aaron Braves	Hank Aaron , Mickey Mantle (Lee Trevino)	15	10	+ 20
9/70	Johnny Bench Reds	Billy Williams , O.J.Simpson , Pete Maravich Nolan Ryan Derek Sanderson , Reggie Jackson (Johnny Unitas -v-8)	22	15	+ 20
10/70	Plunkett/Kern/ Theismann Manning Stanford, Ohio St, ND, Ol Miss	Tony Perez , Alex Johnson , Jim Bouton , Vince Lombardi	15	10	Varies
11/70	Dick Butkus Bears	Dick Butkus , Clemente/Oliva , Bud Harrelson Jim Merritt	25	10	+ 20
12/70	Roman Gabriel Rams	Bob Lilly , Roman Gabriel , Joe Namath , Luis Aparicio (Dodge Charger, Triump GT)	12	6	+ 10
1/71	Larry Brown/ Mike Lucci Redskins	Detroit Lions , Jerry Lucas , Frank Robinson/ World Series , Keith Magnuson , Bill Bradley	10	6	+ 10
2/71	Dave Bing Pistons	Dave Bing , Bobby Orr	15	6	+ 10
2/71	Bobby Orr Bruins (regional)	Dave Bing , Bobby Orr , Merv Rettenmund	40	20	+ 30
3/71	Pete Maravich Hawks	Walt Frazier , Pete Maravich , Muhammad Ali , Pete Rose , Manny Sanguillen	35	15	+200 (d)
4/71	John Havlicek Celtics	Phil Esposito , Pete Rose , John Havlicek , History of the NHL Stanley Cup (Paul Newman-Coke, Phil Esposito-Gillette, Ed Giacomin, Brooks Robinson)	15	10	+ 20
5/71	Ted Williams/ D. McLain/ C. Flood Senators	Dave DeBusschere , Joe Frazier , Lew Alcindor , Sam McDowell	20	10	Varies
6/71	Boog Powell Orioles	Calvin Murphy , Billy Martin , Maury Wills	15	10	+ 10
7/71	Carl Yastrzemski Red Sox	Bob Gibson , Yaz , Seaver/Hodges/ Swoboda , Cesar Cedeno (Yaz, Bob Gibson, Coke)	15	10	+ 20
8/71	Mike Curtis Colts	Willie Stargell , Vida Blue , Jim Bouton , Bobby Hull	10	6	+ 10
9/71	Willie Mays Giants	Joe Torre , Top Performers of 1946-1971 (Coke , Joe Dimaggio (Sports Special 25th Anniversary Issue)	25	15	+ 35

SPORT

DATE	COVER/Team	MAJOR FEATURE STORIES (Ads)	NM	EM	AUTO
10/71	Vida Blue A's	Top Performers of 1946-1971, Vince Lombardi, Willie Davis Bill Russell	10	6	+ 10
11/71	Ken Willard 49ers	Ken Willard , Top Performers of 1946-1971 Roberto Clemente / Bill Mazeroski , Catfish Hunter	10	6	+ 10
12/71	Bob Griese Dolphins	Bob Griese , Pete Maravich , Ernie Banks , Jackie Robinson	12	6	+ 20
1/72	Larry Brown Redskin	Satchel Paige, Artis Gilmore	10	6	+ 10
2/72	Spencer Haywood Supersonics	Tony Esposito, Lance Alworth, Sandy Koufax Kareem Abdul- Jabbar	10	6	+ 10
2/72	Tony Esposito (regional)		15	10	+ 15
3/72	Wilt Chamberlain Lakers	Larry Csonka, Johnny Bench, Rod Gilbert, Wilt Chamberlain, Gene Washinton (Ford Mustang-mach1)	15	9	+ 75
4/72	Bobby Orr Bruins	Joe Theisman, Connie Hawkins, Lee Trevino, (Cowens, Staubach)	25	15	+ 35
5/72	Bobby Hull Blackhawks	Richie Allen, F. Robinson, Bobby Hull (Blackhawk), (Richard Petty-Sunglasses-Mustang) Walt Frazier, Tom Seaver	15	8	+ 15
6/72	Brooks Robinson Orioles	Hank Aaron, Steve Prefontaine, (Ford Mustang)	15	10	+ 10
7/72	Joe Namath Jets	Freguson Jenkins	15	10	+ 35
8/72	Tom Seaver Mets	Bobby Orr	20	10	+ 20
9/72	Frank Robinson Orioles		15	10	+ 15
10/72	Jim Plunkett Stanford	Willie Mays, Johnny Bench	10	6	+ 10
11/72	Johnny Bench Reds		25	12	+ 20
11/72	Otis Taylor Chiefs (regional)	Red Auerbach	15	10	+ 10
12/72	Fran Tarkenton Viking	Lakers, Dick Allen (Bob Griese) , Duke Snider	15	8	+ 20
1/73	Merlin Olson Rams		10	6	+ 10
2/73	Rick Barry Warriors (regional)	Mark Spitz, Knicks	15	10	+ 10
2/73	Willis Reed Knicks (regional)	Mark Spitz, Bobby Fisher, OJ Simpson, Knicks Carlton Fisk	15	10	+ 10
3/73	Ken Dryden Canadians	Nate Archibald, Dr J, Yankees (Mustang)	12	6	+ 10
4/73	Oscar Robertson Bucks (regional)	Steve Carlton, Lakers, 76ers, Roberto Clemente, Super Bowl VII	12	6	+ 20
4/73	Steve Carlton Phillies (regional)		20	12	+ 15
5/73	Dave Cowens Celtics		10	6	+ 15
6/73	A.J. Foyt Car Racing	Nolan Ryan, Dr J (Mustang)	12	9	+ 15
7/73	George Foreman Boxing		12	9	+ 40
8/73	Bobby Murcer Yankees	Joe Morgan	12	7	+ 10
9/73	Gaylord Perry Indians	Cards	12	6	+ 10
10/73	Pete Rose * Reds	Pete Rose, Ferguson Jenkins, Cowboys (*also Ron Blomberg-Yanks, John Mayberrry -Royals Ferguson Jenkins - Cubs, Ken Holtzman-A's)	15	10	+ 20
11/73	Franco Harris Steelers	Anthony Davis, Dave Bing	12	6	+ 10

SPORT

Value Guide

DATE	COVER/Team	MAJOR FEATURE STORIES (Ads)	NM	EM	AUTO
12/73	Joe Namath Jets	(Flap-Norm Snead-Giants, John Huarte -Chiefs) Pete Maravich, Philadelphia Flyers	15	8	+ 40
1/74	Larry Little/ Manny Fernandez Dolphins	SF Giants, Jackie Stewart, Reggie Jackson, Dolphins, Gordie Howe, M. Fernandez	10	6	+ 10
2/74	Karem Abdul Jabbar Bucks	Secretariat, Dr J, Arthur Ashe	10	6	+ 35
3/74	Bill Russell Wilt Chamberlain Celtics/Lakers	(B Robinson-Rawlings), Giants, Bill Russell, Buffalo Braves, Dave Thompson	10	6	+200
4/74	Dave Debusschere Knicks	Jerry Tarkanian, Dodgers, Fran Tarkenton, Gaylord Perry	10	6	+ 10
5/74	Hank Aaron Braves (#715)	Phil Esposito, Babe Ruth, John Havlicek Home Run Record	25	15	+ 20
6/74	Pete Rose Reds	Johnny Miller, Rod Carew (B. Robinson-Rawlings)	15	10	+ 20
7/74	Chris Evert Jimmy Connors Tennis	Charlie Finley, Yogi Berra, Thurmon Munson, Dr J, Johnny Bench	12	6	+ 20 each
8/74	Larry Csonka/Calvin Hill Dolphins/Cowboys		12	8	+ 20
9/74	Muhammad Ali Boxing		14	8	+ 75
10/74	Reggie Jackson A's	Jackie Jensen, Mario Andretti	16	8	+ 35
11/74	Joe Namath* Jets	(*also Palmer, Chamberlain),(VW-Earl Monroe)	12	8	+ 40
12/74	O.J. Simpson, Bills	(Ed Giacomin-VW, Rick Barry, Wilt Chamberlin Pistol Pete Spalding Poster promotion -life size) Pro Keds shoes - Kareem & Others) Rangers, Mike Schmidt, Knicks, Notre Dame	12	9	+ 30
1/75	Fran Tarkenton Viking	Maury Wills, Wilt Chamberlain, Moses Malone (Lee Roy Jordan-Cowboys-VW) Rollie Fingers	12	8	+ 25
2/75	Muhammad Ali Boxing	NC State, Bobby Hull, Don Sutton, Dr J, Suns	12	8	+ 75
3/75	Julius Erving 76ers	Jim Palmer, ABA	25	15	+ 40
4/75	Rick Barry Warriors	Bill Sharmon (Kareem & Others- Pro Keds)	12	6	+ 10
5/75	Frank Robinson Indians	Bobby Orr, Tom Heinsohn, Tony Conigliaro	12	6	+ 15
6/75	Johnny Miller Golf	Steve Garvey, (Joe Torre-VW Bug)	10	6	+ 10
7/75	Bobby Bonds Yankees		12	9	+ 10
8/75	Billy Martin Rangers	Mickey Mantle, Bill Walton	12	9	+ 50 (d)
9/75	Jimmy Connors Tennis		10	5	+ 20
10/75	James Harris Rams	World Series, Reggie Jackson	10	6	+ 10
11/75	Joe Namath Jets	Fran Tarkenton, Rick Barry	12	9	+ 35
12/75	Joe Greene Steelers	Green Bay Packers	10	6	+ 15
1/76	Super Bowl Preview	Superbowl	10	6	-
2/76	Fran Tarkenton Viking		10	6	+15
3/76	George McGinnis 76ers	Bob Gibson	10	6	+10
4/76	Steve Garvey Dodgers	National League 100th Anniversary Issue	15	8	+5

SPORT

Value Guide

DATE	COVER/Team	MAJOR FEATURE STORIES (Ads)	NM	EM	AUTO
5/76	Tom Seaver Mets	Celtics	15	8	+10
6/76	Ronald Reagan/Gerald Ford Jimmy Carter/George Wallace Presidential Hopefuls		10	6	
7/76	Bruce Jenner Track	Olympic Issue	10	6	+ 10
8/76	Pete Rose/ Joe Morgan Reds		15	10	+ 20 each
9/76	Franco Harris Steelers	Arthur Ashe	10	6	+ 10
10/76	Bert Jones Colts		10	6	+ 10
11/76	George Simpson		10	6	+ 5
12/76	Pill-Popping	Pete Maravich, Jack Lambert	10	4	
1/77	Roger Staubach Cowboys		15	8	+ 25
2/77	Julius Erving 76ers	Performer of the Year	25	10	+ 30
3/77	Joe Namath Bobby Orr OJ Simpson		15	6	+ 30
4/77	Bill Walton Trailblazers	Bill Walton, Tom Lasorda, Dr J (Magic Johnson-McDonalds) OJ-Dingo, Raiders, Roger Staubach- Hagger, Johnny Bench -Batter up, Lou Brock -Converse, Coke)	15	6	+ 20
5/77	Jan Stephenson Golfer	Reds, Knicks (see through shirt on cover)	20	12	+ 20
6/77	Greed in Sports	George Brett, Vida Blue, Reggie Jackson (Coke)	15	6	
7/77	Mark Fidrych Tigers	Suns, Bill Cosby (Coke)	10	6	+ 10
8/77	Boxing	Davey Lopez, Muhammad Ali, Sugar Ray Leonard, Carlton Fisk	10	6	
9/77	Leonard Willis* Vikings	Dan Pastorini-Oilers, Raiders, Broncos (*Also Floyd Rice - Raiders)	10	6	+ 5
10/77	Rod Carew Twins	Rod Carew, World Series, Bruce Sutter	10	6	+ 15
11/77	Earl Monroe* Bulletts	Curt Flod, Joe Namath, Tony Dorsett (*also Woodie Allen)	10	6	+ 10
12/77	Ken Stabler Raiders		10	6	+ 15
1/78	Tony Dorsett Cowboys	Superbowl	10	6	+ 15
2/78	Kareem Abdul-Jabbar Lakers	Performer of the Year	10	6	+ 35
3/78	Maurice Lucas Trailblazers	Marice Lucas, Tarkanian, Mario Andretti, OJ-Dingo	8	6	+ 10
4/78	Rich Gossage & Jim Hunter Yankees	Lou Brock-Cards	8	6	+ 10 each
5/78	Graig Nettles Yankees	Celtics, Paul Westphal, (R Jackson-Rabbit)	8	6	+10
6/78	Julius Erving 76ers	NBA Finals	20	12	+ 30
7/78	Jim Rice Red Sox	Ted Simmons, Bobby Bonds	10	6	+ 10
8/78	Tom Seaver Reds	Bob McAdoo, Nolan Ryan	15	9	+ 20
9/78	Cliff Branch Raiders	Football Preview Issue	10	6	+ 10

SPORT

DATE	COVER/Team	MAJOR FEATURE STORIES (Ads)	Value Guide		
			NM	EM	AUTO
10/78	Carl Yastrzemski Red Sox	Gary Carter, Yaz, (Dr J), (Tony Dorsett-Underwear)	12	8	+ 20
11/78	O.J. Simpson 49ers	Earl Campbell, Jack Clark	12	8	+ 25
12/78	Jack Lambert Steelers	Don Shula, Paul Newman, Kyle Macy , Larry Bird	12	6	+ 10
1/79	Harvey Martin Raiders	Howard Cosell, Cowboys (*Also Jim Hart/Cardinals)	12	6	+ 10
2/79	Julius Erving 76ers		25	12	+ 30
3/79	John Drew Hawks	NBA Basketball Issue	10	6	+ 5
4/79	Pete Rose Reds	Baseball Preview Issue	12	9	+ 20
5/79	Ron Guidry Yankees	Elvin Hayes, Jim Palmer, Joe Lewis	8	6	+ 5
6/79	Dave Parker Pirates	Red Auerbach	8	6	+ 5
7/79	Graig Nettles Yankees (regional)		12	6	+ 5
7/79	J.R. Richard Astros (regional)		12	6	+ 15
8/79	Rod Carew Angels		10	6	+ 15
9/79	Tony Dorsett Cowboys		10	6	+ 15
10/79	Reggie Jackson Yankees	World Series Issue	15	8	+ 30
11/79	Raiders/Patriots Raiders	NBA Basketball Preview	8	6	
12/79	Pat Haden Chargers	College Basketball Preview	8	6	+ 5
1/80	Jack Ham Steelers	Playoff	10	4	+ 5
2/80	Magic Johnson Lakers		25	16	+ 40
3/80	Larry Bird Celtics		20	12	+ 40
4/80	Willie Stargell Priates (regional)	Pro Baseball Preview Issue Nolan Ryan	15	6	+ 10
4/80	Nolan Ryan Astros (regional)	Pro Baseball Preview Willie Stargell	30	15	+ 25
5/80	Lou Piniella Yankees (regional)		8	6	+ 5
5/80	Steve Garvey Dodger (regional)		8	6	+ 5
5/80	George Brett Royals (regional)		20	10	+ 40
6/80	Bill Russell Dodgers	Indy 500	6	4	+ 5
7/80	Gorman Thomas Brewers	Muhammad Ali, Roger Staubach	6	4	+ 5
8/80	Terry Bradshaw Steelers	Pro Football Issue	10	4	+ 10
9/80	Tommy John White Sox(regional)	Bear Bryant, College Football Issue	6	4	+ 10
9/80	Art Schlicter Ohio State (regional)		6	4	+ 5
10/80	Earl Campbell Oilers	Terry Bradshaw, Pro Basketball Preview	10	4	+ 15
11/80	Lee Roy Selmon Tampa Bay Buccaneers	Pro Basketball Preview	6	4	+ 5

SPORT

DATE	COVER/Team	MAJOR FEATURE STORIES (Ads)	Value Guide		
			NM	EM	AUTO
11/80	**Dan Pastorini** Chiefs (regional)		10	5	+ 10
12/80	**Louie Gicmmon** Eagles	FB's Special Teams, Col Basketball Issue	6	4	+ 10
12/80	**Herschel Walker** Georgia	(Regional Cover) Col Baskeball Preview	10	5	+ 15
1/81	**Billy Sims** Lions	Al Davis, Wayne Gretzky	6	4	+ 5
2/81	**Danny White** Cowboys		6	4	+ 10
2/81	**Ron Jaworski** Eagles	Danny Whiet	6	4	+ 5
3/81	**Kelly Tripucka** Notre Dame (regional)	Dave Winfield, Final Four	6	4	+ 5
3/81	**Rod Foster** UCLA (regional)	Boxing, Final Four, Dave Winfield	10	5	+ 5
4/81	**Tug McGraw** Phillies(regional)	Baseball Issue	8	4	+ 5
4/81	**George Brett** Royals(regional)		10	5	+ 40
5/81	**Billy Martin** A's	Mike Schmidt, Reggie Jackson	8	6	+ 50 (d)
6/81	**Don Sutton** Astros (regional)		10	4	+ 10
6/81	**Dave Parker** Pirates(regional)		10	4	+ 5
7/81	**Goose Gossage or Bruce Sutter** Yankees(regional) or Cubs (regional)		10	4	+ 5
8/81	**Jim Plunkett** Raiders	Frank Robinson	6	4	+ 5
9/81	**Earl Campbell** Oilers	Football Preview	7	4	+ 10
10/81	**Doug Plank**-Bears Jackle Slater - Rams		6	4	+ 5
11/81	**Lester Hayes** Raiders		6	4	+ 5
12/81	**Steve Bartowski** Falcons	College Basketball Issue	6	4	+ 5
1/82	**Tony Dorsett** Cowboys	NFL Playoff Preview	16	4	+ 10
2/82	**Magic Johnson** Lakers		20	10	+ 40
3/82	**Gerry Cooney** Boxing		6	4	+ 20
4/82	**Fernando Valenzuela*** Dodgers	(*also Larry Bird in corner) Baseball Preview Issue	6	4	+ 10
5/82	**Reggie Jackson** Angels	[Wayne Gretzky in corner] NBA Issue	12	6	+ 35
6/82	**Tom Seaver** Reds	Nolan Ryan	8	6	+ 20
7/82	**Billy Martin** A's	Cowboys	8	5	+ 50 (d)
8/82	**Joe Montana** 49ers	NFL Preview	20	10	+ 50
9/82	**Herchel Walker** Georgia	College Football Issue	12	6	+ 20
10/82	**Los Angeles Rams***	[* Reggie Jackson in corner] World Series	8	5	
11/82	**Lawrence Taylor** Giants	Magic Johnson	10	5	+ 20
12/82	**Patrick Ewing** Georgetown	Baskeball Preview	10	5	+ 35

SPORT

DATE	COVER/Team	MAJOR FEATURE STORIES (Ads)	NM	EM	AUTO
1/83	John Elway* Stanford	Fearless Predictions (*Also Kareem abdul-Jabbar, Walker, Garvey, Leonard, Evert)	6	4	+ 25
2/83	Tony Dorsett* Cowboys	(*Kurt Rambis in Corner)	10	6	+ 20
3/83	Moses Malone Gary Carter*	Top 100 Salaries (*Martina Navratilova, Angel Cordero)	6	4	Varies
4/83	Steve Garvey Padres	Baseball Issue	6	4	+ 5
5/83	Steve Carlton* Phillies	(* Also Wayne Gretzky)	6	4	+ 10
6/83	Gary Carter* Mike Schmidt Expos/Phillies	(*Also Robin Yount, Andre Dawson)	8	6	+ 10 + 40
7/83	Reggie Jackson Angels		8	6	+ 35
8/83	Marcus Allen Raiders	NFL Preview	6	4	+ 15
9/83	Marcus Dupree Oklahoma	College Football Preview	6	4	+ 10
10/83	Mark Gastineau Jets	NHL preview, John Elway	6	4	+ 10
11/83	Franco Harris Pirates	NBA Preview	6	4	+ 10
12/83	Lyle Alzado Raiders	Colege Basketball Preview	6	4	+ 50 (d)
1/84	Dan Marino Dolphins	Playoffs	20	10	+ 40
2/84	Mary Decker * Runner	(*also Dickerson, Hagler, Landry, Ewing, Cosell, Rose, Noah) Fearless Predictions Issue	6	4	-
3/84	Marina Navratilova* Tennis	(*also Dale Murphy, Joe Theisman, Magic Johnson, Mavin Hagler, Herschel Walker) Salaries Issue	6	4	-
4/84	Cal Ripken Jr. Orioles	Baseball Preview Issue	30	15	+ 40
5/84	Wayne Gretzky Oilers		20	15	+ 40
6/84	Dale Murphy Braves	NBA Playoff	6	4	+ 10
7/84	Tom Lasorda,* Sparky Anderson	(*Also Herzog, Joe Torre)	6	4	Varies
8/84	Eric Dickerson Colts	NFL Preview	6	4	+ 10
9/84	Darryl Clack ASU	College Football Preview	6	4	+ 5
10/84	Walter Payton Bears		6	4	+ 30
11/84	Betting Football	NBA Preview	6	4	-
12/84	Chris Mullin & Patrick Ewing St Johns/Georgetown	College Basketball Preview	6	4	Varies
1/85	Dan Marino Dolphins		15	10	+ 40
2/85	Mary Lou Retton* Gymnast	Fearless Predictions (*also Ralph Samson, Alzado, Gooden, Joe Montana)	6	4	-
3/85	Joe Montana Magic Johnson Gary Carter	Salaries Preview USFL	6	4	+ 10
4/85	Dwight Gooden Mets	Baseball Issue	8	6	+ 10
5/85	Gary Matthews & Keith Hernandez Cubs/Mets		6	4	+ 10

SPORT

DATE	COVER/Team	MAJOR FEATURE STORIES (Ads)	Value Guide		
			NM	EM	AUTO
6/85	George Brett		12	6	+ 30
	Royals	Baseball Issue			
7/85	Model	Baseball season	6	4	
		(Regional cover)			
7/85	Kirk Gibson		6	4	+ 10
	Tigers (regional)	Baseball Issue			
8/85	Joe Montana	NFL Preview Issue	15	10	+ 35
	49ers				
9/85	John Maarleveld/Rick Badanjek		6	4	+ 5
	Maryland (Regional)				
9/85	Robbie Bosco	College Football Issue	6	4	+ 5
	BYU				
10/85	Dan Marino	Football Issue	10	6	+ 40
	Dolphins				
11/85	Lawrence Taylor &		8	5	+ 20 each
	Marcus Allen	NHL Preview			
	Giants/Raiders				
12/85	Patrick Ewing		6	4	+ 15
	Knicks	College & Pro Basketball Preview			
1/86	Jim McMahon		6	4	+ 10
	Bears				
2/86	William Perry		6	4	+ 10
	"The Fridge"				
	Bears				
3/86	Stacy Oversier	"The Most Beautiful Women In Sports	6	4	Varies
	Gymnast	(See Through Swimsuit)			
4/86	Bret Saberhagen		6	4	+ 10
	Royals				
4/86	Dwight Gooden		6	4	+ 10
	Mets	Baseball Preview Issue			
5/86	George Brett		8	4	+ 30
	Royals	Larry Bird			
6/86	Wayne Gretzky*	"Top 100 Salaries"	6	4	-
	Oilers	(*Cover Includes others)			
7/86	Hall of Fame Prospects		6	4	-
8/86	Howie Long		6	4	+ 15
	Raiders				
9/86	Jim Harbaugh		6	4	+ 10
10/86	Dan Marino		25	15	+ 35
	Dolphins				
10/86	Magic Johnson		15	10	+ 40
	Lakers (regional)				
11/86	Pervis Ellison		10	5	+ 5
	Louisville	College/Pro Basketball Preview			
11/86	Terry Cummings		6	4	+ 10
12/86	40th Anniversary		10	5	-
	Issue				
1/87	John Elway		10	5	+ 30
	Broncos				
2/87	Montana/Dent/		10	5	Varies
	M. Allen	Superbowl Issue			
	49ers/Raiders/Bears				
3/87	M. Jordon/M. Schmidt/		25	15	Varies
	R. Clemens/Eric Davis				
4/87	Darryl Strawberry Cal Ripken Jr, baseball Preview		6	4	+ 10
	Mets				
5/87	Dominique Wilkins		6	4	+ 10
	Hawks	NBA/ NHL Playoff			

SPORT

155

DATE	COVER/Team	MAJOR FEATURE STORIES (Ads)	NM	EM	AUTO
6/87	Michael Jordan* Bulls	(*also Tyson, Conner, Woodard, Schmidt Hogan, Flutie, Madden, Joyner, Graf) "Top 100 Salaries"	6	4	-
7/87	Dave Parker vs. Mike Scott Pirates/Astros		6	4	+ 10
8/87	Roger Craig & The 49ers 49ers	NFL Preview	6	4	+ 10
9/87	Lawrence Taylor Giants	College Football Preview	6	4	+ 10
10/87	Jim Kelly Bills	NHL Preview	6	4	+ 25
11/87	Larry Bird Celtics	NBA Preview	25	15	+ 35
12/87	"10 Most Intriguing Sports Stories"		6	4	-
1/88	Boomer Esiason		6	4	+ 10
2/88	NFL's All -Time Greatest Coaches		6	4	-
3/88	Jack McDowell/ Greg Jefferies/ Don Lovell Mets/Indians/White Sox		6	4	Varies
4/88	Don Zimmer (Regional Cover)	Baseball Preview Issue	6	4	+ 10
4/88	K. Hernandez/ W. Clark Mets/Giants (regional Cover)	Baseball Preview Issue	6	4	+ 10 each
5/88	Isaiah Thomas Pistons		6	4	+ 15
6/88	"Top 100 Salaries"		6	4	-
7/88	Mike Tyson Boxing		8	5	+ 40
8/88	Howie Long & Marcus Allen & Todd Christianson Raiders		6	4	Varies
9/88	Troy Aikman Cowboys	College Football Preview	12	8	+ 40
10/88	Cornelius Bennett Bills	Football Issue	6	4	+ 5
11/88	Michael Jordan Bulls	NBA Preview	20	10	+ 40
12/88	Stacey King Oklahoma	College Basketball Issue, Wayne Gretzky	6	4	+ 5
1/89	Dennis Gentry Bears		6	4	+ 5
2/89	Cindy Crawford Swimsuit Issue	Swimsuit	25	15	+ 40
3/89	Orel Hershiser Dodgers	Baseball Spring Training Issue	6	4	+ 10
4/89	Don Mattingley Yankees*	Baseball Preview Issue (*also Eckersley, Gibson, Hernandez)	10	6	+ 15
5/89	Magic Johnson Lakers	NBA/NHL Playoff Preview	10	5	+ 40
6/89	Wayne Gretzky Oilers	Top 100 paid athletes (* also Tyson, Marino, Graff, Ewing, Clemens)	20	10	+ 40
7/89	Jose Canseco A's				
8/89	Joe Montana 49ers*	NFL Preview (also Randall Cunningham, Troy Aikman)	10	5	+ 30

SPORT

DATE	COVER/Team	MAJOR FEATURE STORIES (Ads)	NM	EM	AUTO
9/89	Emmitt Smith* Gators	(* also Scott Mitchell, Tony Rice) College Football preview	25	10	+ 25
10/89	Dan Marino Dolphins	43rd Anniversary Issue (*also Dwight Gooden)	10	5	+ 30
11/89	Michael Jordan Larry Bird Magic Johnson		20	10	+ 40 + 35 + 35
12/89	Hank Gathers Loyola*	College Basketball Preview (*also Trevor Wilson, David Butler)	8	5	+100 (d)
1/90	Jim Everett Rams	NFL Playoff Issue	8	5	+ 10
2/90	Swimsuit Model	Swimsuit Issue	20	10	+ 20
3/90	Bo Jackson Royals	Baseball Spring Training Issue	10	6	+ 25
4/90	Jose Canseco A's	Baseball Issue (*Orel Hershiser, Wally Joyner)	7	4	+ 10
5/90	Rickey Henderson A's	Baseball Preview	7	4	+ 10
6/90	Michael Jordan* Bulls	100 Top paid players (*Montan, Gretzky, Stockton, etc)	15	9	+ 40
7/90	Will Clark Giants		7	4	+ 10
8/90	Joe Montana 49ers	Football Issue (* also Willie Anderson, Bobby Humphry)	12	8	+ 30
9/90	John Elway* Broncos	NFL Preview (*also Roger Craig, Jim Everett, Bo Jackson	12	8	+ 20
10/90	Joe Montana 49ers	'100 best sports stories) (*also Wayne Gretzky, Michael Jordan, others)	12	8	+ 20
11/90	Joe Montana 49ers	NHL Preview, Swimsuit Calendar	8	5	+ 20
12/90	Randall Cunningham Lawrence Taylor*	NBA/College Basketball Issue (*KJ, Thomas, others)	6	4	+ 10
1/91	Michael Jordan Bulls	NFL Playoff Preview	10	5	+ 40
2/91	Rowanne Swimsuit	Swimsuit Issue	20	10	+ 15
3/91	Ken Griffey Jr. Mariners		20	10	+ 40
4/91	Jose Canseco A's*	Baseball Issue (* also Ryan Sandberg, Dwight Gooden)	6	4	+ 10
5/91	Matt Williams Giants*	Baseball Poster of Nolan Ryan, Ken Griffey Jr (* also Eddie Murray, Benito Santiago)	6	4	+ 10
6/91	Darryl Strawberry Dodgers	Sports Salary Survey	6	4	+ 10
7/91	Joe Montana 49ers*	NFL Hottest Cheerleader poster, NFL Preview (* also Lenny Dykstra, Elliott, King)	10	6	+ 20
8/91	Ronnie Lott Raiders	Football Poster	6	4	+ 10
9/91	Joe Montana 49ers*	NFL & College Preview (* also Marcus Allen, Jim Everett, Bobby Humphrey)	10	6	+ 20
10/91	Bo Jackson Raiders	45 Great years of Sport	6	4	+ 10
11/91	Michael Jordan Bulls*	NBA Preview (Swimsuit Calendar) (*also C. Drexler, David Robinson, Magic Johnson, Charles Barkley)	10	5	+ 40
12/91	Michael Jordan Bulls		15	10	+ 30
1/92	Jim Kelly Bills	NBA Pictorial	10	5	+ 25
2/92	Charles Barkley 76ers		12	7	+ 10

SPORT

DATE	COVER/Team	MAJOR FEATURE STORIES (Ads)	NM	EM	AUTO
				Value Guide	
3/92	Swimsuit Model	Swimsuit Issue	15	10	+ 15
4/92	Eric Davis, Darry Strawberry, Brett Butler Dodgers	Baseball Preview issue	6	4	+ 10 each
5/92	Michael Jordan Bulls	NBA Playoff Issue, Cheerleaders (*also Tim Hardaway, Patrick Ewing	10	5	+ 40
5/92	Cal Ripken Jr. Orioles	NBA Playoff Issue, Cheerleaders	10	5	+ 40
6/92	Michael Jordan Scottie Pippen Bulls	(*also Magic Johnson)	10	5	+ 40
7/92	Troy Aikman Cowboys	NFL Preseason	10	5	+ 30
8/92	Mark Rypien Redskins*	NFL Hottest Cheerleaders (*also Jerry rice, Tommy Maddox)	6	4	+ 10
9/92	Eric Dickerson Raiders	Football Preview Issue	6	4	+ 10
10/92	Larry Johnson Hornets	NBA Issue	6	4	+ 10
11/92	Tim Hardaway Warriors*	NBA PREVIEW (*also Pete Rose)	6	4	+ 10
12/92	Chargers/Steelers	Swimsuit Calendar	6	4	+ 5
1/93	Charles Barkley* 76ers	(*also Jerry Rice, Magic Johnson,others) Top 40	6	4	Varies
2/93	Jill Model	Swimsuit Issue (Newstand version)	25	10	+ 15
2/93	Charles Barkley Model	Swimsuit Issue Hank Aaron	25	10	+ 15
3/93	Dave Winfield* Toronto Blue Jays	Inside Baseball Issue	6	4	+ 10
4/93	Barry Bonds Giants	Baseball 12993 preview edition (* also Bonila, Canseco, Clemens)	6	4	+ 15
5/93	Michael Jordan Bulls	NBA PLAYOFF ISSUE (*also Pat Ewing)	15	5	+ 40
6/93	Michael Jordan Bulls	NBA Final Edition (*also C. Barkley, D. Robinson, P. Ewing)	6	4	+ 40
7/93	Troy Aikman Cowboys	Football Issue	10	5	+ 20
8/93	Steve Young 49ers	(*also Joe Montana, Reggie White, Troy Aikman) Football Preview Issue	10	5	+ 20
9/93	Joe Montana Chiefs	Football Issue	10	5	+ 20
10/93	Steve Young 49ers*	Whos the Best QB? (*also Troy Aikman, Joe Montana, Randall Cunningham, Dan Marino)	6	3	+ 15
11/93	Michael Jordan Bulls	NBA Preview (*also Barkley, Shaq, Ewing)	10	4	+ 30
12/93	Michael Jordan Bulls	10 years of Michael Jordan (swimsuit Calendar)	20	10	+ 40
1/94	Steve Young 49ers	The Best 40 (* also Bonds, Barkley, Jordan, Thomas, Smith)	10	5	+ 20
2/94	Joe Montana Chiefs*	SuperBowl (*also Troy Aikman, Jerry Rice)	10	5	+ 20
3/94	Alison Armitage Actress	Swimsuit Issue	15	10	+ 15
4/94	Barry Bonds Giants*	Baseball 1994 issue (* also Joe Carter, David Justice, Juan Gonzalez)	10	6	+ 20
5/94	Mike Piazza Dodgers	NBA Showtime Pictorial	12	6	+ 15
6/94	Scottie Pippen Bulls	NBA Playoffs (*background with Jordan)	8	5	+ 25

SPORT

DATE	COVER/Team	MAJOR FEATURE STORIES (Ads)	Value Guide		
			NM	EM	AUTO
7/94	**Aikman/Smith** Cowboys	NBA Draft Preview, Swimsuit	8	6	+ 25
8/94	**Dan Marino** Dolphins*	Football Preview (*Thurman Thomas, Jerry Rice, Troy Aikman)	12	8	+ 30
9/94	**75th Pro Football** Cowboys*	75 Yeras of Pro Football (Mail Version) (* also Walter Payton, Joe Montana, Joe Namath, Jim Brown)	12	8	+ 20
9/94	**Troy Aikman** Cowboys*	75 Yeras of Pro Football (Store Verison) (* also Walter Payton, Joe Montana, Joe Namath, Jim Brown)	12	8	+ 20
10/94	**Marcus Allen** Chiefs	NBA Preseason	8	5	+ 10
11/94	**Michael Jordan** Bulls*	Basketball Preview (*Charles Barkley, Patrick Ewing, Hakem Olajuwon)	10	6	+ 30
12/94	**Shaq** Magic	College Basketball Preview Swimsuit Calendar	10	6	+ 30
1/95	**Frank Thomas** White Sox*	Athlete of the Year (*Emmit Smith, Ken Griffey Jr, Troy Aikman, Olajuwon)	10	6	+ 20
2/95	**Jerry Rice** 49ers*	SuperBowl Issue, Swimsuit sneak Peek (*also Troy Aikman & others)	6	4	+ 20
3/95	**Shanna** Model	Swimsuit Issue	15	10	+ 10
4/95	**Michael Jordan** White Sox*	 (*also Thomas, Bonds, Ripken)	6	4	+ 30
5/95	**Charles Barkley** Suns	Baseball predictions (*Rodman)	6	4	+ 15
6/95	**Michael Jordan** Bulls	NBA Playoff Preview	6	4	+ 25
7/95	**Steve Young** 49ers*	Swimsuit Special (*Troy Aikman)	6	4	+ 15
8/95	**Steve Young** 49ers*	Football Preview (*Jeff Hosteler, Emmitt Smith, John Elway)	6	4	+ 15
9/95	**Steve Young** 49ers*	Pro Football 95 (*Marino, Aikman, Cunnigham, Elway)	6	4	+ 15
10/95	**Dan Marino/Jerry Rice/Irvin/Warren Moon** 49ers*	Subsription Version	6	4	+ 15
10/95	**Steve Young** 49ers*	 (*also Jerry Rice) Store Version	6	4	+ 15
11/95	**Michael Jordan** Bulls*	Pro preview Issue (*also Shaq, Olajuwon, Johson, Exel)	6	4	+ 15
12/95	**Dennis Rodman** Spurs*	Baslektball Preview (* UCLA)	6	4	+ 15
1/96	**Michael Jordan** Bulls		6	4	+ 15
2/96	**Dan Marino/Troy Aikman** Dolphins/Cowboys	Superbowl Dream Team	6	4	+ 15
3/96	**Swimsuit**	Swimsuit Issue	6	4	+ 15
4/96	**Penny Anfernee Hardaway** Magic	Baseball Issue	6	4	+ 15
5/96	**Magic Johnson/Dennis Rodman/Michael Jordan** Lakers/Bulls	NBA Playoff	6	4	+ 15
6/96	**Michael Jordan/Scottie Pippen/Dennis Rodman** Bulls		6	4	+ 15

CHAPTER EIGHT:
TIME AND LIFE MAGAZINE

TIME MAGAZINE

Time magazine has been covering historical events for seven decades through portraits of individuals who impact our history. Along side presidents, villains, artists, scientists and a load of politicians is a significant representation of movie stars and athletes. Since this audience is more interested in athletes than Marilyn Monroe, I will cover the likes of Marilyn's ex, Joe Dimaggio, and the like.

Time began making sports covers in 1923 with a dummy issue that featured a boxer name Floyd Johnson. There are 170 sports related covers. Baseball and football players dominate the sports pages followed by tennis and boxing. However, the most popular *Time* magazine covers for collectors are baseball players and then golfers.

The most popular issue of Time is the 1936 Joe Dimaggio because of the immense demand to get the issue autographed. An exmt issue of Joe Dimaggio went for over $500 in a recent auction. Just as valuable but rarely seen are the two Bobby Jones Time magazines. Both of these are on every golf magazine collectors want list. The rarest issue of all the sports covers is the Dummy issue which rarely trade hands.

I have diligently compiled a listing of all the sports covers by subject for you below. However, if you are serious about collecting *Time* magazines you need to obtain the book "The Faces of History-- TIME magazine covers 1923-1991".

GRADING OF TIME MAGAZINES

Grading of *Time* magazines is similar to *Sports Illustrated*. However, labels were placed on the back of the magazine before 1945. After 1945 you will find magazines with the label on the front. Most collectors want the magazine to be ex-mt or better with or without the label. Issues used for autograph purposes are preferred without a label. Most of the magazines will be used for framing purposes, so it is critical that the cover be clean without any major flaws. However, the early issues (pre 1940) may be acceptable in excellent grade. The most common flaw with *Time* magazines is flaking along the spine. The paper stock is excellent, so the issues that have survived the paper drives over the years tend to be in good condition.

COLLECTING TIME MAGAZINES

Collecting every sports issue of *Time* is a challenge because there is no easy source. You can contact sports publication dealers across the country and discover that they only have a handful in stock at any given time.

For example, I have seen only three George Sisler issues in the last four years. Some of the most advanced sports collectors usually have a George Sisler on their want list.

Many, people only collect their favorite player. A few people collect every baseball cover and even fewer collect every sport cover. However, the challenge is fun and rewarding and you will meet a lot of interesting people on the way.

Another important aspect of *Time* magazine collecting is the variations that are available. *Time* magazine began to make variations as early as WWII with the 1945 Pony editions. I do not know all of the variations, that exist but I have compiled the variations of which I am aware of:

1. Pacific Edition - Currently produced for the Far East.
2. Pacific Edition (Pony) small used during and after WWII. Mel Ott was on a cover.
3. Time International - Currently produced for Europe.
4. Atlantic Edition (Pony) small used during and after WWII. Mel Ott was on a cover in 1945.
5. Latin American Edition - These started as early as 1948 with Joe Dimaggio on the cover. The paper is thinner, different stock.
6. Canadian Edition - These have Canada written on them. In the earlier years a Canadian maple leaf was on the center page. I also have a version with different red color variation than the American version. Later editions of Canadian Time have a small maple leaf. From the late 1950's through today the Canadian versions just state "Canada" on them.
7. Atlantic/East Coast Edition - In the 1960's it stated Atlantic Edition on the cover.
8. Classroom Edition - This was design for school education and it had a statement across the middle saying Classroom Edition.

AUTOGRAPHED TIME MAGAZINES

Time magazines are one of the most popular magazines in the world to have autographed. A collection of autographed *Time* magazine 'covers' sold for over $170,000 in a 1996 auction. Many great men and woman of this century have appeared on the cover and were willing signers through the mail. The autograph price list is based on complete magazines, however, autographed covers of deceased players will still command a quality price.

My success at getting *Time* magazines signed through the mail has been just as good or better than getting my *Sports Illustrated* signed. Many collectors treasure their *Time* autographed issues. I recommend that you review the autograph *Sports Illustrated* chapter for further details on how to obtain autographs.

As for values of current issues, most Autographed *Time* magazines will retain the cumulative value of the magazine. The older issues have extreme limits on availability and thus an increasing in demand for key covers. Values for autographed covers of deceased athletes are estimates and may go for higher prices on clean magazines.

TIME MAGAZINE

VALUE GUIDE

BASEBALL COVERS		NM	EM	Ex	+Auto
3/30/25	George Sisler - Browns	$700	$500	$200	+$300 (d)
4/11/27	Connie Mack - A's	$300	$250	$100	+$400 (d)
7/09/28	Roger Hornsby - Braves	$300	$200	$100	+$400 (d)
7/29/29	Jimmy Foxx - A's	$200	$150	$ 65	+$300 (d)
10/14/29	W. Wrigley Jr - Cubs	$150	$100	$ 50	+$200 (d)
8/25/30	W. Robinson - Dodgers	$150	$125	$ 50	+$250 (d)
3/28/32	Gabby Street-Cardinals	$150	$100	$ 45	+$200 (d)

TIME MAGAZINE

VALUE GUIDE

BASEBALL COVERS

		NM	EM	Ex	+Auto
9/19/32	Col Jacob Ruppert	$100	$ 75	$ 40	+$250 (d)
7/09/34	Lefty Gomez-Yankees	$100	$ 75	$ 45	+$150 (d)
4/15/35	Dizzy Dean - Cardinals	$100	$ 75	$ 40	+$150 (d)
10/07/35	Mickey Cochrane-Tigers	$100	$ 75	$ 40	+$150 (d)
7/13/36	Joe Dimaggio - Yankees	$550	$450	$150	+$250 (d)
10/05/36	Lou Gehrig-Yankees/ Carl Hubbell-Giants	$300	$250	$100	+$1000/+$250(d)
4/19/37	Bob Feller - Indians	$150	$100	$ 50	+$ 50
8/01/38	Happy Chandler - Commissioner	$ 75	$ 65	$ 35	+$150 (d)
7/02/45	Mel Ott - Giants	$ 75	$ 50	$ 20	+$250 (d)
7/02/45	Mel Ott - Giants (pony East/West Edition)	$ 75	$ 65	$ 35	+$250 (d)
4/14/47	Leo Durocher - Dodger	$ 50	$ 40	$ 25	+$200 (d)
4/14/47	Leo Durocher (Classroom ed)	$100	$ 75	$ 25	+$200 (d)
9/22/47	Jackie Robinson - Dodgers	$150	$ 85	$ 30	+$300 (d)
10/04/48	Joe Dimaggio - Yankees	$350	$200	$ 75	+$175
9/ 05/49	Stan Musial - Cardinals	$175	$150	$ 50	+$ 30
4/10/50	Ted Williams - Red Sox	$300	$200	$ 75	+$150
10/01/51	Bert Lahr - (comedy)	$ 40	$ 30	$ 15	+$ 50 (d)
4/28/52	Eddie Stanky - Cardinals	$ 45	$ 35	$ 15	+$ 25
7/01/53	Mickey Mantle - Yankees	$250	$125	$ 75	+$250 (d)
7/26/54	Willie Mays - Giants	$250	$200	$ 75	+$ 50
6/13/55	Gwen Verdon (actress) Damn Yankees	$ 35	$ 25	$ 10	+$ 50
7/11/55	A. Busch - owner Cardinals	$ 35	$ 25	$ 5	+$ 50 (d)
8/08/55	Roy Campanella - Dodgers	$ 75	$ 65	$ 25	+$250 (d)
10/03/55	Casey Stengel - Yankees	$ 50	$ 40	$ 15	+$200
5/28/56	Robin Roberts - Phillies	$ 50	$ 40	$ 10	+$ 20
7/08/57	Berdie Tebbetts - Reds	$ 35	$ 25	$ 5	+$ 45
4/28/58	Walley O'Malley - Dodgers	$ 35	$ 25	$ 10	+$150 (d)
8/24/59	Rocky Colavito - Indians	$ 40	$ 30	$ 10	+$ 35
9/11/64	Hank Bauer - Orioles	$ 40	$ 30	$ 10	+$ 15
6/10/66	Juan Marichal - Giants	$ 75	$ 40	$ 15	+$ 20
9/13/68	Denny Mclain - Tigers	$ 40	$ 30	$ 15	+$ 15
9/05/69	Mets	$ 40	$ 30	$ 5	Varies
8/23/71	Vida Blue - A's	$ 40	$ 25	$ 5	+$ 15
7/10/72	Johnny Bench - Reds	$ 40	$ 25	$ 5	+$ 20
6/03/74	Reggie Jackson - A's	$ 50	$ 30	$ 5	+$ 40
8/18/75	Charlie Finley - A's	$ 20	$ 15	$ 5	+$100 (d)
4/26/76	Babe Ruth	$ 15	$ 10		
7/18/77	Rod Carew - Twins	$ 30	$ 15		+$ 20
5/11/81	Billy Martin - A's	$ 20	$ 10		+$ 75 (d)
8/19/85	Pete Rose - Reds	$ 20	$ 10		+$ 20
4/07/86	Dwight Gooden - Mets	$ 15	$ 5		+$ 5
7/10/89	Pete Rose - Reds	$ 15	$ 5		+$ 20
1/06/92	Ted Turner - Owner	$ 10	$ 5		+$ 20
8/22/94	Strike	$ 5			
9/11/95	Cal Ripken Jr - Orioles (corner only)	$ 5			

BASKETBALL COVERS

10/20/58	Nonagenarian Stagg	$ 40	$ 25	$ 5	+$150 (d)
3/17/61	Oscar Robinson (Cinc)	$ 40	$ 20	$ 5	+$ 40
3/18/85	Larry Bird/Wayne Gretzky	$ 40	$ 30	$ 5	+$ 60/+$50
2/12/96	Magic Johnson - Lakers	$ 10	$ 4		+$ 40

TIME MAGAZINE

VALUE GUIDE

BOXING COVERS		NM	EM	Ex	+Auto
2/27/23	Floyd Johnson (dummy)	$600	$400	$250	+$ 500(d)
9/17/23	Jack Dempsey	$200	$150	$ 75	+$ 200(d)
8/30/26	James Tunney	$125	$ 75	$ 50	+$ 200(d)
6/24/29	Max Schmeling	$150	$100	$ 35	+$ 50
10/01/31	Primo Carnera	$ 45	$ 35	$ 15	+$ 150(d)
9/29/41	Joe Louis	$ 75	$ 50	$ 25	+$ 250 (d)
6/25/51	Sugar Ray Robinson	$ 50	$ 35	$ 20	+$ 250 (d)
3/22/63	Cassius Clay - Boxing	$100	$ 50	$ 35	+$ 95
3/08/71	Ali vs Frazier	$ 35	$ 25	$ 15	+$ 95/$25
2/27/78	Muhammad Ali	$ 30	$ 20	$ 10	+$ 95
6/14/82	Gerry Cooney	$ 10	$ 5		+$ 20
6/27/88	Mike Tyson	$ 5	$ 2		+$ 25

FOOTBALL COVERS					
10/05/25	Red Grange	$300	$200	$100	+$ 300 (d)
11/07/27	Knute Rockne (Notre Dame)	$250	$150	$ 75	+$ 500 (d)
9/23/29	Christian Cagle (army)	$ 75	$ 50	$ 25	+$ 125 (d)
11/17/30	Football Crowd	$ 35	$ 25	$ 10	
11/21/31	Captain Wood (Harvard)	$ 50	$ 40	$ 20	+$ 125
11/14/32	Howard Jones (USC)	$100	$ 75	$ 20	+$ 250 (d)
11/11/33	Football Crowd	$ 40	$ 20	$ 10	
11/11/35	Football Crowd	$ 40	$ 20	$ 10	
10/25/37	Duke Wade (Football)	$ 40	$ 30	$ 15	+$ 100
11/06/39	Tom Harmon (Michigan)	$ 50	$ 40	$ 25	+$ 100 (d)
11/12/45	Blanchard/Davis(Army)	$ 50	$ 35	$ 15	+$ 20 each
10/14/46	Frank Leahy (Notre Dame)	$ 40	$ 30	$ 15	+$ 50
11/03/47	Chappuis (Michigan)	$ 45	$ 35	$ 20	+$ 40
11/19/51	Dick Kazmaier (Princeton)	$ 45	$ 35	$ 15	+$ 15
11/09/53	Lattner - Notre Dame	$ 45	$ 35	$ 20	+$ 10
5/24/54	Clint Murchison (owner)	$ 25	$ 15	$ 5	+$ 50 (d)
11/29/54	Bobby Layne(Lions)	$ 40	$ 25	$ 15	+$ 50 (d)
10/08/56	Daugherty (Michigan St)	$ 40	$ 30	$ 15	+$ 35
11/30/59	Sam Huff (Giants)	$ 40	$ 20	$ 5	+$ 25
6/16/61	Clint Murchison (owners)	$ 25	$ 15	$ 2	+$ 50 (d)
12/21/62	Vince Lombardi (Packers)	$ 45	$ 20	$ 5	+$ 250 (d)
10/18/63	Roger Staubach -Navy	$ 40	$ 20	$ 10	+$ 25
11/20/64	Parshian (Notre Dame)	$ 35	$ 25	$ 10	+$ 25
11/26/65	Jimmy Brown (Browns)	$ 40	$ 30	$ 15	+$ 25
10/28/66	Seymour/Hanratty(Notre Dame)	$ 35	$ 20	$ 15	+$ 15 each
1/17/72	Staubach & Griese	$ 35	$ 25	$ 15	+$ 25 each
10/16/72	Joe Namath (Jets)	$ 50	$ 35	$ 15	+$ 50
12/11/72	Don Shula (Dolphins)	$ 35	$ 25	$ 10	+$ 20
12/08/75	White, Greene, Holmes, Greenwood (Steelers)	$ 35	$ 25	$ 10	+$ 15 each
1/10/77	Superbowl (Raiders vs Vikings)	$ 20	$ 10		Varies
1/10/78	Superbowl (Denver vs Cowboys)	$ 25	$ 15		Varies
9/29/80	Bear Bryant - Alabama	$ 25	$ 15		+$ 100
1/12/82	Joe Montana - 49ers	$ 25	$ 15		+$ 40
1/27/86	Payton & Fridge	$ 10	$ 5		+$ 35/+$10
6/27/ 94	OJ Simpson	$ 10	$ 5		+$ 30

GOLF COVERS					
8/30/25	Bobby Jones	$600	$400	$250	+$1200 (d)
9/21/30	Bobby Jones	$600	$400	$250	+$1200 (d)
6/06/38	Johnny Goodman	$ 45	$ 35	$ 15	+$ 150 (d)
1/10/49	Ben Hogan	$150	$ 75	$ 35	+$ 200 (l)

TIME MAGAZINE

VALUE GUIDE

GOLF COVERS		NM	EM	Ex	+Auto
6/21/54	Sam Snead	$100	$ 45	$ 15	+$ 35
5/02/60	Arnold Palmer	$100	$ 35	$ 15	+$ 50
6/29/63	Jack Nicklaus	$100	$ 35	$ 15	+$ 60
7/19/71	Leo Trevino	$ 60	$ 25	$ 10	+$ 35

HOCKEY

		NM	EM	Ex	+Auto
2/11/35	Lorne Chabot - Blackhawks	$ 50	$ 35	$ 15	+$ 50 (d)
3/14/38	Dave Kerr - Rangers	$ 50	$ 35	$ 15	+$ 50 (d)
3/01/68	Bobby Hull - BlackHawks	$ 50	$ 35	$ 15	+$ 25
10/09/72	Phil Esposito (Canadian only)	$ 50	$ 30	$ 15	+$ 25
10/14/74	Mele - Gordie Howe (Canadian only)	$ 50	$ 25	$ 10	+$ 25
2/24/75	Bernie Parent	$ 25	$ 15	$ 10	+$ 15
6/26/78	Woman in Sports Field Hockey	$ 10	$ 5		+$ 15
3/18/85	Wayne Gretzky	$ 35	$ 25	$ 15	+$ 40

OTHER SPORTS COVERS

		NM	EM	Ex	+Auto
9/05/27	Deverux Milburan (Polo)	$ 25	$ 15		+$ 100 (d)
1/13/30	Domingo Ugalde (Jai Alai)	$ 20	$ 10		+$ 100 (d)
3/03/30	Pointer Mary Blue (Hunting)	$ 25	$ 15		+$ 100 (d)
5/26/30	Edward Statley (Horse Owner)	$ 25	$ 15		+$ 100 (d)
9/15/30	Mike Vanderbilt (Yachting)	$ 20	$ 10		+$ 50
3/14/31	David Ingalls (Polo)	$ 25	$ 15		+$ 50
7/11/32	Ben Eastman - Stanford (Track)	$ 20	$ 10		+$ 50
3/27/33	John Whitney (Polo)	$ 20	$ 10		+$ 50
5/07/34	Edward Bradley (Horse Owner)	$ 20	$ 10		+$ 100(d)
8/20/34	Calvalcade (Horse)	$ 35	$ 15		
5/10/37	Matt Winn (Horse Owner)	$ 35	$ 15		+$ 100(d)
	Horses [Blue Grass,Bourbon,Bands,Build Up]				
5/17/48	Eddie Arcaro - Jockey	$ 30	$ 15		+$ 25
8/02/48	Mel Patton (Olympic Hurdler)	$ 20	$ 10		+$ 20
5/39/49	Ben Jones (Horse Owner)	$ 20	$ 10		+$ 100(d)
7/21/52	Bob Mathias (Track)	$ 25	$ 10		+$ 25
5/31/54	Native Dancer (Horse)	$ 35	$ 25		
12/03/56	Parry O'Brian (Track)	$ 20	$ 10		+$ 15
2/10/58	Willie Hartak (Jockey)	$ 20	$ 10		+$ 25
8/29/60	Rafer Johnson (Decathlon)	$ 20	$ 10		+$ 25
7/09/65	Jim Clark (Car Racing)	$ 20	$ 10		+$ 20
9/11/72	Mark Spitz (Swimmer)	$ 20	$ 10		+$ 15
6/11/73	Secretariat (Horse)	$ 35	$ 15		
9/01/76	Nadia Comaneci (Gymnastics)	$ 20	$ 10		+$ 15
6/13/77	Steve Cauthen (Jockey)	$ 15	$ 5		+$ 15
5/29/78	Steve Cauthen (Jockey)	$ 15	$ 5		+$ 15
7/28/84	Carl Lewis (Track)		$ 10	$ 5	+$ 20
8/13/84	Carl Lewis (Track)		$ 10	$ 5	+$ 20
2/09/87	Dennis Conners- American Cup	$ 5			+$ 10
9/19/88	Jackie Joyner Kersee (Track)	$ 10	$ 5		+$ 20
Special	Michael Johnson (Track)	$ 5			
8/05/96	Kerri Stug/Bela Karolyi (Gymnastics)	$ 5			
8/12/96	Michael Johnson (Track)	$ 5			

WINTER SPORT COVERS

		NM	EM	Ex	+Auto
2/17/36	Leni Riefenstahl (Skiing)	$ 35	$ 25	$ 10	+$ 200(d)
7/17/39	Sonja Henie (Ice Skating)	$ 65	$ 45	$ 20	+$ 200(d)

TIME MAGAZINE

VALUE GUIDE

WINTER SPORTS COVERS		NM	EM	Ex	+Auto
2/03/48	Barbara Ann Scott (Ice Skating)	$ 25	$ 15	$ 10	+$ 25
1/21/52	Andrea Lawrence (Skiing)	$ 25	$ 20	$ 10	+$ 20
2/02/76	Dorthy Hamill (Ice Skating)	$ 15	$ 10		+$ 10
2/12/80	Eric Heiden (Speed Skating)	$ 10	$ 5		+$ 10
10/17/83	Peter Ueberroth (Olympics)	$ 10	$ 5		+$ 10
1/30/84	Phil Mahre & Tamara Mckinney	$ 10	$ 5		+$ 10 Each
2/15/88	Debbie Thomas (Ice Skating)	$ 5	$ 2		+$ 15
1/24/94	Tony Harding/Nancy Kerrigan	$ 5	$ 2		+$ 15 Each

TENNIS COVERS

7/16/26	Helen Wills	$100	$ 50	$ 25	+$ 100 (i)
6/31/29	Helen Wills	$100	$ 50	$ 25	+$ 100 (i)
7/06/31	Betty Nuthall	$ 35	$ 25	$ 15	+$ 100 (d)
8/01/32	Ellsworth Vines Jr.	$ 35	$ 25	$ 15	+$ 100 (d)
9/04/33	Jack Crawford	$ 35	$ 20		+$ 100 (d)
9/03/34	Fred Perry	$ 35	$ 15		+$ 100 (d)
9/02/35	Donald Budge	$ 35	$ 15		+$ 25
9/14/36	Helen Jacobs	$ 35	$ 15		+$ 25
9/13/37	Gottfried Von Cramm	$ 30	$ 15		+$ 100 (d)
9/02/46	Pauline Betz	$ 25	$ 15		+$ 25
9/01/47	Jake Kramer	$ 30	$ 15		+$ 15
8/27/51	Dick Savitt	$ 25	$ 10		+$ 15
8/26/57	Althea Gibson	$ 25	$ 15		+$ 35
6/10/73	Bobby Riggs	$ 15	$ 5		+$ 100 (d)
4/28/75	Jimmy Conners	$ 15	$ 5		+$ 25
6/30/80	Bjorn Borg	$ 15	$ 5		+$ 20

LIFE MAGAZINE

Life Magazine is an icon like *Time* but it is more known for pictures and covers. *Life* is heavily collected by non sport magazine collectors for the purpose of getting autographed and framed. While this is popular to do, only a few *Life* magazines are used heavily for this purpose. Joe Dimmaggio, Mickey Mantle, Ted Williams and Ben Hogan are the four most popular *Life* magazines used for autographing. The other issues are also used but clean copies are required for the avid autographed magazine collector.

Life is more common than any other magazine from the 1930's - 1960's period. This is because people love to save these big picture magazines. However, this also keeps the price of these magazines down compared to *Time* or other publications of the same era.

The magazine was a weekly but went down to semi-annual in the 1970's. It was reintroduced as a monthly in 1978 and has continued on that track since.

VALUE GUIDE

BASEBALL COVERS		NM	EM	EX	+Auto
4/25/38	John Thomas Winsett - Dodgers	25	15		+$ 40
5/01/39	Joe Dimaggio - Yankees	150	100	50	+$195
4/01/40	John Rucker - Giants	25	15		+$ 40
9/01/41	Ted Williams - Red Sox	150	75	25	+$150
4/01/46	Charles "Red" Barrett - Cardinals	25	15		+$ 40
4/05/48	Dodgers Rookies	20	10		

LIFE MAGAZINE

VALUE GUIDE

BASEBALL COVERS

Date		NM	EM	Ex	+Auto
5/02/49	Arnold Galiffa- Army	20	10		+$ 40
8/01/49	Joe Dimaggio - Yankees	150	55	20	+$150
5/08/50	Jackie Robinson- Dodgers	60	40	15	+$300 (d)
6/08/53	Roy Campanella- Dodgers	60	40	10	+$300 (d)
9/14/53	Casey Stengel- Yankees	45	25	5	+$300 (d)
6/25/56	Mickey Mantle- Yankees	75	55	20	+$200 (d)
10/14/57	Milwaukee Braves Victory Parade	30	20	5	Varies
4/28/58	Willie Mays - Giants	45	25	5	+$ 40
7/21/58	Roy Campanella - Dodgers	60	40	20	+$300 (d)
8/18/61	Mickey Mantle & Roger Maris- Yankees	75	45	20	+$200(d)/ +$500 (d)
4/13/62	Richard Burton & Liz Taylor (Baseball cards of Mickey Mantle/Maris)	200	125	85	
9/28/62	Don Drysdale - Dodgers	40	20	5	+$100 (d)
8/02/63	Sandy Koufax - Dodgers	40	25	10	+$ 50
7/30/65	Mickey Mantle - Yankees	60	40	10	+$150 (d)
9/08/67	Carl Yastrzemski - Red Sox	45	25	5	+$ 25
9/26/69	Jerry Koosman - Mets	35	15	5	+$ 10

BASKETBALL COVERS

Date		NM	EM	Ex	+Auto
1/15/40	Ralph Vaughn/Tom McGarvin - USC	25	15	5	+$ 20 each
1/22/45	Bill Kotsores/Ivor Summer - St Johns	25	15	5	+$ 20 each
3/24/72	Kareem Jabbar/Wilt Chamberlain	25	15	5	+$ 40/+$75

BOXING COVERS

Date		NM	EM	Ex	+Auto
5/16/49	Child Boxer	15	10	5	
4/07/58	Sugar Ray Robinson	25	15	5	+$150 (d)
7/20/59	Ingemar Johansson / Birgit Lundgren	20	10	5	+$ 35/+$20
3/06/64	Cassius Clay	45	35	5	+$100
10/23/70	Muhammad Ali	30	20	5	+$100
3/05/71	Muhammad Ali/Walt Frazier	30	20	5	+$100/+$25
3/19/71	Joe Frazier / Muhammad Ali	30	20	5	+$100/+$25
1/19/81	Muhammad Ali	20	10	5	+$100

FOOTBALL COVERS

Date		NM	EM	Ex	+Auto
10/11/37	Chuck Williams -USC	25	15	5	+$ 40
10/24/38	Sid Luckman-Columbia	25	15	5	+$ 40
10/09/39	Child Football Player	15	5		
11/11/40	Tom Harmon-Michigan	35	25	5	+$ 75 (d)
11/17/41	Texas Football Players	25	10	5	
10/22/45	Paul Sarringhaus-Ohio State	20	10	5	+$ 20
9/16/46	Glen Davis/Doc Blanchard-Army	40	25	5	+$ 40
9/29/47	Johnny Lujack-Notre Dame	35	15	5	+$ 25
10/25/48	Football Crowd	15	5		
9/27/48	Doak Walker - SMU	35	20	5	+$ 25
10/03/49	Charles Justice-UNC	20	10	5	+$ 20
11/13/50	Kyle Rote-SMU	20	10	5	+$ 20
12/05/60	Pro Football Kickoff	15	5		
11/17/61	Minnesota Vikings Team	30	15	5	Varies
12/10/65	Tommy Nobis -Texas	30	15	5	+$ 20
4/08/66	Pete Dawkins -Army	25	15	5	+$ 20
10/14/66	Brown vs Packers	25	15	5	
12/13/68	Baltimore Colts	25	15	5	
6/20/69	Joe Namath -Jets	25	15	5	+$ 65

LIFE MAGAZINE

VALUE GUIDE

FOOTBALL COVERS		NM	EM	Ex	+Auto
12/03/71	Baltimore Colts	25	15	5	
1/14/72	Roger Staubach & Tom Landry	25	15	5	+$ 25 each
10/06/72	Football's Tough Guys	15	10	5	
11/03/72	Joe Namath –Jets	25	15	5	+$ 65

TENNIS COVERS

		NM	EM	Ex	+Auto
2/01/37	Tennis at Vassar College	15	10	5	
8/28/39	Alice Marble	15	10	5	+$ 25
7/06/59	Gardner McKay	15	10	5	+$ 10
9/20/68	Arthur Ashe	25	15	5	+$100 (d)
Jan /83	Jimmy Conners	20	10	5	+$ 25

OLYMPIC SPORTS COVERS

		NM	EM	Ex	+Auto
08/02/48	Mel Patton - Track	25	15	5	+$ 25
07/11/49	Bob Mathias- Track	25	15	5	+$ 25
07/23/51	Mary Freeman- Swimming	15	10	5	+$ 10
02/11/52	Henri Oreiller- Skiing	15	10	5	+$ 10
12/10/56	Bobby Morrow -Track	25	10	5	+$ 10
02/08/60	U.S. Skiers	15	10		
02/29/60	Tamas Sudar- Ski Jumping	15	10		
08/22/60	Chris Von Saltza &Lynn Burke	15	10		+$ 10 each
09/12/60	Doris Fuchs &Sharon Richardson	15	10		+$ 10 each
02/14/64	Ski Jumper	15	10		
07/31/64	Diver	15	10		
10/09/64	Donna de Varona- Swimming	15	10		+$ 10
10/30/64	Don Schollander- Swimming	15	10		+$ 10
02/23/68	Peggy Fleming- Figure Skating	15	10		+$ 15
02/18/72	Yukio Kasaya- Ski Jumping	15	10		+$ 15
05/05/72	Cathy Rigby- Gymanastic	15	10		+$ 10
08/18/72	Mark Spitz- Swimmer	15	10		+$ 15
09/15/72	Munich Murders	15	10		
09/22/72	Frank Shorter- Marathon	15	10		+$ 15
Sum/ 84	Mary Decker -Track	15	10		+$ 10
Jan/ 85	Mary Lou Retton-Gymastics	25	10		+$ 10
Feb/ 88	Bonnie Blair- Speedskating	15	10		+$ 10

MISC. SPORTS COVERS

		NM	EM	Ex	+Auto
12/07/36	Skier	15	10		
03/08/37	Skier	15	10		
07/26/37	Polo Horse	15	10		
01/03/38	Vivi-Anne Hulten-Figure Skating	15	10		+$ 20
01/24/38	Skiers	15	10		
03/21/38	Squash Players	15	10		
06/19/39	Payton Jordan - USC	25	15	5	+$ 20
08/05/40	Sailer	15	10		
12/02/40	Balloonist	15	10		
01/20/41	Army Ski Patrol	15	10		
07/14/41	Sand Sailors	15	10		
04/17/44	Esther Williams- Skiing	15	10		+$ 20
02/19/45	Ski Fashions	15	10		
03/26/45	Carol Lynn -Figure Skating	15	10		+$ 20

LIFE MAGAZINE

CHAPTER NINE:
BECKETTS PRICE GUIDE

Becketts Price guide is the only monthly guide that has obtained a premium value for its original issues. At shows across the nation, *Becketts* is the most recognized price guide used by collectors and dealers alike. The reason it is listed in this guide is because many young collectors have been getting their *Becketts* autographed.

Back issues of *Becketts* can be ordered through *Becketts* and/or through magazine dealers (see Appendix IV). The early Baseball *Beckett* issues are the hardest issues to obtain and are the only ones that command a premium. The value outside of the earlier issues has remained rather flat over the last few years because of the card industry. The first six issues are actually the toughest to find since most were destroyed after use.

Autograph collectors tend to like the glossy covers of their favorite players and may only find them on one of the four *Becketts* monthly price guides. Issues not listed tend to have only a nominal value.

Beckett Baseball Card Price Guide

Beckett #	Cover Feature	Date	NrMt Value	Autograph Add Value	
1	R. Clemente/D.Murphy	9/84	$ 200	(d)	/+10
2	M.Mantle/C.Ripken		$ 150	+$175(d)/+40	
3	W. Mays/D. Winfield		$ 75	+$ 50	/+20
4	H. Aaron / G. Carter		$ 50	+$ 35	/+15
5	S. Musial/E. Murray		$ 50	+$ 20	/+15
6	J. Bench/W.Boggs		$ 50	+$ 20	/+15
7	Steve Garvey		$ 30	+$ 15	
8	Rick Suttcliff		$ 35	+$ 10	
9	Cal Ripken Jr		$ 50	+$ 40	
10	Reggie Jackson	1/85	$ 35	+$ 40	
11	Pete Rose		$ 35	+$ 20	
12	Dwight Gooden		$ 25	+$ 10	
13	Vince Coleman		$ 25	+$ 10	
14	Don Mattingley		$ 25	+$ 15	
15	Dwight Gooden		$ 25	+$ 10	
16	George Brett		$ 25	+$ 25	
17	Wade Boggs		$ 25	+$ 15	
18	Dale Murphy		$ 20	+$ 15	
19	Mickey Mantle		$ 30	+$150(d)	
20	Roger Clemens		$ 20	+$ 15	
21	Pete Rose		$ 20	+$ 20	
22	Wally Joyner	1/86	$ 15	+$ 10	
23	Don Mattingly		$ 15	+$ 15	
24	Wade Boggs		$ 15	+$ 15	
25	Roger Clemens		$ 10	+$ 15	
26	Mike Schmidt		$ 10	+$ 25	
27	Kirby Puckett		$ 15	+$ 25	
28	Eric Davis		$ 10	+$ 10	
29	Willie Mays		$ 10	+$ 35	

Beckett Baseball Card Price Guide

Beckett #	Cover Feature	Date	Mint Value	Autograph Add Value
30	Bo Jackson		$ 10	+$ 25
31	Andre Dawson		$ 10	+$ 15
32	Mark McGwire		$ 10	+$ 15
33	Gary Bell		$ 10	+$ 10
34	Kirby Puckett	1/87	$ 15	+$ 20
35	Don Mattingly		$ 10	+$ 15
36	Kevin Seitzer		$ 10	+$ 10
37	Bernin Sanitigo		$ 07	+$ 10
38	Eric Davis		$ 07	+$ 10
39	K. Nokes		$ 07	+$ 10
40	Jose Canseco		$ 07	+$ 15
41	Dave Winfield		$ 07	+$ 15
42	Dale Strawberry		$ 05	+$ 10
43	Don Mattingly		$ 05	+$ 15
44	Jose Canseco		$ 05	+$ 15
45	Orel Hershiser		$ 05	+$ 10
46	Will Clark	1/88	$ 05	+$ 15
47	Mike Greenwell		$ 05	+$ 10
48	Mark Grace		$ 05	+$ 10
49	Gregg Jefferies		$ 05	+$ 10
50	Bob Clemente		$ 10	(d)
51	Bo Jackson		$ 05	+$ 20
52	Will Clark		$ 05	+$ 10
53	Kevin Mitchell		$ 04	+$ 10
54	Jim Abbott		$ 04	+$ 10
55	Nolan Ryan		$ 15	+$ 25
56	Kevin Mitchell		$ 03	+$ 10
57	Ricky Henderson		$ 03	+$ 10
58	Rubin Sierra	1/89	$ 04	+$ 10
59	Bo Jackson		$ 04	+$ 15
60	Robin Yount		$ 04	+$ 15
61	Mark Grace		$ 04	+$ 10
62	Don Mattengly		$ 03	+$ 10
63	Bo Jackson		$ 03	+$ 15
64	Ken Griffey		$ 10	+$ 25
65	Ryan Sandberg		$ 10	+$ 15
66	Ricky Henderson		$ 03	+$ 10
67	Jose Canseco		$ 03	+$ 15
68	Barry Bonds		$ 05	+$ 25
69	Nolan Ryan		$ 10	+$ 25
70	Cecil Fielder	1/90	$ 03	+$ 10
71	George Brett		$ 10	+$ 20
72	Ken Griffey Jr		$ 10	+$ 25
73	Ricky Henderson		$ 03	+$ 10
74	Cal Ripken		$ 10	+$ 20
75	Dimaggio/Mantle		$ 10	+$100/+$150(d)
76	Clemens, B. Robinson		$ 03	+$ 10/+$10
77	Gwynn/McGriff, Dawson		$ 03	+$ 10 each

Beckett Baseball Card Price Guide

Beckett #	Cover Feature		Mint Value	Autograph Add Value
78	Justice, Erickson		$ 03	+$ 05 each
79	F. Thomas, Winfield		$ 03	+$ 20/+$10
80	B. Jackson, H. Johnson		$ 03	+$ 15/+$05
81	Fielder, Ventura		$ 03	+$ 05 each
82	Ryan, Avery/Glavine	1/91	$ 03	+$ 15/+05 each
83	O. Smith, Bagwell		$ 03	+$ 10 each
84	Ripken, Plantier		$ 03	+$ 20/+$05
85	F. Thomas, Gant		$ 03	+$ 20/+$05
86	Avery, R. Alomar		$ 03	+$ 10/+$05
87	Puckett, Sierra		$ 03	+$ 10/+$05
88	D. Sanders , Perez/Rose/Bench		$ 03	+$ 10 each
89	McGwire, McDowell		$ 03	+$ 05 each
90	Yount, Kruk		$ 03	+$ 10/+$05
91	Sheffield, Juan Guzman/R. Alomar		$ 03	+$ 05 each
92	Glavine, Mussina		$ 03	+$ 10/+$05
93	Gonzalez, Karros		$ 03	+$ 05 each
94	F. Thomas, Knoblauch		$ 03	+$ 20/+$05
95	Griffey Jr., Listach		$ 03	+$ 20/+$05

Beckett's Basketball Card Price Guide

#	Cover Feature	Mt Price	Autograph
1	Jordan, Ewing	$ 12	Price Varies
2	Robinson, K. Malone	$ 05	By Player
3	Magic Johnson, K. Johnson	$ 03	
4	Barkley, Dumars, Green	$ 03	
5	Robinson, Olajuwan	$ 05	
6	Ewing, Stockton	$ 03	
7	Bird, Kemp	$ 03	
8	Drexler, R. Miller	$ 03	
9	D. Wilkins, Hardaway	$ 03	
10	Jordan, Coleman	$ 05	
11	K. Johnson, B. King	$ 03	
12	Abdul-Jabbar, Pippen	$ 03	
13	Magic Johnson, Shaw	$ 03	
14	Jordan, L. Johnson	$ 05	
15	K. Malone, I. Thomas	$ 03	
16	Robinson, Drexler	$ 03	
17	Coleman, Mullin	$ 03	
18	Mutombo, S. Smirth	$ 03	
19	Hardaway, Simmons	$ 03	
20	L. Johnson, D. Brown	$ 03	
21	Pippen, Price	$ 03	
22	Augmon, Rodman	$ 03	
23	Owens, O'Neal, Laettner	$ 03	
24	Magic Johnson, K. Malone, Ewing, Jordan, Barkley	$ 03	

Beckett's Basketball Card Price Guide

25	Jordan, Bird, Parrish, McHale	$	05
26	Magic Johnson, Gill	$	03
27	S. O'Neal, C..Barkley	$	03
28	L.Bird, S. Kemp	$	03
29	L. Johnson, K. Malone	$	03
30	C. Laettner, L. Ellis	$	03
31	M. Jordan, W. Williams	$	03

Beckett's Football Card Price Guide

Beckett #	Cover Feature	Mt Price		Autograph
1	B. Jackson, Marino	$	12	Price Varies
2	Montana, Dickerson	$	12	By Player
3	Elway, Cunningham	$	05	
4	B. Sanders, Okoye	$	10	
5	Ware, Taylor	$	05	
6	Rice, Everett	$	05	
7	Majkowski, Payton	$	03	
8	B. Jackson, Moon	$	03	
9	Montana, Humphrey	$	03	
10	B. Jackson, Lombardi/Starr	$	05	
11	Cunningham, N. Anderson	$	03	
12	T. Thomas, E. Smith	$	03	
13	Ismail, Lott	$	03	
14	B. Smith, J. Johnson	$	03	
15	Esiason, Butts	$	03	
16	Rice, George	$	03	
17	B. Sanders, D. Thomas	$	03	
18	Moon, Rison	$	03	
19	Aikman, Carrier	$	03	
20	Lott/Craig, Sharpe	$	03	
21	E. Smith, B. Thomas	$	03	
22	Kelly, Namath	$	03	
23	Rypien, H. Williams	$	03	
24	Marino, Russell	$	03	
25	T. Thomas, Elway	$	03	
26	Howard, Swilling	$	03	
27	Ervins, Irvin	$	03	
28	B. Sanders, D. Sanders	$	03	
29	D. Thomas, McGwire	$	03	
30	E. Smith, Cunningham	$	03	
31	Monk, Nagle	$	03	
32	D. Sanders, Moon	$	03	
33	Marino, H. Walker	$	03	
34	Watters, L. Taylor	$	03	

Beckett's Hockey Card Price Guide

Becketts Future Stars

CHAPTER 10:

PLAYER ALPHA MAGAZINE LISTING

Many players have appeared on the cover of *Sports Illustrated, Time, Life, Becketts, Sport* and *Sports Illustrated for Kids* that it took more than 35 pages to complete this alpha index. The index is not totally complete. It does not include some issues that a player is in the background for *SI* and *Sport*. It also does not list every *Becketts* issue released. This tool is a quick reference guide to the cover issues of your favorite player. The index lists each player covers by the magazine it is (si = *Sport Illustrated*), then the date of the magazine. *Sports Illustrated* will also have a few with initials' YIS for Year in Sports, and Com for commemorative.

The magazine references are coded below:
      si=Sports Illustrated   sk=Sports Illustrated for Kids
      sp=Sport Magazine   ti=Time
      li=Life   bk=Becketts (all sports)
      sip=Sports Il. Present   YIS= Year In Sports (SI)

<u>Name/Team</u>   <u>Title</u>   <u>Publications listing</u>

Aaron, Hank   si} 8/18/69, 5/25/70, 4/15/74, 9/19/94 sp} 6/62, 7/68, 8/70,
                                         5/74 bk} #4

Abbott, Jim   sk} 9/94 bk} #54
Abdul-Jabbar, Kareem   si} 12/5/66, 4/3/67, 1/29/68, 4/1/68, 3/31/69, 10/26/69,
 (Lew Alcindor)   3/9/70, 4/27/70, 2/8/71, 4/19/71, 4/24/72, 2/19/73
                                         10/14/74, 2/14/77, 5/23/77,5/5/80, 12/15/80, 5/9/83
                                         6/10/85, 6/17/85, 12/23/85, 5/26/86, 6/22/87,4/18/88,
                                         1/23/89, 83 YIS, sp} 2/74, 2/78 bk} #12 li} 3/24/72

Abele, John   si} 6/18/62
Abercrombie, Walter   si} 1/7/85
Adams, Alvin   si} 6/7/76
Adcock, Joe   si} 7/30/56 sp} 8/57
Adleman, Rick   si} 10/15/73
Agassi, Andre   si} 7/13/92, 3/13/95
Agganis, Harry   sp} 11/50, 11/52
Aquirre, Mark   si} 12/1/80
Aikman, Troy   si} 8/21/89, 8/27/90, 2/8/93, 8/1/94, 1/16/95 95 SIP Pro Ft
                                     sk} 3/93, 10/94, sp} 9/88, 7/92, 7/93, 8/93, 10/93, 2/94, 7/94, 8/94,
                                     9/94, 1/95, 2/95, 7/95, 9/95 bk} #19

Ainge, Danny   si} 5/2/83, 3/30/90
Akers-Stahl, Michelle   sk} 9/92
Alarie, Mark   si} 12/1/80
Albright, Tenley   si} 1/30/56
Alcindor, Lew   sp} 4/67, 3/68, 2/70
Alexeyev, Vasilli   si} 4/14/75
Ali, Muhammad   si} 6/10/63, 2/24/64/, 3/9/64,11/16/64, 5/24/65, 6/7/65, 11/2/65,
 (Cassius Clay)   4/11/66, 2/6/67, 7/10/67, 12/22/67 (flap), 5/5/69, 3/1/71
                                         3/15/71, 7/26/71, 4/23/73,2/4/74, 10/28/74, 11/11/74,12/23/74,
                                         9/15/75, 10/13/75, 3/1/76, 10/10/77, 9/25/78, 4/14/80, 9/29/80,
                                         10/13/80, 77YIS, 4/25/88, 11/15/89, 1/13/92, 9/19/94
                                     li} 3/6/64, 1023/70, 3/5/71, 3/19/71, 1/91
                                     sp} 3/64, 9/74, 2/75 ti} 3/22/63, 3/8/71, 2/27/78

Name/Team	Title Publications listing
Allen, Dick (Richie)	si} 3/23/70, 6/12/72, sp} 7/67
Allen, George	si} 7/9/73
Allen, Marcus	si} 10/5/81, 12/13/82, 12/16/85
	sp} 8/83, 11/85, 2/87, 8/88,9/91, 10/94
Allen, Ray - CT	si} 95 sip Col Basket
Alomar, Roberto	si} 10/26/92 sk} 4/92 bk} #86,#91
Alomar, Sandy Jr.	sk} 4/92
Alson, Joe	si} 3/7/55
Alston, Walt	si} 9/26/55, 5/15/67, 5/19/69, sp} 3/56
Alt, Carol (swimsuit)	si} 2/8/82
Alworth, Lance	si} 12/13/65
Alzado, Lyle	si} 7/8/91 sp} 12/83
American Cup	si} 5/12/58, 7/9/62, 8/24/64
Anderson, Bob (Army)	si} 11/24/58, sp} 11/58
Anderson, Don	si} 12/16/68
Anderson, Mary	si} 11/5/62
Anderson, N.	Bk) f#71
Anderson, Otis	si} 1/28/91
Anderson, Rotnei	si} 11/16/87
Andrie, George	si} 9/9/63
Antonelli, Johnny	sp} 6/55, 1/58
Aparicio, Luis	si} 8/10/59, 9/22/59, 4/30/62 sp} 7/60
Arcaro, Eddie	si} 6/17/57 ti} 5/17/48
Archer, George	si} 4/21/69
Archibald, Tiny	si} 10/15/73
Armour, Tommy	si} 3/30/59
Armstrong, Debbie	si} 2/20/84
Arnett, John	si} 10/23/61
Artist's View /Spring Training	si} 3/7/60
Ashburn, Richie	si} 5/19/53
Ashe, Arthur	si} 8/29/66, 7/14/75, 12/21/92, 2/15/93, li} 9/20/68
Atkins, Ace	si} 1993 Alabama Com.
Augmon, Stacey	si} 4/2/90, 11/19/90 bk} #22
Austin, Tracy	si} 3/22/76, 9/17/79, 1981 YIS
Australia:World's Sports C.	si} 5/16/60
Auto Racing at Lime Rock	si} 10/19/59
Autograph Madness	si} 8/13/90
Autumn Leaves in Nova Scotia	si} 10/28/57
Avery, Dan	bk} #82, 86
Babashoff, Shirley	si} 7/19/76
Bailey, Damon	si} 12/13/93
Bailey, Thurl	si} 4/11/83
Baird, Amy	si} 12/16/57
Baiul, Oksana	sk} 2/94
Bagwell, Jeff	bk} #83
Baker, Terry	si} 10/16/61, 1/7/63
Ballesteros, Steve	si} 4/21/80
Bamberger, George	si} 4/30/79
Bando, Sal	si} 10/21/74
Banks, Ernie	si} 7/7/58, 9/8/69 sp} 9/69
Banks, Gene	si} 3/13/78, 4/3/78
Banks, Tyra	si} 1/29/96
Bannister, Roger	si} 1/3/55
Barber, Jerry	si} 2/18/63
Barkley, Charles	si} 12/12/88, 2/18/91, 11/9/92, 6/21/93, 11/7/9, 94 Hot Shot Com
	sk} 2/91, 5/94,bk} #4, #24, #27, sp} 11/91, 2/92, 1/93, 11/93,
	1/94, 11/94, 5/95
Barnes, Marvin	si} 3/26/73
Barrett, Charles	li} 4/1/46

Name/Team	Title Publications listing
Barry, Rick	si} 2/13/67, 4/24/67, 8/24/70, 12/16/74, 2/19/79 sp} 2/73, 4/75
Bartowski, Steve	sp} 12/81
Barzini, Beredette	si} 11/17/69
Baseball Boom	si} 8/11/75
Baseball Crowd/LA Coliseum	si} 6/15/59
Baseball Error Sign	si} 5/18/92
Baseball Jubilee Issue	sp} 5/51
Baseball Managers	sp} 7/84
Baseball Painting	sp} 4/51
Baseball Preview	si} 4/9/56, 4/15/57, 4/14/58, 4/19/65
Baseball Sluggers	sp} 5/62
Baseball Strike	si} 6/22/81
Baseball's Minors	si} 7/23/90
Basilio, Carmen	si} 2/25/57, 9/16/57, 3/24/58
	sp} 2/58
Basilio, Sotela	si} 10/21/68
Basketball Coaches	sp} 3/74
Basketball Painting	sp} 1/51
Bathgate, Andy	si} 1/12/59
Battle for the NCAA Title	si} 3/20/72
Bauer, Hank	si} 7/22/57 , 10/10/66, sp} 5/59 ti} 9/11/64
Bavaro, Mark	si} 12/15/86, 9/1/87
Bayi, Filbert	si} 5/26/75
Baylor, Elgin	si} 10/24/66, 4/29/68 sp} 3/69
Beach Explosion in California	si} 9/3/62
Beamer, Buzz	sk} 1/93, 7/95
Bean, Bubba	si} 12/8/75
Beard, Ralph	sp} 1/48, 3/49
Beatles	li} 8/28/64
Beatty, Jim	si} 7/11/60
Beban, Gary	si} 9/19/66, 11/20/67
Beck, Corey	si} 4/3/95
Becker, Boris	si} 7/15/85, 9/18/89
Becker, Jamee	si} 1/13/69
Beeman, John	si} 6/18/62
Beer and Sports	si} 8/8/88
Belinsky, Bo	si} 3/1/65
Beliveau, Jean	si} 1/23/56
Bell, Gary	bk} #33
Bell, Greg	si} 11/21/88
Bell, Gus	si} 7/16/56
Bell, Ricky	si} 1/7/80
Bell, William	si} 11/12/90
Belle, Albert	si} 5/6/96
Bellino, Joe	si} 11/28/60
Beman, Deane	si} 9/11/61
Bench, Johnny	si} 3/11/68, 7/13/70, 3/13/72, 10/20/75, 11/3/75, 11/1/76
	sp} 9/70, 10/72 ti} 7/10/72, bk} #6, #88
Bennett, Cornelius	sp} 10/88
Benson, Kent	si} 12/1/75, 3/29/76
Bentley, Doug & Max	sp} 2/47
Bentley, Scott	si} 8/30/93
Benvenuti, Nino	si} 9/25/67
Berbick, Trevor	si} 12/1/86
Berenson, Red	si} 4/7/69
Berns, Rick	si} 11/20/78
Berra, Yogi	si} 7/11/55, 7/9/56, 3/3/58, 3/2/64,4/2/84 sp} 8/51, 10/55, 5/58 ,5/63
Berry, Ken	si} 5/8/67

Name/Team	Title Publications listing
Berry, Walter	si} 2/4/85
Best 18 Holes in the U.S.	si} 2/22/65, 2/15/65
Best and Worst of 1992	si} 8/31/92
Betting Football	sp} 11/84
Betting Scandal /Belmont Park	si} 11/14/77
Bettis, Jerome-Rams	si} 95 SIP pro Football
Betz, Pauline	ti} 9/2/46
Biakabutuka, Tshimanga - Mich	si} 95 sip Col Football
Bias, Len	si} 6/30/86
Bichette, Dante - Rockies	si} 96 SIP Baseball
Big Boom in Family Bowling	si} 3/14/60
Big Game Hunting in Idaho	si} 10/22/62
Bill Talbert on Mixed Doubles	si} 6/30/58
Billingham, Jack	si} 3/3/75
Bionda, Jack	si} 1/28/57
Biondi, Matt	si} 9/1/88 sk} 7/92
Bippus, Sunny	si} 1/17/66
Bird, Larry	si} 11/28/77, 3/26/79, 4/28/80, 5/11/81, 11/9/81, 81 YIS, 5/2/83, 10/29/84, 6/10/85, 3/3/86,6/9/86, 5/25/87 (insert), 6/8/87, 3/21/88, 12/11/89, 3/23/92, 12/14/92, 9/19/94 sp} 3/80, 11/87
	ti} 3/18/85 bk} #7, #25, #28
Black Athlete Special Series	si} 7/1/68
Black, Jimmy	si} 11/30/81
Blackledge, Todd	si} 10/4/82
Blackman, Rolando	si} 3/23/81
Blackmon	si} 12/7/92
Blackwell, Ewell	sp} 7/48, 7/51
Blair, Bonnie	si} 2/24/92, 2/28/94, 12/19/94,
Blanchard, Doc	sp} 10/46 ti} 11/12/45, Li} 9/16/46
Blanda, George	si} 11/23/70, 7/19/71
Blass, Steve	si} 7/3/72
Bledsoe, Drew- Patriots	si} 95 sip Pro Football
Bleier, Rocky	si} 6/9/75, 12/6/76, 1/29/79
Blomberg, Ron	si} 7/2/73
Blount, Mel	si} 1/3/77
Blue, Vida	si} 5/31/71, 3/27/72 sp} 10/71, ti} 8/23/71
Blume, Ray	si} 3/23/81
BMX Champs	sk} 7/91
Bobsledder Kids	sk} 1/91
Boggs, Wade	si} 4/14/86, 3/6/89 bk} #6, #17,#24
Boitano, Brian	si} 2/29/88
Bol, Manute	sk} 11/91
Bold Americans Special Issue	si} 12/24/62
Bolt, Tommy	si} 6/8/59
Bonds, Barry	si} 5/4/92, 5/24/93 sk} 8/93, bk} #68 sp} 4/93, 1/94, 4/94, 4/95
Bonds, Bobby	sp} 7/75
Bonilla, Bobby	si} 10/1/90
Borg, Bjorn	si} 7/11/77, 7/16/79, 7/14/80, 6/15/81, 1981 YIS, 5/6/91 ti} 6/30/80
Boros, Julius	si} 7/1/63, 3/25/68
Bossy, Mike	si} 5/14/84 bk} #5
Boston College	si} 11/29/93
Bosworth, Brian	si} 9/1/86, 1/5/87
Boudreau, Lou	sp} 2/49, 7/49
Bouie, Tony	si} 8/29/94
Bourne	si} 12/21/87
Bowe, Riddick	si} 11/23/92
Bowie, Sam	si} 12/5/83, 83 YIS
Bowl Games Preview	si} 1/3/66
Boxing	sp} 8/77

Name/Team	Title Publications listing
Boyd, John	si} 5/30/66
Boyd, Oil Can	si} 8/4/86
Boyer, Ken	si} 7/9/56, 7/30/62 sp} 9/62
Brabham, Jack	si} 10/31/60
Bradley, Bill	si} 12/7/64, 9/11/67, 3/18/68
Bradley, Dudley	si} 3/12/79
Bradley, Edward	ti} 5/7/34
Bradshaw, Terry	si} 2/9/70, 7/29/74, 1/20/75, 10/9/78, 1/15/79, 12/24/79, sp} 8/80
Branch, Cliff	sp} 9/78
Braxton, Dwight	si} 3/28/83
Brayshaw, Gary	si} 6/18/62
Brazil Wins World Cup	si} 7/25/94
Breaud, Francine	si} 12/25/61
Brett, George	si} 6/21/76, 4/13/81, 8/10/81,3/12/84, 10/5/92 sp} 5/80, 4/81, 5/85, 5/86 bk} #16, #71
Breunig, Bob	si} 8/24/81
Brewer, Gay	si} 8/7/67
Brewer, Dale (baseball)	si} 7/9/56
Brimsek, Frank	sp} 2/48
Brinkley, Christie (Swimsuit)	si} 2/5/79, 2/4/80, 2/9/81
Broadway Hit: The Changing Room	si} 3/5/73
Brock, Lou	si} 10/16/67, 4/15/68, 10/7/68, 7/22/74, 8/27/79
Brodie, John	si} 9/20/71 sp} 11/66
Broglio, Ernie	si} 6/26/61
Brown, Bob	si} 10/28/68
Brown, Dale	si} 11/18/85 bk} #20
Brown, James - Texas	si} 95 sip Col Football
Brown, Jim	si} 9/26/60, 12/12/83, 9/19/94 sp} 1/62, 12/62, 12/64 9/94 ti} 11/26/65
Brown, Larry	si} 11/6/72 sp} 1/71, 1/72
Brown, Paul	si} 10/8/56, 8/12/68
Brown, Tim - Raiders	si} 8/31/87, 95 SIP Pro Football
Browner, Delrick	si} 11/12/79
Browner, Ross	si} 9/5/77, 12/4/78
Brumel, Valeri	si} 7/17/61, 2/4/63
Brundage, Avery	si} 9/30/68
Brunfield, Don	si} 5/16/66
Bruschi, Tedy	si} 8/29/94
Bryan, Jim	si} 5/27/57
Bryant, Joe	si} 6/13/77
Bryant, Paul Bear	si} 8/15/66, 12/3/73, 11/23/81, ti} 9/29/80
Buckey, Dave and Don	si} 10/30/72
Buckner, Bill	si} 10/21/74
Buckner, Brentson	si} 12/5/94
Budge, Donald	ti} 9/2/35
Buerkle, Dick	si} 2/6/78
Buffalo Bills	si} 12/16/91
Buhner, Jay	si} 3/18/96
Bukich, Rudy	si} 9/12/66
Bulaich, Norm	si} 11/8/71
Bull, Ronnie	si} 10/14/63
Bumbry, Al	si} 8/25/80
Bunning, Jim	si} 3/1/65
Burch, Elliot	si} 2/22/60
Burdette, Lew	sp} 3/58
Bure, Pavel	si} 6/20/94 bk} #17, #24
Burleson, Dyrol	si} 5/30/60, 10/5/64
Burleson, Tom	si} 11/29/71, 3/25/74
Burton, Ernest	si} 11/14/55
Busch, Anhiser	ti} 7/11/55

Name/Team	Title　　　Publications listing
Busch, Gussie	si} 5/20/57
Bush, George	si} 8/19/91
Butkus, Dick	si} 10/12/64, 9/21/70 sp} 11/70
Butler, Brett (Dodgers)	sp} 4/92
Butler, Keith	si} 12/13/82
Buzz to the Future	sk} 1/90
Butts	bk} #15
Cagle, Christian	ti} 9/23/29
Calabria, Don Te - UNC	si} 95 sip Col Baseketball
Calcagni (Arkansas FB)	si} 9/11/78
Caligiuri, Paul	sk} 6/90
Callison, Johnny	si} 8/10/64 sp} 7/65
Calvalcade (Horse)	ti} 8/20/34
Campanella, Roy	sp} 10/53 ti} 8/8/55 li} 6/8/53, 7/21/58
Campaneris, Bert	si} 10/22/73, 10/21/74
Campbell, Earl	si} 12/5/77, 12/4/78, 9/3/79, sp} 10/80, 9/81
Campton	si} 12/7/92
Canadians Win the Stanley Cup	si} 6/2/86
Candlestick Park - Giants	si} 7/18/60
Cangelosi, John	si} 5/23/94
Canonero II - The Belmont	si} 6/14/71
Canseco, Jose	si} 10/17/88, 8/20/90 bk} #40, #44, #67
	sp} 7/89, 4/90, 4/91
Capriati, Jennifer	si} 3/19/90
Carbo, Carlos	si} 10/19/70
Carew, Rod	si} 7/1/74, 7/18/77, 4/10/78, 6/13/83. 83 YIS sp} 10/77, 8/79
	ti} 7/18/77
Carey, Andy	si} 3/3/58
Carlisle, Duke	si} 10/21/63
Carlos, Cisco	si} 3/11/68
Carlton, Steve	si} 4/9/73, 7/21/80, 10/3/83, 1983 YIS, sp} 4/73, 5/83
Carnera, Primo	ti} 10/1/31
Carpenter, Bobby	si} 2/23/81
Carr, Henry	si} 10/5/64
Carrasquel, Chico	sp} 4/52
Carrier	bk} #19
Carroll, Clay	si} 3/3/75
Carruth, Rae	si} 10/3/94
Carter, Anthony	si} 1/18/88
Carter, Gary	si} 10/6/80, 8/17/81, 4/4/83, 10/27/86 sp} 6/83, 3/85 bk} #4
Carter, Joe	si} 4/6/87, 11/1/93 sp} 4/94
Carter, Rubin	si} 10/17/77
Cartwright, Bill	si} 1/31/77, 5/31/93
Casanova, Tommy	si} 9/13/71
Casey, Mike	si} 12/2/68
Cash, Norm	sp} 4/62
Casper, Billy	si} 2/20/61, 2/7/66, 6/27/66, 6/12/67, 4/20/70
Cassady, Howard	si} 10/24/55
Cauthen, Steve	si} 3/7/77, 12/19/77, 5/15/78, 6/19/78 ti} 6/13/77, 5/29/78
Cecil, Chuck	si} 10/11/93
Cepada, Orlando	si} 10/7/68 sp} 10/67
Chabot, Lorne	ti} 2/11/35
Chamberlain, Wilt	si} 10/30/61, 4/12/65, 1/27/69, 5/15/72, 10/16/72, 2/19/73
	2/22/88 sp} 1/57, 3/60, 3/62, 4/63, 3/67, 3/69, 3/72l, li} 3/24/72
Chambers, John	si} 10/22/56
Champion Barrage of Quality Hill	si} 2/11/57
Champion Bulldog	si} 7/4/55
Chance, Dean	sp} 4/65

Name/Team	Title Publications listing
Chandler, Happy	ti} 8/1/38
Chappas, Harry	si} 3/19/79
Chappuis	ti} 11/3/47
Chavez, Julio Cesar	si} 9/20/93
Cheeks, Maurice	si} 5/11/81
Cheeks, Mo	si} 5/31/82, 3/5/84
Cheevers, Gerry	si} 5/9/77
Chenier, Phil	si} 4/16/73
Chicago Bears	sp} 12/57
Chicago White Sox	si} 9/28/59
Chinaglia, Giorgio	si} 5/21/79
Christianson,	sp} 8/88
Chuvalo, George	si} 2/1/65, 4/11/66, 7/10/67
Clack, Darryl	sp} 9/84
Clark, Dwight	si} 1/18/82
Clark, Gary	si} 10/14/91
Clark, Jim	ti} 7/9/65
Clark, Will	si} 4/4/88, 5/28/90 sp} 4/88,7/90, bk} #46, #52
Clarke, Bobby	si} 5/6/74, 2/23/76
Clayburn, Jill	si} 11/7/77
Clayton (Dolphins) Superbowl	si} 9/10/84
Clemens, Roger	si} 5/12/86, 5/13/91 sp} 3/87, bk} #20, #25, #76
Clemente, Bob	bk} # 50, si} 7/3/67 sp} 8/67 bk} #1
Clements, Tom	si} 9/30/74
Clinton, Bill (President)	si} 3/21/94
Cobb,Ty	sp} 5/69
Cochrane, Mickey	ti} 10/7/35
Coe, Charlie	si} 9/14/59
Coe, Sebastian	si} 7/30/79, 8/11/80
Coghlan, Eamonn	si} 2/26/79, 7/9/79
Colavito, Rocky	sp} 4/59, 9/60, 7/61, 8/62, 7/63, ti} 8/24/59
Coleman, Derrick	si} 1/30/95 bk} #10, #17
Coleman, Vince	bk} #13
College Basketball Preview	si} 12/9/57,12/8/58,12/7/59,12/12/60,12/4/67, 12/2/74,12/3/79
College Football Preview	si} 9/24/56, 9/23/57, 9/22/58, 9/21/59, 9/18/61, 9/24/62, 9/10/73, 9/4/89
College/Pro Football Preview	si} 9/1/82
Collins, Becky	si} 7/13/59
Collins, Carry - Carolina	si} 95 sip Pro Football
Collins, Doug	si} 1/15/73, 6/13/77
Collins, Jim	si} 3/16/70
Collins, Ray	si} 9/28/87
Collinsworth, Cris	si} 12/14/81
Comiskey Park	si} 7/4/60
Comaneci, Nadia	si} 8/2/76 ti} 9/1/76
Comby, Marcus - Mass	si} 95 sip Col Basketball
Cone, Carin	si} 4/16/60
Cone, David	si} 4/5/93, 96 sip baseball
Conerly, Chuck	si} 12/3/56
Conigliaro, Tony	si} 6/22/70 sp} 7/69
Conner, Dennis	si} 2/16/87
Conners, Jimmy	si} 3/4/74, 7/15/74, 5/5/75, 9/20/76, 9/18/78, 7/12/82,9/20/82, 9/16/91 sp} 7/74, 9/75, ti} 4/28/75, li} 1/83
Cooney, Gerry	si} 5/4/81, 6/7/82, 6/21/82, sp} 3/82 ti} 6/14/82
Cooper, Earl	si} 12/21/81, 2/1/82
Cooper, Gary (Skin diving)	si} 6/1/59
Cooper, Michael	si} 5/24/82, 6/17/85
Cooper, Wayne	si} 5/9/83
Coopman, Jean-Pierre	si} 3/1/76

Name/Team	Title Publications listing
Dawson, Andre	si} 7/18/83, 7/20/87 bk} #31, #77
Dawson, Len	si} 11/24/69, 1/19/70
Day, Laraine	si} 4/11/55
Dean, Dizzy	ti} 4/15/35
Debusschere, Dave	sp} 4/74
DeJesus, Esteban	si} 1/30/78
DeVarona, Donna	si} 4/16/62, 10/5/64
DeVicenzo, Roberto	si} 4/22/68
Decinces, Doug	si} 10/22/79, 10/20/86
Decker, Mary	si} 2/18/80, 7/26/82, 12/26/83, 7/29/85, li} sum 84
Deer, Rob	si} 4/27/87
Delak, Tony - Kentucky	si} 95 sip Col Basketball
Delaney, Ron	si} 2/2/59
Dembo, Fennis	si} 11/1/87
Dempsey, George	si} 1/20/58
Dempsey, Jack	ti} 9/17/23
Dempsey, Rick	si} 10/24/83, 10/31/88
Dent, Bucky	si} 8/25/80 sp} 2/87
Detmer, Ty	si} 12/10/90
Devaney, Bob	si} 9/11/72
Devers, Gail	si} 8/10/92
Devine, Dan	si} 9/29/75
Di Bugnano, Betty	si} 2/21/55
Dickerson, Eric	si} 10/17/83, 12/17/84, 9/1/85, 93 YIS,11/9/87, 8/12/91
	sp} 8/84, 9/92 bk} #2
Diebol, Nelson	si} 8/3/92
Dietzel, Paul	si} 11/26/62 sp} 11/59
Discus Thrower	si} 12/30/91
DiMaggio, Dom	sp} 9/47
DiMaggio, Joe	si} 5/3/93 sp} 9/46, 9/47, 9/48, 9/49, 9/61, 8/64, 9/65, 5/69
	ti} 7/13/36, 10/4/48 li} 5/1/39, 8/1/49 bk} #75
Divac, Vlade	si} 5/8/95
Dixon, Hewitt	si} 1/8/68
Dobler, Conrad	si} 7/25/77
Doby, Larry	sp} 4/56
Dodger Rookies	li} 4/5/48
Doherty, Matt	si} 11/30/81
Donohue, Mark	si} 6/5/72
Dorsett, Tony	si} 11/8/76, 1/10/77, 12/7/81, 82 YIS, 8/29/83, 8/12/85, 8/1/88
	sp} 1/78, 9/79, 1/82, 2/83
Double Eagle II	si} 8/28/78
Douglas, Buster	si} 2/26/90
Douglas, Leon	si} 2/19/79
Downing, Al	si} 9/30/63
Downs, Kelly	si} 10/30/89
Downs, Steve	si} 3/26/73
Doyle, Brian	si} 10/23/78
Dozier, D.J.	si} 11/11/85
Dr. Z's Picks	si} 2/1/93
Drew, John	si} 5/7/79 sp} 3/79
Drexler, Clyde	si} 5/11/92, 6/19/95 sk} 2/93 bk} #8, #16, sp} 11/91
Dryden, Ken	si} 2/14/72, 11/25/74, 5/29/78, sp} 3/73
Drysdale, Don	si} 8/20/62, 5/15/67, 6/17/68, sp} 6/60, 9/68, li} 9/28/62
Duckworth, Kevin	si} 12/17/90
Dudek, Joe	si} 12/2/85
Dumars, Joe	si} 11/6/89 bk} #4
Duncan, Dave	si} 5/3/71
Dunleavy, Mike	si} 2/19/79, 12/10/84
Duper, Mark	si} 11/19/84

Name/Team	Title Publications listing
Dupree, Marcus	si} 6/20/83 sp} 9/83
Duran, Roberto	si} 9/26/77, 1/30/78, 7/2/79, 6/16/80, 6/30/80, 6/27/83
	11/7/83, 11/21/83,
Dureson, Dave	si} 11/25/85
Durham, Bull	si} 6/11/84
Durocher, Leo	si} 4/11/55, 2/28/66, 9/28/70, sp} 4/47, 1/58, 9/69 ti} 4/14/47
Dyer, Ed	sp} 7/47
Dyer, Louise	si} 12/5/55
Dykstra, Lenny	si} 6/4/90
Eason (Patriots)	si} 2/3/86
Eastman, Ben	ti} 7/11/32
Eckersley, Dennis	si} 10/22/90, 96 sip Baseball
Edberg, Stefan	si} 9/21/92
Edwards, Glen	si} 1/3/77
Edwards, Harry	si} 9/30/68
Edwards, Phil	si} 7/18/66
Elder, Lee	si} 3/10/75
Eldorado, the Ryder Golf C.	si} 11/2/59
Eller, Carl	si} 11/3/69
Elliot, Bill	si} 9/9/85
Elliott, Harry	si} 3/5/56
Elliott, Herb	si} 11/10/58, 5/30/60
Ellis, L.	Bk} #30
Ellison, Pervis	si} 4/7/86 sp} 11/86
Ellsworth, Rex	si} 2/25/63
Elmore, Len	si} 12/10/73
Elway, John	si} 11/8/82, 8/15/83, 10/13/86, 9/21/87, 1/25/88, 1/22/90
	8/2/93 sk} 10/93 sp} 1/87, 9/90, 8/95, 9/95, bk} #3, #25
Emanuel, Frank	si} 8/8/66
Engram, Bobby - Penn State	si} 95 sip College Football
Enriqueta, Norma	si} 10/21/68
Erdelatz, Eddie	sp} 11/55
Erickson, Craig	si} 1/8/90
Erickson, Dennis	si} 5/15/95
Erickson, Victor	si} 6/18/62
Erickson	bk} #78
Erving, Julius	si} 1/14/74, 5/17/76, 10/25/76,4/28/80, 81 YIS, 5/31/82, 2/28/83
	3/5/84, 5/4/87 sp} 3/75, 2/77, 6/78, 2/79
Esaisson, Boomer	si} 8/7/89, 10/4/93 sk} 9/89, sp} 1/88 bk} #15
Espana, Ernesto	si} 8/2/82
Esposito, Phil	si} 3/29/71, 5/8/72, 11/19/73, ti} 10/9/72
Esposito, Tony	si} 3/29/71 sp} 2/72 bk} #23
Etchebarren, Andy	si} 7/11/66
Eurick, Terry	si} 1/9/78
Evans, Bryan - Indiana	si} 95 sip Col. Basketball
Evans, Darrell	si} 10/19/87
Evans, Dwight	si} 9/26/88
Evans, Janet	sk} 6/89, 7/92
Evert, Chris	si} 7/15/74, 12/20/76, 82 YIS, 8/28/89, sp} 7/74
Evertt, Jim	sp} 1/90, 10/90, 9/91 bk} #6
Ewing, Patrick	si} 3/22/82, 4/5/82, 11/29/82, 3/19/84, 11/26/84, 4/1/85,4/8/85,
	5/20/85, 2/13/89, 2/18/91, 2/10/92, 5/25/92,5/31/93, 6/20/94
	95 sip Basketball, sk} 11/92, sp} 12/82, 12/84, 12/85
	bk} #1, #6, #24 sp} 5/93, 11/93, 11/94
Exel, Nick - Lakers	sp} 11/95, si} 95 sip Pro Basketball
Face, Roy	si} 6/24/63
Fain, Ferris	sp} 7/53

Name/Team	Title Publications listing
Fairly, Ron	si} 9/2/63
Falch, Helmut	si} 11/23/64
Faldo, Nick	si} 4/17/89
Favre, Brett- Packers	si} 1/15/96, 95 sip Pro Football
Faust, Gerry	si} 11/5/84
Fearless Predictions	sp} 1/83, 2/84, 2/85
Fedorou, Sergei	si} 6/5/96 (Canadian SI Only)
Feller, Bob	sp} 6/47, 4/49 ti} 4/19/37
Ferguson, Vagas	si} 9/24/79
Fernandez, M.	sp} 1/74
Ferragamo, Vince	si} 12/8/80, 7/20/81
Ferries, Chuck	si} 3/11/63
Fetisov, Viacheslav	si} 10/9/89
Fichtner, Ross	si} 11/21/66
Fidrych, Mark	si} 6/6/77, 4/24/78 sp} 7/77
Fielder, Cecil	sk} 4/91 bk} #70, #81
Final Four	si} 3/31/86
Fingers, Rollie	si} 10/21/74, 3/16/81, 4/27/81
Finley, Charlie	ti} 8/18/75 bk}(ML) #1
Finsterwald, Dow	si} 6/8/59, 6/13/60
Fischer, Bobby	si} 8/14/72
Fisk, Carlton	si} 9/25/72, 7/30/73, 5/31/76
Flanigan, Jim	si} 11/22/93
Fleming, Peggy	si} 5/2/66, 2/19/68, LI 2/23/68
Fletcher, Simon	si} 2/2/87
Float, Jeff	si} 7/9/84
Flood, Curt	si} 8/19/68, 10/7/68 sp} 5/71
Flournou, Hem	si} 3/28/66
Flowers, Richmond	si} 3/14/66
Floyd, Raymond	si} 4/19/76, 6/23/86
Flutie, Doug	si} 9/26/83, 12/3/84, 2/25/85
Flynn, Mike	si} 3/31/75
Football Crowd	ti} 11/17/30, 11/11/33, 11/11/35
Football Painting	sp} 12/50
Football's Special Team	sp} 12/80
Ford, Chris	si} 5/31/82
Ford, Gerald (President)	si} 7/8/74
Ford, Phil	si} 3/17/75
Ford, Whitey	si} 9/10/56, 9/30/63 sp} 11/63
Foreman, Chuck	si} 10/18/76
Foreman, George	si} 6/18/73, 10/28/74,11/11/74,12/15/75, 7/17/89, 4/29/91, 11/14/94
	sp} 7/73
Fortenberry, Dick	si} 8/13/62
Foster, Alan	si} 3/11/68
Foster, George	si} 10/11/76, 4/10/78
Fox, Nellie	si} 8/10/59, 9/28/59 sp} 4/58, 9/60
Foxx, Jimmy	ti} 7/29/29
Foyt, A.J.	si} 6/1/64, 2/28/72, 5/19/75, 5/25/81 sp} 6/73
Franklin, Andra	si} 1/24/83, 83 YIS
Franklin, Ron / Spec. Bid	si} 5/14/79
Frazier, Joe	si} 7/10/67, 3/1/71, 3/15/71, 2/4/74, 9/15/75, 10/13/75
	6/1/81 ti} 3/8/71
Frazier, Tommy	si} 12/25/95 reg, 96 Nebraska com.
Frazier, Walt	si} 12/8/69, 2/7/72, 4/16/73, 5/7/73
Free, Lloyd	si} 12/15/80
Freehan, Bill	si} 4/14/69
Freeman, Steve	si} 1/12/81
Fregosi, Jim	si} 5/3/71

Name/Team	Title	Publications listing
Frenn, George	si} 7/6/70	
Friar, Matt	si} 1/10/94	
Friend, Bob (Pirates)	si} 7/9/56	
Frontiere, Georgia (Rams)	si} 5/10/82	
Fullmer, Gene	si} 4/29/57	
Furgol, Ed	si} 6/20/55	
Fusina, Chuck	si} 11/13/78	
Gabriel, Roman	si} 10/3/66, 12/18/67, 12/7/70, sp} 12/70	
Gadsby, Bill	si} 4/25/66	
Gagne, Greg	si} 10/19/87	
Galiffa, Arnold - Army	li} 5/2/49	
Galimore, Willie	si} 11/25/63	
Gant, Ron	si} 9/27/93	
Garcia, Mike	sp} 9/52	
Gardne, Cal	si} 1/28/57	
Garner, Phil	si} 10/22/79	
Garnett, Kevin	si} 6/26/95	
Garrett, Mike	si} 8/10/70 sp} 1/68	
Garris, Keyana - Ill	si} 95 sip col Basketball	
Garrison, Walt	si} 9/18/72	
Garrity, Greg	si} 1/10/83	
Garver, Ned	sp} 7/55	
Garvey, Steve	si} 10/21/74, 4/7/75, 4/12/82,4/25/83 sp} 4/76, 4/83 bk} #7	
Gastineau, Mark	si} 9/29/86 sp} 10/83	
Gather, Hank	sp} 12/89	
Gaubatz, Dennis	si} 11/29/65, 12/16/68	
Gehrig, Lou	sp} 10/48, 9/65 ti} 10/5/36	
Genuine Risk	si} 5/12/80	
Gentry, Dennis	sp} 1/89	
George, Ed & Tony	sk} 5/90	
George, Jeff	si} 4/30/90, Bk #16	
Giacomin, Eddie	si} 3/2/70	
Giardello, Joey	si} 5/18/64	
Gibbs, Sonny	si} 10/15/62	
Gibson, Althea	si} 9/2/57 ti} 8/26/57	
Gibson, Bob	si} 7/19/93	
Gibson, Kirk	si} 3/24/80, 12/9/85, 3/7/88, sp} 7/85	
Gifford, Frank	si} 12/17/62	
Gilbert, Rod	si} 1/30/67	
Gill, J	si} 95 sip Pro Basketball, bk} #26	
Gilliam, Joe	si} 9/23/74	
Gilmer, Harry	sp} 10/47	
Gilmore, Artis	si} 3/30/70	
Girls in Sports	sk} 9/93	
Gissy, Doris & Ruth	si} 8/27/56	
Givens, Goose	si} 4/3/78	
Givens, Robin (w/ Tyson)	si} 6/13/88	
Gladden, Dan	si} 10/26/87, 10/26/91	
Glassell, Alfred	si} 3/19/56	
Glavin, Tom	bk} #82,92	
Gminski, Mike	si} 2/4/85	
Goalby, Bob	si} 4/22/68	
Goetz, Lois (Cheerleader)	si} 9/19/60	
Golden Eagle in Flight	si} 6/29/59	
Gomez, Lefty	ti} 7/9/34	
Gonzales, Poncho	si} 6/16/58	
Gonzalez, Juan	sk} 4/94 bk} #93 bk}(FS) #3, #19 sp} 6/94	
Gooden, Dwight	si} 9/24/84, 4/15/85, 9/2/85, 3/22/93, 2/27/95 sp} 4/85, 4/86 ti} 4/7/86 bk} #12, #15	
Goodman, Johnny	ti} 6/6/38	

Name/Team	Title Publications listing
Haddon, Dayle (Swimsuit)	si} 1/29/73
Hagler, Marvin	si} 10/18/82, 11/7/83,11/21/83, 4/22/85, 3/24/86, 3/30/87 4/13/87, 7/2/90
Hall, Jim	si} 5/1/67
Hall of Fame Prospects	sp} 7/86
Ham, Jack	sp} 1/80
Hamill, Dorthy	ti} 2/2/76, 77 YIS
Hamilton, Scott	si} 2/6/84
Hampton (Bears) Superbowl	si} 2/3/86
Hanah, Joan	si} 2/5/62
Haney, Fred	si} 3/2/59
Hannah, John	si} 8/3/81
Hanratty, Terry	si} 11/7/66, 9/11/67 ti} 10/28/66
Hansen, Fred	si} 10/5/64
Harbaugh, Jim	si} 9/14/92 sp} 9/86
Hardaway, 'Penny'	si} 2/13/95 , 94 Hot shot Com, bk} #9, #19, sk} 12/95
Hardaway, Tim	sp} 11/92
Harding, Tonya	ti} 1/24/94
Hardy, Bruce	si} 4/29/74
Harmon, Claude	si} 4/27/64
Harmon, Tom	sp} 12/46 ti} 11/6/39, li 11/11/40
Harrelson, Bud	si} 9/7/70
Harrelson, Ken	si} 9/2/68
Harrington, Stan	si} 9/6/65
Harris, Franco	si} 1/6/75, 1/12/76, 11/5/79, 8/23/82 sp} 11/73, 9/76
Harris, James	sp} 10/75, 11/83
Harris, Joe	si} 6/19/67
Harris, Major	si} 11/27/89
Harris, Roy	si} 8/18/58, 9/1/58
Harris, Sean	si} 8/29/94
Hart, Jim	si} 11/27/67
Hartack, Bill	si} 6/8/64
Hartack, Willie	si} 9/17/56 ti} 2/10/58
Havilcek, John	si} 3/27/61, 5/9/66, 5/12/69, 11/13/72, 2/18/74, 5/20/74 sp} 2/68, 4/71
Hayes, Elvin	si} 5/8/78, 5/7/79
Hayes, Lester	sp} 11/81
Hayes, Woody	si} 9/15/69
Haywood, Spencer	sp} 2/72
Hazzard, Walt	si} 3/30/64
Head, Don	si} 1/15/62
Heard, Garfield	si} 11/12/73, 4/28/75
Hearns, Thomas	si} 9/14/81, 9/28/81, 4/22/85, 6/19/89
Hebert, Bobby	si} 10/7/91
Hedberg, Dorris	si} 1/24/55
Heiden, Eric	si} 2/11/80, 2/25/80 79 YIS, ti} 2/12/80
Heinsohn, Tommy	si} 10/26/64
Heiss, Carol	si} 2/7/55
Hemingway's "An African Betrayal	si} 5/5/86
Henderson, Rickey	si} 9/6/82, 82 YIS, 7/28/86, 10/16/89, bk} #57, #66, #73 sp} 5/90
Hendricks, Elrod	si} 10/20/69
Hendricks, Ted	si} 9/11/67
Henie, Sonja	ti} 7/17/39
Henning, Annie	si} 1/31/72
Henrich, Tommy	sp} 2/50
Hernandez, Keith	si} 4/7/80 sp} 6/85, 4/88
Herrerias, Rene	sp} 1/50
Hershiser, Orel	si} 10/31/88, 12/19/88, 7/1/91, bk} #45 sp}3/89, 4/90
Heuga, Jimmy	si} 2/5/68
Heyman, Art	si} 10/28/63

Name/Team	Title Publications listing
Hilgenberg, Wally	si} 1/5/76
Hill, Calvin	si} 8/16/71, 8/16/76 sp} 1/70
Hill, Graham	si} 5/13/68
Hill, Grant	si} 4/8/91, 95 SIP Pro Basketball, sk} 4/95
Hill, Kent	si} 8/24/81
Hill, Phil	si} 3/16/59
Hoad, Lew	si} 9/3/56, 6/16/58
Hodge, Dan	si} 4/1/57
Hodges, Gil	si} 9/28/70 sp} 5/59, 2/70
Hoffman, Jim	si} 8/29/94
Hogan, Ben	si} 4/4/55, 3/11/57 ti} 1/10/49
Hogan, Hulk	si} 4/29/85
Holleder, Don	si} 11/28/55
Hollingworth, Cindy	si} 11/18/63
Hollyfield, Larry	si} 2/5/73
Holman, Nat	sp} 2/51
Holmes, Larry	si} 10/8/79, 11/16/81, 6/7/82, 1982 YIS, 1983 YIS, 6/21/82, 5/30/83, 7/1/85, 9/30/85
Holtz, Lou	si} 9/11/78, 9/4/89
Holyfield, Evander	si} 4/29/91, 11/23/92,11/15/93
Homan, Dennis	si} 10/30/67
Hope, Bob	si} 6/3/63
Hord, Roy	si} 10/23/61
Hornsby, Roger	ti} 7/9/28
Hornung, Paul	si} 10/29/56, 5/20/63, 8/22/66, sp} 11/56, 11/61, 1/63, 4/66
Horse Racing	sp} 5/47
Hosteler, Jeff	sp} 8/95
Houtteman, Art	sp} 8/50
Howard, Desmond	si} 9/23/91, 12/9/91, bk} #26
Howard, Elston	si} 3/3/58
Howard, Frank	si} 5/25/64 sp} 7/60, 4/61
Howard, Juwan	si} 4/12/93, 95 sip Pro Basketball
Howe, Gordie	si} 3/18/57, 3/16/64, 3/11/74, 1/21/80 ti} 10/14/74
Howley, Chuck	si} 9/9/63
Hrbek, Kent	si} 7/5/82
Huard, Damon - Washington	si} 95 sip Col Football
Huarte, John	si} 11/2/64
Hubbard, Marv	si} 12/17/73
Hubbell-Gia, Carl	ti} 10/5/36
Hudson, Lou	si} 11/12/73
Huff, Sam	sp} 12/61 ti} 11/30/59
Hull, Bobby	si} 11/14/60, 2/3/64, 1/25/65, 2/12/68, 6/19/72 sp} 4/68, 5/72 ti} 3/1/68 bk} #3
Hull, Brett	si} 3/18/91 bk} #2, #13
Hunter, Brice - Georgia	si} 95 sip Col Football
Hunter, Jim "Catfish"	si} 10/23/72, 10/7/74 sp} 4/78
Hunter, Rachel	si} 2/14/94
Humphrey, Bobby	sp} 8/90, 9/91 bk} #9
Hurdle, Clint	si} 3/20/78
Hurley, Bobby	si} 4/13/92, 3/29/93
Hutchinson, Fred	sp} 2/65
Iavaroni, Marc	si} 2/28/83
Imhoff, Darrall	si} 1/27/69, 3/9/70
Ingalls, David	ti} 3/14/31
Indianapolis 500 Preview	si} 5/25/59, 5/29/61, 5/29/67
Ireland, Kathy	si} 2/1/89, 3/9/92, 2/14/94, 95 Best in Swimsuit Comm
Irvin, Michael	si} 2/1/93, 10/25/93, 93 Cowboy Comm., 12/12/94, bk} # 27
Irwin, Hale	si} 6/24/74, 6/25/79, 6/25/90
Ismail, Raghib	si} 9/25/89, 2/25/91 bk} #13 bk} (FS) #6
Issel, Dan	si} 3/16/70

Name/Team	Title Publications listing
Izo, George	si} 10/26/59
Iverson, Allen - Georgetown	si} 95 sip col Basketball
Jacklin, Tony	si} 6/29/70
Jackson, Bo	si} 12/2/85, 7/14/86, 12/14/87, 6/12/89 sk} 1/92
	bk}(base) #30, #51,#59, #63, #80 bk}(Foot)#1,#8, #10
	sp}3/90, 9/90, 10/91
Jackson, Chris	si} 2/20/89,
Jackson, Phil	si} 11/11/91, 1/1/93, 1993 Bulls Com. , 5/27/96
Jackson, Reggie	si} 7/7/69, 6/17/74, 10/6/75, 8/30/76, 77 YIS, 5/2/77, 8/4/80,3/15/82,
	4/20/87, 5/11/87 sp} 10/74, 10/79, 5/82, 7/83 ti} 6/3/74 bk} #10
Jackson, Sonny	si} 6/6/66
Jacobs, Helen	ti} 9/14/36
Jacobs, Louie (Mafioso)	si} 5/29/72
James Thurber	si} 11/7/60
James, Craig	si} 1/13/86
Jankowski, Bruce	si} 11/11/68
Jansen, Dan	si} 2/28/94
Jastremski, Chet	si} 1/29/62
Javier, Julian	si} 10/7/68
Jaworski, Ron	sp} 2/81
Jay, Joey	si} 10/9/61
Jazy, Michel	si} 8/30/65
Jeffcoat, Jim	si} 12/12/94
Jefferies, Gregg	si} 7/24/89, 96 sip Baseball, sp} 3/88 bk} #49, bk}(ML) #1, #6
Jefferson, John	si} 8/20/79
Jenkins, Ferguson	si} 8/30/71
Jenkins, Hayes	si} 1/30/56
Jenner, Bruce	si} 8/9/76 sp} 7/76
Jensen, Jackie	si} 6/23/58, 7/7/58
Joao, Maria (Brazil)	si} 1/16/78
Johansson, Ingemar	si} 6/22/59, 7/6/59, 1/4/60, 6/20/60 sp} 2/60, Li 7/20/59
John, Tommy	sp} 9/80
Johnson, Alex	si} 7/5/71
Johnson, Ben	si} 10/30/88
Johnson, Bill	si} 2/27/84
Johnson, Charley	si} 12/14/64, 11/1/65 sp} 1/66
Johnson, Dennis	si} 6/4/84, 6/9/86, 2/23/87
Johnson, Ervin "Magic"	si} 11/27/78, 4/2/79, 11/19/79, 5/26/80, 3/9/81, 5/24/82
	3/5/84, 6/4/84, 5/13/85, 2/23/87, 4/18/88, 5/23/88, 6/27/88
	8/22/88, 4/17/89 inset, 12/18/89, 12/3/90, 2/18/91, 6/10/91, 11/18/91
	12/14/92, 9/19/94 2/12/96 sk} 12/89,
	sp} 2/80, 2/82 5/89, 11/91, 6/92, 1/93, bk} #3, #13, #24, #26
Johnson, Floyd	ti} 2/27/23 (Dummy Issue)
Johnson, Gus	si} 5/10/71, 10/25/71
Johnson, Howard	bk} 80
Johnson, Jimmy	si} 3/20/89 5/11/96 bk} #14
Johnson, Kevin	sk} 12/90, 3/93 sp} 10/92 bk} #3, #11
Johnson, Keyshawn	si} 8/28/95
Johnson, Larry	si} 11/19/90 bk} #14, #20, #29, bk}(FS) #3 sp} 10/92
Johnson, Magnus	si} 6/13/55
Johnson, Michael	si} 5/20/91
Johnson, Rafer	si} 1/5/59, 8/6/84 sp} 2/59, ti} 8/29/60
Johnson, Ted	si} 11/15/65
Johnston, Neil	si} 1/20/58
Jones, Bert	si} 9/13/76, 5/10/82 sp} 10/76
Jones, Bobby	ti} 8/30/25, 9/21/30
Jones, Calvin	si} 9/27/54
Jones, Cobi	sk} 6/94
Jones, Deacon	si} 1/5/70 sp} 1/69
Jones, Harry	si} 11/8/65

Name/Team	Title	Publications listing
Jones, Howard	tl} 11/14/32	
Jones, Jimmy	si} 9/29/69	
Jones, Randy	si} 7/12/76	
Jones, Robert Tyre	si} 4/6/59	
Jones, Too Tall	si} 8/11/86	
Joradan, Bryce	sk} 3/94	
Jordan, Jimmy	si} 11/12/79	
Jordan, Lee Roy	si} 9/9/63, 12/18/72	
Jordan, Michael	si} 11/28/83, 7/23/84, 12/10/84,11/17/86, 12/28/87, 5/16/88, 3/13/89,	

si} 11/28/83, 7/23/84, 12/10/84,11/17/86, 12/28/87, 5/16/88, 3/13/89,
5/15/89, 8/14/89, 11/6/89, 11/9/87 inset, 5/21/90, 12/17/90,
2/18/91, 6/3/91, 6/10/91, 6/17/91, 8/5/91, 11/11/91,12/23/91,
5/11/92, 5/25/92, 6/15/92, 6/22/92, 1/1/93, 93 Bulls Comm.
6/7/93, 6/21/93, 6/28/93,10/18/93, 3/14/94, 3/20/95,3/27/95,
5/22/95, 96 Bulls Com. 95 SIP Basketball 5/27/96, 6/17/96,
6/3/96 sk} 1/89, 5/92

sp} 3/87, 11/88, 6/90, 10/90, 1/91, 11/91, 12/91, 5/92, 6/92, 5/93,
11/93, 12/93, 1/94, 6/94, 11/94, 4/95, 6/95, 11/95, 1/96, 6/96

bk} #1, #10, #14,#24, #25, #31

Jordan, Steve	si} 3/17/80	
Joyner, Florence Griffith	si} 7/25/88, 10/10/88,12/26/88	
Joyner-Kersee, Jackie	si} 9/14/87, 10/10/88, 7/22/92, sk} 3/90 ti} 9/19/88	
Joyner, Wally	bk} #22, sp} 4/90	
Jauntorena, Alberto	si} 9/12/77	
Julen, Emil	si} 7/25/55	
Jurgensen, Sonny	si} 7/28/69 sp} 12/65, 10/69	
Justice, David	si} 1995 Braves Commerative, sp} 4/94	
Justice, Charlie	sp} 11/49 bk} #78 li} 10/3/49	
Kaab, Vyto	si} 12/6/82	
Kaftan, George	sp} 3/48	
Kaline, Al	si} 5/14/56, 5/11/64, 6/5/67, 9/23/68 sp} 7/57, 3/59, 7/63	
Kalule, Ayub	si} 7/6/81	
Kansas City/World Series	si} 11/4/85	
Kansbod, Lena (Maui)	si} 1/24/77	
Kapp, Joe	si} 7/20/70	
Karlis, Rich	si} 1/19/87	
Karras, Alex	si} 11/30/64, 10/12/70 bk}(FS)#18	
Karros, Eric	bk} #93	
Karten, Maud	si} 1/24/55	
Kazmaier, Dick	ti} 11/19/51	
Kearns, Jack/ Dempsey- Willard	si} 1/13/65	
Keenan, Mike	si 11/27/95 (Canadian issue only)	
Keino, Kip	si} 9/30/68, 12/21/87	
Kelly, Jim	si} 7/21/86 sp} 10/87 ,1/92 bk} #22	
Kelso Races	si} 11/6/61	
Kemp, Bruce	si} 10/12/69	
Kemp, Shawn	sk} 12/94 bk} #7, #28	
Kendall, Pete - Boston Col.	si} 95 sip Col Football	
Kennedy, John F./Jackie	si} 12/26/60	
Kentucky Derby	si} 7/18/55, 5/6/57, 5/2/60, 5/1/61, 3/12/62, 5/7/62, 5/6/63, 5/4/64	

si} 7/18/55, 5/6/57, 5/2/60, 5/1/61, 3/12/62, 5/7/62, 5/6/63, 5/4/64
5/3/65

Keogh, Matt	si} 4/27/81	
Kern, Rex	si} 9/15/69 sp} 10/70	
Keron, Larry	si} 3/26/73	
Kerr, Dave	ti} 3/14/38	
Kerrigan, Nancy	si} 1/17/94 ti} 1/24/94	
Keyes, Leroy	si} 9/9/68	
Keys, Randolph	si} 12/11/89	
Khan, Aly	si} 3/23/59	
Kidd, Billy	si} 3/8/65, 2/5/68	
Kidd, Jason	si} 3/29/93	

Name/Team	Title Publications listing
Kids of Famous Fathers	sk} 6/91
Klick, Jim	si} 8/7/72, 7/28/75
Killebrew, Harmon	si} 4/8/63 sp} 5/60, 11/64, 6/70
Killy, Jean-Claude	si} 2/21/66, 3/27/67, 11/18/68
Kim, Duk Koo	si} 11/22/82
Kimberly, Jim	si} 9/13/54, 3/26/56
Kimble, Bo	si} 3/26/90
Kiner, Ralph	sp} 5/50, 6/52
King, Albert	si} 3/17/80, 12/1/80
King, Billie Jean	si} 12/25/72, 7/16/73, 9/19/94
King, Don	si} 9/15/75
King, JB	si} 12/21/87
King, Stacey	sp} 12/88
Kingman, Brian	si} 4/27/81
Kinmont, Jill	si} 1/31/55
Kirby, Clay	si} 3/3/75
Kite, Tom	si} 6/29/92
Kitt, A.J.	si} 1/27/92
Klammer, Franz	si} 2/16/76
Klinger, David	si} 8/26/91
Kluszewski, Ted	si} 7/16/56 sp} 5/54
Knicks, The	si} 10/23/67
Knievel, Evel	si} 9/2/74
Knight, Bobby	si} 1/26/81, 3/23/87
Knight, Chris	si} 4/2/90
Knight, Phil	si} 8/16/93
Knight, Ray	si} 11/3/86
Knoblaugh	bk} #94
Koosman, Jerry	si} 4/13/70, li} 9/26/69
Korbut, Olga	si} 3/19/73, 9/19/94
Kosar, Bernie	si} 9/1/84, 8/26/85, 8/29/88
Koss, Johann Olav	si} 12/19/94
Koufax, Sandy	si} 3/4/63, 4/13/64, 12/20/65, 5/15/67 sp} 9/63, 2/64, 5/65, 10/65, 2/66, 10/66, 5/69 li} 8/2/63
Koy, Ernie	si} 1/11/65
Kramer, Jake	ti} 9/1/47
Kramer, Jerry	si} 1/22/68
Kramer, Ron	si} 11/12/56
Krebs, Jim	si} 2/18/57
Kristofferson, Kris	si} 11/7/77
Krone, Julie	si} 5/22/89
Kubiak, Gary	si} 1/19/87
Kuenn, Harvey	si} 5/14/56, 7/9/56 sp} 8/62
Kuhn, Bowie	si} 6/28/76
Kush, Rod	si} 1/12/81
Kuznetsov, Vasily	si} 7/20/59
Labine, Clem	si} 6/3/57
Lackey, Bob	si} 11/9/59
Lacy, Lee	si} 10/23/78
Laettner, Christian	si} 11/25/91 bk} #23, #30
Lafleur, Guy	si} 2/7/77
Lahr, B.	ti} 10/1/51
Laimbeer, Bill	si} 6/27/88, 11/5/90
Lakers Team Photo	si} 4/18/88
Lalas, Alexi	sk} 6/94
Lambert, Jack	si} 1/17/83, 7/30/84 sp} 12/78
Lamonica, Daryl	si} 11/23/70
Landry, Tom	si} 11/14/88
Landy, John	si} 5/21/56
Lane, Lisa	si} 8/7/61

Name/Team	Title　　　Publications listing
Langford, Rick	si} 4/27/81
Lanier, Bob	si} 3/16/70
Larkin, Barry- Reds	si} 96 sip Baseball
Larussa, Tony	si} 3/12/90
Lary, Frank	si} 4/9/62
Laskowski, John	si} 2/3/75
Lasorda, Tommy	si} 3/14/77
Lassic, Derek	si} 1993 Commerative
Lattner, Johnny	sp} 11/53 ti} 11/9/53
Lavagetto, Cookie	si} 5/15/61
Laver, Rod	si} 8/26/68
Law, Vernon	si} 10/10/60
Lawrence, Andrea	ti} 1/21/52
Layne, Bobby	sp} 1/61 ti} 11/29/54
Leach, Rick	si} 9/6/76
Leahy, Frank	sp} 11/46 ti} 10/14/46
LeBaron, Eddie	sp} 1/54
Lee, Butch	si} 4/4/77
Lee, Johnny	si} 1/21/57
Leisenring, James	si} 3/28/60
Lema, Tony	si} 3/23/64, 3/15/65
Lemieux, Mario	si} 2/6/89, 6/8/92, 4/19/93,sk} 12/93 bk} #4, #10
Lemon, Bob	sp} 6/50, 5/53, 5/56
Lemond, Greg	si} 7/31/89, 12/25/89, 7/30/90
Lendl, Ivan	si} 9/15/86
Leonard, Sugar Ray	si} 12/10/79, 6/30/80,11/24/80, 7/6/81, 9/28/81, 12/28/81
	1981 YIS, 11/15/82, 9/8/86, 3/30/87, 4/13/87, 6/19/89
Lewis, Carl	si} 8/22/83, 6/25/84, 8/20/84, 8/17/92, 1/4/93 ti} 7/28/84,
	8/13/84, 83 YIS, 92 Year In Pictures
Lewis, Reggie	si} 8/9/93
Light, Donald	si} 6/18/62
Lilly, Bob	si} 9/9/63
Lindsay, Ted	si} 3/18/57
Lindros, Eric	si} 10/9/95 Canadian
Liquori, Marty	si} 5/24/71
Liston, Sonny	si} 2/12/62, 9/17/62, 3/25/63, 7/29/63, 3/9/64, 11/16/64
	4/26/65, 5/24/65, 6/7/65
Listach	bk} #95
Little, L.	sp} 1/74
Little League	sk} 8/89
Littler, Gene	si} 5/14/62
Lofgran, Don	sp} 1/50
Logan, Dave	si} 9/8/80
Lombardi, Vince	si} 1/22/68, 3/3/69, 7/28/69, 1/1/89 , 1989 Superbowl Special
	ti} 12/21/62 bk} #10
Long, Chuck	si} 12/2/85
Long, Dale	si} 7/9/56
Long, Dallas	si} 4/25/60
Long, Howie	si} 7/22/85 sp} 8/86, 8/88
Longden, Johnny	si} 2/16/59
Longhorns Beat Oklahoma	si} 10/19/81
Look at Spring Training	si} 3/6/61
Look at the World Series	si} 9/29/58
Lopes, Dave	si} 11/2/81
Lopez, Danny	si} 2/12/79
Lopez, Felipe	si} 11/28/94
Lopez, Nancy	si} 7/10/78
Los Angeles Rams	sp} 10/82
Lott, Ronnie	bk} #13,#20 sp} 8/91
Louis, Joe	si} 9/16/85 sp} 6/48 ti} 9/29/41

Name/Team	Title Publications listing
Lovell, D.	sp} 3/88
Lowe, Jeff	si} 12/11/78
Lowe, Paul	si} 12/16/63
Lowe, Sidney	si} 4/11/83
Lucas, Jerry	si} 1/11/60, 3/27/61, 1/8/62,10/28/63
Lucas, Maurice	si} 6/13/77, 10/31/77 sp} 3/78
Lucci, Mike	sp} 1/71
Luce, Clare Boothe	si} 8/11/58, 5/22/61
Luckett, Walter	si} 11/27/72
Luckman, Sid	sp} 12/49. Li} 10/24/38
Lujack, Johnny	sp} 11/46, 11/47, 12/48, 12/49, 12/51
Lunn, Bob	si} 2/17/69
Luzinski, Greg	si} 8/29/77, 6/8/81
Lyle, Sparky	si} 8/21/72
Lynch, George	si} 4/12/93
Lynn, Carol	li} 3/26/45
Lynn, Fred	si} 7/7/75, 3/18/85
Macauley, Ed	sp} 1/49
Mack, Connie	ti} 4/11/27
Mackey, Malcom	si} 3/30/92
Maclaine, Shirley(Football Film)	si} 7/20/64
Macon, Mark	si} 3/28/88
MacPherson, Elle	si} 2/10/86, 2/9/87, 2/15/88, 2/14/94
Maddux, Greg- Braves	si} 8/14/95, 96 sip Baseball
Maddux, Tommy	sp} 8/92
Maentz, Tom	si} 11/12/56
Magic Views of Speed on Skis	si} 12/4/61
Maglie, Sal	si} 3/17/58
Magnuson, Keith	si} 4/6/70
Mahaffey, Art	si} 4/29/63
Mahre, Phil	si} 2/6/84 ti} 1/30/84
Major League Salaries	si} 4/20/87
Majkowski	bk} #7
Malloy, Mike	si} 12/2/68
Malone, Karl	si} 5/23/88, 11/7/88, 2/18/91
	sk} 11/89, 6/93 bk} #2, #15 #24, #29
Malone, Frank	si} 7/7/58
Malone, Moses	si} 2/19/79, 5/3/82, 11/1/82, 2/28/83, 6/6/83
Mancini, Ray	si} 8/2/82, 11/22/82
Mandarich, Tony	si} 4/24/89, 9/28/92
Manges, Mark	si} 10/4/76
Manley, Dexter	si} 11/23/87
Manning, Archie	si} 9/14/70
Manning, Danny	si} 2/17/86, 4/11/88
Manning, Peyton - Tenn	si} 95 Col Football
Mantle, Mickey	si} 6/18/56, 7/9/56, 10/1/56, 3/4/57, 7/7/58, 7/2/62, 6/21/65, 5/8/67 3/25/85, 5/27/91, 4/18/94, 8/21/95, 95 Mantle Comm.
	sp} 4/53, 10/56, 3/57, 6/59, 8/59, 8/60, 5/61, 9/61,7/62, 5/63, 10/63, 9/64, 8/65, 7/66, 5/67, 4/69 ti} 7/1/53, bk} #2, #19, #75 Li} 6/25/56, 8/18/61, 7/30/65
Maradona, Diego	si} 7/7/86
Maravich, Pete	si} 3/4/68, 12/1/69, 11/12/73, 79YIS, sp} 3/71
March, Babette	si} 1/20/64
Marciano, Rocky	si} 9/19/55 sp} 1/53, 6/54, 3/55
Marichal, Jaun	si} 8/9/65 ti} 6/10/66
Marinaro, Ed	si} 11/1/71
Marino, Dan	si} 11/14/83, 83 YIS, 9/1/84, 1/14/85,1/21/85, 1/14/91, 9/12/94 9/4/95 5/11/96 sk} 9/90, 10/95 sp} 1/84, 1/85, 10/85, 10/86 10/89, 10/93, 8/94, bk} #1, #24, #33
Marinovich, Todd	si} 9/3/90

Name/Team	Title Publications listing
Maris, Roger	si} 10/2/61, 10/7/68, 5/27/91, li} 8/18/61 sp} 11/60, 2/62
Marlin, Sterling	si} 7/24/95
Marshall, Mike	si} 8/12/74
Marston, Ann	si} 8/8/55
Martin, Billy	si} 4/23/56, 7/21/69, 6/2/75, 7/31/78, 5/6/85 sp} 8/58, 8/75, 5/81, 7/82 ti} 5/11/81
Martin, Christy	si} 4/15/96
Martin, Harvey	si} 1/23/78 sp} 1/79
Martin, Rod	si} 2/2/81
Martinez, Ramon	si} 9/30/91
Maryland, Russell	si} 10/24/88, 12/12/94
Maryland Football	sp} 9/85
Masco, Judit in the Greenlands	si} 2/12/90
Mason, Tommy	si} 9/28/64, 9/18/67 sp} 11/65
Masters Tournament	si} 4/3/61
Masters Golf Clubs	si} 8/23/54
Masters Golf	si} 4/7/58, 4/4/60
Mateer, Diehl	si} 2/10/58
Mathews, Eddie	si} 8/16/54, 8/15/55, 8/20/56, 6/2/58, 8/15/94 sp} 2/54, 4/57, 9/58, 8/59
Mathewson, Christy	sp} 10/49
Mathias, Bob	ti} 7/21/52, li} 7/11/49
Matson, Ollie	si} 10/7/57
Matte, Tom	si} 1/6/69
Matthews, Gary	sp} 6/85
Mattingly, Don	si} 7/13/87 , 7/27/87 inset bk} #14, #23, #35, #43,#62 sp 4/89
Matuszak, John	si} 8/6/73
Mau, Turia	si} 1/15/68
Mauldin, Bill	si} 1/13/58
Maute, Charles	si} 2/13/56
Maxwell, Bill	si} 10/7/68
May	si} 10/19/70
May, Scott	si} 4/5/76, 7/19/76
Mayer, Dick	si} 6/9/58
Mays, Willie	si} 4/11/55, 7/9/56, 7/7/58, 4/13/59, 6/26/61, 6/4/62, 7/27/70, 5/22/72 3/25/85, 8/1/92, sp} 6/56, 1/58,6/58, 8/59, 3/60, 9/60, 6/61, 10/62, 8/63, 8/64, 10/64, 6/65, 4/66, 9/66, 6/67, 5/68, 5/69, 9/71 ti} 7/26/54 li} 4/28/58, bk} #3, #29
Mazza, Valeria	si} 1/29/96
McAdoo, Bob	si} 3/8/76
McAlister, Barbara	si} 7/23/62
McAlister, James	si} 5/17/71
McCallum, Napoleon	si} 9/1/85
McCantey, Steve	si} 4/27/81
McCarthy, James	si} 10/20/58
McCarver, Tim	si} 9/4/67, 10/7/68
McClain, Dwayne	si} 4/1/85
McClain, Gary	si} 3/16/87
McColl, Bill	sp} 11/51
McCovey, Willie	sp} 5/60
McCray, Rodney	si} 5/19/86
McDonald, Ben	si} 7/18/94
McDonald, Ray	si} 11/11/85
McDonald, Tommy	si} 10/8/62, 7/27/64
McDougald, Gil	si} 3/3/58, 5/5/58, sp} 3/52
McDowell, J.	si} 96 sip Baseball, sp} 3/88
McDowell, Sam	si} 5/23/66
McElhenny, Hugh	sp} 12/55
McEnaney, Will	si} 11/3/75

Name/Team	Title Publications listing
McEnroe, John	si} 12/18/78, 9/15/80, 7/13/81, 79 YIS, 81 YIS, 83 YIS 9/21/81, 7/11/83, 7/16/84, 9/17/84
McGee, Max	si} 1/23/67
McGinnis, George	si} 10/27/75, 3/21/77, 11/19/79 sp3/76
McGraw, Tug	sp} 4/81
McGriff	bk} #77
McGuire, Allie	si} 2/21/72
McGuire, Dick	si} 10/30/61
McGuire, Steve	si} 12/4/89
McGuirk, Michael	si} 6/18/62
McGwire, Mark	si} 4/4/88, 6/1/92 bk} #32, #89,
McHale, Kevin	si} 5/11/81, 6/16/86, 6/15/87, bk} #25
McIntire, Barbara	si} 8/22/60
McIntyre	si} 2/5/90
McKay, John	si} 10/2/67
McKinney, Tamara	si} 2/6/84 ti} 1/30/84
McKyer, Tim	si} 12/5/94
McLain, Denny	si} 7/29/68, 9/23/68, 2/23/70,7/19/93 sp} 12/69, 5/71 ti} 9/13/68
McMahon, Jim	si}10/21/85, 1/20/86, 9/1/86, 8/24/87, 9/12/88, 12/2/91 sp} 1/86
McManus, Kitty (Cheerleader)	si} 1/2/67
McMillan, Jim	si} 4/24/72
McMillan, Roy	si} 9/9/57
McMillen, Tom	si} 2/16/70
McNair, Steve	si} 9/26/94
McNeeley, Tom	si} 11/13/61
McNerty, Gerry	si} 8/31/64
McQueen, Steve (Motorcycling)	si} 8/23/71
McTear, Houston	si} 3/6/78
Means, Natrone	si} 10/17/94
Melton, Bill	si} 3/12/73
Member of the Oklahoma Band	si} 10/11/54
Mercein, Chuck	si} 1/8/68
Meredith, Don	si} 9/16/68 sp} 1/67, 11/68
Meriwether, Del	si} 2/22/71
Messier, Mark	si} 6/13/94 bk} #2, #10, #15
Mets	ti} 9/5/69
Meyers, Dave	si} 4/24/72, 2/17/75
Miami Beats Oklahoma	si} 1/11/88
Miami Football	si} 6/12/95
Michigan Beats Notre Dame	si} 9/22/86
Michigan State/Football Issue	sp} 12/53
Middlecoff, Cary	si} 6/10/57
Mikan, George	sp} 3/50
Mikita, Stan	si} 1/31/66, 4/25/66, 3/20/67
Milburan, Deverux	ti} 9/5/27
Mildenberger, Karl	si} 7/10/67
Miller, Cheryl	si} 11/1/85
Miller, Johnny	si} 6/25/73, 6/10/74 sp} 6/75
Miller, Ralph	si} 2/6/56
Miller, Reggie	si} 95 sip Basketball, bk} #8
Milner, John	si} 10/22/73
Minnesota Vikings	li} 11/17/61
Minoso, Minnie	sp} 8/54
Mira, George	si} 9/23/63
Mirer, Rick	si} 9/24/90
Mitchell, Dennis	si} 8/17/92
Mitchell, Kevin	bk} #53, #56 bk}(ML) #9
Mizell, Vinegar Bend	sp} 8/56

Name/Team	Title	Publications listing
Moceanu, Dominique	sk} 1/95	
Model	si} 10/17/60	
Moe, Tommy	si} 2/21/94	
Moeller, Gary	si} 5/15/95	
Mohns, Doug	si} 3/20/67	
Moncrief, Sidney	si} 2/13/78, 2/22/82, 12/10/84	
Monk	bk} #31	
Monroe, Earl	si} 11/4/68, 1/25/71, 4/16/73 sp} 11/77	
Montana, Ashley	si} 3/11/91	
Montana, Joe	si} 81 YIS, 1/25/82, 1/21/85, 10/2/89, 12/18/89, 2/5/90, 8/6/90, 12/24/90, 7/27/92, 4/26/93, 9/13/93, 1/24/94, 4/24/95 sp} 8/82, 8/85, 2/87, 8/89, 6/90, 8/90, 10/90, 11/90, 7/91, 9/91, 8/93,9/93, 10/93, 2/94, 9/94 ti} 1/12/82, bk} #2, #9	
Montross, Eric- Celtics	si} 4/12/93, 95 sip basketball	
Monzon, Carlos	si} 8/8/77	
Moon, Wally	si} 3/5/56, 4/22/57 sp} 10/61	
Moon, Warren	sk} 10/92, Bk} #18, #32	
Moore, Davey	si} 6/27/83	
Moore, Kirby	si} 9/11/67	
Morgan, Joe	si} 6/6/66, 4/12/76, 3/14/83, sp} 8/76	
Morrall, Earl	si} 11/25/68, 1/25/71	
Morris, Larry	sp} 11/54	
Morris, Mercury	si} 1/8/73	
Morrow, Bobby	si} 7/2/56, 1/7/57 sp} 12/56, li} 12/10/56	
Morton, Craig	si} 1/18/71	
Mosbacher, Bob & Bus	si} 5/18/59	
Moseby, Lloyd	si} 10/5/87	
Moses, Edwin	si} 9/12/83, 12/24/84, 83 YIS	
Most Beautiful Women of Sports	sp} 3/86	
Mount, Rick	si} 2/14/66	
Mourning, Alonzo	si} 11/8/93, 94 Hot Shot Comm.	
Mugabi, John	si} 3/24/86	
Mulder, Marie	si} 5/10/65	
Mullin, Chris	si} 4/1/85, 2/10/92 sk} 11/91, sp} 12/84 bk} #17	
Mullins, Gerry	si} 1/12/76	
Mullins, Jeff	si} 3/30/64, 3/24/69	
Muncie, Chuck	si} 11/24/75, 1/12/81, 1/17/83	
Munson, Thurmon	si} 10/24/77	
Murcer, Bobby	si} 7/2/73 sp} 8/73	
Murchison, Clint	ti} 5/24/54, 6/16/61	
Murphy, Calvin	si} 11/16/70	
Murphy, Dale	si} 8/9/82, 7/4/83, 83YIS, 12/21/87 sp} 6/84, bk} #1, #18	
Murray, Eddie	bk} #5	
Murtaugh, Danny	si} 9/28/70, 9/24/73 sp} 2/61	
Musial, Stan	si} 3/5/56, 7/9/56, 7/8/57, 12/23/57, 7/7/58, 4/10/61 sp} 8/48, 7/50, 7/52, 7/54, 9/59, 9/62, 4/63 bk} #5, ti} 9/5/49	
Mussina, Mike	si} 7/18/94	
Musso, Johnny	si} 12/6/71	
Mutombo, D.	Bk} #31	
NFL Injuries	si} 11/10/86	
NFL Troubles	si} 11/12/84	
NFL's Greatest Coaches	sp} 2/88	
Nagel, Cathy	si} 2/11/63	
Nagle,	bk} #31	
Nagy, Steve	si} 3/28/55	
Namath, Joe	si} 7/19/65, 10/17/66, 12/22/67 flap, 12/9/68,1/20/69, 6/16/69, 8/11/69, 8/17/70, 10/9/72 sp} 6/66, 11/67, 7/72, 12/73, 11/74, 11/75, 3/77, 9/94, ti} 10/16/72, bk} #22, li} 6/20/69, 11/3/72	
Nance, Jim	si} 12/12/66	
Nash, Cotton	si} 12/10/62	

Name/Team	Title Publications listing
Olmedo, Alex	si} 9/7/59
Olson, Greg	si} 10/26/91
Olson, Merlin	sp} 1/73
Olszewski, Johnny	sp} 12/52
Olympic Games Preview	si} 11/19/56, 8/28/72, 7/28/80
Olympic Sailing	si} 8/13/56
Olympic '84 Preview	si} 7/1/84
One Day in Baseball	si} 7/6/87
Open at Oakmont Preview	si} 6/11/62
Opening Ceremonies in Rome	si} 9/5/60
Opening Day Squaw Valley	si} 2/29/60
Organa, Marvin - Alabama	si} 95 sip Col. Football
Orr, Bobby	si} 12/11/67, 2/3/69, 5/4/70, 12/21/70, 5/8/72
	sp} 12/69, 2/71, 4/72
Osborn, Dave	si} 1/5/70
Osborne, Tom	si} 1/9/95
Osteen, Claude	si} 8/20/73
Ott, Mel	ti} 7/2/45
Outboarding	si} 5/90/60
Owen, Laurence	si} 2/13/61
Owens, Steve	si} 11/10/69
Ownes, Billy	si} 11/1/88 Bk #23
Page, Alan	si} 11/3/69
Paige, Stephone	si} 12/31/90 Pictures
Palermo, Steve	si} 7/6/92
Palmer, Arnold	si} 6/13/60, 1/9/61, 4/2/62, 11/12/62, 7/15/63, 6/15/64
	4/5/65, 7/26/65, 4/4/66, 3/6/67, 6/12/67, 6/10/68
	9/1/69, 6/1/70 ti} 5/2/60
Palmer, Jim	si} 7/21/75
Palomino, Carlos	si} 7/2/79
Parent, Bernie	ti} 2/24/75
Parish, Robert	si} 5/31/82, 5/2/83, 2/11/91, 82 YIS
Park, Brad	si} 5/9/77
Parker, Dave	si} 5/30/77, 4/9/79 sp} 6/79, 6/81, 7/87
Parker, Harry	si} 6/28/65
Parker, Wes	si} 3/22/71
Parkins, Hef	si} 11/29/54
Parrish, Robert	sk} 5/91 bk} #25
Parry, Zale	si} 5/23/55
Parshian	ti} 11/20/64
Passarella, Daniel	si} 7/3/78
Pastorini, Dan	si} 1/14/70
Pastrano, Willie	si} 3/22/65
Paterno, Joe	si} 12/22/86
Patrick, Dave	si} 6/3/68
Patterson, Floyd	si} 6/4/56, 7/29/57, 9/1/58, 7/6/59, 3/13/61, 5/28/62, 11/22/65
Patterson, Steve	si} 4/5/71
Patton, Mel	ti} 8/2/48
Paul, Bob	si} 12/15/58
Paultz, Billy	si} 4/25/77
Payne, Billy	si} 1/8/96
Payton, Gary	si} 3/5/90, 5/2/94, 6/10/96
Payton, Walter	si} 11/22/76, 77 YIS, 8/16/82,10/15/84, 12/8/86 sp} 10/84, 9/94
	ti} 1/27/86, bk} #7
Peace, Wayne	si} 9/13/82
Pearce, Mary	si} 8/23/93
Pearson, Preston	si} 1/5/76
Peck, A. Wells	si} 4/8/57
Peeples, George	si} 1/24/66
Peete, Rodney	si} 11/28/88

Name/Team	Title	Publications listing
Peirson, John	si} 1/28/57	
Pele	si} 6/23/75	
Pellegrini, Bob	si} 11/7/55	
Pendleton, Terry	si} 5/23/94	
Penn State falls to Colorado	si} 10/5/70	
Pennant Time	sp} 10/73	
Perez, Tony	si} 10/19/70, 3/14/83 bk} # 88	
Perkins, Sam	si} 11/30/81, 3/29/82, 11/28/83, 3/26/84	
Perreault, Gilbert	si} 2/26/73	
Perry, Fred	ti} 9/3/34	
Perry, Gaylord	si} 9/26/66, 8/27/79, 5/17/82, sp 9/73	
Perry, William	si} 8/11/86 sp} 2/86 ti} 1/27/86	
Pestova, Daniela	si} 2/20/95	
Pet Pals	sk} 7/94	
Peters, Jon	si} 5/8/89	
Peterson, Mike	si} 8/9/71	
Peterson, Sue (Swimsuit)	si} 1/18/65	
Phillip, Andy	sp} 1/47	
Phillips, Kristie	si} 9/1/86	
Phillips, Lawrence - Nebraska	si} 95 Nebraska Com, 95 sip Col. Football	
Phillips, Pamela	si} 10/31/55	
Phipps, Mike	si} 10/9/67	
Physical Fitness in Siviet Union	si} 12/2/57	
Piazza, Mike- Dodgers	si} 7/5/93, 4/4/94, 96 sip Baseball, sk} 6/95 sp} 5/94	
Pierce, Billy	si} 5/13/57 sp} 10/57	
Piersall, Jimmy	sp} 7/59	
Pietrosante, Nick	si} 11/19/62	
Pihos, Pete	sp} 1/55	
Pill-Popping	sp} 12/76	
Pinckney, Ed	si} 4/8/85	
Pinder, Fred & Art	si} 9/5/55	
Pine Valley - Golf	si} 8/25/58	
Pinella, Lou	si} 5/31/76 sp} 5/80	
Pinson, Vada	sp} 4/62	
Pippen, Scottie	si} 5/16/88, 11/11/91, 5/25/92, 6/28/93, 94 Hot Shot Comm.	
	sk} 5/93 bk} #12, #21, sp} 6/92, 6/94, 6/96	
Pit Bull Terrier	si} 7/27/87	
Pitno, Rick	si} 2/26/96	
Pittsburgh Celebration	bk} #22	
Plante, Jacques	si} 2/17/58 sp} 2/57	
Player, Gary	si} 5/8/61, 3/21/66, 4/4/66, 4/22/74, 4/17/78, 5/1/78	
Plunkett, Jim	si} 2/15/71, 9/7/81 sp} 10/70,10/72, 8/81	
Podres, Johnny	si} 1/2/56	
Point Shaving at Boston Col.	si} 2/16/81	
Pointer: Mary Blue	ti} 3/3/30	
Porizkova, Paulina	si} 2/13/84, 2/11/85	
Porter, Darrell	si} 6/9/80, 10/27/80	
Post, Wally	si} 7/16/56	
Postema, Pam (Umpire)	si} 3/14/88	
Potvin, Denis	si} 4/16/79	
Poulus, Ron - Notre Dame	si} 95 sip col Football	
Powell, Boog	si} 10/19/70, 4/12/71 sp} 6/71	
Powell, Mike	si} 9/9/91	
Power Boating	si} 8/2/65	
Prefontaine, Steve	si} 6/15/70	
Price, Mark	si} 11/1/85 bk} #21	
Princeton's Marching Band	si} 10/17/55	
Pro Football Strike	si} 8/5/74, 9/27/82	
Pro Football's War Ag. Roughness	si} 11/11/63	
Prothro, Tommy	si} 7/24/72	

Name/Team	Title	Publications listing
Prudden, Bonnie	si} 8/5/57	
Pruitt, Greg	si} 10/2/72	
Puckett, Kirby	si} 4/20/87,9/10/87 inset variation ,10/21/91, 4/6/92 sk} 8/92, bk} #27, #34, #87	
Pyland, Lynn	si} 3/20/61	
Quast, Anne	si} 8/17/59	
Racing at Santa Anita	si} 1/10/55	
Radford, Mark	si} 3/23/81	
Rafting Down the Colorado Rapids	si} 8/1/77	
Ralston, Dennis	si} 8/26/63	
Rambis, Kurt	si} 6/4/84, 5/26/86, 6/15/87, 4/18/88	
Ramirez, Manny	si} 4/1/96	
Ramsey, Frank	si} 12/9/63	
Randall, Mark	si} 4/1/91	
Randle, Sonny	si} 11/1/65	
Ratterman, George	si} 10/8/56	
Rawls, Betsy	si} 8/3/64	
Reagan, Ronald (President)	si} 11/26/84, 2/16/87	
Reavis, Phil	si} 2/24/58	
Red Sox #23	si} 8/22/94	
Reds at Spring Training	si} 3/5/79	
Redwine, Jarvis	si} 11/12/79	
Reed, Willis	si} 4/27/70, 2/8/71, 4/19/71, sp} 4/70, 2/73	
Reese, Brian	si} 3/8/93	
Reese, Don (Cocaine Habit)	si} 6/14/82	
Reese, Pee Wee	sp} 10/52, 1/58	
Reeves, Byron - Grizzlies	si} 95 sip Pro Basketball	
Reeves, Dan	si} 11/6/67, 8/2/93	
Regan, Larry	si} 1/28/57	
Regan, Mike as Casey at the Bat	si} 7/18/88	
Reid, J.R.	si} 3/2/87	
Reilly, Mike	si} 10/26/92	
Report on Gambling in Las Vegas	si} 5/11/59	
Report on Grizzly Bears	si} 5/26/69	
Report on National Field Trials	si} 11/30/59	
Repulski, Rep	si} 3/5/56	
Results of the Melbourne Games	si} 12/10/56	
Retton, Mary Lou	si} 8/13/84, 12/24/84, life 1/85	
Reuschel, Rick	si} 7/10/89	
Revson, Pete	si} 6/7/71	
Reynolds, Allie	sp} 8/52, 11/52	
Reynolds, Burt	si} 11/7/77	
Rice, Glen	si} 4/10/89	
Rice, Jerry	si} 1/30/89, 1/15/90, 9/7/92,12/26/94 sk} 12/92, bk} #6,#16 Sp} 8/92, 1/93, 2/94, 9/94, 2/95, 10/95,	
Rice, Jim	si} 4/9/79, 10/27/86 sp} 7/78	
Rice, Tony	si} 10/24/88, 12/5/88, 1/9/89, 11/27/89	
Richard, Henri	si} 4/2/73	
Richard, J.R.	si} 8/18/80, 3/2/81 sp} 7/79	
Richard, Maurice	si} 3/21/60 sp} 1/59	
Richards, Paul	sp} 8/55	
Richardson, Clint	si} 3/5/84	
Richardson, Nolan	si} 1/1/93, 94 Arkansas Comm.	
Richter, Mike	si} 6/20/94, 94 Rangers Comm.	
Riefenstahl, Leni	ti} 2/17/36	
Rigby, Bob	si} 9/3/73	
Rigby, Cathy	li 5/5/72	
Riggins, John	si} 2/7/83, 12/19/83, 83 YIS	
Riggs, Bobby	si} 5/21/73 ti} 6/10/73	
Riley, Pat	si} 3/28/66, 4/18/88	

Name/Team	Title	Publications listing
Rinchlott, Janis	si} 4/20/64	
Riodar, Mike	si} 11/13/72	
Ripken, Billy	si} 3/9/87, 5/2/88	
Ripken, Cal, Jr.	si} 3/9/87, 7/29/91, 5/1/95, 8/7/95, 9/11/95 , 95 Ripken Com.	
	96 sip Baseball, sp} 4/84, 4/95 bk} #2, #9, #74, #84 sk} 6/92, 8/95,	
Rivalry Between the AFC & NFC	si} 11/21/77	
Rivesq	si} 12/21/87	
Rivers, Doc	si} 5/18/87	
Rivers, Mo	si} 3/17/75	
Rison	bk} #18	
Rizzoti, Jennifer	si} 4/10/95	
Rizzuto, Phil	sp} 11/53	
Roach, Hal (Hunter)	si} 1/19/59	
Roach, Jessee	sk} 7/89	
Roberts, Bill	si} 1/28/57	
Roberts, Fred	si} 6/15/87	
Roberts, Robin	sp} 9/53, 5/57 ti} 5/28/56	
Robertson, Alvin	si} 11/17/86	
Robertson, Oscar	si} 10/26/70, 5/10/71 sp} 3/61,4/64, 4/73	
Robinson, Brooks	si} 8/31/64, 10/10/66,10/20/69, 10/19/70 sp} 6/72 bk} #76	
Robinson, David	si} 11/1/86, 1/29/90, 3/7/94, 4/29/96	
	sk} 10/90, Bk} #2,5,16 sp} 11/91	
Robinson, Earl	si} 8/31/64	
Robinson, Eddie	si} 10/14/85	
Robinson, Flynn	si} 4/24/74	
Robinson, Frank	si} 10/10/66, 10/5/69,10/18/71,sp} 9/65, 8/66, 2/67, 9/72, 5/75	
Robinson, Jackie	sp} 8/49, 10/51, 10/52, 11/52, 3/60 ti} 9/22/47 li} 5/8/50	
Robinson, Larry	si} 5/24/76, 5/29/78	
Robinson, Len	si} 5/7/84	
Robinson, Oscar	ti} 3/17/61	
Robinson, Rumeal	si} 4/10/89, 11/20/89	
Robinson, Sugar Ray	si} 4/29/57, 9/6/65 sp} 6/51, 2/52 ti} 6/25/51, li} 4/7/58	
Robinson, Tony	si} 10/7/85	
Robinson, W.	ti} 8/25/30	
Roche, John	si} 1/4/71	
Rockne, Knute	ti} 11/7/27	
Rodgers, Bill	si} 10/30/78, 10/29/79	
Rodgers, Phil	si} 1/14/63	
Rodman, Dennis	si} 5/29/95, 3/4/96, sp 5/95,12/95, 6/96 bk} #22,	
Rodriguez, Rafael	si} 1/17/55	
Rodriguez, Ricardo	si} 3/26/62	
Rollins, Tree	si} 5/2/83	
Romack, Barbara	si} 4/16/56	
Rome Olympics Preview	si} 8/15/60	
Roscoe, Sheila (Swimsuit)	si} 1/17/72	
Rose, Murray	si} 8/14/61	
Rose, Pete	si} 5/27/68, 9/8/69, 9/7/70,4/8/74, 12/22/75, 8/7/78, 79 YIS,	
	5/28/79, 8/27/79, 7/19/82, 3/14/83, 8/27/84, 8/19/85, 8/10/87 inset	
	5/9/88, 4/3/89, 7/3/89, 8/27/89 inset, 9/4/89,	
	sp} 9/67, 8/68, 6/74, 8/76, 4/79, 11/92 ti} 8/19/85, 7/10/89	
	bk} #11, #21, #88	
Rosen, Al	si} 4/18/55 sp} 10/54	
Rote, Kyle	li} 11/13/50	
Rote, Tobin	si} 12/16/63	
Roundfield, Dan	si} 5/7/79	
Rozelle, Pete	si} 1/6/64	
Rozier, Mike	si} 9/5/83, 83 YIS	
Roy, Patrick	si} 6/17/96 reg, bk 1,6	
Rubiano, Tannia (Swimsuit)	si} 2/1/71	
Ruby, Lloyd	si} 5/31/65	

Name/Team	Title	Publications listing

Name/Team   **Title**   **Publications listing**

Rucker, John   li} 4/1/40

Ruddock, Razor   si} 3/25/91

Rudi, Joe   si} 4/11/77

Rudometkin, John   si} 3/19/62

Runyan, Paul   si} 8/6/62

Rupp, Adolph   si} 3/7/66

Ruppert, Col. Jacob   ti} 9/19/32

Russell, Bill   si} 10/25/65, 12/23/68,4/28/69, 8/4/69, 8/20/73, 10/24/77
10/29/84, 2/22/88, 11/8/93, sp} 3/66, 6/80

Russell, Campy   si} 12/11/72

Russell,   bk}#24

Ruth, Babe   si} 3/18/74 sp} 5/48, 10/60, 5/69, ti} 4/26/76

Rutherford, Johnny   si} 6/3/74, 6/2/80

Rutledge, Gary   si} 12/3/73

Ryan, Frank   si} 1/4/65, 9/27/65

Ryan, Nolan   si} 6/16/75, 7/23/79, 5/1/89, 4/15/91 sk} 9/91 sp} 4/80
bk} #55, #69, #82

Rypien, Mark   si} 2/3/92 bk} #23 sp} 8/92

Ryun, Jim   si} 9/14/64, 6/20/66, 8/1/66, 12/19/66, 9/30/68, 5/24/71
7/17/72 sp} 7/67

Saberhagen, Bret   sp} 4/86

Sabo, Chris   si} 10/29/90

Safe Driving Series   si} 1/30/61

Sailing   si} 9/6/54, 7/25/60

Sakai, Yoshinori   si} 10/19/64

Salazar, Alberto   si} 11/3/80

Salmon Fishing on the Miramichi   si} 9/8/58

Saluan, Henri   si} 2/10/58

Sampras, Pete   si} 9/17/90, 7/11/94

Sampson, Ralph   si} 12/17/79, 12/1/80, 3/30/81, 11/29/82,12/20/82,10/31/83

Sandberg, Ryan   si} 3/16/92, 96 sip Baseball, bk} #65 sp} 4/91

Sanders, Barry   si} 9/10/90, 12/25/95 Regional, sk} 10/91 bk} #4, #17, #28
bk} (FS) #20

Sanders, Brandon   si} 8/29/94

Sanders, Deion   si} 11/13/89, 4/27/92, 8/24/92, sk} 8/94 bk} #88 bk}(FS) #4, 28,32

Sanders, Doug   si} 1/22/62

Sanderson, Derek   si} 4/26/71

Sandstrom, Thomas   si} 4/23/90, 6/14/93

Santiago, Benito   si} 4/1/89

Santo, Ron   si} 6/30/69 sp} 9/69

Sapporo Olympic Games Preview   si} 11/15/71

Sauer, Hank   sp} 6/53

Savitt, Dick   ti} 8/27/51

Saxton, Jimmy   si} 11/27/61

Saxton, Johnny   si} 2/25/57

Sayers, Gale   si} 9/12/66 sp} 12/66, 11/69

Scandal in Amateur Track   si} 3/10/69

Sceptre, The English   si} 9/15/58
America's Cup Entry

Schaddelee, Hugh   si} 2/4/57

Schaeffler, Willy   si} 11/25/57

Schenk, Christian   si} 91 pictures

Schleeh, Russell   si} 8/12/57

Schlicter, Art   si} 11/12/79, 11/26/79 sp} 9/80

Schloredt, Bob   si} 10/3/60

Schmeling, Max   ti} 6/24/29

Schmidt, Jerry   si} 4/23/62

Schmidt, Mike   si} 5/3/76, 10/27/80, 4/13/81,8/10/81, 3/4/85, 4/20/87
sp} 6/83, 3/87, bk} #26

Schneider, Mathieu   si} 6/14/93

Schoendienst, Red	si} 6/6/60, 10/7/68
Schollander, Don	si} 10/5/64, lIFE 10/30/64
Schoolboy Hockey in the U.S.S.R.	si} 1/25/60
Schott, Marge	si} 5/20/96
Schultza, Helga	si} 8/27/62
Schumate, John	si} 2/5/73
Schwarzenegger, Arnold	si} 12/7/87
Score, Herb	si} 5/30/55 sp} 7/58
Scott, Barbara Ann	ti} 2/3/48
Scott, Byron	si} 6/15/87, 4/18/88
Scott, Charlie	si} 12/2/68, 4/25/77
Scott, Freddie	si} 10/24/94
Scott, Mike	sp} 7/87
Scott, Steve	si} 7/7/80
Scurry, Rod	si} 4/9/90
Seagren, Bob	si} 2/20/67
Sears, Ken	si} 12/20/54
Seau, Junior	si} 9/6/93 sk} 11/94
Seaver, Tom	si} 12/22/69, 7/21/75, 6/27/77, 7/27/81, 4/18/83
	sp} 5/70, 8/72, 5/76, 8/78, 6/82
Secretariat (Horse)	si} 6/11/73, ti} 6/11/73
Secrets of the Shuffle Offense	si} 12/11/61
Seles, Monica	si} 6/18/90, 5/10/93, 7/17/95, sk} 3/91
Sellers, John	si} 8/28/61
Sellers, Joyce	si} 10/4/54
Selmon, Dewey	si} 10/1/79
Selmon, Lee Roy	sp} 11/80
Seltzer, Kevin	bk} #36
Seymour,	ti} 10/28/66
Shannon, Bill	si} 10/7/68
Shantz, Bobby	sp} 2/53
Sharpe	bk} #20
Shavers, Ernie	si} 10/10/77, 10/8/79
Shaw, Brian	bk} 12
Shaw, Tim	si} 8/4/75
Shealy, Steadman	si} 11/12/79
Sheehan	si} 12/21/87
Shelby, Carroll	si} 3/25/57
Shell, Donnie	si} 1/17/83
Shepfield, Gary	si} 96 sip Baseball, bk} 91
Shelton, Lonnie	si} 5/3/82
Sherry, Larry	sp} 10/60
Shields/Fairbank Ballooning	si} 5/9/55
Shoemaker, Bill	si} 1/27/58
Shofner, Del	sp} 12/63
Shor, Toots (Party)	si} 7/27/59
Shorter, Frank	si} 8/3/70, 7/5/76, 7/19/76, life 9/22/72
Shula, Don	si} 12/20/93 ti} 12/11/72
Shy, Les	si} 8/31/70
Sidle, Jimmy	si} 9/21/64
Sierra, Rubin	bk} #58, #87
Sievers, Roy	si} 3/31/58
Sikma, Jack	si} 5/22/78, 5/3/82
Silas, Paul	si} 3/21/77
Silky Sullivan	si} 4/28/58
Silver Anniversary Issue	si} 8/13/79
Silver Spoon	si} 4/27/59
Sime, Dave	si} 7/2/56
Sime, Wes and Betty	si} 1/14/57
Simms, Phil	si} 2/2/87
Simmons	bk} 19

Name/Team	Title Publications listing
Simonton, Ann	si} 1/28/74
Simpson, George	sp} 11/76
Simpson, Johnny	si} 8/19/57
Simpsom, O.J.	si} 11/20/67, 10/14/68,7/14/69, 8/25/69, 10/29/73, 9/16/74
	10/8/90, 6/27/94
	sp} 12/68, 2/69, 8/69, 12/69, 12/74, 11/78
Simpson, Scott	si} 6/29/87
Sims, Billy	si} 10/3/77, 9/10/79, 9/22/80, sp} 1/81
Sisler, George	ti} 3/30/25
Singletary, Mike	si} 1/27/86
Singleton, Larry	si} 1/27/86
Sistrunk, Otis	si} 1/12/76
Sixkiller, Sonny	si} 10/4/71
Sizemore, Ted	si} 5/19/69
Skiing	si} 11/13/67, 12/19/55, 11/23/59, 12/1/58
Slager, Rick	si} 9/29/75
Slaughter, Enos	si} 3/3/58 sp} 5/49
Smith, Billy	si} 5/23/83, 83 YIS
Smith, Bruce	si} 9/2/91, 95 sip Pro Football
Smith, Bubba	si} 1/6/75 bk} #14
Smith, Dave	si} 5/11/70
Smith, Dean	si} 11/30/81, 3/1/93, 93 UNC Com.
Smith, Emmitt	si} 11/27/89, 1/25/93, 1/31/94, 2/7/94, 8/1/94, 12/12/94,
	9/18/95 1/22/96, 2/5/96, 94 Cowboys Comm,
	96 Cowboys Comm sp} 9/89,1/94,7/94,1/95, 8/95
	sk} 10/94, 9/95 bk} #12, #21, #30
Smith, Janell	si} 5/10/65
Smith, Jeff	si} 10/1/84
Smith, Lonnie	si} 10/25/82
Smith, Ozzie	si} 9/23/85, 10/28/85, 4/20/87, 9/28/87, bk} #83
Smith, Randy	si} 4/28/75
Smith, Robyn	si} 7/31/72
Smith, Scott	bk} #18
Smith, Steve	si} 2/12/73
Smith, Tommie	si} 5/22/67
Smoltz, John	si} 10/26/92
Snead, Sam	si} 6/11/56, 12/5/60, 11/12/62, ti} 6/21/54
Sneakers	si} 5/14/90
Snider, Duke	si} 6/27/55, 7/9/56 sp} 9/54, 9/55, 9/57, 1/58, 4/60
Snipes, Renaldo	si} 11/16/81
Snite, Betsy	si} 2/1/60
Snow Boarding	sk} 2/90
Snow Champion Afghan	si} 3/12/56
Snyder, Cory	si} 4/6/87
Solich, Frank	si} 9/20/65
Sonners vs. Nebraska	si} 11/22/71
Souchak, Mike	si} 1/16/56
Soviets Boycott Olympic Games	si} 5/21/84
Spahn, Warren	si} 6/25/56 sp} 8/53, 5/57, 10/59, 8/61, 5/64
Sparrow	si} 12/21/87
Special Double Issue	si} 12/24/56
Special Holiday Double Issue	si} 12/21/59
Special Report on Gambling	si} 3/10/86
Special Year End Double Issue	si} 12/22/58
Speier, Chris	si} 4/30/73
Spinks, Leon	si} 2/27/78, 9/25/78
Spinks, Michael	si} 3/28/83, 9/30/85, 6/20/88, 7/4/88
Spitball:Who Throws it and How?	si} 7/31/67
Spitz, Mark	si} 7/22/68, 9/4/72, 5/14/73, li} 8/18/72, ti} 9/11/72
Split-Second Action in Baseball	si} 7/31/61

Name/Team	Title	Publications listing
Spoonbill Duck	si} 11/15/54	
Sport Magazine 10th	sp} 9/56	
Sporting Life of Southern Cal.	si} 9/7/87	
Sports Fans	si} 7/22/91	
Sports in China	si} 8/15/88	
Sports Painting	sp} 3/51	
Spurrier, Steve	si} 12/4/72, 8/23/76, 1/1/96 reg	
Squirek, Jack	si} 1/30/84	
Stabler, Kenny	si} 1/17/77, 9/19/77, 8/6/79, sp} 12/77	
Stackhouse, Jerry	si} 3/6/95	
Stadler, Craig	si} 4/19/82	
Stagg, Nonagenarian	ti} 10/20/58	
Stallings, Gene	si} 93 Alabama Comm. , 8/14/95, 8/14/95 regional,	
Stallworth, John	si} 1/28/80	
Stanky, Eddie	si} 2/28/66 ti} 4/28/52	
Stanley Cup Playoffs	si} 4/8/68	
Stanley, Allan	si} 1/28/57	
Stanley, Fred	si} 8/25/80	
Stargell, Willie	si} 8/2/71, 8/27/79, 12/24/79	
Starikov, Sergei	si} 10/9/89	
Starks, John	si} 5/30/84	
Starr, Bart	si} 9/25/61, 10/31/66, 1/9/67, 8/25/75 sp} 12/67, 7/70 bk} #10	
Start of a Hialeah Race	si} 2/28/55	
Statley, Edward	ti} 5/26/30	
Staubach, Roger	si} 12/2/63, 9/4/78 sp} 1/77, ti} 10/18/63, 1/17/72 li} 1/14/72	
Steele, Lanny	si} 5/23/77	
Steeplechase at Belmont Park	si} 10/18/54	
Steinbrenner, George	si} 6/18/90, 3/1/93	
Stemkowski, Pete	si} 5/6/74	
Stengel, Casey	si} 3/2/59, 3/5/62, 3/2/64, sp} 4/50, 3/54 ti} 10/3/55, li} 9/14/53	
Stephenson, Don	sp} 11/57	
Stephenson, Jan	sp} 5/77	
Stewart, Dave	sk} 4/90	
Stewart, Ernie	si} 7/4/94	
Stewart, Jackie	si} 9/6/71, 12/24/73	
Stewart, James- Jacksonville	si} 95 sip Pro Football	
Stieb, Dave	si} 7/18/83	
Stockton, John	sp} 6/90 bk} #6	
Stoudamire, Damon - Raptors	si} 95 sip Pro Basketball	
Stones, Dwight	si} 6/14/76, 7/2/84	
Stowe, William	si} 6/18/62	
Strake, George	si} 12/19/83	
Strange, Curtis	si} 6/26/89	
Strategies (Golf) Forest Hills	si} 9/4/61	
Strawberry, Darryl	si} 4/23/84, 10/6/86, 7/13/87, 7/11/88, 7/9/90, 3/4/91 2/27/95 sk} 8/91 sp} 4/87, 6/91, 4/92 bk} #42	
Street, Gabby	ti} 3/28/32	
Street, James	si} 12/15/69	
Stroud, Marcus	sl} 2/19/96	
Stuart, Dick	sp} 6/64	
Stunyo, Jeanne	si} 8/6/56	
Sudakis, Bill	si} 5/19/69	
Sugar Bowl; The Tide Sinks Penn	si} 1/8/79	
Sullivan, Danny	si} 6/3/85	
Sullivan, Ed	si} 3/9/59	
Summer Sport on Nantucket Is.	si} 8/4/58	
Summer Surfers Invade Hawaii	si} 7/24/67	
Sumners, Rosalynn	si} 2/6/84	
Sunny's Halo Wins the K.D.	si} 5/16/83	
Super Bowl	ti} 1/10/77, 1/10/78	

Name/Team	Title	Publications listing
Super Bowl Preview	sp} 1/76	
Super Ski Runs in the U.S.	si} 11/14/66	
Surfcasting	si} 11/8/54	
Surfing	si} 3/10/58, 3/8/82	
Sutcliffe, Rick	si} 9/24/84 bk} #8	
Sutter, Bruce	sp} 7/81	
Sutton, Don	sp} 6/81	
Swann, Lynn	si} 1/26/76	
Sweikert, Bob	si} 5/28/56	
Swilling	bk} #26	
Swimsuit Issues	sp} 2/90, 2/91, 3/92, 2/93, 3/94, 3/95, 3/96	
Swink, Jim	si} 12/26/55	
Swiss Ski Resort of Klosters	si} 12/27/54	
Switzer, Barry	si} 9/8/75, 2/27/89, 8/1/94, 12/12/94,	
Swoboda, Ron	si} 5/6/68	
Silvander Twins (Swimsuit)	si} 1/19/76	
TV Sports are in Big Trouble	si} 2/24/86	
Tainted Title	si} 5/16/94	
Talbert, Bill	si} 4/20/59, 4/15/63, 7/13/64, 7/5/65	
Tarantino, Jon	si} 7/8/63	
Tarkenton, Fran	si} 10/29/62, 9/13/65, 7/17/67, 10/8/73, 1/7/74, 11/10/75	
	sp} 12/65, 10/68, 12/72, 1/75, 2/76	
Tasker, Steve	si} 12/25/95 regional	
Tatum, Jack	si} 11/9/70	
Taylor, Jim	si} 9/10/62, 1/10/66, 8/22/66, 8/14/67 sp} 11/62, 1/64	
Taylor, Lawrence	si} 9/29/86, 1/26/87 sp} 11/82,11/85, 9/87	
	bk} #5, #34	
Taylor, Otis	sp} 11/72	
Taylor, Marice - Michigan	si} 95 sip Col Basketball	
Tebbetts, Birdie	ti} 7/8/57	
Ter-Ovanesyan, Igor	si} 7/16/62	
Terrell, Ernie	si} 7/10/67	
Terrio, Bob	si} 1/10/72	
Testaverde, Vinny	si} 11/24/86, 8/3/87	
Texas Tech #20 basketball	si} 3/25/96	
Thackaberry, Richard	si} 6/18/62	
Theismann, Joe	si} 11/9/70, 1/11/71,1/16/84, 9/3/84 sp} 10/70	
Thomas, B	bk} #21	
Thomas, Debbie	ti} 2/15/88	
Thomas, Duane	si} 1/24/72, 8/27/73 bk} #17, #29	
Thomas, Frank	si} 8/8/94 sk} 7/93 bk} #79, #85,#94 bk}(Fs} #2, #12	
	sp} 1/94, 1/95, 4/95	
Thomas, Frank (Pirates)	si} 7/28/58	
Thomas, Gorman	sp} 7/80	
Thomas, Isaiah	si} 4/6/81, 5/18/87, 6/11/90, sk} 3/92 sp} 5/88 bk} #15	
Thomas, Thurmon	si} 1/20/92 bk} #12, #25 sp} 8/94	
Thomforde, Chris	si} 2/27/67	
Thompson, Anthony	si} 11/27/89	
Thompson, Charles	si} 2/27/89	
Thompson, David	si} 11/26/73, 4/1/74, 11/15/76	
Thompson, Jennie	sk} 1/95	
Thompson, John	si} 11/26/84	
Thompson, Michael	si} 11/17/86	
Thomson, Bobby	sp} 5/55	
Thomson, Peter	si} 6/8/59	
Threat to Sports from Drugs	si} 6/23/69	
Threats to the Environment	si} 2/2/70	
Tiant, Luis	si} 10/20/75	
Tiegs, Cheryl	si} 1/12/70, 1/27/75, 2/14/83, 83 YIS	
Tilden, Bill	si} 1/13/75	

Name/Team	Title Publications listing
Tillmon, Mark	si} 3/28/88
Tindall, Marilyn	si} 1/16/67
Tittle, Y.A.	si} 11/22/54, 11/20/61, 9/7/64, 8/16/65
Todd, Richard	si} 8/1/83
Tomjanovich, Rudy	si} 2/19/79
Toney, Andrew	si} 2/28/83
Top 100 Salaries	sp} 3/83, 3/84, 6/86, 6/87, 6/88
Torluemke, Judy	si} 8/21/61
Toronto Blue Jays	si} 11/2/92
Torre, Joe	si} 4/10/72
Torrez, Mike	si} 3/11/68
Trabert, Tony	si} 8/29/55
Trammell, Alan	si} 5/28/84, 10/22/84, 8/17/87, 10/12/87 inset
Tresh, Tom	sp} 7/64
Trevino, Lee	si} 6/24/68, 6/9/69, 6/28/71, 8/19/74 ti} 7/19/71
Triandos, Gus	si} 7/7/58
Trippi, Charley	sp} 12/47
Tripuka, Kelly	si} 5/7/84 sp} 3/81
Trottier, Bryan	si} 12/12/77
Trotting Champ Nevele Pride	si} 8/5/68
Troy, Mike	si} 8/1/60
Trull, Don	si} 8/17/64
Tunney, James	ti} 8/30/26
Turley, Bob	si} 5/4/59 sp} 4/55, 10/58
Turner, Curtis	si} 2/26/68
Turner, Jim	si} 9/22/69
Turner, Ted	si} 7/4/77
Tuttle, Harry	si} 1/11/82
Tweedy, Penny with Secretariat	si} 6/11/73
Twins - World Series	si} 11/2/87, 11/4/91
Twyman, Jack	sp} 3/61
Tyler, Wendell	si} 8/24/81
Tyson, Mike	si} 1/6/86, 12/1/86, 8/10/87,2/1/88, 6/13/88, 7/4/88 2/19/90, 3/25/91, 6/24/91, 2/17/92, 7/3/95 sp} 7/88 ti} 6/27/88
U.S. Yacht Championships	si} 9/16/63
U.S. Hockey Team Beats Soviets	si} 3/3/80
U.S. Olympic Hockey Team	si} 12/22/80
U.S. Open Preview	si} 6/14/65
U.S. Open at Oakland Hills	si} 6/12/61
UCLA Press and How to Beat It	si} 12/6/65
Ueberroth, Peter	si} 3/25/85 ti} 10/17/83
Uelses, John	si} 2/26/62
Ugalde, Domingo	ti} 1/13/30
Unbeaten Sooners of Oklahoma	si} 11/18/57
Underwater World of Swimmer	si} 7/3/61
Unitas, Johnny	si} 10/5/59, 7/10/72 sp} 12/58,12/59, 12/60, 12/62, 1/65, 11/65, 10/67, 7/70
Unseld, Wes	si} 5/10/71, 6/11/79 sp} 12/69
Unser, Al	si} 6/8/70, 6/7/71, 6/5/78
Utz, Jay	si} 11/11/57
Vachon, Rogie	si} 2/10/75
Valenzuela, Fernando	si} 5/18/81, 81 YIS, 7/8/85 sp} 4/82
Vallely, John	si} 3/16/70
Valvano, Jim	si} 1/11/93
Van Brocklin, Norm	si} 12/19/60
Van Eeghen, Mark	si} 1/2/78, 1/19/81
Vanderbilt, Alfred	si} 8/12/63
Vanderbilt, Harold S.	si} 10/15/56
Vanderbilt, Mike	ti} 9/15/30

Name/Team	Title	Publications listing
Vanderkelen, Ron	si} 8/19/63	
Vann, Pete	sp} 12/54	
Vasquez, Jaciata Foolish Pleasure Kent	si} 5/12/75	
Vaughn, Jacque - Kansas	si} 95 College Basketbal	
Vaughn, Mo	si} 10/2/95, 96 sip Baseball	
Veeck, Bill	si} 5/17/65, 3/15/76	
Vendela (Swimsuit)	si} 2/22/93	
Venturi, Ken	si} 6/13/60, 4/1/63, 6/29/64 12/21/64, 6/13/66	
Verdon, Gwen	ti} 6/13/55	
Versailles, Zoilo	si} 10/4/65	
Vines Jr., Ellsworth	ti} 8/1/32	
Violent Face of Pro Football	si} 10/24/60	
Virdon, Bill	si} 3/5/56	
Viruet, Edwin	si} 9/26/77	
Volk, Rick	si} 12/16/68	
Von Cramm, Gottfried	ti} 9/13/37	
Von Saltza, Chris	si} 7/21/58, Life 8/22/60	
Vonderheide, Nancy	si} 8/5/63	
Voronin, Gennady	si} 2/15/60	
Wade, Duke	ti} 10/25/37	
Wadkins, Lanny	si} 8/22/77	
Wagner, Barbara	si} 12/15/58	
Walker, Antonie	si} 4/8/96	
Walker, Doak	si} 10/3/55 sp} 11/48, 11/52,1/56, li} 9/27/48	
Walker, Harry	si} 9/5/66	
Walker, Herschel	si} 11/17/80, 8/31/81, 3/1/82, 82 YIS, 3/7/83, 83 YIS, 5/27/85, 8/18/86, 10/23/89 sk} 10/89 sp} 9/82, bk} #33	
Walker, Kenny	sk} 5/89	
Wall, Art	si} 6/8/59, 1/18/60	
Walls, Everson	si} 2/4/91	
Walsh, Steve	si} 10/12/87	
Walters, (Army)	si} 11/24/58	
Walters, George	si} 2/27/67	
Walther, Marie	si} 10/5/64	
Walters, Shawn - UCS	si} 95 sip College Football	
Walton, Bill	si} 3/6/72, 4/3/72, 2/5/73,3/26/73, 12/10/73, 2/25/74 3/25/74, 4/1/74, 10/14/74, 12/13/76, 5/23/77, 6/13/77 8/21/78, 10/15/79 sp} 4/77,	
Ware, Andre	si} 11/27/89 bk} #5	
Warfield, Paul	si} 7/28/75	
Was Dancer's Image Drugged?	si} 5/20/68	
Washington, Joe	si} 11/4/74, 9/8/75, 10/10/83	
Wasserman Family	si} 1/6/58	
Watanabe, Hisanobu	si} 10/31/94	
Watson, Tom (Golfer)	si} 4/18/77, 6/4/79, 4/20/81, 6/28/82, 7/25/83, 83 YIS	
Watson, Tom (Skiing Family)	si} 12/14/59	
Watters, Ricky	si} 11/21/94, 95 sip Pro Football, bk} #34	
Wayne, John (Party)	si} 7/27/59	
Weatherford, Jimmy	si} 10/30/67	
Weaver, Earl	si} 6/18/79	
Webb, Spud	sk} 3/89	
Webber, Chris	si} 4/12/93, 95 SIP Basketball	
Webster, Marvin	si} 5/22/78, 10/16/78	
Weinbrecht, Donna	sk} 2/92	
Weiner, Suzy	si} 5/14/73	
Weiskoph, Tom	si} 7/23/73	
Weiss, Bob	si} 12/8/69	
Weiss, Walt	si} 10/19/92	

Name/Team	Title Publications listing
Wepner, Chuck	si} 3/24/75
Werner, Buddy	si} 3/14/55, 1/27/64
Werner, Skeeter	si} 11/21/55
West, Jerry	si} 2/8/65, 4/29/68, 5/7/73, sp} 3/65, 3/69, 3/70
Westbrook, Michael	si} 10/3/94
Westminster Preview	si} 2/8/60
Westphal, Paul	si} 10/20/80
Weurffel, Danny	si} 9/25/95
Wharram, Kenny	si} 3/20/67
Whitaker, Pernell	si} 9/20/93, 10/10/94
White, Charles	si} 10/2/78, 9/10/79
White, Danny	si} 11/25/85 sp} 2/81
White, Randy	si} 1/23/78, 8/24/81
White, Reggie	si} 3/15/93 sk} 12/91, sp} 8/93
Whitney, John	ti} 3/27/33
White Sox Team	si} 9/28/59
Whittenburg, Dereck	si} 4/11/83
Wicks, Sidney	si} 3/30/70, 11/30/70, 4/25/77
Wiggins, Al	si} 4/2/56
Wiggins, Rod	si} 11/7/88
Wild Cats on Probation	si} 5/29/89
Wiley, Hugh	si} 11/3/58
Wilkens, Gerald	si} 5/25/92
Wilkes, Jamaal	si} 6/6/83
Wilkes, Keith	si} 2/5/73
Wilkins, Dominique	si} 5/2/83, 4/28/86 sp} 5/87
Wilkins, Rick	si} 8/22/94
Wilkinson, Bud	si} 9/12/55
Wilkinson, Dan	si} 4/25/94
Willard, Ken	si} 10/11/65 sp} 11/71
Willett, Gerald	si} 2/25/74
Williams, Chucky	si} 5/17/76
Williams, Dick	si} 8/17/81
Williams, Doug	si} 2/8/88
Williams, Edward	si} 7/25/66
Williams, Erik	si} 12/12/94
Williams, Gus	si} 6/11/79
Williams, H.	Bk} #23
Williams, Matt	si} 6/5/95, sp 5/91
Williams, R	si} 12/21/87
Williams, Ted	si} 8/1/55, 7/8/57, 7/8/68, 3/17/69, 7/18/77, 4/16/90
	sp} 8/47, 4/48, 9/48, 9/51,7/56, 6/59, 9/59, 6/69, 5/71
	ti} 4/10/50, li} 9/1/41
Williams, Walt	bk} #31
Williamson, Corliss	si} 4/11/94
Willie, Herb	si} 1/22/79
Willis, Leonard	sp} 9/77
Wills, Bump	si} 3/28/77
Wills, Helen	ti} 7/16/26, 6/31/29
Wills, Maury	si} 7/12/65, 4/17/67, 5/15/67, 9/27/71 sp} 2/63, 6/63, 10/65,5/66
Wilson, Otis	si} 11/25/85
Winder, Sammy	si} 10/8/84
Winfield, Dave	si} 1/5/81, 4/20/87, 10/19/92 bk} #3, #41, #79 sp} 3/93
Winn, Matt/ Horses	ti} 5/10/37
Winner of Westminister Show	si} 2/24/75
Winsett, John	li} 4/25/38
Winston, Roy	si} 11/3/69
Winter Fun in Colorado	si} 2/9/59
Winter Olympic Preview	si} 1/1/88
Winter Racing at Hialeah Park	si} 1/26/59

Name/Team	Title	Publications listing
Winter Wonderland in Montana	si} 12/3/62	
Wise, Mike	si} 8/27/90	
Witt, Katrina	SI 3/7/88	
Wolford, Will	si} 9/5/94	
Women in Sports	si} 5/28/73	
Women in Sports: Field Hockey	ti} 6/26/78	
Wood, Captian	ti} 11/21/31	
Wood, Wilbur	si} 6/4/73	
Wooden, John	si} 12/25/72	
Woods, Ickey	si} 1/16/89	
Woosnam, Ian	si} 4/22/91	
World Bobsled Champions	si} 12/27/61	
World Series	sp} 10/59	
World Series Painting	sp} 10/50	
World Series Scouting Report	si} 9/30/57	
World Series: Yanks vs. Who?	si} 10/1/62	
World's Best Marlin Ground	si} 4/22/63	
Worster, Steve	si} 11/9/70, 12/14/70	
Worthy, James	si} 11/30/81, 3/29/82, 4/5/82, 5/18/86, 4/18/88, 6/5/89	
Wright, Larry	si} 5/7/79	
Wright, Mickey	si} 2/19/62	
Wrigley, W. Jr.	ti} 10/14/29	
Wuerffel, Danny - Florida	si} 95 sip Col Football	
Wynn, Early	sp} 6/57	
Wynn, Jim	si} 5/27/74	
Yachting Flags, The Sailors Alphabet	si} 7/1/57	
Yale-Dartmouth Game Preview	si} 11/5/56	
Yamaguchi, Kristi	si} 3/2/92	
Yang, C.K.	si} 12/23/63	
Yarborough, Cale	si} 2/28/77, 78 YIS	
Yastrzemski, Carl	si} 8/21/67, 12/25/67, 8/27/79, 7/19/82 sp} 7/64, 2/68, 6/68, 7/71, 10/78 li} 9/8/67	
Yeager, Steve	si} 10/21/74	
Year in Sports	si} 1/1/77, 1/1/78, 2/15/79, 3/13/80, 2/12/81, 2/10/82 2/16/83, 1/1/84	
Yepremian, Garo	si} 1/3/72	
Young, Earl	si} 6/19/61	
Young, Howie	si} 1/28/63	
Young, Sheila	si} 2/2/76	
Young, Steve	si} 1/18/93, 1/16/95, 1/23/95, 2/6/95, 95 sip Pro Football sk} 11/93 sp} 1/94, 7/95, 8/95, 9/95, 10/95	
Yount, Robin	si} 10/11/82, 10/25/82, 82 YIS, bk} #60,#90	
Zimmer, Don (Baseball Preview)	sp} 4/88	
Zimmerman, Chick	si} 10/27/58	
Zimmermann, Egon	si} 2/10/64	
Zoeller, Fuzzy	si} 4/23/79	
10 Most Intriguing Sports Stories	sp} 12/87	
40th Anniversary Issue	sp} 12/86	

APPENDIX I:
PERIPHERAL SECTION

In addition to rare publications, some collectors also accumulate items sponsored and sold by *Sports Illustrated*. In this category are posters, lithographs, films, games, books, and puzzles. The estimated value for these items will range depending upon player and demand. However, many of these items are tough to find. It should be noted that this is not a comprehensive list of material and that more is added daily through the *Sports Illustrated Store*.

Books

Books are a natural fit for *Sports Illustrated*. Many Times books were released, sponsored, and promoted, in *Sports Illustrated* pages and outside of the magazine. I compiled a very short list of books and the first year they were promoted within the pages of Sports Illustrated.

1957

"Spectacle of Sports",
"Book of the Outdoors"
"Modern Fundamentals of Golf " Ben Hogan
"Bonnie Prudden's Fitness Book
"The Best 18 Golf Holes in America"
"The Wonderful World of Sport"

"The Pros"
"Golf is My Game" Bob Jones
"Tips from the Top"
"Wind on My Wings"
"Jack Nicklaus - Take a Tip From Me"

1966 - 1976

Sports Illustrated Library of Book series was created to help instruct people on how to play different sports. The books were promoted over a period of time. Listed below is a partial list of the many book subjects:

* Badmitton,
* Diving ,
* Football,
* Gaited Riding,
* Ice Hockey,
* Safe Driving,
* Soccer,
* Tennis ,
* Wet Fly Fishing

* Baseball,
* Dog Training,
* Football Defense,
* Golf,
* Judo,
* Skiing ,
* Squash,
* Track & Field,

* Basketball,
* Fencing,
* Football Offense,
* Handball,
* Junior Sailing,
* Skin Diving,
* Swimming/Diving,
* Training - Weights,

* Boating,
* Fly Fishing,
* Football Quarterback,
* Horseback Riding,
* Powerboating,
* Small Boat Sail,
* Table Tennis,
* Volleyball

1971

"Golf lessons"   " Inside Major League Baseball"

1977 SI Book club - Many different Time -Warner books were promoted and advertised through the SI Book club.

Calendars

Today's Sports Illustrated Swimsuit Calendar is one of the top ten most recognized calendars made in America. Outside of the traditional large swimsuit calendar is the daily box calendar and the monthly regular size calendar. The most collectable calendar is the Swimsuit calendars which can range from $10 - $100 depending upon year and demand. There are Sports Illustrated calendars that date back to 1970.

Games/Puzzles

From 1978-1987 Sports Illustrated offered board games. The games are collected by game collectors and tend to range in value from $15 - $50 depending upon the game and the condition. Some of the games were released each year with the ability to buy updated cards of there favorite sport. Games originally sold between $15-$20 each. Games are listed on the next page.

BOARD GAMES

All Time All Star Baseball
Football Strategy
Challenge Golf
Baseball Strategy
Bowl Bound
Superstar Baseball
Speed Circuit
Horse Racing
Pro Tennis

College Football
Golf for the Green
Paydirt
Statis-Pro Football
Statis- Pro Baseball
Title Bout
Auto Racing
Regatta
Decathlon

Puzzles: 1969   Ski, Best 18 Holes
            1977   Oscar Robertson, and others

Learning Programs

1975: This package contained SI posters, boxes, and SI education books. It may not have lasted long because it was only advertised a few years.

Posters

Posters is one area that *Sports Illustrated* pushed throughout its history. Many of these earlier posters are now sought after by advanced collectors.

1957:   *Sports Illustrated* offered your choice of any color photograph or painting, which ever appeared in *Sports Illustrated*. The cost was $1.00 half page, $1.50 full page and $2.50 for a two page spread. Therefore many photo's of the original *Sports Illustrated* covers may exist.

1961:   Russell Hoban paintings prints were offered in 1961 for $1 each. These 3 feet by 12 inch color prints are seldom seen in the market and therefore are classified as scarce. The prints were offered only through *Sports Illustrated* in 1961. I would estimate the value around $100 -$300 each
            1. Carol Heiss skating at Squaw Valley
            2. Ted Williams hitting home run #500
            3. Johnny Unitas winning the championship
            4. Rafer Johnson wins the Olympic Decathlon
            5. Arnold palmer winning second Masters title
            6. Floyd Paterson beating Ingemar Johansson

1963:   Posters are from the pages of Sports Illustrated. These are beautiful sports scenes range in sizes from 27 x 20 to 36 x 34. The value of them is unknown but I would estimate them around $25-$50 each
            "Skiing in the Sangre De Cristo Mountains Taos N.M."
            "Tennis at Wimbledon"
            "Harness Racing ' High stepping trotters at Goshen" 36x14
            "Sports Car Racing ' the start of the 24 hour race at Le Mans" 36 x24
            "Ocean Racing" 27 x 20 cover of si 7/4/60
            "Crew ' on the Seventh River" 27 x 20
            "Golf - The 12th hole at Augusta" 27x 20

<u>1968- 1972</u>: The most popular sports posters. These were done over a four year period and were marketed through various means. Originally, there were Baseball, Football, Basketball and Hockey individual player posters. This expanded into team and other types of SI posters. This book lists the baseball posters, but only list the stars in the other major sport groups.

SI Posters had an insert poster that had pictures of 54 different players that were going to be on a *Sports Illustrated* Poster. These pictures were all baseball players. The major players were: Mantle, Aaron, Mays, Kaline Clemente, Seaver, Banks, Rose, Gibson, Robinson, Killebrew, and Mantle. The value of this insert poster ranges from $5 to $10.

1968-1972 SI BASEBALL POSTER

Player- Team	Yr	Price	Player- Team	Yr	Price
Hank Aaron - Braves	68	$ 50	Tommy Agee- Mets	68	$ 20
Richie Allen - Phillies	68	$ 20	Gene Alley- Pirates	68	$ 15
Felipe Alou - Braves	68	$ 12	Max Alvis- Indians	68	$ 20
Mike Andrews - Red sox	69	$ 12	Bob Aspromonte -Astros	68	$ 15
Ernie Banks - Cubs	68	$ 25	Glen Beckett - Cubs	70	$ 20
Gary Bell - Indians	68	$ 25	Gary Bell - Pilots	68	$ 15
Bobby Bonds - Giants	70	$ 25	Clete Boyer - Braves	68	$ 15
Lou Brock - Cards	68	$ 20	Johnny Callison - Phillies	68	$ 20
Bert Campaneris-A's	68	$ 20	Leo Cardenas - Reds	68	$ 12
Rod Carew - Twins	70	$ 25	Paul Casanova- Orioles	68	$ 15
Orlando Cepeda-Card	68	$ 15	Roberto Clemente - Pirates	68	$350
Tony Conigliaro-Red Sox	68	$ 20	Mike Cuellar - Orioles	70	$ 15
Tommy Davis Pilots	68	$ 15	Willie Davis - Dodgers	68	$ 20
Don Drysdale -Dodgers	68	$ 30	Mike Epstein - Senators	70	$ 15
Al Ferrara-Dodgers	68	$ 15	Curt Flood - Cards	68	$ 15
Bill Freeham-Tigers	68	$ 20	Jim Fregosi - Angels	68	$ 12
Bob Gibson - Cards	68	$ 20	Bud Harrelson - Mets	68	$ 15
Ken Harrelson-Red Sox	68	$ 15	Ken Holtzman -Cubs	70	$ 12
Joe Horlen -White Sox	68	$ 15	Tony Horton-Indians	68	$ 15
Frank Howard - Senators	68	$ 20	Reggie Jackson - A's	68	$150
Ferguson Jenkins - Cubs	69	$ 50	Tommy John - White Sox	68	$ 30
Cleon Jones - Mets	68	$ 25	Al Kaline - Tigers	68	$ 25
Harmon Killebrew - Twins	68	$ 25	Jerry Koosman-Mets	68	$ 15
Lets Go Mets - Mets	69	$ 35	Mickey Lolich - Tigers	68	$ 25
Jim Lonborg - Red Sox	68	$ 20	Jim Maloney - Reds	68	$ 25
Mickey Mantle - Yankees	68	$300	Juan Marichal-Giants	68	$ 25
Willie Mays - Giants	68	$200	Willie Mays - Mets	72	$100
Bill Mazeroski -Pirates	68	$ 12	Tim McCarver - Cards	68	$ 12
Mick McCormick - Giants	68	$ 25	Willie McCovey - Giants	68	$100
Sam McDowell - Indians	68	$ 25	Denny McLain -Tigers	68	$ 15
Don Mincher - Angels	68	$ 30	Don Mincher - Pilots	69	$ 20
Rick Monday-A's	68	$ 12	Bobby Murcer - Yankees	68	$ 20
Phil Niekro - Braves	68	$ 20	John Odom - A's	70	$ 20
Tony Oliva - Twins	68	$ 17	Wes Parker - Dodgers	68	$ 25
Tony Perez - Reds	70	$ 25	Rico Petrocelli-Red Sox	68	$ 20
Boog Powell - Orioles	68	$ 25	Rich Riechart - Angels	68	$ 12
Brooks Robinson - Orioles	68	$100	Frank Robinson - Orioles	68	$ 50
Pete Rose - Reds	68	$ 50	Ron Santo - Cubs	68	$ 20
Tom Seaver - Mets	68	$100	Chris Short- Phillies	68	$ 15
Bill Singer -Dodgers	68	$ 20	Reggie Smith - Red Sox	68	$ 20
Rusty Staub - Astros	68	$ 15	Mel Stottlemyre- Yankees	68	$ 20
Ron Swobada- Mets	68	$ 15	Cesar Tovar - Twins	68	$ 20
Roy White -Yanks	68	$ 20	Walt Williams - White Sox	68	$ 15
Earl Wilson - Tigers	68	$ 20	Jim Wynn -Astros	68	$ 15
Carl Yastrzemski - Red Sox	68	$ 25			

1968-1972 SI BASKETBALL POSTER

Basketball was not the most popular sport during the 1968 era. However a few superstars still had a poster made.

Bill Bradley - Knicks	68	$100	Billy Cunningham - 76ers	68	$ 15
John Havlicek -Celtics	68	$ 40	Evin Hayes - Bullets	70	$ 40
Spencer Hayward - Bullets	71	$ 12	Willis Reed - Knicks	71	$ 20
Oscar Robertson - Bucks	71	$ 45			

1968-1972 SI FOOTBALL POSTER

There are many Football SI Posters made during this era and it would take a page to list all of the common posters. The common posters value around $15-$25 based on demand and scarcity. Some of the posters are more scarce than others. Star posters tend to go between $40-$50 with a few notable exceptions. The star posters are listed below:

Lance Alworth $100	Fred Biletnikoff,	George Blanda,	John Brodie,
Dick Butkus $100,	Larry Csonka,	Len Dawson,	Roman Gabriel,
Joe Greene,	Bob Griese,	Sonny Jorgenson,	Joe Kapp,
Jack Kemp $50	Daryle Lamonica,	Bob Lilly,	Don Maynard
Archie Manning $50,	Craig Morton,	Ray Nitschke,	Joe Namath $150,
Merlin Olsen,	Alan Page,	Jim Plunkett,	Gale Sayers $75,
OJ Simpson $65,	Bart Starr $60,	Roger Staubach $100,	
Charley Taylor,	Otis Taylor,	Paul Warfield,	Larry Wilson

1968-1972 SI HOCKEY POSTERS

These are tougher than the baseball and football posters. Common posters tend to be between $15-$20 each. The tougher ones are the superstars which go between $40-$50 each:

Red Berenson (70)	$40	Phil Esposito(71)	$40
Gordie Howe (68)	$50	Bobby Hull (68)	$50
Bobby Orr (68)	$50		

1973-1983 SI POSTERS

Sports Illustrated continues to offer a variety of posters between the two large poster series offers. In fact, the list of superstars expands during the 1975 SI Poster series and the 1979 SI Signature Sports Poster series.

1971: Ali vs Frazier fight poster   1972: Nature posters
1972: Secretariat SI Poster
1975: More Sports Posters - Basketball, Horseracing, etc.
1976: Montreal Olympic Poster   1976: 28 small olympic posters
1979: SI Signature Sports Posters

1983 Sports Illustrated Posters

These posters were handled by Marketcom and were advertised in 1983 in Sports Illustrated. The posters had the name of the athlete at the top with a border around the player. These posters do appear from time to time. Commons tend to go around $10-$15 and superstars go for $25-$50. Most of the posters were big name sports (Football, baseball, basketball) however, this generation of Sports Illustrated posters had many different types of sports offered. Listed below is the key posters and a total listing of posters by sport:

Football 53 posters: Superstars (Walter Payton, Tony Dorsett, Roger Staubach, Joe Montana)
Baseball 44 posters: Superstars (Rod Carew, Reggie Jackson, Robin Yount, Tom Seaver, Jim Palmer, Pete Rose, Mike Schmidt, Johnny Bench, George Brett)
Basketball 26 posters:

Superstars (Larry Bird, Magic Johnson,Kareem Abdul Jabbar, Isiah Thomas, Julius Erving, Moses Malone)

Tennis 11 posters,	Boxing 1 poster - Sugar Ray Leonard,
Hockey 1 poster - Wayne Gretzky	US Ski Team - 5 posters
Golf 4 posters	Bowling 5 posters
Body Building 1 poster	

1987: *Sports Illustrated* Quacker Chewy Granola Bars (3" x 5") Mini posters
These posters are similar to the 1983 posters except in size. Values range from $5 to $30 based on player and condition.
Football 57 posters: (Payton, Killy, Elway, Dorsett, Staubach,Walker, Marino, Montana, Taylor, Largent, Bradshaw,)
Baseball 40 poster: (Jackson, Yount, Sandberg, Ripken, Gwynn,Schmidt, Bench, Rose, Brett)
Basketball: 28 posters: (Jordan, Bird, Johnson, Jabbar, Thomas, Barkley, Erving)

Ice Skating & Running 5 posters	Surfing 2
Water Skiing 2	Snowmobile 2
Golf 4	Racquetball 2
Hockey 1 Dave Maloney	Boxing - Sugar Ray Leonard,
US Ski Team 5	Soccer 2

Prints:

Sports Illustrated twice offered limited edition autographed lithograph of great atheletes during great events. These were all signed in pencil by the great athletes. The original price when they were released were $100 each. The litho's were limited to 1,000 or 1,500 each. The most valuable ones will be of the great deceased players.

1974:

Prints	Est. Price Ranges
Jack Dempsey/Gene Tunney	$250 - $400
Joe Louis vs Max Schmiling	$400 - $600
Arnold Palmer	$150 - $250
Eddie Aracado	$ 75 - $100
Joe Dimaggio	$250 - $500
Johnny Unitas	$100 - $150

1976:

Jack Nicklaus	$150 - $250
Chamberlain/Havlicek	$100 - $200
Stan Musial	$ 75 - $150
Billie Jean King	$ 50 - $100
Rod Laver	$ 75 - $150
Red Grange	$250 - $350

Promotional Items

These are salesman representatives giveaways, samples and the like that have various Sports Illustrated logo's on them. I have found belt buckles, buttons, pins, magazines and books as some of the items that were developed for this purpose. The demand for these items is low because they usually don't directly relate to a particular person or sport. Some of the neatest items are special posters of players that were used in displays.

Videos

The *Sports Illustrated* Store continues to offer new and exciting video's on a range of subjects. The ones that are offered exclusively by *Sports Illustrated* are the ones heavily collected by Sports Illustrated collectors. Two very popular series produced by *Sports Illustrated* is "The Year in Sports" and "The Swimsuit Issue".There were also Beta *Sports Illustrated* (no longer made) videos (the smaller cartridge that didn't make it) that do exist in the market. In earlier years action films (1971) and SI highlight films were released.

APPENDIX II:

SI COVER APPEARANCE LEADERS*

*SOURCE: *Sports Illustrated*'s "35 Years of Covers" issue and updated through 1996.

APPENDIX III:

DEALERS AND SUPPLIERS

Magazine Supplies
Larry E. Krein Co.
3725 Portland Ave So.
PO Box 7126
Minn. Minn 55407

Specialty Dealers
The Sports Illustrated Store
Dept. #A4GA
P.O. Box 60042
Tampa, FL 33660-0042
1-800-274-5200

Sports Publication Dealers
Concord Collectibles - (Lou Madden)
15875 Greenway-Hayden Loop, Suite 112
Scottsdale, AZ 85260
1-800-345-7474

Horance "Ace" Martchant
232 Rockrimmon Rd.,
Belchertown, MA 01007

Atlanta Sports Collectibles- (Barry Sanders)
4732-D North Royal Atlanta Dr.
Tucker GA 30084

Baseball Dreams - (Ed Taylor)
982 Monterey St.
San Luis Obispo, CA 93401
805-541-6432

B & E Collectibles, Inc - (Joe & Jay Esposito)
950 Broadway
Thornwood, NY 10594
914-769-1304

Sportslore - (Joe Campius)
P.O. Box 43256
Upper Montclair, NJ 07043
(201) 783-7451

Sports Publications Clearinghouse -(Phil Regl)
P.O. Box 26596
Las Vegas, NV 89126-0596
(702) 228-9902

Adelson Sports
13610N Scottsdale,
Scottsdale, AZ 85254

Scott Smith - Signed Issues Only
53 Sherwood Ave.
Englewood Cliffs, NJ 07632
(201) 567-2723

Todd Mueller- Signed Issues Only
PO Box 701182,
Dallas, TX 75370-1182
(214) 385-0055

Wayne Greene
945 W. End Ave, 5d
NY, NY 10025
(212)-662-2104

Headline Sports
Kurt Backhaus
3404 Nottingham
Pearland, TX 77581
713-485-7622

Scott Daloisio Sports
12475 Cnetral Ave #286
Chino, CA 91710
(909) 628-9730

The Golf Hounds
16612 Green Dolphin Lane
Cormelius, NC 28031
(704) 892-5116

YesterYear Sports
Bill Harris
4 Cedar Way
Charleroi, PA 15022
(412) 483- 8508

Jeff Baseball Books
5536-A Port Royal Rd
Springfield, VA 22151

Rick Mattel
5922 E. Emile Zola
Scottsdale, AZ 85254
(602) 494-4606

Bailey's Collectible
2910-B Girad NE
Albuquerque, NM 87107
(505) 269-0963

George Kaufer
4104 E. 14th st.,
Vancouver, WA 98661
1-800-896-6751

Paul Cards & Collectible
3879 E. 120th Ave #308
Thornton, Co 80233
1-800-757-4620

Robert Dick
3 Ambrose Lane
South Barrington, IL 60010
847 - 304-5579

R. Plapinger- Baseball Books
po box 1062
Ashland, Or 97520
(503) 488-1220

Label Removal Service
Greg York c/o
Speciality Sports
15213 S. W. Freeway #115
Sugarland, TX 77478
713-491-0997